Heinrich von Kleist Studies

Hofstra University
Cultural & Intercultural Studies: 3

Other titles in this series:

No. 1. George Sand Papers. Conference Proceedings (1976). 1980
No. 2. George Sand Papers. Conference Proceedings (1978). 1981
No. 4. William Cullen Bryant Studies. 1981.

ISSN 0195-802X

Heinrich von Kleist Studies

Editorial Board
Alexej Ugrinsky
Frederick J. Churchill
Frank S. Lambasa
Robert F. von Berg

Joseph G. Astman, Director
University Center for Cultural
& Intercultural Studies

AMS PRESS, INC.
NEW YORK, N.Y.

Library of Congress Cataloging in Publication Data
Main entry under title:

Heinrich von Kleist studies.

(Hofstra University cultural & intercultural studies; 3)
Articles in English and German.
Includes bibliographical references and indexes.
 1. Kleist, Heinrich von, 1777-1811—Criticism and
interpretation—Addresses, essays, lectures.
 I. Ugrinsky, Alexej. II. Hofstra University, Hempstead, N.Y.
Center for Cultural & Intercultural Studies.
 III. Series: Hofstra University, Hempstead, N. Y. Hofstra
University cultural & intercultural studies; 3.
PT2379.Z5H37   838'.6'09   79-8846
ISBN 0-404-61653-4

Published simultaneously as "Heinrich von Kleist-Studien"
by Erich Schmidt Verlag, 1000 Berlin 30,
Genthiner Str. 30 G, West-Germany

Copyright © 1980 by AMS Press, Inc.
All rights reserved.

MANUFACTURED IN THE UNITED STATES
OF AMERICA

Foreword

The Heinrich von Kleist bicentennial almost coincides with the bicentennial of the birth of our own nation. I find it intriguing to note that Heinrich von Kleist, who was born into a family of generals, was more at home with friends who were writers, painters, and patrons of the arts. It is more than interesting too, that, like the founding fathers of the very young nation that emerged on this side of the Atlantic, Heinrich von Kleist was very much concerned about the individual in society. His plays and stories testify to the individual's struggle for his rights, the conquest of class and racial barriers, and the aspirations of women for a better place in society. Understandably, Heinrich von Kleist was misunderstood by his contemporaries and by some generations that came after his time. Like many great persons, he spoke and wrote for posterity. As one scholar has noted, the twentieth century was the first to recognize itself in him. But Heinrich von Kleist is no longer relegated just to German scholarship or German culture. His greatness is of the caliber that transcends national boundaries. His works are read in translation in many nations and have been brought to the attention of millions through film and television.

Among the contributors to this volume are representatives of Canada, West Germany and West Berlin, England, Japan, Switzerland, and of many of the States of our own country. I would like to thank them all for joining us in this tribute to a remarkable writer, a contemporary of Schiller and Goethe, whose works profoundly transformed German drama and changed the very scope of European literature. His honesty, his feeling for reality, his concern for the individual, appeal to us today as they did to the realists, the expressionists, the nationalists, and the existentialists. Heinrich von Kleist truly belongs to the ages; as it has been said, no man is truly great who is great only in his lifetime. The test of greatness is the page of history.

JAMES M. SHUART
President, Hofstra University

Contents

Foreword   v
    JAMES M. SHUART

Introduction

Homage to a Misfit: Heinrich von Kleist (1777/1977)   3
    ILSE GRAHAM

Dramas

Kleist's Tragic Roots   27
    KLAUS AICHELE

Rethinking Kleist's *Hermannsschlacht*   33
    JEFFREY L. SAMMONS

"Ein Traum, was sonst?" Kleist's *Prinz Friedrich von Homburg*   41
    LAWRENCE RYAN

Fünf Thesen zu *Prinz Friedrich von Homburg*   47
    HANS-JÜRGEN SCHLÜTTER

Adam und Frau Marthe: polare Verfahrensweisen in Kleists   59
    Der zerbrochne Krug
    LILIAN HOVERLAND

Der Zerbrochne Krug: Juggling of Authorities   69
    WOLFGANG WITTOWSKI

Novellas

Unglück und Verwirrung: Bemerkungen zu Kleists Erzählungen   83
    BARBARA MECK

Kleist's "Der Zweikampf" as Comedy   87
    JAMES M. McGLATHERY

Kleist's "Der Findling"—The Pitfalls of Terseness   93
    ROLF N. LINN

Marionettes

Heinrich von Kleist und die Marionette 103
 WOLFGANG KUROCK

Marionette und Gewölbe. Zur Differenzierung der Sinnbilder bei Kleist 109
 SHIRO NAKAMURA

Kleist and Mathematics: The Non-Euclidean Idea in the Conclusion of the *Marionettentheater* Essay 117
 SYDNA STERN WEISS

Schwerpunkt Kleist: Motive des Marionettentheaters im 20. Jahrhundert 127
 RALF R. NICOLAI

Comparative Studies

Diderot and Kleist 139
 HILDA M. BROWN

Michael Kohlhaas in New York: Kleist and E. L. Doctorow's *Ragtime* 147
 MARION FABER

E. L. Doctorow's *Ragtime:* Kleist Revisited 157
 ROBERT E. HELBLING

An Echo of Kafka in Kleist 169
 MARK HARMAN

Affinities in Romanticism: Kleist's Essay "Über das Marionettentheater" and Keats's Concept of "Negative Capability" 177
 HAL H. RENNERT

Education, Linguistics, and Science

Bemerkungen zum Kleistverständnis im Deutschunterricht an Gymnasien der Bundesrepublik Deutschland 189
 KARL SCHWEIZER

A Report on Two Statistical Surveys of Kleist's Syntax 197
 TE-MAY SO

CONTENTS

Heinrich von Kleist's Poetic Technique: Is It Based on the 203
Principle of Electricity?
HERMINIO SCHMIDT

New Perspectives

Kleist in Thun 217
HERMANN RESKE

Literaturrezeption als Spiegel ihrer Zeit: Die Frankfurter Kleist- 229
Feier von 1927 und die politische Rolle der Kleist-Gemeinde in
der Weimarer Republik
ROLF BUSCH

Regie as Interpretation—Kleist's *Homburg* and *Käthchen* on the 243
Current West German Stage
DONALD H. CROSBY

Thesen zur Aktualität Kleists in Westdeutschland 251
FRIEDRICH ROTHE

Unified Vision: The Struggle for the Center 257
VALENTINE C. HUBBS

Appendix: Exhibition Catalogue 265

Index 289

Introduction

Homage to a Misfit
HEINRICH VON KLEIST
(1777/1977)

ILSE GRAHAM
Kings College
University of London

1

Heinrich von Kleist was born two hundred years ago. This is where the mystery begins. Characteristically, we do not know the date. The official entry says on the 18th of October. He himself maintained that it was the 10th. He was the eldest son of an old family of Prussian officers. One of his forbears was Lessing's friend, the poet Ewald von Kleist who died of wounds received—and welcomed by an ineradicably melancholy temperament—in the battle of Kunersdorf. Heinrich was expected to take up a soldier's calling and to add luster to his family's name in the defence of king and country. He took these expectations seriously. To add honor to the family fortunes was a driving motive throughout his short life. When he was ten years old, his father died; his mother, when he was sixteen. At fourteen he entered the regiment of the guards at Potsdam. In between soldiering he studied philosophy and mathematics—the most unsuited disciplines for one like him—and played the clarinet. He took part in the siege of Mainz under General Kalckreuth, and, in due course, became a second lieutenant. Around this time, he met some of his closest friends, Ludwig von Brockes, Ernst von Pfuel, and Rühle von Lilienstern. In the spring of 1799, after having lost seven precious years, Kleist quit his army career and matriculated as a student at the university of Frankfurt an der Oder. That year saw his engagement to Wilhelmine von Zenge, a demure girl who clearly did not know what she had let herself in for. Her fiancé bombarded her with 'Denkübungen,' exercises devised for the betterment of his beloved's mind, and with incessant doubts of her loyalty and love. All was not well with this suitor, as readily attested by the fact that, during the time of his courtship, preceding the actual betrothal, he confessed to being plagued by an acute sense of physical unease plainly connected with his role in the Zenge set-up (to Ulrike von Kleist, 12 November, 1799, S. No. 6).[1] In August he sets out, with his friend Brockes, on a mysterious trip to Würzburg, undertaken to be cured of some impediment which in his own eyes made him unfit for marriage. Speculations as to the nature of his ailment have been legion—they range from the supposition that it was a stammer to the suspicion that he suffered from impotence. There is a good deal of evidence to suggest that what ailed him were the guilt feelings aroused by earlier sexual, perhaps homosexual, experiences during his military career combined with those about the possible consequences of masturbation: the treatment meted out to him—cold baths at bedtime, followed by the unflinching perusal of uplifting literature until overcome by sleep would suggest a condition that was primarily psychological.

The only authentic portrait we have of Kleist dates from about this time. Its features, set in a compact but stapely and very round head, are a strange blend of childlike innocence and a sensual sweetness that is quite overpowering and might easily be mistaken for those of a young woman at the first dawning of arousal.

It is around the time of the enigmatic Würzburg episode that his resolution to become a poet crystallized and that he started keeping an "Ideenmagazin"—a file to store ideas, images, etc. for future poetic use. By way of a bread-and-butter job he resolved to enter the civil service. A steady job was certainly what he needed, though he never succeeded in holding one down for any length of time. He was always in financial trouble, sometimes for telling and touching reasons. Family tradition has it that one day he came to his sister—not Ulrike for once, but Wilhelmine—to ask for money, which she duly gave him. The following day, he repeated his request. "But Heinrich, I gave it to you only yesterday," says the sister, to which Heinrich replies: "Ach, Minette, ich traf einen Freund, der es noch viel notwendiger brauchte wie ich, dem habe ich alles gegeben."— "Und das hatte seine Richtigkeit," the informant adds succinctly.[2]

In March of the year following—it is now 1800—the so-called Kant-crisis broke. Kleist had known Kant's work since the previous autumn. Now, all of a sudden, he complains that Kant's philosophy has shattered his most sacred beliefs: the philosopher's phenomenalistic account of knowledge had robbed him of his cherished conviction that "what we call the truth is truly truth" and that we are able to gather an imperishable store of knowledge that will follow us into the grave. Sick of mentation and restless, he sets out with his half-sister, Ulrike, a mannish, resolute, and loyal woman traveling in male clothing on a trip which eventually takes them to Paris, a destination that seems incongruous to the point of being paradoxical on two counts: Kleist is an ardent hater of Napoleon and the French; and it is in the French capital that he wants, of all things, to propagate the philosophy of Kant whose teaching has struck "at the most sacred core of my self." After some months, he parts from Ulrike and sets out for Switzerland, where he wants to buy some land and become a farmer. He breaks off his engagement to Wilhelmine, who does not fancy becoming a farmer's wife, and spends some idyllic months, first in Bern, then on the Deloesa-Inseli just outside Thun. It is during those months that his first drama, *Familie Ghonorez,* together with *Robert Guiskard* and *Der zerbrochne Krug* are taken in hand, the last named by way of a literary competition with his fellow poets Gessner and Zschokke. The idyll abruptly ends as Heinrich suffers a breakdown and is medically treated during the summer months in Bern, an interlude of which we know little and from which he is returned into public view by the advent of the loyal Ulrike. The beginning of the new year—1803—finds him at Ossmannstedt as the cherished guest of old Wieland who, having coaxed his *Guiscard* out of him, sets the highest hopes on him, prophesying that he will achieve a synthesis unheard of in European letters of Aeschylus, Sophocles and Shakespeare. This idyll ends, too, probably because Kleist did not ward off, or respond to, the affections of Wieland's fourteen-year-old daughter Luise; and again he gravitates to France, this time wandering, clearly in a disturbed state of mind, from Lyon via St. Omer to Boulogne where he tries to sneak his way into the French infantry massed to invade England. Despatched back to Germany—he has meanwhile, in a brainstorm, burnt the manuscript of *Guiscard*—he reports to a doctor by the name of Wedekind in Mainz that he feels ill and is nursed by him, in a grave mental condition, over a number of weeks. He considers becoming a carpenter. Meanwhile his friend Pfuel, whom he had repeatedly pestered for a suicide-pact,[3] has daily and desperately looked for his vanished friend in the morgue in Paris.[4]

On returning to Berlin and being interrogated about his treasonable activities by the king's adjutant von Köckeritz, Kleist pleaded that some idée fixe had saddled him with a headache so splitting that he would have agreed to having the earth's axis reversed to rid himself of the pain. Reinstated this time as a civil servant, he was presently sent to Königsberg, where he met his ex-fiancée, now—of all ironical coincidences—the wife of Kant's successor, Professor Krug! The autumn of 1805 and the beginning of 1806 saw him ailing, yet slogging away at his chores amid furious work on his dramas; and in August of that year he was granted a six months' leave of absence on grounds of poor health. In October 1806, Napoleon won the battle of Jena. Prussia collapsed. On his way to Dresden, Kleist, together with Pfuel and some other friends, was arrested on a charge of attemped spying and kept under lock and key during some six months, first in Fort de Joux near Besançon and later in a prisoner-of-war camp in Châlons sur Marne. Returned to Dresden, again through the plucky Ulrike's intervention, Kleist, together with Adam Müller, launched the literary journal *Phöbus,* having completed *Penthesilea* and published *Amphitryon* and "Das Erdbeben in Chili." The journal folded up after twelve issues, after Goethe's unsuccessful staging of Kleist's comedy, which proved a severe knock to his growing literary reputation. During its short lifetime, however, *Phöbus* had printed "Die Marquise von O.," the *Guiscard* fragment, two *Käthchen* fragments and one of "Michael Kohlhaas." *Die Hermannsschlacht* was completed. The year 1809 saw the entry of Austria into the war against Napoleon, the mobilisation of Prussia, the victory of Aspern and the Austrian defeat of Wagram. After Aspern, Heinrich, wandering over the battlefield, was once again suspected of being a spy and, to convince the soldiers otherwise, pulled his anti-French poems out of his pocket and proceeded to recite them to a jeering audience, an episode which his companion Dahlmann described as being tragicomical.[5] The reason he continually attracted suspicion, a later commentator surmises, is that he was so easily embarrassed, stuttered, had a child's face and spoke French more fluently than his mother tongue.[6]

Drawn towards the hard core of patriotic resistance in Austria, deeply cast down by the French victory at Wagram and the ensuing armistice, Kleist made his way to Prague, where he altogether disappeared from view for weeks on end. Rumor spread among his friends that he was dead. To their surprise, he turned up again, very much alive but shattered at the eclipse of the national fortunes. He settled in Berlin, from October 1810 edited the *Berliner Abendblätter,* which ran into editorial censorship troubles, incurred the displeasure of the king and folded on March 30, 1811. In June, *Prinz Friedrich von Homburg* was completed, in August, the second volume of his stories appeared. During this last period, his cousin Marie von Kleist is his main anchorage in life, trying to help him to obtain a post, a pension, and possibly his reinstatement as an officer. None of these moves proved successful. A desperate Kleist formed a close friendship with Henriette Vogel, a married woman suffering—or so it was believed—from terminal illness, and gradually the idea of a suicide pact crystallized. This was by no means the first time Kleist had reached out for such a solution: we have reports that as a mere boy he made such a pact with his cousin, Karl von Pannwitz,[7] that he roundly proposed a double suicide to Karoline von Schlieben,[8] periodically pestered Ernst von Pfuel and Rühle von Lilienstern,[9] and made an oblique offer to the poet Fouqué,[10,11] the last two suggestions being oddly enough made at the spot at which he was actually to end his life. But now he had met a woman who had nothing to lose. On November 21, 1811, having burnt all Kleist's papers and written ecstatic

INTRODUCTION

farewell messages, the two were watched by the innkeeper near Potsdam where they had turned in, running hand in hand down the incline towards the lake (the Kleine Wannsee), jumping, fooling, skipping flat pebbles across the water's surface and sporting upon the shore, chasing one another like two children, as they had indeed addressed one another while still within the hearing of a witness.[12] A little later, two shots rang out. Kleist had shot his companion through the heart, himself through the mouth.

Towards the end of Kleist's short life a family conference had declared him a good-for-nothing who had brought dishonor to an illustrious name. On the day of the 100th anniversary of his birth, representatives of that same family laid a wreath, saying, "Dem Besten ihres Geschlechts." This was replaced in 1936 by a tombstone bearing his name and dates and the simple inscription:

> Nun,
> O Unsterblichkeit,
> Bist Du Ganz Mein.

2

From this short sketch it will be apparent that we have no biography in any proper sense of the word of a brief life lived out in the glare of the contemporary literary scene, a span encompassed by more than twenty years on either side by that of Goethe whose every step and passing thought is documented by others as well as by himself. Time and again, the trail of this life is lost in discontinuity and darkness—in sickness, voluntary and involuntary exile, and supposed death—and when we pick it up again, it is without any clues as to the intervening links. Undoubtedly the event of which we know by far the most is that double shot ringing out across the shores of the Kleine Wannsee which was trotted out in the newspapers and in private letters for weeks and months on end. Unless we are prepared to maintain, as some have done, that Heinrich von Kleist's death was his surpassing work of art, we are none the wiser.

Indeed, Kleist is not merely an artist without an outer biography. We have pitifully few clues as to what went on inside him. It is entirely characteristic that an autobiographical novel in two volumes entitled *Geschichte meiner Seele* which would have been invaluable source material was destroyed or more probably lost and that no trace of it has shown up to this day. Indeed we are lucky to possess what collected works we do have. *Homburg* turned up by the merest of chances, and we owe it to the untiring efforts of Ludwig Tieck and a few other admirers that we have a substantial opus warranting to be commemorated up and down the country, indeed all over the civilized world, in the first place. And it is largely due to the dedicated labors of Helmut Sembdner in this century that we have colorful if intermittent documentation of the impact made by Kleist's works and personality on his own and later times.

Nonetheless, to reconstruct something of that inner biography of Kleist's in which man and work supplement and illuminate one another must, for the most part, remain a matter for conjecture. We may profitably set out on this task by asking what was the dominant impression left by him and of him. The answer that immediately springs to mind is that it was one of suffering, and suffering of a peculiarly helpless and radical kind, such as is sometimes seen in the eyes of children. The last words virtually he penned to his half-sister Ulrike "on the morning of my death" were these: "die Wahrheit ist, daß mir auf Erden nicht zu helfen war."[13] The tenor of such words is matched by K. von Holtey who speaks of the "unhappiest of all *great German poets*"[14] or by Friedrich Hebbel's homage to "dieses außerordentliche, zu Tode gemarterte Genie,"[15] not to speak of the lines from the poem which that writer—like an astonishing number of others—dedicated to Kleist:

> An Kraft sind wenige ihm zu vergleichen,
> An unerhörtem Unglück, glaub ich, keiner.[16]

Nor is it only shadowed by death's wing that Kleist himself assessed his condition on this earth to be radically incurable. Much, much earlier already, when he was a young man of 23, as the Kant-crisis was breaking over his head, he spoke of his warm, impressionable heart "das unaufhörlich sich sehnt, immer wünscht und hofft, und niemals genießen kann, das etwas ahndet, was es nirgends findet,"[17] words which are echoed in December of that year when scolding "mein töricht überspanntes Gemüt, das sich nie an dem, was ist, sondern nur an dem, was nicht ist, erfreuen kann."[18] And eight weeks before his death he sums up this strain, saying that it is indescribably wretched "immer an einem anderen Orte zu suchen, was ich wohl an keinem, meiner eigentümlichen Beschaffenheit wegen, gefunden habe."[19]

At this point some of my listeners may show signs of impatience, seeing before their minds' eye the interminable "blue flower" of Kleist's fellow contemporaries, the Romantics, or even hearing in their inner ear the crushing end of Schubert's song *Der Wanderer,* from the song-cycle *Die Winterreise*: "Da, wo du *nicht* bist, da ist das Glück. . . ." If so, this is the time to leave the room; for, remembering Rahel von Varnhagen's lovely words: "es ging streng um ihn her, er war wahrhaft und litt viel. . . ."[20] I shall press on and ask, in his own words, what ineradicable condition made his lot on this earth incurable? And to ask this question seriously and in depth,

INTRODUCTION

we must ask "wie sich die Welt in diesem Kopfe spiegelt," a problem of communication which, since the disquieting investigations of R. D. Laing, may no longer strike us as flippant or superfluous.

By way of a preliminary answer, let me quote a couple of descriptions, one, or really two, by Kleist himself, the other by a sensitive commentator of the last century. In one of his earliest letters, in which he tries to sell his half-sister Ulrike his own concept of a life's plan, Kleist speaks of life as a journey: "Ein Reisender, der das Ziel seiner Reise, und den Weg zu seinem Ziele kennt, hat einen Reiseplan. Was der Reiseplan dem Reisenden ist, das ist der Lebensplan dem Menschen."[21] The day before his death, Kleist took up the image again. And now it appeared in immeasurably deepened form, the form, in fact, in which we know it from the last monologue of Prinz Friedrich von Homburg. He is once more putting pen to paper "in dieser Stunde, da unsere Seelen sich, wie zwei fröhliche Luftschiffer, über die Welt erheben," words which clearly cut deep, seeing that they are echoed by his companion in death who adds the postscript of "zwei wunderlichen Menschen, die bald ihre große Entdeckungsreise antreten werden."[22] The other description stems from the autobiography of one Johann George Scheffner. "Wie ein der Meerestiefe entsteigender Taucher sich wenigstens in den ersten Augenblicken nicht auf alles Große und Schöne besinnt, was er in der Wasserwelt gesehen, und es nicht zu erzählen vermag, so schien es bisweilen bei Heinrich von Kleist der Fall zu sein."[23] These are beautiful and resonant words, and they make the mind hum with a host of assonances. They recall the profound abstractedness evinced by some of Kleist's characters, Penthesilea, Achilles, or by the speaker at the end of the essay "Über das Marionettentheater," or again those strange words recounting the way that thought is dredged up from the deep, from the essay "Über die allmähliche Verfertigung der Gedanken beim Reden": "Denn nicht *wir* wissen, es ist allererst ein gewisser *Zustand* unsrer, welcher weiß."[24] But here Scheffner's words arrest the attention because they so patently tie in with the tenor of Kleist's own: in both, he is pictured as an explorer, indeed as a denizen of another world in which altogether different conditions obtain: a world presupposing different impression, sensations, and experiences from the ones that are familiar to us and governed by laws which are different, and contrary, to those to which we are beholden. For, to mention only one thing, both the astronaut and the deep-sea diver are exempt from gravity, the one because of the buoyancy of the water, the other because that of the air. And both are basically lonely.

I would suggest that Kleist's mind inhabited a world radically different from ours, that consequently our own world was mirrored in the most bizarre way in his shapely and childlike head—his farewell letter still marvels "Ja, die Welt ist eine wunderliche Einrichtung"[25]—and that he quit it because he could neither understand it nor accommodate himself to its rules. He was a congenital misfit and the suffering that meant turned out to be too great. If we entertain this hypothesis for a moment, a number of things that are otherwise puzzling slot into place. First, his high-handed way of dealing with the basic laws governing our terrestrial existence. We have seen in passing that he was ready to reverse the earth's axis to get rid of the headache that plagued him when he strayed through France. This is by no means a unique thought pattern. In his poetic world, the basic laws of our physical and mental universe—the law of gravity and the law of contradiction—are constantly and very readily rescinded. Rivers flow upstream—the image occurs time and again to express a given character's sense of stupefaction at the ways of this, our, world—and two variables that equal a third one, nonetheless contradict one another. A passage that is entirely characteristic in this respect is the one in which Odysseus, in *Penthesilea,* expresses his puzzlement at the war strategy of the Amazons, like the Greeks the enemies of the Trojans, yet equally implacable vis-à-vis the Greeks:

> So viel ich weiß, gibt es in der Natur
> Kraft bloß und ihren Widerstand, nichts Drittes.
> Was Glut des Feuers löscht, löst Wasser siedend
> Zu Dampf nicht auf und umgekehrt. Doch hier
> Zeigt ein ergrimmter Feind von beiden sich,
> Bei dessen Eintritt nicht das Feuer weiß,
> Obs mit dem Wasser rieseln soll, das Wasser,
> Obs mit dem Feuer himmelan soll lecken.[26]

True, this speech is in character. It is the rationalistic Greek who mentally measures what is credible against the law of contradiction (and, for that matter, that of gravity). But illustrations of this kind could be multiplied and their cumulative effect is to induce a slight sense of giddiness suggesting that Kleist has a secret vantage point in some other world, seen from which our own physical and mental universe seems gently to sway on its hinges.

A second feature which becomes clear is the sense of puzzlement communicated by him and by so many of his characters. This is the description Clemens Brentano gave of Kleist's personality. It impresses itself as peculiarly authentic. "Der Phöbus *Kleist,*" he writes, "ein sehr kurioser, guter, grober, bornierter, dummer, eigensinniger, mit langsamem Konsequenztalent herrlich ausgerüsteter Mensch,"[27] and this characterisation is mirrored in a deft thumbsketch of Kleist's characters, again by the shrewd Brentano: "Er denkt sich alle Personen halb taub und dämlich, so kömmt dann durch Fragen und Repetieren der Dinge der Dialog heraus."[28]

Very few commentators have had the pluck to call Kleist, or his characters, plain stupid. Gundolf is one of the few, in a book which otherwise misses the mark. But that is precisely what he is and what they are: only we are better advised to translate *dumm* into *tumbe*, stupid into stupified: he, and they, are figures set into a world so alien that they appear, like Amphitryon, perpetually to have "fallen from the clouds," nonplussed in a world the very cogency of which to them bristles with paradox and whose seemingly most nonsensical manifestations are wearily accepted as inevitable, seeing that it is "eine wunderliche Einrichtung"—"a wondrous institution"—crazily topsy-turvy compared with the world that their minds inhabit. Our world, the fragile world, "on which the Gods but gaze down from afar," to Kleist's figures appears to be as puzzling as the Amazon state does to the Greeks; and yet the natives of that strange institution who solemnly and ludicrously replenish their young "according to annual calculations" feel everything about their state to be perfectly rational and in order.

But, you will ask, what world is it which Kleist and his figures inhabit, and how can we know anything of its constitution? My answer is that it is a "verkehrte Welt:" more precisely speaking, the world of Kant in reversal, and that we may get a perfectly clear view of it by calling to mind the world of experience as Kant envisaged it. Not indeed that Kleist's inner universe was a philosophical construct. To say this would be as far from the truth as is ever possible. His world was there, latent long before the encounter with Kant. But that encounter served as a catalyst which made Kleist's own vision jell, and gave it the contour and density in which it was henceforth to govern his structuring imagination, leaving its unmistakably Kleistean imprint upon its every creation.

I have just said that the characteristically Kleistean world was there, latent, before the cathartic encounter with Kant's philosophy. This I must now seek to show, and to do so will mean delving into the pathology of Kleist. That done, we shall see the emergent model of the world crystallize into full articulation in the clarifying contact with that of Kant; and at this point, what started as being a deeply pathological and private pattern takes on the dignity of an artistic archetype and becomes the matrix on which Kleist's dramatic and narrative structures are recorded, public, accessible, and, in their way, unbetterable.

To explain this twofold course, a very beautiful passage from Goethe's Notes and Treatises on the *Westöstliche Divan* serves. Explicating an oriental legend which has for its subject Christ's compassion for a dead dog—Jesus points out to the disgusted bystanders that its teeth are as white as pearls—Goethe comments: "Ein faulendes Geschöpf wird, durch das Vollkommene was von ihm übrigbleibt, ein Gegenstand der Bewunderung und des frömmsten Nachdenkens."[29] To illustrate this transition—which is the transition we shall have to make—Goethe then adduces the following simile. In some regions, he relates, a vital building material is produced by slowly burning sea shells stacked between layers of firewood. "Der Zuschauende kann sich das Gefühl nicht nehmen, daß diese Wesen, lebendig im Meere sich nährend und wachsend .... jetzt, nicht etwa verbrennen, sondern durchgeglüht, ihre völlige Gestalt behalten, wenn gleich alles Lebendige aus ihnen weggetrieben ist. Nehme man nunmehr an, daß die Nacht hereinbricht und diese organischen Reste dem Auge des Beschauers wirklich glühend erscheinen, so läßt sich kein herrlicheres Bild einer tiefen, heimlichen Seelenqual vor Augen stellen."[30] This transfiguration of living, squirming, and agonised matter being burnt clean into the "völlige Gestalt"—the pure form—of suffering it is now our business to trace.

3

"In mir ist nichts beständig, als die Unbeständigkeit,"[31] Kleist is supposed to have said, and the tenor of this remark is borne out time and again in his letters. "Ach, was ist das Leben eines Menschen für ein farbenwechselndes Ding,"[32] he exclaims during his stay in Paris and asks his fiancée to be satisfied with a rather tatty letter, giving her nothing but snatches of his interior state, for "Es ist darin so wenig bestimmt, daß ich mich fürchten muß, etwas aufzuschreiben, weil es dadurch in gewisser Art bestimmt *wird*."[33]

If such lability reflects the early Goethe of, say, the anacreontic *Die Freuden* with its iridescent dragonfly, or *Unbeständigkeit*, so does, up to a point, his deployment of water imagery. "Pfeilschnell"—dartlike—the river Rhine speeds to its destination, impatient of earthly obstacles—the image occurs twice (to Karoline von Schlieben, Paris, 18 July, 1801, S. No. 48 and to Adolfine von Werdeck, Paris, 28 and 29 July, 1801, S. No. 50); while the river Elbe is described—again twice—as kissing now one bank of its darling Dresden, then "tottering"—"wanken"—over to the other, and fleeing from both, "als würde ihr die Wahl schwer;"[34] and the same image is twice used, in a less euphoric fashion, of the river Main.[35] Images of ambivalence culminate in one that is expressive of pure transcience, as Kleist remembers lying in the bottom of a boat and letting himself be carried downstream, unresisting. "Wie diese Fahrt," he reflects, "so war mein ganzes damaliges Leben ... Ach, das Leben des Menschen ist, wie jeder Strom, bei seinem Ursprunge am höchsten. Es fließt nur fort, indem es fällt—In das Meer müssen wir alle—Wir sinken und sinken..."[36]

But whereas the Goethe of say, "An den Mond," was able mentally to sustain, and to transfigure, the phenomenon of sheer flux in tranquil recollection, so that it became shaped into song, Heinrich von Kleist is in a less favored position. He lacks the capacity to hold things in memory. "Aber

INTRODUCTION 13

zu schnell wechseln die Erscheinungen im Leben," he laments, "und zu eng ist das Herz, sie alle zu umfassen und immer die vergangnen schwinden, Platz zu machen den neuen, und matt gibt es sich Eindrücken hin, deren Vergänglichkeit es vorempfindet—Ach, es muß öde und leer und traurig sein, später zu sterben als das Herz...."[37] The same lament is repeated ten days later, but this time with a telling preamble of which I quote only a small excerpt: "Ach, die Liebe entwöhnt uns von ihren Freuden, wie die Mutter das Kind von der Milch, indem sie sich Wermut auf die Brust legt—Und doch ist die Erinnerung selbst an das Bitterste noch süß. Ja, es ist kein Unglück, das Glück verloren zu haben, das erst ist ein Unglück, sich seiner nicht mehr zu erinnern...."[38]

The inability to hold experience in memory is a deep and very early impairment incurred, as we now know, and as Kleist seems to know in this very passage, in the feeding situation with the mother and in later life accountable for a damaged sense of identity and an inability to experience symbolically. Nonsense, my readers will think: an inability to experience symbolically in relation to the animal symbolicum par excellence, the poet! Yet this is precisely how it is and Kleist himself knew it, too. He is quite alone, he writes to his cousin Marie von Kleist in the summer of his last year. "Sie helfen sich mit Ihrer Einbildung und rufen sich aus allen vier Weltgegenden, was Ihnen lieb und wert ist, in Ihr Zimmer herbei. Aber diesen Trost....muß ich *unbegreiflich unseliger* Mensch entbehren. Wirklich, in einem so besondern Fall ist noch vielleicht kein Dichter gewesen..."[39]

Then he goes on to relate how an object to him is either one to his five live senses or fails to be an object. "Every one who thinks differently on this point," he categorically states, must draw upon a store of experience radically incompatible with his, Kleist's own. When people are absent, they are as good as dead to him, and he mourns them as though they were in fact dead; "and if I didn't know that you are going to return, I'd feel the same way about you." And statements such as this one could be readily multiplied.

An exceptional impressionableness making him a plaything of momentary impingements, a sense of being in interminable flux like the river that carries him downstream, combined with a startling lack of holding power to sustain the awareness of abiding pattern in the absolutely ephemeral—such are the elements of which Kleist's dominant character trait is compounded; a deep ontological insecurity, born of a defective sense of identity.

The question arises what sort of a world a person needs who so profoundly lacks an anchorage within himself. The answer is that he requires a world that shall be a stable and solid vis-à-vis to his own mutability. He needs a world of objects that are reliably "there" so as to demarcate the fluctuating frontiers of his self.

So paramount is this need in the case of Kleist that it leads his mind continually to hypostasize, i.e. to make substantial and to reify, that is to endow with thing-character, what is living and mutable. No single image renders these twin tendencies quite as graphically as do his descriptions—repeated threefold and virtually verbatim—of the impression made upon him by the towns of Würzburg, Dresden, and Mainz. The circumstance that the picture he conveys of three quite different towns is identical testifies to the fact that he is here exteriorizing a model of his way of seeing, determined by his overriding need. Here is the first of those inscapes, of the panorama of Würzburg, dating from before the encounter with Kant: "In der Tiefe . . . . liegt die Stadt." (The account of Mainz speaks of "eine konkave Wölbung, wie von der Hand der Gottheit eingedrückt"), "wie in der Mitte eines Amphitheaters. Die Terrassen der umschließenden Berge dienten statt der Logen, Wesen aller Art blickten als Zuschauer voll Freude herab und sangen und sprachen Beifall, oben in der Loge des Himmels stand Gott. Und aus dem Gewölbe des großen Schauspielhauses sank der Kronleuchter der Sonne herab. . . ."[40] God and his heavenly hosts have become endowed with material substance, living nature—the valley, the terraced hills, the sky, the sun—have been frozen into so many reliably static objects: a globular solid vault scooped out by the hand of God, encasing a grand tier, a royal box and, for good measure, a chandelier! Such is the need for concretion on the part of his mercurial and unstable mind. And indeed, the picture remains unchanged wherever we look in Kleist's letter: truth and virtue become a precious hoard to be stowed away, guaranteeing immortality; the living heart is described as "that quaint thing of which one only needs to let oneself be robbed for it to bear interest;" that most intangible of assets, his fiancée's loyalty, is likened to a banknote, real or faked; and living love becomes—of all things he might have thought of—an icefloat that is safely carried past all obstacles to the eternally chilly sea.

4

Into such a psychological constellation—and a very sick configuration it is—burst the picture of the world as Kant insisted that it must be. It is, in short, a world which has been denuded of its thinghood. To explain the possibility of such universal predictive judgments as we do make about objects outside us and their behavior, Kant had resorted to the notion that it is our minds which are instrumental, in the first instance, in creating, or constituting, the very objects we thus know. Through the forms of our pure sensibility—time and space—and the categories of our understanding, such as causality, we ourselves construe the sensa that assail us into meaningful patterns of objective experience or—and this comes to the same—into such objects as may fall within the range of our possible experiencing. What such things might be in themselves, unconditioned by the synthesizing mind, we have no way of knowing. These fall outside the boundaries of our knowing and can only be approximated by our doing. What we can know is the world of objects capable of being empirically experienced: and this world of phenomena is mind-imbued through and through, insolubly interlaced with the intelligence that helps interpret and, indeed, construct it in the first instance. It is within a mental time-space continuum and within intellectual categories of our own contributing that we experience objects which are by definition germane to our mind and transparent to it. The 'outer space' enveloping the area of experience mapped out by this joint subject-object enterprise to us remains terra incognita, a void filled by our doing and believing.

To a Kleist relying on a solid object world to help define, and prop, a gravely defective sense of self, this picture of the world must have been, and indeed was, shattering. To him the epistemological question of how we come by universal a priori judgments was of no interest whatever. What was of burning interest to one fluctuating like him was the unadulterated object-status of the world outside, its reliable thinghood. He had no earthly use for a theory postulating a collusion between subject and object, knower and known. On the contrary, his radical insecurity clamored for a direct, and reassuring, awareness of things, absolutely uninfected by the mutability of the knowing self, as-they-are-in-themselves. And thus, bruised by the literally world-shaking encounter with Kant's critical philosophy, he retreated into the thick-walled fortress of an obdurately naive realism. To him, phenomena were things were things were things. They could not possibly be effects of the noumenal as they were to Kant, or translucent veils of it as they were to Goethe, in an experiential encounter involving and modifying subject and object alike and marking out, as it were, a familiar and humanised zone in an interior time-space continuum. Phenomena, to him, were as real as bricks—and as opaque, and they hit him out of the blue either with the impact of numinous visitations or, in this world of ours in which our subjectivity does ineluctably modify our perceptions, with the trickery of witchcraft and delusion. Against a fluid world in which dreams need to be distinguished from actuality, in which the same water seems tepid to the cool hand and cold to the warm one, he pitted the immutable universe of immutable objects his idiosyncratic vision demanded: a solid continuum of things par excellence, mind-independent entities experienced unconditionally and alike inscrutable whether they were "Erscheinungen" in one or the other sense available to Kleist—

visionary apparations of the Absolute or surface appearances tricking credulous senses.

This, then, is the shape of the world as he envisaged it in the recesses of his innocent and untempered mind: a world in some dark outer space, dark because unillumined by mind and outer because not construed within the time-space continuum provided by mind; an assemblage of discrete, opaque, and utterly alien objects unrelated either to one another or to the experiencing self and impinging on it with terrible immediacy. Whether those objects were other selves or things made no difference. In either case, the navel cord of mutual involvement in the experiential encounter being severed, they were wholly "other" and alike intractable. The paradigm of such an experiential encounter of non-knowing is to be found in *Penthesilea*, in two descriptions of the head-on meeting between the Amazon and the man she loves. There we read:

> Jetzt, eben jetzt, da ich dies sage, schmettern
> Sie wie zwei Sterne aufeinander ein!

And, even more poignantly:

> Achill und sie, mit vorgelegten Lanzen
> Begegnen beide sich, zween Donnerkeile,
> Die aus Gewölken in einander fahren.[41]

In Kleist's world, the experiential encounter between two sentient selves is tantamount to a frontal collision between discrete projectiles in outer space—stars, thunderbolts, meteoric fragments, what have you—each ramming the other in an unmitigated impact of unparalleled force and either destroying it utterly or else glancing off its impermeable shell. And the symbol for the impenetrable integrity of the self, a windowless monad if any, unknowing and unknown, is always the gem.

Apparition or appearance, penetration or surface rebound: these are the alternative forms the encounter between two unrelated "things-in-themselves" can take. They span the two ends of Kleist's experiential spectrum. Take apparition and penetration first: always, these betoken the annihilating inroads made by one unmediated self into the other. Of this nature is the impact of Achilles on Penthesilea and of her on him; of Ottokar on Agnes; of Graf Wetter vom Strahl on Käthchen; of Jupiter on Alkmene; and of Count F. on the Marquise von O. And such is the aura of numinosity felt to surround the direct apparition of the absolutely "other" that the poet deploys all the magic of his poetry to evoke cosmic distances and thunderous over-proximity, otherworldly illumination and inky darkness, consuming splendor and faceless, brooding presence, as in young Agnes' description of Ottokar in the poet's first drama, *Die Familie Schroffenstein*:

INTRODUCTION

>   Sein Antlitz
> Gleicht einem milden Morgenungewitter,
> Sein Aug dem Wetterleuchten auf den Höhn,
> Sein Haar den Wolken, welche Blitze bergen,
> Sein Nahen ist ein Wehen aus der Ferne,
> Sein Reden wie ein Strömen von den Bergen
> Und sein Umarmen—
>
> *(11,1: 693-699)*

Or again, here is Penthesilea's description of Achilles as she first set eyes on him:

>   Wie aber ward mir,
> O Freund, als ich dich selbst erblickte!
> Als du mir im Skamandros-Tal erschienst,
> Von den Heroen deines Volks umringt,
> Ein Tagsstern unter bleichen Nachtgestirnen!
> So müßt es mir gewesen sein, wenn er
> Unmittelbar mit seinen weißen Rossen
> Von dem Olymp herabgedonnert wäre,
> Mars selbst, der Kriegsgott, seine Braut zu grüßen!
> Geblendet stand ich, als du jetzt entwichen,
> Von der Erscheinung da—wie wenn zur Nachtzeit
> Der Blitz vor einen Wandrer fällt, die Pforten
> Elysiums, des glanzerfüllten, rasselnd,
> Vor einem Geist sich öffnen und verschließen.[42]

And finally, listen to the second description of Achilles which actually accompanies the frontal collision of these two "luminaries:"

> Seht, seht, wie durch der Wetterwolken Riß,
> Mit einer Masse Licht, die Sonne eben
> Auf des Peliden Scheitel niederfällt!
>
> Auf einem Hügel leuchtend steht er da,
> In Stahl geschient sein Roß und er—der Saphir,
> Der Chrysolit wirft solche Strahlen nicht!
> Die Erde rings, die bunte, blühende,
> In Schwärze der Gewitternacht gehüllt;
> Nichts als ein dunkler Grund nur, eine Folie,
> Die Funkelpracht des Einzigen zu heben![43]

This is Kleist's nature imagery at its most magnificent. Such grandeur is at the poet's bidding because nature, alongside the selves that make their appearance in it, is herself experienced as pregnant with the Numinous, partaking of its distance and its dynamism, its sheer "otherness" and, with it, its threatening closeness, if anything, magnifying the consuming glory and the annihilating violence of its impingement.

The very space in which such descriptions as I have quoted are set is as "unmental" as could ever be: concrete, looming, a huge vault but a vault nonetheless, like those amphitheatres of nature in which the young Kleist embedded his interior panoramas. There is no air inside this dome, nor does it shade off into a felt infinity: the sky is a close-fitting hood made of steel, like the armor in which Achilles is sheathed.

Even time, in Kleist, is represented as though it were solid. The poet evokes it in curious concretion by setting side by side two or more sequential events, say, Penthesilea's mind outpacing the horse she rides and the army that follows her, or Achilles overtaking her by the length of three arrow shots. The slower moving of these sequences in their graphic presentation become the visible yardstick, as it were, against which the faster one can be read off spatially, like the mercury column of a thermometer climbing up along its scale. One illustration will make my point:

> Seht! wie sie mit den Schenkeln
> Des Tigers Leib inbrünstiglich umarmt!
> Wie sie, bis auf die Mähn herabgebeugt,
> Hinweg die Luft trinkt lechzend, die sie hemmt!
> Sie fliegt wie von der Senne abgeschossen:
> Numidsche Pfeile sind nicht hurtiger!
> Das Heer bleibt keuchend hinter ihr, wie Köter,
> Wenn sich ganz aus die Dogge streckt, zurück!
> Kaum daß ihr Federbusch ihr folgen kann![44]

You can see how time is measured out in space, as the hound draws ahead to overtake the mongrels. Such is the precipitate, on the poetic plane, of Kleist's "Naive Realism," that is to say, his literal envisagement of time and space, together with the object world, as ontologically self-sufficient external entities enjoying the status of full "thinghood."

That the direct encounter of such impermeable forces—like diamonds they shatter or deflect one another—is from the start destructive and allows of no true communication needs no spelling out. Their meeting signifies no "taking in" of the other in an act of loving relatedness—how could incapsulated "things-in-themselves" open up so as to take in the wholly alien other—but an orgy between strangers, which, at best, issues in a swoon or death and, at worst, in atavistic modes of physical ingestion.

5

The wholly "other" experienced as mystic apparition—such an encounter is soul piercing and incandesced with suffering. And yet these invasions from the yonder are also luminous—one thinks of the fairytale loving of

Käthchen or Homburg's dream visions, or of the visitations of Alkmene or the Marquise von O. by their demonic lovers—and while they last, Kleist's figures move with ease in their own world, and are exempt from gravity, like those pebbles he made to dance across the water's surface before they sank and died. The real agony begins when what had been hailed as the immediate perception of the truth becomes unmasked as a delusion of the senses, when the Absolute can no longer be plucked like a juicy fruit from the nearest tree. This is, of course, the situation in the Garden of Eden when Adam and Eve, reaching out to "see" what is strictly invisible—the knowledge of good and evil—end up eating apples, a tragicomical debacle insistently touched on in the essay on the puppet show and paradigmatic for the poet as the model of experiencing in this world or ours:

> ... die gebrechliche,
> Auf die nur fern die Götter niederschaun.[45]

For with the Absolute becoming withdrawn and intractable to naively innocent perception, Kleist's primordial world fractures as our complex one rudely encroaches on it, confounding the percipient with its contingency. Signs no longer betoken their significances, what was experienced as direct apparition is now experienced as oblique appearance, the glance that was ecstatically felt to be penetrating the unknown "other" to the core, in a lightning flash in stupified incomprehension bounds off the surface of a now impermeable shell. This is the rude "Fall" suffered by the prince, as the procession of those he loved and sought to grasp is swallowed up in darkness, as the "sun" of the elector's grace is hidden behind a bank of heavy clouds. This is Gustav's tragedy as he wakes up bound hand and foot by the girl he thought he knew. This is the trauma of Penthesilea as the man whose radiance filled her vision incomprehensibly and maddeningly challenges her to do battle.

It is in such situations of reversal when Kleist's figures are jolted out of their involuntary grace, and startled perception splinters against the surface of a reality become patently inscrutable, that Kleist's proclivity to hypostasize the unsubstantial and to reify what is living runs amok. What a strange conflation of disparate things! Spiritual imponderables such as Amphitryon's honor, Alkmene's or Eve's or Littegarde's integrity, Kohlhaas' justice or Homburg's aspirations are compacted into an honest-to-goodness object—a diadem, a pitcher or a ring, a pair of blacks, a glove, and snatching at the reliable "thinghood" of such "articles of faith," the nonplussed seekers of Kleist's poetic universe try to fool themselves into believing in the veracity of objects still irridescent with the Numinous which they can thus directly grasp.

Even that most elusive of phenomena, "the enigma of a feeling heart," relatedness in love, becomes reified and is subjected to a coldly positivistic scrutiny, as though it were a thing among others, an object to be sized up, held, and weighed. Like a criminologist or torturer, Amphitryon puts Alkmene's loving on the rack, interrogating and dissecting it and coming away empty-handed and angry. Natalie to the prince becomes a barterable pawn, in a cruel game to which in his disillusionment he imagines the elector to be a party. With the dispassion of a chartered surveyor he measures his own immortal share in terms of the space his physical body occupies, first two spans above the earth and then two spans below ground.

Simple Simons all and sundry who would know directly an "other" to which, by definition, they can have no access, their rage as their concussed sensibility glances off that impermeable "other," however tantalisingly close at hand, is measureless. And always this rage finds vent in their abuse of sense organs which have so dismally failed them, in a tangled world in which direct apparition has turned into a degrading surface encounter with appearance. This is how Amphitryon despairs of a spiritual challenge to which he has proven shamefully unequal:

> In Zimmern, die vom Kerzenlicht erhellt,
> Hat man bis heut mit fünf gesunden Sinnen
> In seinen Freunden nicht geirret; Augen,
> Aus ihren Höhlen auf den Tisch gelegt,
> Vom Leib getrennte Glieder, Ohren, Finger,
> Gepackt in Schachteln, hätten hingereicht,
> Um einen Gatten zu erkennen. Jetzo wird man
> Die Ehemänner brennen, Glocken ihnen,
> Gleich Hämmeln, um die Hälse hängen müssen.[46]

This rage, this bitter suffering is Kleist's own, in a world where knowledge is not possible; not, ultimately, because it is a phenomenal world, the world of a Goethe or a Kant, but because knowledge is a tragic fiction in a universe peopled by contact-less and discontinuous beings, untarnished, yes, but also untempered by the interlacing of knower and the known. It is a precarious self, routed in its first security, as incapable of being related as of being distinct, repelling the "other" in a frozen stance of clinically viewing it or else devouring it, that has wrought this world out of its sickness; a world of isolates incapsulated in the oyster-shell of their selfhood and only sometimes, very rarely, flowing out in a total communion that is throat-catchingly sweet in its simple grace. This second innocence mirrors the primordial one, that of the virgin soul moving in the virgin territories of things as they are in themselves. But now an arctically pure landscape of the interior has melted and the contours of selves harshly opposed at long last blend in one melodious thaw.

Yet how bravely he lived his deep-sea longing for the absolutely pristine "other," how furiously he incarnated his characters who share his childlike and quixotic vision of unadulterated knowing, in the vice of a real that is forever conditioning! Nowhere perhaps has Kleist forged the anguish of life lived in a world where everything nauseatingly touches and interlocks with everything else more consummately than he did in his narrative prose; in those intricate plots where the simple vision is forever tricked by the wickedest twists of ambiguity and paradox, hallmarks of our bewildering world but not of his, in these labyrinthine periods where the subject is forever waylaid by impingements machine-gunning its consciousness to the point of fragmentation, preventing it, almost, from completing its utterance, from making its statement in life and about it.

They go to the point of fragmentation, but not quite. In the maze of a world into which this poet has placed them, his characters keep a tenuous hold on their vision, and they die face to face with it, content, whether what they see be love or justice, heaven or hell; and so did their creator. And because in the white-heat of the creative engagement, the shell of his being was cauterized of all sick and squirming matter, it is incandesced with a glow all its own. It has become—to quote Goethe once again—the pure vessel "the perfect form of a deep and secret agony," ours, surely, the agony of sentient souls isolated and imprisoned in a world that has become a technological and bureaucratic machinery altogether too abstruse for our feeling at home in it.

Let Wordsworth speak the concluding words:

> The thought of our past years in me does breed
> Perpetual benediction: not indeed
> For that which is most worthy to be blest—
> Delight and liberty, the simple creed
> Of Childhood, whether busy or at rest,
> With new-fledged hope still fluttering in his breast:
> Not for these I raise
> The song of thanks and praise;
> But for those obstinate questionings
> Of sense and outward things,
> Fallings from us, vanishings;
> Blank misgivings of a Creature
> Moving about in worlds not realised....[47]

Let us give thanks and praise to Kleist, for keeping faith to the simple creed of Childhood he retrieved from the under-water world of the unconscious, for those obstinate questionings and blank misgivings of a Creature moving about in worlds not realised which he would and could not stifle, and for those precious intimations of immortality he sometimes soared aloft to glimpse, intrepid astronaut that he was.

NOTES

1. Heinrich von Kleist, *Sämtliche Werke und Briefe*, Ed. Helmut Sembdner, 2nd ed. (Munich, 1961), Hanser Vlg. Vol II p. 493.
2. *Heinrich von Kleists Lebensspuren, Dokumente und Berichte der Zeitgenossen* 2., veränderte und erweiterte Auflage, Ed. Helmut Sembdner, (Bremen: Carl Schünemann, 1957). No. 4.
3. Ibid., No. 112.
4. Ibid., No. 119b.
5. Ibid., Nos. 316 & 317.
6. Ibid., No. 155.
7. Ibid., No. 5.
8. Ibid., No. 108.
9. Ibid., Nos. 53 & 112.
10. Ibid., No. 515a.
11. *Heinrich von Kleists Nachruhm. Eine Wirkungsgeschichte in Dokumenten.* (Bremen: Schünemann, 1976). No. 58.
12. *Lebensspuren*, No. 532.
13. Sembdner, Vol. II # 226, p. 887.
14. *Nachruhm*, No. 174d.
15. Ibid., No. 173.
16. Ibid., No. 296.
17. Sembdner, Vol. II #48, p. 659 to Karoline von Schlieben, (Paris, 18 July 1801).
18. Ibid., #59 p. 708 to H. Lohse, (Liestal, 23 (-29) December, 1801).
19. Ibid., #215 p. 877 to Marie von Kleist (Berlin, 17 September 1811).
20. *Nachruhm*, #51.
21. Sembdner, #5 p. 486 to Ulrike von Kleist, (Frankfurt a.d. Oder, Mai, 1799).
22. Ibid., #224 p. 885 to Sophie Müller, (Berlin, 20 November 1811).
23. *Lebensspuren*, No. 142.
24. Sembdner, Vol. II, p. 323.
25. Ibid., #224 p. 885 to Sophie Müller, (Berlin, 20 November 1811).
26. Sembdner, Vol. I, Penthesilea 1: 125-132.
27. *Lebensspuren*, No. 420a.
28. *Nachruhm*, No. 76.
29. *Goethes Werke*, Hamburger Ausgabe in 14 Bänden, ed. E. Trunz, 9th edition, Munich, 1972, Vol. 2, p. 164.
30. Ibid.
31. *Lebensspuren*, No. 108.
32. Sembdner, Vol. II No. 50, p. 671, to Adolfine von Werdeck (Paris 28(and 29) July, 1801).
33. Ibid., No. 46 p. 654/55, to Wilhelmine von Zenge (Göttingen, 3 June, 1801).
34. Ibid., No. 48 p. 662 to Karoline von Schlieben (Paris 18 July, 1801) and # 44 p. 647 to Wilhelmine von Zenge (Dresden, 4 May, 1801).
35. Ibid., No. 24 p. 579 to Wilhelmine von Zenge (Würzburg, 10 (and 11) October, 1800).
36. Ibid., No. 50 p. 674 to Adolfine von Werdeck (Paris 28 (and 29) July, 1801).

37. Ibid., No. 48 p. 661 to Karoline von Schlieben (Paris, 18 July, 1801).
38. Ibid., No. 50 p. 672 to Adolfine von Werdeck (Paris 28 (and 29) July, 1801).
39. Ibid., No. 210 p. 873 to Marie von Kleist (Berlin, Summer 1811).
40. Ibid., No. 24. p. 579/80 to Wilhelmine von Zenge (Würzburg 10 (and 11) October 1800). Cf. also: No. 48, to Karoline von Schlieben (Paris, 18 July, 1801); and: No. 50 to Adolfine von Werdeck (Paris, 28 (and 29) July, 1801).
41. Ibid., Vol. I Penthesilea 7: 1079/80, 8: 1123-1125.
42. Ibid., 15: 2203-2211.
43. Ibid., 7: 1033-1035, 1037-1043.
44. Ibid., 3: 395-403.
45. Ibid., 24: 2854/55.
46. Ibid., *Amphitryon* III, 1: 1681-1689.
47. *The Works of William Wordsworth*, with an introduction by Mark Van Doren, (Roslyn, 1951), p. 545.

Dramas

Kleist's Tragic Roots

KLAUS AICHELE
Brooklyn College

Kleist's closeness to Classical Greek drama is clearly evident in as much as half of his dramatic work: *Guiskard, Der zerbrochne Krug, Amphitryon, Penthesilea*. Modern interpreters of these plays, in most cases, seem to be content to demonstrate the literary relation, without too much concern for Kleist's specific tragic affinity to Greek tragedy.

The two pivotal authorities on tragedy, Aristotle and Nietzsche, seem to regard Euripides and Kleist respectively as the foremost tragedians of their national literatures.[1] In the work of both, women very frequently play the role of protagonists. It seems, therefore, that a closer look at the women protagonists in Kleist's and Euripides' work might offer a few new hints as to Kleist's specific tragic sensibility.

My point of departure is the protagonist in Kleist's "Marquise von O...." The novella presents the story of a woman who gets caught in a war, literally between the lines; she narrowly escapes rape by a hoard of enemy soldiers and is rescued by an enemy officer, in whose arms she faints; then she finds herself mysteriously pregnant without having had a sexual encounter in years. She suffers considerable embarrassment and hardship because of this, and eventually finds that her savior, the enemy officer, used her during her fainting spell, an act which has to be regarded as a form of rape. When he asks for her hand, quite understandably she shows him the door. Finally, when the Count has shown total contrition by giving her complete control over his person, she relents and accepts him as her husband.

The Marquise, it seems to me, has not received enough attention from her predominantly male interpreters who, understandably, concentrate on her male antagonist, Count F., and his problems. One of the key passages of the novella, the Marquise's musings about her predicament, at the very center of the novella, seems to me to bear closer scrutiny.

The Marquise, thrown out by her parents, finds herself literally *mutterseelenallein*, totally isolated. Strong woman, however, that she is, in this very crisis she regains her peace of mind. "Nur der Gedanke war ihr unerträglich, daß dem jungen Wesen, das sie in der größten Unschuld und Reinheit empfangen hatte, und dessen Ursprung, eben weil er geheimnisvoller war, auch göttlicher zu sein schien, als der anderer Menschen, ein Schandfleck in der bürgerlichen Gesellschaft ankleben sollte." Being sure of her own innocence, she worried about the child being born with a stigma, although its origin seemed to her in its very mystery all the more divine.

The surprising element here seems to be the word, "göttlich." How can the Marquise claim "divine origin" for her unborn child? Does she speak of her baby the way we speak of, for instance, a piece of music or even a gourmet dish as divine? That is, does she use the word metaphorically? This would sound like rather verbose sentimentalism coming from such a laconic woman. I believe that Kleist, or rather his heroine, have to be taken literally.

An earlier passage in the story seems to give a clue, namely the conversation with the midwife from whom the Marquise received the confirmation of her pregnancy. "Die Marquise . . . fragte, mit gebrochener Stimme, wie denn die Natur auf ihren Wegen walte? Und ob die Möglichkeit einer unwissentlichen Empfängnis sei?" She asked, in her anguish, what the midwife knew about the course of nature, and whether there was any possibility of "unwissentliche Empfängnis," unconscious conception. "Die Hebamme versetzte, daß dies, außer der heiligen Jungfrau, noch keinem Weibe auf Erden zugestoßen wäre . . . Nein, nein, antwortete die Marquise, sie habe wissentlich empfangen, sie wolle nur im allgemeinen wissen, ob diese Erscheinung im Reiche der Natur sei?" The midwife assures her that that had only happened to the Virgin Mary. The Marquise denies having thought of herself, she only wanted to know whether such a possibility existed in nature.

"Unconscious conception in the realm of nature?" Obviously, this would be a physiological rather than a psychological problem. She must be thinking of spontaneous generation which had been observed since Aristotle in lower animals such as worms, polyps, spiders. Plutarch[2] mentions an Egyptian myth that proclaimed that the vultures are all female and inseminated by the wind. The myth became part of the *Physiologus-Bestiary* tradition, and the Marquise could have known it from Amyot's Plutarch or any number of books. In any case, she still tries to rationalize what she cannot comprehend. We should not assume that the Marquise, devout Catholic and mother of two children that she is, has the presumption to see herself as a type of the Virgin who gave birth to the Messiah.

Christian mythology, therefore, does not furnish an explanation for the child's "divine origin." There remains Classical mythology. The Marquise is well read, Kleist mentions her library at three different occasions. He might have fancied his own books in her slender white hands. She could have read his *Amphitryon* or of course, for that matter, Plautus's or

Molière's, and now be reminded of Alkmene who after all went through something very similar. Having had the misfortune to incite the sexual appetite of a God, she had to suffer a lot of anguish until the father of her son to be born acknowledged his peccadillo. We might be reminded of the instant where Kleist uses the morpheme "god" on the father of the child. Toward the beginning of the story when the Count returns from the front and he and the Marquise, for the first time, have a good look at each other, Kleist calls him "schön wie ein junger Gott."

The Marquise is, I believe, a sort of Alkmene, only slightly more tragic. After all, even Kleist's *Amphitryon* is still a comedy. Whereas his Marquise of O. . . can hardly be seen as a comic heroine. Being caught in a siege, being nearly raped, finding herself mysteriously pregnant, being nearly shot by her own father, and cast out by her family, and eventually finding that the very person whom she considered her savior, in fact raped her and allowed seven men to be shot for having only attempted the crime that he committed. This is definitely not a comic plight.

Here it comes to mind that the first dramatic version of the Amphitryon myth is by the tragedian Euripides. There is little more than the title left of Euripides' *Alcmene*; but we know of a whole gallery of Euripidean heroines like Alkmene and the Marquise. Melanippe, Alope, Auge, Danaë, Antiope, and Krëusa who appears in the drama *Ion*, which has been preserved, all get in trouble because of their illegitimate children begotten by gods.

In all of these Euripidean tragedies, the heroines suffer because they are desired by males who are used to following their impulses without consulting anyone. Euripides deeply sympathizes with these suffering women.[3] Euripides the woman-hater is a comedy joke, just like Socrates counting flea's legs or Sappho killing herself on account of an unresponsive fisher lad.

Looking at Kleist's work, we find this scenario abounding; most of his heroines get in trouble being desired by men who concern themselves very little with their wishes. In fact what all Kleistian heroines share is suffering and humiliation, directly or indirectly caused by men. The heroes on the other hand suffer and cause suffering more or less of their own accord, usually by a mistake of judgment, a *hamartia* according to Aristotle.

The *Marquise of O. . .* furthermore, it seems to me, contains a series of situations that are typically Euripidean and have close counterparts in, for instance, Euripides' *Ion*. Ion's mother Krëusa does not conceive without her knowledge, but against her will, overpowered by the god Apollo. She exposes her son and then meets him again as a young man without recognizing him. In the course of events, mother and son are pitted against each other and almost kill each other. The recognition leads to their reconciliation. Hostile encounters of closely related characters abound in Euripides' plays; the heroines Auge and Danaë were threatened by their fathers just as was the Marquise of O. . . Eventually, at the end of *Ion*, the child's father, Apollo "der junge Gott," is revealed by the deus ex machina as the father is in Kleist's novella.

Ion's father Apollo, by the way, does not have the courage to show up in person; he sends his brother Hermes. He has every reason to hide because he has been very explicitly criticized by his own son:

> . . . Ein mächtiger Herr wie Du
> Soll Tugend üben. Wenn ein Sterblicher
> Ein Bösewicht ist, so strafen ihn die Götter;
> Wer soll die Götter strafen, wenn sie Böses tun?

This seems to me very close to the Marquise's sentiment about the Count whom she considers and actually exorcises as the Devil only because originally he had appeared to her as an angel. The tertium quid is of course the demand for higher moral responsibility that divine beings should be expected to feel.

Kleist's familiarity with Euripides' *Ion*, it seems to me, can be assumed. I believe we can even pinpoint the German version that Kleist read. The German translation just quoted is Christian Martin Wieland's. According to his own statement, Wieland had finished his translation of Euripides' *Ion* in the spring of 1802. The publication was delayed until 1803 when it appeared in his periodical *Attisches Museum*.[4] He kept it in his desk for a year using this time for further improvement ("Ausfeilung"). Kleist spent several months at the beginning of 1803 as a guest at Wieland's estate in Ossmannstedt near Weimar. At one point he overcame his usual shyness and recited to his older friend passages from his tragedy *Robert Guiskard*. Wieland is overwhelmed and feels reminded of Aeschylus and Sophocles.[5] Are we not almost compelled to conclude that he took it upon himself to introduce the young dramatist to the third great tragedian, who happened to be his own favorite, by showing him the *Ion* translation on which he was working just then?

I also believe that Kleist's specific concept of fate, of the "große, heilige und unerklärliche Einrichtung der Welt," the great, holy, and inexplicable constitution of the world, is deeply indebted to Euripides and his interpreter Wieland. In his notes to *Ion*,[6] Wieland characterizes Euripides' concept of fate with the following words:

> Aber was war denn der Begriff, den sich die Alten von diesem Schicksal machten? Sobald sie sich denselben klar zu machen suchten, gewiß kein anderer als eben derselbe, den wir Neuern mit diesem noch immer allgemein und täglich gebrauchten Worte verbinden—nämlich der Begriff des allgemeinen Zusammenhangs aller Dinge und Ereignisse in der Welt, in so fern als er notwendig, von dem Verstand und Willen der Sterblichen unabhängig, und eben darum unbegreiflich ist; eines Zusammenhangs, der gerade deswe-

gen, weil von dem Unerklärbaren und außer unserer Vorsicht und Willkür Liegenden in demselben so häufig das Glück oder Unglück einzelner Menschen und ganzer Völker abhängt, ein dunkles Gefühl in uns erregt, daß etwas Göttliches in ihm sei, daß er das Werk einer unumschränkten, unerforschlichen Macht sei, welche zu hoch über uns throne, als daß es so schwachen und beschränkten Wesen, wie wir Sterblichen, möglich und ziemlich sein könnte, sie zu fragen, was machst du.

The sentence seems to me to express the very sentiments of the Marquise of O . . . at the point where she submits to the "große, heilige und unerklärliche Einrichtung der Welt." This, as we have seen, suggests to her that her child's origin, since it is more mysterious ("geheimnisvoller"), is also more divine ("göttlicher") than that of other people.

We have thus come full circle from Kleist to Euripides, from Euripides to Wieland, and back to Kleist. What I tried to do was not to establish another literary source for the "Marquise von O . . .," but rather to show the spiritual kinship between the two tragic poets. I could have mentioned other points of contact, as for instance their conspicuous lack of success among their contemporaries. Even the particulars of the criticism they encountered are remarkably similar. They are too dialectical, Euripides for Nietzsche's as well as Kleist for Goethe's taste, to quote their most prominent German critics. They seem to be incongruous, Euripides, according to Nietzsche, in his mixing "kühle paradoxe Gedanken" and "feurige Affekte;" Kleist, according to Goethe, in his forcing together "Antikes" and "Modernes." What is probably most disquieting in the work of the two poets, is the intellectual tension, the result of a traumatic encounter with a high-powered philosophy, Sophism, and Kant, respectively. Wieland brilliantly characterizes this intellectual vibrancy in Kleist when he observes that "ein einziges Wort eine ganze Reihe von Ideen in seinem Gehirn wie ein Glockenspiel anzuziehen schien." The same could be said of Euripides. This intellectual tendency makes both of them play with tradition. Euripides wrote an *Antigone* in which the heroine got married to Haimon and moved with him to the countryside, Kleist parodies *Oedipus Rex* in his comedy *Der zerbrochne Krug*. It is obviously this "dallying" with a venerable tradition that Goethe and Nietzsche for specific reasons could not stomach. Both, Euripides and Kleist, are "Berufsliteraten," that is they live on their writing, with all the consequences. Both are highly patriotic, although their fellow-countrymen make them miserable. And, in conclusion, both are *tragikotatoi*, "utterly tragic," Euripides according to Aristotle, Kleist according to Wieland and Nietzsche. On the other hand, both have inspired comedies, Euripides *Amphitryon* and later Attic comedy in general, Kleist's "Marquise von O . . ." Eric Rohmer's movie.

These have to remain hints. In closing, I would like to strike one more chord on Kleist's carillon. The Marquise's musings about her child's father seem to be reminiscent of another character's musings about the identity of his own father, a character who will have to face the most horrible revelation imaginable; I mean Sophocles' Oedipus. The Oedipus speech in question follows Iocaste's final exit (107ff.); it might be paraphrased like this: "Let everything go to pieces. I want to know my origin, be it ever so humble. She (he is speaking of Iocaste) might be embarrassed by my low birth—she is a woman and such things mean a lot to her. I consider myself a son of the generous goddess Tyche (fortune) and am not ashamed of it. She is my mother. The months, my brothers, have seen my small beginnings and my rise. This is the way I am. I will not change and never give up the search for my origin."

The Marquise shares with Oedipus the apprehension concerning the social stigma of low birth, the determination to uncover it in spite of this, and the ever so slightly facetious claim of divine origin—at this point the Marquise and Oedipus are smiling. These are too many similarities, it seems to me, to be purely accidental. And let us not forget that *Oedipus Rex* was Kleist's favorite drama. It is almost as if he had put Oedipus's speech into prose and indirect discourse and given it to a woman.

NOTES

1. Aristotle in chapter 13 of his Poetics calls Euripides the most tragic of poets. That Nietzsche saw in Kleist the most tragic German author, can be seen clearly by interpolating his various statements on Kleist (cf. Oehler's index). Most indicative is the following aphorism: "What Goethe sensed in Kleist, was his tragic sensibility that he turned away from. It was the incurable side of nature. He himself was conciliatory and curable. Tragedy concerns incurable, comedy concerns curable suffering." (Nietzsche, *Die Unschuld des Werdens,* Der Nachlass ed. A. Bämler, Leipzig 1931, I 185)
2. Quaestiones Romanae no. 93.
3. My understanding of Euripides is deeply indebted to Philip Vellacott, *Ironic Drama, A Study of Euripides' Method and Meaning*, (Cambridge, 1975).
4. *Attisches Museum* IV 3 (1803), cf. "Vorbericht zu Ion". The lines quoted are 535ff.
5. Wieland's impressions of Kleist in his letter to Frh. von Wedekind in Mainz (Weimar, 10 April 1804).
6. *Attisches Museum* IV 3, 161f.

Rethinking Kleist's *Hermannsschlacht*

JEFFREY L. SAMMONS
Yale University

In the current atmosphere of German literary studies, one from time to time hears an assertion that our subject has, in the past, been hedged in with tabus that are now being triumphantly broken by the radical and the brave. This is certainly true, but the pervasive truth of it may slightly obscure the likelihood that the reorientation might generate here and there a new tabu as a reversal of repudiated allegiance. If one were to search for examples, it would be hard to find one so manifest as Kleist's *Hermannsschlacht*, which is one of the handful of dramas by a playwright of the highest standing and acutest interest in the modern canon of evaluation; yet it is perceived as a grave and discomforting embarrassment and therefore has been exiled to the periphery of our attention.

To my knowledge, *Die Hermannsschlacht* has not been performed since World War II, and it seems hardly possible that it ever could be, even by the techniques of parody and travesty to which canonical texts are often subjected on the German stage. Of course, it was never a success. The play that Kleist offered in 1809 as a gift to the German people[1] was not premiered until twenty-eight years after his death, and it was performed only sporadically thereafter. Even though it was revived in the Wilhelminian age as a festival play for national anniversaries, and it had some currency in the Nazi period as an ideological resource, apparently primarily in schools,[2] it does not seem even then to have had much life in the theater. The tendency in contemporary Kleist scholarship, with a few exceptions that I shall acknowledge in the course of this discussion, has been to dismiss it[3] or to confront it with succinct outrage.[4] Whatever we may think of *Die Hermannsschlacht*, therefore, it is clearly one area of Kleist's failure to realize his purposes and one of the most enduring aspects of his tragedy as a writer.

Perhaps it is easier for a non-German to be more dispassionate about this play. But it might not be amiss, first, to point out that the reasons for rejecting it have changed significantly through history and, second, to suggest that the biases and evils of past reception ought not wholly to regulate the boundaries of our current work of interpretation. We might begin by trying to be a little more tolerant of Kleist's subject. I understand there is a plan afoot to neutralize the chauvinistic offense given by the Hermann Monument erected in 1875 by carving onto it Heine's disrespectful verses on the Battle of the Teutoburg Forest from *Deutschland, Ein Wintermärchen*, though I see no evidence that the world at large cares much about it one way or the other. When the self-regard of a group of people or a nation burgeons at the same time as those people find themselves to be downtrodden or oppressed, nothing is more natural than to search history for heroes as models of self-esteem—a process that goes on visibly in several parts of the world and in our own society to this very day. (Equally familiar to modern ears are the generation of atrocity propaganda and the argument that the most moral and humane of the enemy are the worst, since they deflect concentration on the primary injustice.[5]) It would have been odd indeed if the Germans under Napoleonic domination had not made much of Arminius the Cheruscan, not so much in his own character, for not a great deal is known about him and not all of that is edifying, but because the historical record makes it very clear that he struck the Romans an exceedingly painful and long-lamented blow.

On the other hand, there are certain difficulties with the employability of Arminius for nationalist inspiration. For it belongs to the whole complex of self-justification that the Germans are purer in heart, more vulnerably ingenuous, and more ethically upright than their treacherous, dissembling enemies.[6] Arminius is a little difficult as a wellspring of such virtues, for, from a certain not unreasonable point of view, he was, not to put too fine a point on it, a traitor. He was a Roman citizen and a Roman officer and he had been elevated into the equestrian caste. He won his famous battle not in open, equal combat but, first of all, by exploiting Quintilius Varus' obviously dimwitted trustfulness and then by falling upon his superior and liege from ambush in a swampy forest. There is no heroic confrontation of Hildebrand and Hadubrand in this story.[7]

It is characteristic of Kleist's temper that he entered the material precisely here, embracing and turning to his own purposes its most inexorable implications. By doing so, he caused much of the trouble that we all have with the play.[8] For I think it must be faced that the play's suspension of our normal, shared ethical restraints in favor of a hierarchy of values in which one purpose commands all others is inextricable from its import. Kleist confronts his projected audience with the same question that Hermann sets his fellow chiefs: how much does the liberation of the nation matter to you? With this techique of stripping down and abstracting human responses and reordering them around a single sharply honed purpose, the play reminds one strongly of Brecht's *Die Maßnahme*. Indeed, I hope it will not be considered an impropriety to remark that *Die Hermannsschlacht* seems to me the most Brechtian of all of Kleist's dramas in tone and strategy. Hermann, with his pragmatic combination of obliqueness and directness, of wry realism and adamant concentration on the larger purpose, with his unshadowed confidence in his perspicacity and interpretation of the world, might remind us, not so much of any character of Brecht, than of Brecht himself. My reason for venturing such a comparison, attenuated though it may be, will emerge presently.

Hermann is the locus of that comic quality of the play to which Rolf Linn has usefully drawn attention.[9] His humor, however, is cerebral. Kleist shapes Hermann in the greatest possible contrast to that type of Teutonic lummox of whom Heine—rather unfairly—made Fouqué's Sigurd the exemplar: "so viel Mut wie hundert Löwen und so viel Verstand wie zwei Esel."[10] Hermann is courageous enough, but primarily he makes his rebellion with his head. He has thought about and defined the issue, estimating the possibility of defeat with equanimity. He has a philosophical and historical vision. He can think several steps ahead and order circumstances and situations according to their relative significance. Much of his lightheartedness remarked by Linn is owing to the fact that he knows what he is doing; there is gaiety in competence, especially mental competence. In short, he is an intellectual, exhibiting, one might remark parenthetically, that peculiar capacity of the intellectual to set a one-dimensional logic of purpose above compassion and probity, of which there have been so many gruesome examples in modern times.

Hermann not only thinks out his rebellion; he *stages* it. He lucidly recognizes that his main problem is not with his enemies but with his allies and competitors. He therefore maneuvers them into dramatic situations that induce them to act out his script. With his allies he plays the sardonic fool for a time in order to draw them into their appropriate roles; with Ventidius and Varus he is the puppet master, allowing them to think that they are the main actors; he arouses the emotions of the population by directing a theater of cruelty charged to the Roman account; with Thusnelda he stages a grim comedy of recognition and with Marbod a classical drama of heroic renunciation. He oversees the action and directs it to its climactic conclusion.

By now you see what I am driving at. In Hermann, Kleist projects as the hero of historical action a man of his own type: intellectual and artist. This is important, as I shall endeavor to show. For it is obvious that Kleist was not daydreaming his way into an archaic past. The modern unacceptability of *Die Hermannsschlacht* is not without a degree of paradox in view of the universal lament that German literature in its great age failed to involve itself with social and political concerns, for, as Richard Samuel has shown,[11] here is a play of explicit relevance to major political events composed at a distance from them measured in weeks, perhaps in days. Whatever the details of Kleist's connections to the Stein circle may have been, it is evident that *Die Hermannsschlacht* acts out a scenario of conduct for King Frederick William III and Kaiser Franz.[12] The audacity of his procedure is impressive. For not only is the *Dichter* putting himself forward as a volunteer preceptor to the king; he is demonstrating a means by which the king's dishonorable policy could be redeemed *post hoc*. The solution is one of exquisite irony, for honor is to be recovered by transforming previous actions and commitments into dissimulation. It is hardly possible that Kleist thought the stolid king had actually conducted himself in this way; he is therefore proposing not only that the king should alter his policy but that he should become a *different kind of man*.

Samuel argues that Hermann is a portrait of Stein.[13] I read the situation differently. In Hermann, Kleist has combined political leadership of historical import with an intellectual's mentality. Hermann stands in not so much for Stein or for Kleist personally as for a whole newly alert and dynamic segment of the population seeking participation in the governance of the nation. In the synthesis of his character, Hermann *symbolizes* what the play attempts to do, namely to articulate the claim of the *Dichter* in his representative capacity to function as the king's advisor and partner. The single most remarkable thing about *Die Hermannsschlacht* is that it is a public literary work by a citizen without office or delegated authority that endeavors to tell the King of Prussia what he should do in a matter of the gravest significance. Actually it goes further. It attacks the king's very morality by implying that his conduct has been so shameful that it can only be redeemed by making it appear to have been guile and duplicity.

I recommend this view for two reasons. First, it seems to me to shed some light on at least part of the meaning of *Prinz Friedrich von Homburg* and, second, it contributes something to locating Kleist and the tragedy of his career in a historical continuum. There is a sense in which the king and the court are the ideal audience projected by *Prinz Friedrich* as well as by *Die Hermannsschlacht*; Kleist wrote to the Prince of Prussia that he hoped that the play would show him worthy of the grace of the royal house.[14] I cannot see that anything is gained by trying to argue that *Prinz Friedrich* is not a patriotic play;[15] of course it is, but of a particular kind. In it, the synthesis symbolized by Hermann has broken apart again into its antagonistic component parts, with authority embodied in the Elector, and the representative modern self in Prince Friedrich, not, however, in its intellectual aspect, but in regard to sensibility and the claim to a loyal personal autonomy. At the same time, the theme of partnership, of sharing in the responsibility for the welfare of the state, implied by the strategy of *Die Hermannsschlacht*, is internalized in the action of *Prinz Friedrich*. I do not wish to venture here into the contentious interpretive issues generated by this much more difficult play, but it is a plain fact of the plot that the Elector receives a great deal of assistance, much of it unwanted and some of it a little drastic, in governing at a crucial historical juncture. He is balked and lectured to; a mere girl borrows his authority to order his troops about; at least the potential of mutiny hangs in the air; and he is driven by circumstances to improvise a situation in which Friedrich's moral autonomy is formally acknowledged. None of the Elector's authority is lost, but by his resilience he incorporates into his larger purpose—to some extent under duress—the dialogue of other selves, so that out of the acknowledgement and resolution of differences a shared political decision is forged and the bonds of loyalty are strengthened. It needs hardly be said that nothing like this characterized the Prussian style of government in Kleist's time, and therefore we find the poet and intellectual once again asserting his claim to partnership by offering a model of how Prussia ought to be governed.

In retrospect this kind of purpose may seem naive and futile. Certainly it is sad, because Kleist pursued it with his peculiar intensity and addiction to the absolute, as the most disturbing features of the *Hermannsschlacht* text amply testify, and its failure seems to me to have been an important component of his defeat in life. But it was not really eccentric. Rather it seems to me to exemplify a recurrent theme in the German educated class in the nineteenth century: the urge to offer to the royal authority a participating, patriotic loyalty that was not wanted by the royal authority and was therefore met by suspicion and rebuff. In the course of time it becomes a longing to democratize monarchy by supplanting the aristocracy. The theme has many variations and would bear tracing through literature and literary life. For example, there is Heine in 1832 writing in a letter: "es geschieht den Königen ganz recht, sie haben die Liberalen, die nur gegen Adel und Pfaffenherrschaft eiferten, nicht hören wollen, und jetzt bekommen sie den blutigsten Jakobinismus auf den Hals,"[16] and one of his late lyrical themes is lament over the divorce of poetry and power. One might regard as the satyr play to Kleist's personal tragedy Georg Herwegh's embarrassing experience in 1842, when he took an episode of amiability on the part of Frederick William IV as an invitation to admonish the king on the subject of freedom of the press, with unfortunate consequences. Then there was Bettina von Arnim, badgering that same king with advice and commands year after year, pursuing with dogged persistence the chimera of a benevolent and progressive *Volksmonarchie*. Or one might consider Willibald Alexis, who wanted nothing more than to write patriotic novels about the Prussian nation, who ran afoul of the censorship, who appealed loyally to the king only to find himself ludicrously classified as a subversive, the consequence of all of which was one of the bitterest German political novels of the century, *Ruhe ist die erste Bürgerpflicht*.

Kleist with his *Hermannsschlacht* is in this sequence. It is largely for this reason that I regard as useless all attempts to perceive Kleist's consciousness as that of an erratic *Junker*. Class origin is not the determining factor here; what is significant is the involvement with the burgeoning modern thought and sensibility. Kleist is an ally of the German middle-class intellectuals, whose efforts at constructive citizenship were met with decades of frustration, with far-ranging consequences for the history of the world. For this reason it seems to me necessary to read *Die Hermannsschlacht* on more than one level, or at least to sense in it different kinds of inchoate purposes struggling for expression.

This is not to say that we must accept the level that offends us. With all respect for Sigurd Burckhardt's uncommonly thoughtful and helpful interpretation, I cannot share his apologetic view that Kleist cannot have meant what the text appears to project and that he wanted us instead "to see ... a *descent*, unredeemed and unrevoked, into bestiality."[17] I see no warrant in the text or in Kleist's literary practice for taking this view. But if we could get out of the habit, now endemic in German literary studies, of evaluating texts according to their faithful representation of how things are or ought to be, and think of them as fictions, as experiments, probing positions and, in Kleist's case as in Brecht's, carrying them to their utmost implications, as contexts that do not require of us total submission and assent, but a dialogic response out of our own autonomy as competent selves, we might come to a more relaxed view of *Die Hermannsschlacht*. Then we would be freer to reintegrate its terrifying extremity of gesture into an interpretation of Kleist's cast of mind that could encompass such texts as "Katechismus der Deutschen," "Penthesilea," and "Michael Kohlhaas." We divest ourselves of some of our interpretive resources if we insist that we need fully to assent to the implications of a text in order to get it into view, or that its subsequent historical resonances wholly define its meaning in its own context.

I would be the last person to proscribe an ethical judgment on a text as a segment of our apprehension of it, and this part of our response to *Die Hermannsschlacht* must, no doubt, be a refusal. Beyond this, it is probably in texture and subtlety the least of Kleist's seven completed dramas. But from the point of view of scholarly integrity there can be no such thing as a Kleist without *Die Hermannsschlacht*. It was important to him, and if Kleist is important to us, it must be also. Even if its patriotic excess appears as an episode among Kleist's complicated affects,[18] historically, it was not a momentary faux pas but a significant intersection of poetic imagination with political reality. Otherwise, we run the risk of manipulating the authors we claim to care about, of making them disposable for our own purposes, and since the whole catalogue of atrocities in literary criticism, which we have no difficulty identifying in retrospect, is in one way or another traceable to this vice, we need to learn to exercise some discipline on ourselves in order to avoid perpetuating it.

NOTES

1. Heinrich von Kleist, *Sämtliche Werke und Briefe,* ed. Helmut Sembdner, 4th ed. (Munich: Hanser, 1965), I, 943.
2. See Helmut Sembdner, "Nachruhm als Missverständnis," *In Sachen Kleist: Beiträge zur Forschung* (Munich: Hanser, 1974), pp. 254-55; Rolf Busch, *Imperialistische und faschistische Kleist-Rezeption 1890-1945: Eine ideologiekritische Untersuchung* (Frankfurt am Main: Akademische Verlagsgesellschaft, 1974), 134-55.
3. E.g., Jochen Schmidt, in *Heinrich von Kleist: Studien zu seiner poetischen Verfahrensweise* (Tübingen: Niemeyer, 1974), states that he does not wish to shut the play out of our consideration of Kleist (46-47), but he treats it disparagingly throughout as a regrettable aberration, claiming, incorrectly, it seems to me, that Kleist repudiated it (250). Robert E. Helbling, *The Major Works of Heinrich von Kleist* (New York: New Directions, 1975), devotes but eight pages to it (183-90), tentatively suggesting undercurrents flowing against the grain of the text but ultimately discarding it.
4. E.g., Hermann Reske, *Traum und Wirklichkeit im Werk Heinrich von Kleists* (Stuttgart: Kohlhammer, 1969), 75: "ein Hetz- und Tendenzstück reinsten Wassers"; Adolf D. Klarmann, "Kleist und die Gegenwart," *Festschrift für Detlev W. Schumann zum 70. Geburtstag,* ed. Albert R. Schmitt (Munich: Delp, 1970), 235-36: "[die] kaum noch ertragbaren Haß- und Perversitätsexzesse seiner *Hermannsschlacht.*" It is of some interest that the relatively recent nationalist emphasis in East Germany has led to an acceptance and even praise of Kleist's "nationaler Leidenschaft." See Robert Müller-Sternberg, "Der grenzenlose Preusse. Nation und Staat bei Heinrich von Kleist," *Deutsche Studien* 12 (1974): 234. For some history of this development see Manfred Lefèvre, "Kleist-Forschung 1961-67," *Colloquia Germanica* (1969): 33-34.
5. *Die Hermannsschlacht,* III, 2; IV, 3-6; IV, 9; V, 13. *Sämtliche Werke* I, 564-65; 584-91; 593-94; 612.
6. Splendid examples in Heinz Ludwig Arnold, *Deutsche über die Deutschen: Auch ein deutsches Lesebuch* (Munich: Beck, 1972), passim. It is among the nicer ironies of the play that Ventidius misreads Hermann as an honest simpleton and that Varus is astonished that blond hair and blue eyes can be false (III, 6; V, 9; *Sämtliche Werke* I, 576, 608).
7. Grabbe sensed the problem but dealt with it by shouting at it. To the question raised about the propriety of deception and betrayal he has his Hermann reply: "Halts Maul mit deinen kleinen Bedenklichkeiten. Geh in deine Rotte."

Christian Dietrich Grabbe, *Werke und Briefe*, ed. Alfred Bergmann, III (Emsdetten: Lechte, 1961), 346.
8. We are not alone with these troubles; the chauvinists at the time of World War I had an amusingly difficult time with the morality of Hermann's conduct. See Sembdner, "Nachruhm als Mißverständnis," pp. 254-55.
9. Rolf N. Linn, "Comical and Humorous Elements in Kleist's *Die Hermannsschlacht*," *Germanic Review* 47 (1972): 159-67.
10. Heinrich Heine, *Sämtliche Werke*, ed. Ernst Elster (Leipzig and Vienna: Bibliographisches Institut, [1887-90]), V, 339.
11. Richard Samuel, "Kleists Hermannsschlacht und der Freiherr vom Stein," *Heinrich von Kleist: Aufsätze und Essays,* ed. Walter Müller-Seidel (Darmstadt: Wissenschaftliche Buchgesellschaft, 1967), pp. 412-58.
12. See Beda Allemann, "Der Nationalismus Heinrich von Kleists," *Nationalismus in Germanistik und Dichtung: Dokumentation des Germanistentages in München vom 17. bis 22. Oktober 1966*, ed. Benno von Wiese und Rudolf Henss (Berlin: Erich Schmidt Verlag, 1967), p. 310.
13. Samuel, 449-51.
14. *Dichter über ihre Dichtungen: Heinrich von Kleist,* ed. Helmut Sembdner (Munich: Heimeran, 1969), p. 59.
15. J.M. Ellis, *Kleist's* Prinz Friedrich von Homburg: *A Critical Study* (Berkeley and Los Angeles: University of California Press, 1970), 99. It is important not to allow reception history to obscure the historical fact that in Kleist's time patriotism was *rebellious*. Cf., for example, his citation of Mirabeau in *Über die allmähliche Verfertigung der Gedanken beim Reden, Sämtliche Werke,* II, 320-21.
16. Heinrich Heine, *Säkularausgabe*, XXI, Ed. Fritz H. Eisner and Christa Stöcker (Berlin: Akademie-Verlag and Paris: Editions du CNRS, 1970), 31.
17. Sigurd Burckhardt, *The Drama of Language: Essays on Goethe and Kleist* (Baltimore: Johns Hopkins Press, 1970), p. 129. This particular statement refers to the Thusnelda plot. I think, by the way, that the form of embryonic racism contained in the broad implication that a Roman could not love as deeply as a German and in the account of the longing of greasy-haired Roman ladies for blond German locks (II, 8; III, 3; *Sämtliche Werke* I, 557, 569-71) ought to be more repellent to modern sensibilities than the feeding of Ventidius to the bear, which has worried so many commentators.
18. Sembdner, "Nachruhm als Mißverständnis," 252.

"Ein Traum, was sonst?"—Kleist's
Prinz Friedrich von Homburg

LAWRENCE RYAN
University of Massachusetts

There is a devilish mercy in the judge
If you'll implore it, that will free your life.[1]

These lines sound almost as if they could be, but are in fact not a quotation from Kleist's *Prinz Friedrich von Homburg*. Instead, the Prince's reading out of the letter sent to him by the Elector, promising him pardon if he will but assert his innocence, is followed not by a verbalised response, but by that characteristic Kleistian device, the pause: "*Natalie erblaßt. Pause. Der Prinz sieht sie fragend an.*"[2] As well he might, for the mercy is indeed devilish: the letter is an invitation to the Prince, in effect, to throw himself on the mercy of the Elector by acquiescing in his own conviction. Why does the Elector offer such a choice? His inscrutability leaves his motivation largely unexplained. I should like to explore the possibility of making the whole confrontation more explicable by contrastive reference to one of the acknowledged sources of the play, Shakespeare's *Measure for Measure*, from which the opening quotation is taken. Indeed, in certain respects *Measure for Measure* provides almost a kind of gloss on the pregnant pauses of Kleist's dramatic interplay.

Outwardly, there are numerous points of comparison, which have often been noted.[3] In Shakespeare's play, a kindly and humane Duke, fearing to lose his grip on his people by his overly permissive treatment of their misdemeanors, leaves the country for a time in the charge of one Angelo, a righteous and untainted man whom the Duke has personally chosen to be his substitute. But the Duke returns, disguised as a friar, to observe the outcome of his trick. Now one Claudio, having anticipated marriage by prematurely impregnating his betrothed, is swiftly condemned to death by the meticulous Angelo; but when Claudio's sister Isabella, an aspirant to nunhood, appeals to Angelo for her brother's life, the "angel" duly "falls": the apparently righteous judge is so overcome by the attractions of her person that he demands her sexual favors as the price of granting her appeal. But Isabella, rejecting this way out, prevails upon her brother to accept his death: like Homburg, Claudio—after first begging abjectly for his life—rejects a pardon that will take away his self-respect. In this case, however, the machinations of the Duke behind the scenes see to it that Angelo's villainy is brought to light, indeed that Angelo—a precursor also of Kleist's Adam in *Der zerbrochne Krug*—must preside at a hearing that is destined to uncover his own wrongdoing. Whereas he should by rights be put to death himself for the same crime of lechery for which he has condemned the unfortunate Claudio, Angelo is now punished instead by a kind of equalising "poetic" justice: he is forced to marry a lady he has long ago pledged to wed, but shamefully deserted.

This abbreviated plot summary shows several points of resemblance to Kleist's *Homburg*: tricks of justice are, after all, practically a Kleistian trademark. But the constellation of characters bears closer examination. The function of the "superior," reigning character in Kleist—the Elector— is carried out by two figures in Shakespeare, the Duke and Angelo. Whereas the conflict of the individual with the apparently inexorable workings of the law is centered in Kleist in the figure of Homburg himself, in Shakespeare both Claudio and Isabella are involved. This feature points to a consistent difference in conception between the two plays, which bears upon the relationship of the "individual" to the "political" aspects of the action. It is often still held that Kleist's drama constitutes, as it were, his political testament and that it revolves around a conflict between the state and the individual—but this view seems to me a persistent misconception. It is futile to argue whether he is a tyrannical, an indifferent, or even an "ideal" ruler, for this is not the question at issue. The Elector, it is true, seems determined to apply the letter of the law without discrimination of persons, indeed with a rigor that Homburg perhaps not altogether unjustly compares to the unfeeling inhumanity of a Brutus; he appeals emphatically to the "Satzung" (V. 774, 1143-44)—the laws of the Prussian state—as the only guarantee of the continued survival of the "Vaterland" (V. 1120-21). But if this were all, the matter would be cut and dried and Homburg's life would be forfeit. In fact, the main complications of the action—and its ultimate resolution—are not determined by this political question. For the Elector has "another" relationship to Homburg, beginning with the initial dream scene, whose originally solipsistic nature (underscored by the enclosed garden setting and the mirror imagery used to describe the Prince's mental condition) is translated into the realm of personal, legal, and political conflict only by the Elector's "trick"—the "Scherz" (V. 83) that induces him first to snatch away the laurel wreath, then to intertwine it with the chain he has himself been wearing around his neck, to hand it to Natalie, but finally to reject as premature the Prince's attempt to reclaim the wreath. On the surface, he may seem to be expressing a politically motivated judgment ("Ins Nichts mit dir zurück, Herr Prinz von Homburg ... Im Traum erringt man solche Dinge nicht" [V. 74-78]), but more essentially, he is making himself a partner in the ultimate realization (and partial modification) of Homburg's dream. For it is under the Elector's guidance that in the fifth act Natalie gives back to the Prince the laurel wreath, still entwined with the gold chain of office, that symbolises the content of the Prince's dream. The pronouncements of the Elector on the upholding of the law are subordinated in the last count to his function of providing Homburg with access to a more developed projection of the subjective aspirations by which the Prince is actuated throughout.

It is not thus with Shakespeare's Duke, whose "ruse" is quite differently motivated. *Measure for Measure* begins not with a dream scene in a French garden, but with a discourse upon the "nature of our people, / Our city's institutions, and the terms / For common justice." (I,i) The focus is here upon a purely political and administrative action: the handing over of power to a temporary substitute, one who is described moreover as caring little for self and much for the common weal ("Thyself and thy belongings / Are not thine own so proper as to waste / Thyself upon thy virtues, they on thee." [I,i]) Even though these presumed virtues are then vitiated by the faults that are their obverse, it is the dichotomy between the private self and its administrative and representative role that defines the contours of the play, as it does the whole of Shakespeare's thinking. This is why, for Shakespeare, there cannot be just one ruling figure, but—in the Duke and Angelo—two discrete characters, and why the trick that the Duke plays upon his people is dependent upon disguise and play-acting, whereby two opposing persons can act as ruler in the same situational context.

Similarly, it appears that Kleist contracted two characters into one when creating the figure of Homburg, namely the impetuous brother Claudio, who first pleads for his life in the same self-demeaning way as does Homburg, and the steadfastly pure sister Isabella, who persuades him to accept the apparent certainty of death. (Kleist's Natalie, though she corresponds in some ways to Isabella, undergoes no comparable dramatic conflict.) That Homburg embodies elements that in Shakespeare comprise two different characters does not however mean that he is complex and divided in himself. True, there are moments when he may appear to be so. He says he is "zerstreut—geteilt" (V. 420); others claim that he is "abwesend ganz / Aus seiner Brust" (V. 1704-05); and at the opening of the play he is even physically lost (his friends are seeking him) and seems not to remember where he is. But the point is that at such moments he is precisely "not himself," rather than being divided in himself. This is possible because of his absorption in dream. Homburg's seeming disclaimer of the pardon finally vouchsafed him: "Nein, sagt! Ist es ein Traum?" (V. 1856)—like his apparently disbelieving reception of the Elector's first, conditional offer of pardon: "Es ist nicht möglich! Nein! Es ist ein Traum!" (V. 1305)—conveys a feeling more of joyfully realised anticipation than of shocked surprise; almost from beginning to end he clings to the truth of his inner vision. When for a time that belief seems untenable in the face of the Elector's insistence on the death sentence, he gives way to abject despair, having nothing else to which to cling. But at the moment of crisis the Elector is equal to the task Kleist has set him of enabling Homburg to save himself. For Homburg's acceptance of the Elector's challenge to decide his own fate enables him to assert himself in a different way: his welcoming invocation of the eternity of death ("Nun, o Unsterblichkeit, bist du ganz mein!" [V. 1380]) is but an extension of his continual emphasis on the self, which is now seen to be more fully whole in eternity than in life. This emphasis can again be illustrated with reference to the Shakespearian equivalent. Whereas Shakespeare's Claudio sees the after-life as:

> To be imprison'd in the viewless winds,
> And blown with restless violence round about
> The pendent world
>
> *(III, i).*

Homburg in his final stage envisages a ship, being borne by the wind ("wie ein Schiff, vom Hauch des Winds entführt" [V. 1835]) to freedom, to a sphere in which the self is emancipated from the shackles of earthly existence. It is not likely that even the Elector really feels that Homburg has somehow been aroused from his self-centered dream and is fit once more (after not one, but several failures!) to lead the troops into battle. For the Elector has, more importantly, won a personal victory of another kind: just as Homburg has gambled and won, saving in the process both his life and his self-respect, so has the Elector, gambling on Homburg's gamble, been saved from the predicament in which he would otherwise have been placed—of seeming to grant pardon under pressure and thus seeming to demean his own authority. In any case, it is clear that the Prince has only spun himself more finely—Tasso-like—into his dream world (as Goethe puts it, one cannot forbid the silkworm to spin, even as it spins itself closer to death). The ceremonial conclusion of the play—contrasting with the more prosaic settlement in *Measure for Measure*—simultaneously distracts from and underscores the fact that no politically and legally meaningful settlement has been effected.

If this is so, then one has still to explain the focus of the play upon two main characters, and to ask whether the Elector's role, apart from his function in the development of the Prince, is consistent and meaningful in itself. It might be well to think of comparable figures in Kleist's works. In the play *Amphitryon,* the almighty god Jupiter plays a similar trick upon certain of his subjects. Just as the Elector leads the Prince on, then repels him, but finally—after the Prince's change of heart—accepts him, so does Jupiter in effect translate into reality Alkmene's idolatorous love for her husband Amphitryon, for the sake of which she would only too gladly have had the night of reunion extended indefinitely. Just as the dream of personal glory is at first the centre of Homburg's being, so does Alkmene's all-absorbing devotion to Amphitryon render her incapable of recognising that the all-encompassing divinity of Jupiter is more than just a projection of her idolised husband. Jupiter's "ruse"—to assume the form of Amphitryon, then to test Alkmene by requiring her to differentiate between Jupiter and Amphitryon and thus to modify the restrictive focus of her love—ultimately succeeds, as Alkmene acknowledges the supremacy of the "divine" Amphitryon over the "merely mortal" Amphitryon and thereby becomes aware that her love is not merely a subjective dream, but rather participates in a universal harmony of being that is personified in the all-informing nature of Jupiter. But more exactly, this is another, a universalised dream. As such, it enables Alkmene to re-establish the wholeness of her being in a fashion comparable to the transformation of Homburg, who finds himself again by envisaging his apotheosis in immortality, rather than his glorification in worldly terms. For him—as for Kleist—no credence can be placed in a "political" reconciliation of opposing forces, there is only the spontaneity of subjective being in—respectively—a finite or an infinite context. For those such as Homburg and Alkmene there can never be such a thing as a dichotomous world view, since for them the external is subsumed into their own inner wholeness. This is why the "trick" of contrived duplicity—whether played by an Elector or by a god—results not really in "mediation" (a concept that has virtually no application in Kleist's works), but rather in a "dislocation" of vision. The dramatic function of the god—or of the ruler of god-like mien, as the Elector is described—is not so much to represent and enforce the law and order of society, as rather to project the self-realisation of subjectivity onto a wider plane. There is here no "measure for measure," no balancing of interests or mediation of conflict between the individual and the social order, but rather an intimation of what Kleist calls elsewhere the three chapters of the history of the world.

    A further example might serve to reinforce this point. Kleist's *Michael Kohlhaas* would seem to constitute a prime example of the relationship of the measures and counter-measures of justice: Kohlhaas is punished for his crimes, but obtains the satisfaction of knowing both that recompense is to be made to him (and his heirs) and that those who have wronged him are also to receive their due punishment. But such a "political" mediation as this, taking place as it does within the framework of an established legal order, is no answer for a writer who from the start regards all social systems as inimical to individual spontaneity. It is thus no accident that Kleist introduces the rather grotesque machinery of the gypsy-woman subplot in order to establish his hero's integrity in a realm that transcends the sphere of legal order.

If then there are a number of similarities to *Measure for Measure* in the composition of *Prinz Friedrich von Homburg,* it may help to illuminate the intent of Kleist's work to point out that it refutes precisely that concept of an equalising justice that informs Shakespeare's play. But that is tantamount to saying that Kleist rejects the validity of political order altogether. What have we then at the end of the play? Is it the reality of the body politic? Is it reality at all? And the answer can only be: No, a dream, what else?

NOTES

1. Quotations from *Measure for Measure* are given by act and scene and taken from the following edition: William Shakespeare, *The Complete Works,* edited by Peter Alexander, (London and Glasgow: Collins, 1951). III, i.
2. Quotations from *Prinz Friedrich von Homburg* are given by verse number and are taken from the following edition: Heinrich von Kleist, *Sämtliche Werke und Briefe,* Ed. Helmut Sembdner, (München: Carl Hanser, 1961). V. 1313.
3. The fullest account of Kleist's relations to Shakespeare is still: Meta Corssen, *Kleist und Shakespeare,* (Weimar: Duncker, 1930).

Fünf Thesen zu *Prinz Friedrich von Homburg*

HANS-JÜRGEN SCHLÜTTER
University of Western Ontario

Ob die Beschäftigung mit Heinrich von Kleist und seinem Werk, die in diesem Jahr von Theaterpraxis wie Literaturwissenschaft zu erwarten ist, uns einem Consensus über das Schauspiel *PFvH* irgend näher bringen wird? Festzustehen scheint bisher nur, daß sich der Streit um dieses Stück lohnt, daß diesem letzten Spiel des Dichters hoher, vielleicht höchster Rang zukommt. Die Auffassungsverschiedenheiten reichen bis in das Zentrum der Handlung, betreffen den Protagonisten und den Antagonisten und die Beziehung, in der beide zueinander stehen. Besonders schwer tun wir uns heute mit der Figur des Kurfürsten. Im Jahre 1972 fanden in Berlin gleichzeitig zwei Aufführungen des Schauspiels statt, im Schillertheater unter der Regie von Heinz Lietzau und in der Schaubühne am Halleschen Ufer unter der Regie von Peter Stein. Über die beiden Aufführungen schrieb Hans Mayer, man habe im Schillertheater "einen trockenen, von den Ereignissen oft überrannten Bürokraten" erblickt, bei Peter Stein "einen listigen und herzenskalten Egozentriker." Kleists Bild eines "guten Herrschers" sei zwar historisch einsehbar (als Gegenentwurf zu der "jämmerlichen Realität" Friedrich Wilhelms III.), aber nicht mehr nachvollziehbar. Verliere der Kurfürst seine Funktion eines Antagonisten, so bleibe nur noch Homburg auf der Szene. "Das Stück wandelt sich folglich; es wird zum *Monodrama mit Statisten*. Beide Spielleiter ziehen diese Folgerung...."[1] Im Bereich der literaturwissenschaftlichen Interpretation waren es die beiden 1970 erschienenen Studien von Ellis und Politzer, in denen die Figur des Kurfürsten zum Erstaunen schlecht abschnitt. Beide Autoren griffen einen älteren psychologischen Ansatz[2] wieder auf: nach diesen Deutungen rivalisiert der Kurfürst mit dem Prinzen, bei Ellis geht es um das militärische Ansehen beider, bei Politzer—cherchez la femme!—um die Prinzessin Natalie. So kann man denn bei Politzer lesen, die Worte, mit denen der Kurfürst in der 1. Szene den Traum des Prinzen annulliert und den Träumer auf das Schlachtfeld verweist, schlössen einen Todeswunsch ein;[3] und entsprechend legt Ellis nahe, die Tendenz des Kurfürsten sei es, "to create a situation in which the sentence is justified."[4] Bei der vorbestimmten Kürze dieses Vortrags kann ich natürlich nicht auf die Argumentationen des Aufsatzes von Politzer und des Buches von Ellis näher eingehen; ebensowenig kann eine abgerundete eigene Interpretation versucht werden. Ich lege Ihnen also nur einige Thesen vor und überlasse das Weitere der Diskussion und künftiger Ausführung.

Als 1. These soll gelten: *Die Schwierigkeiten, die sich einem Verständnis (das Aussicht auf einen Consensus der Interpreten hätte) entgegenstellen, liegen im Stück selbst und hängen in manchen Fällen mit seinen besonderen Qualitäten zusammen.* Kleist wußte es von sich und schrieb es in einem Brief vom Sommer 1811, also gerade nach Vollendung des Homburg, wie präzise seine Phantasie bei der Gestaltung seiner Geschöpfe war, "wie so bestimmt in Umriß und Farbe die Gestalten sind, die sie ... hervorbringt."[5] Lebenswahrheit, Komplexität, Facettenreichtum—das sind Eigenschaften, die Kleists Gestalten auszeichnen—und es der Interpretation schwer machen. Die Schwerdurchschaubarkeit des Kurfürsten ist ein solcher Zug unmittelbar überzeugender Wahrheit. Die Figuren sind miteinander verbunden durch Verstehen, Halbverstehen, Mißverstehen in so reichen Schattierungen, wie sie im Leben vorkommen. Vieles davon klärt sich im Laufe des Spiels, anderes bleibt disparat. Sagt z.B. Natalie zum Kurfürsten, Gott habe noch nichts Milderes als ihn geschaffen (V. 1111), und spricht dagegen Hohenzollern vom "stolzen Geist" des Kurfürsten (V. 913), so ist es Sache der Interpretation herauszufühlen, wer Recht hat, oder wer mehr Recht hat, bis zu welchem Grade beides stimmt, oder nicht stimmt, ob Natalies ein argumentum ad hominem ist usw.[6] Oder: Bedenken Sie, wie oft die Figuren dieses Spiels sich verstellen, fast alle Hauptcharaktere tun das irgendwann: der Kurfürst, Hohenzollern, der Prinz, Natalie, die Kurfürstin, Froben (im Bericht), in der Schlußszene der ganze Hofstaat. Wo sollen wir den Kurfürsten wörtlich nehmen und wo verstehen, daß er ironisch spricht?

Man weiß, daß dieses Drama durch manche Anlehnungen an Vorgängerwerke mitgeprägt ist, daß es die Sprache der Dichtung spricht. Bis zu welchem Grade können oder müssen dann diese Originalorte zur Erklärung kleistischer Textstellen herangezogen werden? Die Kenntnis und Bewertung solcher Stellen kann zum Verständnis ebenso unerläßlich sein wie die Bedeutungsgeschichte bestimmter Wörter, deren Bedeutung sich seit Kleists Tagen verändert hat. Der 1. Auftritt schon enthält eine solche schwierige Stelle: die Worte des Kurfürsten: "Ins Nichts mit dir zurück, Herr Prinz von Homburg, / Ins Nichts, ins Nichts! ....." Wer hier nicht auf Tassos Worte: "Bin ich Nichts, / Ganz Nichts geworden?" zurückgeht, der kann die Bedeutung dieser Worte leicht falsch einschätzen, z.B. wie Ellis ihren Ton für "deadly serious" halten.[7] Die Homburg-Dichtung weist in mancher Hinsicht Gestaltungsvorgänge auf, wie sie für ein anderes künstlerisches

Medium spezifisch sind: für die Musik.[8] Musikalisch verstehbar ist die Schlußszene als Wiederholung des Anfangs, sind die scherzogemäßen Wiederholungen in der Szene I,4 (Hohenzollern und Homburg), ist die einzigartige Polyphonie der Paroleszene, ist der Anakoluth, mit dem das Schauspiel beginnt, oder wir sollten vielleicht sagen "einsetzt." Manchmal notiert Kleist geradezu musikalisch und muß dann auch so verstanden werden. Am Ende des Stücks rufen

> Kottwitz
>   Heil, Heil dem Prinz von Homburg!
> Die Offiziere
>   Heil! Heil! Heil!
> Alle
>   Dem Sieger in der Schlacht bei Fehrbellin!

Das hat kein Leser des Textes jemals mißverstanden, daß dieses "Alle" den Prinzen nicht einbegreift, daß er nicht mit einstimmt in den Ruf "Dem Sieger in der Schlacht bei Fehrbellin!"

Im Gegensatz zum Schlußvers. Das ist ja beides klar. Keineswegs klar ist aber, wie das "Alle" des Verses 467 aufzufassen ist. Die Reiteroffiziere beobachten die Schlacht; auf eine bestimmte Bewegung der Schweden hin brechen sie ("Alle") in den Ruf aus: "Triumph! Triumph! Triumph! Der Sieg ist unser!" Unmittelbar darauf folgt Homburgs Aufbruch in die Schlacht: "Auf, Kottwitz, folg mir!" Man hat—sehr zu Unrecht—daraus geschlossen, der Prinz greife jetzt ein, damit er zum Sieg nicht zu spät komme. Eine Auffassung, die nichts für sich anführen kann, als eben diese—zugegeben: zweideutige—Juxtaposition von Triumphruf und Entschluß zum Eingreifen. Das ist aber wiederum aus dem "musikalischen" Duktus zu erklären, aus dem Entscheiden des Komponisten, wieviel Raum einer Motivdurchführung gegeben werden kann und wo eine neue Entwicklung einsetzen muß. Der Ruf "Aller" (*Tutti*) beendet die Teichoskopie, darauf setzt das Homburg-Geschehen (*Solo*) ein.

Als 2. These soll gelten: *Zur Konzeption der beiden Hauptfiguren gehört wesentlich ihr unterschiedliches Lebensalter: Die Jugend des Prinzen und das reife Mannesalter—virtus—des Kurfürsten.* Der Prinz wird oft genug als jung bezeichnet.[9] Wie man weiß, hat Kleist dies der Geschichte gegenüber ebenso geändert, wie die Kinderlosigkeit des Kurfürsten eine Änderung ist, durch die Natalie und der Prinz näher an den Kurfürsten gerückt werden. Vom Alter des Kurfürsten ist nur einmal die Rede: Natalie spricht bei ihrer Fürbitte vom *Herbst* des Onkels, vom friedlich prächtigen (V. 1140f.), die Metapher ist wohl leicht prospektiv gemeint. Welches Alter wäre damit angedeutet? Katharina Mommsen hat in ihrem Buch "Kleists Kampf mit Goethe" nachgewiesen, daß Kleist bei der Gestalt des Kurfürsten an ein bestimmtes Goetheporträt gedacht hat: es stammt von Friedrich Bury und ist im Jahre 1800 entstanden, zeigt Goethe also als etwa Einundfünfzigjährigen.[10] Katharina Mommsen weist auch darauf hin, daß von den sieben in den Phöbus-Heften enthaltenen Kupferstichen fünf das Verhältnis der Generationen zueinander behandeln.[11] Das letzte Heft des Phöbus enthält aus der Feder Basilius von Ramdohrs, aber wohl doch in Übereinstimmung mit dem Denken der Herausgeber, eine "Charakteristik des Jupiters," in der die Rede ist von einem Manne, "dem das reife Alter und lange Erfahrung Herrschaft über seine Leidenschaften ... gegeben haben."[12] Die Jugend Homburgs (wie Penthesileas) dagegen hat zu kämpfen mit dem "verderblichsten der Feind' in uns," dem Trotz, dem Übermut (V. 1756f.). Die Jugend bringt es aber zu dem großen Aufschwung des Gefühls. So sind denn das Heldentum der Unerschütterlichkeit und das Heldentum der leidenschaftlichen Bewegtheit in Kurfürst und Prinz einander entgegengesetzt. Der Kurfürst, in vollkommener Beherrschung seiner selbst, ist in der Schlacht "das Ziel der feindlichen Kanonenkugeln:"[13]

> Granaten wälzten, Kugeln und Kartätschen,
> Sich wie ein breiter Todesstrom daher,
> Und alles, was da lebte, wich ans Ufer:
> Nur er, der kühne Schwimmer, wankte nicht,
> Und, stets den Freunden winkend, rudert' er
> Getrost den Höhn zu, wo die Quelle sprang.[14]

Ganz anders der Prinz. Nach erstem, zum Stehen gekommenem Angriff seine Reiterei sammelnd, sieht er den Reiter des "strahlend weißen" Schimmels fallen.

> Drauf faßt, bei diesem schreckensvollen Anblick,
> Schmerz, unermeßlicher, des Prinzen Herz;
> Dem Bären gleich, von Wut gespornt und Rache,
> Bricht er mit uns auf die Verschanzung los....[15]

Es ist diese Gefühlsmächtigkeit der Jugend, der unermeßliche Schmerz um den Kurfürsten, was ihn zu der Berserkertat veranlaßt, die die Schlacht entscheidet. Und seine Jugend ist es auch, die später zu seinem Zusammenbruch in der berühmten Todesfurchtszene führt. Trotz des bekannten literarischen Einflusses ist sie ganz Kleists Eigentum, sie entspricht der in einem Brief von 1801 geäußerten Erfahrung: "...wenn die Jugend von jedem Eindrucke bewegt wird, und ein heftiger sie stürzt, so ist das nicht, weil sie keinen, sondern weil sie *starken* Widerstand leistet."[16]

These 3: *Der Kurfürst verkörpert das Ideal eines Souveräns.* Daß, wie Hans Mayer schreibt, der Kurfürst "keine Zukunft hat und gehabt hat,"[17] ändert daran absolut nichts und bezeugt lediglich die, wie Kleist es genannt hat, "Gebrechlichkeit der Welt." Wie allerdings ein Ideal in die menschliche Welt der Theateraufführungen zu überführen wäre, das mag wohl ein

Problem sein. Aber nicht unseres. Denn wir sind ja mit dem Verständnis des kleistischen Texts befaßt. Und hier ist nun der Ort, alle Interpretationen, die der vollkommenen Gerechtigkeit dieses Herrschers nicht gerecht werden, für falsch zu erklären. Um die Härte der Entscheidung des Kurfürsten auszuwiegen, legt Kleist in die Waagschale der Schuld des Prinzen zwei früher verscherzte Siege (unhistorisch!); die Ermahnung, sich diesmal wohl zu regieren; den Übergriff Homburgs gegen den 1. Offizier, bei dem er sich auch noch auf die märkischen Kriegsartikel beruft; den strategisch nicht vollkommenen Sieg (historisch!) und in seinem Gefolge die Gefährdung des Glücks nicht nur Homburgs, sondern auch Natalies, deren erwogene Verheiratung mit dem Schwedenkönig der Kurfürst als Opfer, "vom Mißglück nur des Kriegs mir abgerungen," versteht.[18] Keineswegs, wie man oft lesen kann, leider auch bei Arthur Henkel und Richard Samuel, "verurteilt" der Kurfürst den Prinzen in den Worten "... Der ist des Todes schuldig, das erklär ich" und verweist ihn dann erst an ein Gericht "Und vor ein Kriegsgericht bestell ich ihn."[19] Der Kurfürst spricht aus, was öffentlich bekannt ist; soweit entspricht dies genau der entsprechenden Szene in den Piccolomini, in der die Offiziere ebenfalls aussprechen, daß auf dem Brechen der Order der Tod steht. Die Rolle des Kurfürsten ist hier nicht die des Richters, sondern die des Anklägers. Daß er zugleich als Souverän die Begnadigungsinstanz ist, darf und kann hier noch nicht ins Spiel kommen. Er erhebt die Anklage, im Gegensatz zu Wallenstein, der aus Opportunitätsgründen auf den Strafanspruch verzichtet.

Es ist bezeichnend für die Rechtsauffassung des Kurfürsten, daß er die "Satzung" auf die jederzeit lebendige Übereinstimmung Aller gründet. Das Gefängnis des Prinzen ist offen. Dem Feldmarschall Dörfling antwortet der Kurfürst auf seinen Begnadigungsvorschlag, da müsse erst der Prinz selbst befragt werden. Die anderen Fürsprecher fordert er auf, selbst zu urteilen, zu Natalie: "Dich aber frag ich selbst" (V. 1114), zu den Offizieren: "Ja, urteilt selbst, ihr Herrn!" (V. 1818). In demselben Sinne legt er die Entscheidung in die Hände des Prinzen. Mehr noch: er stellt Homburg die Validität der Kriegsartikel anheim, aufgrund deren das Urteil ergangen ist. Das ist der Sinn der so oft als ironisch mißverstandenen Verse:

> Wo werd ich
> Mich gegen solchen Kriegers Meinung setzen?
> ...
>
> Wenn er den Spruch für ungerecht kann halten
> Kassier ich die Artikel: er ist frei![20]

Das Motiv der Begnadigung, zu der sich der Kurfürst im Gespräch mit Natalie spontan entschließt, ist dieses: dem Prinzen darf durch ihn, den Kurfürsten, kein Unrecht geschehen. Der Kurfürst hatte geglaubt, vollkommen rechtlich verfahren zu sein. Homburgs Zusammenbruch bringt ihn in Verwirrung, denn er scheint ihm zu zeigen, daß Homburg sich ungerecht behandelt fühlt. Wir kennen aus der Kohlhaas-Dichtung das Motiv, daß Unrecht als Kränkung empfunden wird. Kann die Todeserwartung auf einen "solchen Krieger" eine so persönlichkeitsverändernde Wirkung ausüben, wie sie Natalie geschildert hat? Der Kurfürst wäre im Interesse des Staates bereit gewesen, die Gewalt der rechtmäßigen Todesstrafe auszuüben; nicht bereit ist er, das Rechtsgefühl des Prinzen, das er so hochhält, zu vergewaltigen. Indem er den Prinzen zum Richter in eigener Sache macht, läßt er seine eigene Rechtsauffassung in Frage stellen. Die 'Milde', die Natalie an ihm rühmt, erweist sich darin, daß der Kurfürst keinen Gebrauch macht von seiner Macht, wenn damit die Möglichkeit eines Unrechts verbunden wäre; daß er das Recht gründet auf die freie Übereinstimmung Aller, die noch den "Beifall" dessen einschließt, der dem Gesetz verfallen ist.

Man hat sich oft gefragt, ob es sich bei der spontanen Entscheidung des Kurfürsten wirklich um Begnadigung handelt, wie er Natalie glauben mache, oder ob die Bedingung, daß der Prinz den Spruch für ungerecht halten müßte, die Begnadigung nicht wieder zurücknimmt, wenn nämlich Homburg den Spruch für gerecht erklärt. Werde die Begnadigung nicht erst später beschlossen, als der Brief des Prinzen eintrifft? Mache nicht Homburgs Annahme des Urteils die Begnadigung überhaupt erst möglich? Oder, im Sinne der pädagogischen Auffassung gefragt: warum, wenn der Kurfürst zur Gnade entschlossen wäre, warum überhaupt diese Bedingung? Will er ihn durch diesen Appell nicht zur Einsicht führen? Erst den Einsichtigen könne er dann begnadigen. Er wisse aber als der gute Pädagoge voraus, wie Homburg sich entscheiden wird.

Beide Auffassungen werden nach meiner Überzeugung der Konsequenz des Kleistischen Denkens nicht gerecht. Der Kurfürst ruft den Prinzen zur Entscheidung auf, ohne Vorbehalt; sein im voraus gefaßter Entschluß, die Kriegsartikel zu kassieren, wenn Homburg sie nicht bestätigt, ist so verbindlich wie später das Versprechen, Homburgs Wunsch, "was es auch sei," zu gewähren. Zwischen Recht und Unrecht gibt es hier kein Drittes. Meint der Prinz, ein Unrecht sei ihm widerfahren, so wird der Kurfürst jeden Strafanspruch aufgeben. Wie aber im anderen Fall? Die Milde des Kurfürsten bestand darin, Homburg von der Rechtsheteronomie zu befreien und ihm die Rechtsautonomie zu gewähren. Führt aber die spontane Rechtsneuschöpfung des Prinzen zur Bestätigung von Kriegsartikel und Spruch, so vertritt er nun auch selbst den Strafanspruch. Der Strafanspruch geht auf ihn über (nach der 'Regel des Gegensatzes,' die, wie Kleist beobachtet hat, auch im Moralischen gilt).[21] Bei dieser Entscheidung des Prinzen tritt der Kurfürst seinen Strafanspruch an den Prinzen ab. Mithin: wie Homburgs Urteil auch ausfällt, der Kurfürst läßt seinen Strafanspruch fallen, das heißt, er begnadigt den Prinzen. Und diese Begnadigung ist an keine Bedingung gebunden und ist unwiderruflich. Dennoch ist Homburg nicht begnadigt. Denn er begnadigt sich selbst nicht. In Konsequenz seiner freien Rechtsfindung hat er beschlossen, das heilige Gesetz des Krieges, das er verletzt, durch seinen Sühnetod zu verherrlichen. Der Kurfürst wird am Ende diesen Sühnetod "kraft angeborner Macht" verhindern.[22]

These 4: *Prinz und Kurfürst sind miteinander verbunden durch Verhaltenserwartungen, die zunächst falsch sind, sich dann aber doch als berechtigt erweisen.* Homburg erwartet, vom Kurfürsten begnadigt zu werden—zu einem Zeitpunkt, an dem der Kurfürst diese Absicht nicht hat. Der Kurfürst verhält sich anders, als Homburg und Natalie aus ihrer vertrauten Kenntnis des Kurfürsten dies annehmen dürfen. Am Ende erst gehen ihre Erwartungen in Erfüllung. Der Kurfürst, der Homburg als Krieger von heldenhafter Tapferkeit kannte, glaubt diesen gefaßt und bereit, die Konsequenzen aus seinem Fehlverhalten bei der Schlacht zu ziehen. Homburgs Zusammenbruch, sein (wie der Kurfürst es versteht) Um-Gnade-Flehen, überrascht ihn. Daß Homburg später das Urteil bestätigt und den Tod erleiden will, gibt nachträglich der Erwartung des Kurfürsten recht.

Die dramaturgisch konstitutive Beziehung zwischen Protagonist und Antagonist läßt sich also mit den drei Stadien Nähe / Ferne / Nähe markieren. Das mittlere Stadium stellt für Prinz wie Kurfürst eine Selbstentfremdung dar; der Zusammenbruch des Prinzen ist ebenso eine Eklipse seiner Tapferkeit, die ihm gleich der erste Vers des Dramas zugesprochen hatte, wie die Strenge des Kurfürsten eine Eklipse seiner Güte darstellt. "Güte" sei hier definiert mit den Worten des letzten Phöbus-Heftes, aus der "Charakteristik des Jupiters:" "Billigkeit gegen die Schwächen andrer." Daß hier wiederum Kleists Wunschdenken in Hinsicht auf Goethe zum Ausdruck kommt, hat Katharina Mommsen wahrscheinlich gemacht.[23]

Das Stadium der Ferne ist das eigentlich dramatische. Kleist macht in ihm die Spannung zwischen Kurfürst und Prinz, die in der anekdotischen Überlieferung nur latent vorhanden war, manifest. Wie schon gesagt: die gegenseitigen Verhaltenserwartungen der beiden Gegenspieler sind zunächst falsch. Es kommt auf beiden Seiten zur Korrektur. Hohenzollern erschüttert die Zuversicht Homburgs. Nun erkennt Homburg, daß der Kurfürst die Vollstreckung des Urteils plant. Aber Homburg kommt zu dieser zutreffenden Ansicht durch einen Motivirrtum, durch die Annahme, der Kurfürst wolle ihn als Verlobten Natalies aus dem Wege haben, um Natalie an den Schwedenkönig verheiraten zu können. Wie Homburg durch die Konfrontation mit Hohenzollern in Bewegung gesetzt wird, so der Kurfürst durch die Konfrontation mit Natalie. Auch der Kurfürst muß seine Vorstellung von Homburg korrigieren. Er erkennt, daß Homburg sich mit dem Urteil nicht abgefunden hat. Aber er kommt zu dieser zutreffenden Ansicht ebenfalls durch einen Motivirrtum, durch die Annahme, Homburg halte das Verfahren für ungerecht. Ist es auf beiden Seiten ein Irrtum, der zur "richtigen" Beurteilung des Gegenspielers führt, so ist dies nur als Kehrseite des vorher festgestellten Verhältnisses zu verstehen, daß die zunächst "falschen" Meinungen voneinander sich am Ende doch bewahrheiten.

Wir bleiben uns bewußt, diese dramaturgisch konstitutiven Vorgänge zwischen Protagonist und Antagonist hier in thesenartiger Verknappung, recht grobschlächtig, wiedergegeben zu haben. Deutlich wird aber, daß eine Reduzierung oder gar Eliminierung des Kurfürsten als Gegenspielers, wie sie Hans Mayer für die beiden Berlinger Aufführungen konstatiert hat, das Schauspiel in dem Maße verkrüppelt, in dem sie geschieht.

These 5: *Die Homburg-Dichtung gestaltet ein Ideal menschlichen Miteinanders.* Botho Strauß, der Dramaturg der Schaubühne am Halleschen Ufer, hatte völlig recht, wenn er von der "Wunsch-und Projektions-Fantasie des Autors Kleist" schrieb, von der "Traum-und Desideratform des 'Homburg.'"[24] Nur darf man dies nicht einengen auf das in Erfüllung gehende Glück-und Ruhmverlangen des Prinzen. Der diese Erfüllung gewährt, der Kurfürst, ist vor allem eine Wunschfigur Kleists. Abzulehnen sind darum alle Verkleinerungen des Kurfürsten, seien sie politischer Herkunft wie in der marxistischen Position Hans Mayers ("Dies ist die Zeit der Könige nicht mehr"),[25] oder seien sie psychologisch motiviert wie in den Rivalitätshypothesen von Ellis und Politzer. Dies ganz und gar utopische Brandenburg ist aus dem Stoff, aus dem die Träume sind, die Wunschträume, nicht die Alpträume, die wir Kleist offenbar leichter zu glauben geneigt sind (gestaltet z.B. in der korrupten Herrschaftswelt des 'Kohlhaas'). Was noch nicht deutlich genug gesehen wird ist, wie personal Kleist den Konflikt gestaltet hat: daß der Prinz die Schlacht aus dem "unermeßlichen Schmerz" um den Kurfürsten gewonnen hat und dann von diesem unter Anklage gestellt wird, eine charakteristisch Kleistische Zuspitzung, die hart ans Unerträgliche heranführt. An den Kurfürsten sind alle wichtigen Mitspieler gebunden. Kottwitz setzt zwar in seiner Replik zunächst Vaterland, Krone und Person des Kurfürsten gleich, aber im Weiterreden zeigt er, daß er sich ganz eigentlich dem Kurfürsten verschrieben hat. Es ist der Kurfürst selbst, der über sich hinaus weist, am deutlichsten im Zwiegespräch mit Natalie. Auch von dem Prinzen wird diese Einsicht verlangt. Die fraglose emotionale Bindung an den Kurfürsten muß er läutern, muß im Kurfürsten den Fürsten sehen und was er repräsentiert. Das geht nicht ab ohne ein Moment des Trennungsschmerzes: ". . . mein Fürst, der einen süßern Namen [Vater!]/Dereinst mir führte, leider jetzt verscherzt . . ."[26] Wie alle dem Kurfürsten ihr Gefühl entgegenbringen, das spricht ebensosehr für sie, wie es für den Kurfürsten spricht, daß er diese Gefühle zu sublimieren sucht, dem "Vaterland" zugute, oder der "Satzung," dem Gesetz als Legitimationsgrund der Herrschaft. Homburg, versöhnten und heiteren Herzens (V. 1771), erkennt dies und vollzieht es mit. Er fleht für den Kurfürsten allen Segen des Himmels herab, wünscht ihm Sieg und Herrschaft mit den Worten: "denn du bists wert."[27] Dieselben Worte werden wenig später zu dem Prinzen gesprochen.[28] Hier wird zeichenhaft explizit, daß es Kleist um Menschenwert geht. Daß Kleist Menschen-entwürfe macht, den großen Gedanken der Schöpfung noch einmal denkt. Die Beglaubigungsformeln heißen etwa: "Hier ward ein Mensch, so hab ich ihn gewollt!" oder "so urgemäß dem göttlichen Gedanken" oder "recht nach der Lust Gottes."[29] Die Wert-erkennungen und-zusprechungen in der Homburgdichtung gehen hervor aus einem einzigartigen Gleichgewicht von inniger Verbundenheit und "interesselosem Wohlgefallen," wie es etwa deutlich wird, wenn der alte Kottwitz erklärt, warum er dem Kurfürsten dient:

>   Meine Lust hab, meine Freude ich,
> Frei und für mich im Stillen, unabhängig,
> An deiner Trefflichkeit und Herrlichkeit....[30]

Und es ist bezeichnend für Natalies Fühlen, in dem Liebe und Freude zugleich sind. So ist ihre Fürbitte zu verstehen (V. 1083-89) und ihre Worte (an denen man Anstoß genommen hat), als Homburg den Spruch bestätigt:

>   Nimm diesen Kuß! — Und bohrten gleich zwölf Kugeln
> Dich jetzt in Staub, nicht halten könnt ich mich,
> Und jauchzt und weint und spräche: du gefällst mir![31]

Wie die Menschen dieses Schauspiels *sind* und (das fließt daraus) wie sie sich zueinander verhalten, darin sehen wir die Vision einer Menschenwelt nach Kleists Herzen. Daß einem, der so träumt, die Wirklichkeit unlebbar werden kann, wer verstünde das nicht? "Dadurch daß ich mit Schönheit und Sitte, seit meiner frühesten Jugend an, in meinen Gedanken und Schreibereien, unaufhörlichen Umgang gepflogen, bin ich so empfindlich geworden, daß mich die kleinsten Angriffe [auf das Gefühl] . . . doppelt und dreifach schmerzen" schreibt er in einem der letzten Briefe.[32] In diesem Brief steht auch: "Mir waren die Gesichter der Menschen schon jetzt, wenn ich Ihnen begegnete, zuwider, nun würde mich gar, wenn sie mir auf der Straße begegneten, eine körperliche Empfindung anwandeln, die ich hier nicht nennen mag."[33] Manches wird zusammengekommen sein, um diese Stimmung zu erzeugen. Aber die Briefstelle ist doch nicht ohne Vorläufer: schon 1801 schrieb Kleist die entwaffnend ehrlichen Sätze, die wir kennen: "Ach, liebe Ulrike, ich passe mich nicht unter die Menschen, es ist eine traurige Wahrheit, aber eine Wahrheit; und wenn ich den Grund ohne Umschweif angeben soll, so ist es dieser: sie gefallen mir nicht."[34] Wer so aus dem Wünschen gelebt, so inständig Menschen geliebt hat, *wie sie nicht sind*, (sondern sein sollten) dem war wohl auf Erden keine Glücksmöglichkeit gegeben.

ANMERKUNGEN

1. Hans Mayer, "Der 'Prinz von Homburg' als Denkspiel und als Traumspiel." In: *H.M., Vereinzelt Niederschläge.* (Pfullingen: Neske.) 1973, 263f.
2. Hellmuth Kaiser, "Kleists 'PFvH'." — *Imago* XVI (1930), 119-137.
3. Heinz Politzer, "Kleists Trauerspiel vom Traum: PFvH," *Euphorion* 64 (1970), S. 204.
4. John M. Ellis, "Kleists's 'PFvH'. A Critical Study." (Berkeley: University of California Press, 1970), S. 13.
5. Br. an Marie von Kleist vom Sommer 1811.-*Heinrich von Kleist, Sämtliche Werke und Briefe,* Hrsg. von Helmut Sembdner. (München: Hanser, 1964), II, S. 873. Alle Zitate nach dieser Ausgabe.
6. Vgl. *Familie Schroffenstein,* V. 835-839.
7. *Torquato Tasso,* V. 3415 ff. - J. Ellis, S. 36. - Vgl. Katharina Mommsen, *Kleists Kampf mit Goethe.* (Heidelberg: Stiehm 1974), 185.
8. Der Aufstaz von Detlef Müller-Hennig "Vom Musikalischen der Kleistschen Dichtung" (Werke Kleists auf dem modernen Musiktheater. Berlin 1977. Jahresgabe der Heinrich-von-Kleist-Gesellschaft 1973/1974) wird dem Problem nicht einmal ansatzweise gerecht. Dichtung und Musik haben zeitliche Extension; von dieser strukturellen Gemeinsamkeit könnte man ausgehen, wenn bestimmte Techniken, oder sagen wir vorsichtiger: Kunstgriffe, verglichen werden sollen. Man wird Müller-Hennig beistimmen, wenn er sich gegen unscharfe Analogien wendet, wie sie gelegentlich vorgebracht worden sind. Was ist aber gewonnen, wenn einerseits unscharfe Analogien und unpräzise Metaphern abgelehnt, andererseits vom Autor selbst benutzt werden, und zwar gerade bei der Bestimmung von Kleists "latenter Musikalität:" darunter sei zu verstehen die "Identität von Form und Inhalt" (S. 50). Wie es mit dieser angeblichen Identität bestellt ist, darauf lassen die weiteren Metaphern schließen. Die klanglich-rhythmische Schicht müsse mit der inhaltlichen Aussage "zur Deckung gebracht werden" (S. 49). Form und Inhalt seien "ineinander verwoben" (S. 50). Wo es so metaphorisch zugeht, da kann ein Drama sich denn wohl auch durch "Schwerelosigkeit" auszeichnen, noch dazu durch eine "hervortretende" (S. 50).
9. Vergleiche auch den Anfang der kleinen Schrift "Was gilt es in diesem Kriege?", wo von einem jungen und unternehmenden Fürsten die Rede ist, "der, in dem Duft einer lieblichen Sommernacht, von Lorbeern geträumt hat." Helmut Sembdner stellt fest, es sei fraglich, ob Kleist hierbei schon an seinen "Prinz von Homburg" gedacht habe (II, 938). Wir brauchen so weit nicht zu gehen, diesen jungen Fürsten mit Homburg zu identifizieren. Die Jugendlichkeit verbindet sich jedenfalls auch hier motivisch mit dem Traum vom Ruhm.

10. K. Mommsen, S. 176-178.
11. K. Mommsen, S. 94.
12. *Phöbus. Ein Journal für die Kunst.* Hrsg. von Heinrich von Kleist und Adam Müller. Neudruck, hrsg. von Helmut Sembdner (Stuttgart: Cotta, 1961), 599. Vgl. dazu K. Mommsen, 191 f. Als Indiz für Kleists innere Beziehung zu Goethe ist dieses Zitat nur mit Vorbehalt zu verwenden. Ramdohr wird in Ferdinand Hartmanns Beitrag angegriffen. Er hatten ein Gemälde C.D. Friedrichs (Landschaft mit Kreuz) auf eine für Hartmann und Gleichgesinnte unannehmbare Weise kritisiert. Hartmann stellt vor allem Ramdohrs Autorität als Kunstkritiker infrage. Durch eine Kompilation von Exzerpten aus seinen Büchern setzt er ihn dem Publikum zur Beurteilung aus. Diese Auszüge sollen ihn bloßstellen. Das letzte dieser Zitate ist die "Charakteristik des Jupiters." Man wolle, schreibt Hartmann, diesen würdigen Freund des klassischen Altertums würdig und klassisch abtreten lassen. Die Schwierigkeit in der Beurteilung des Zitats liegt darin, daß nicht zu entscheiden ist, ob diese Wendung ironisch oder unironisch gemeint ist. Für das erstere sprechen die seitenlang angeführten dekuvrierenden Exzerpte, für das letztere, daß Hartmann eingangs ein Zitat zustimmend, als Motto, verwendet hatte. Auch in seiner Metakritik hatte Hartmann einzelnes Positive angeführt, so daß sich an diesen Stellen Ramdohr der Uneinsichtige mit Ramdohr dem Einsichtigen konfrontiert findet.
13. V. 645.
14. V. 648-653.
15. V. 550-553.
16. Br. an Adolfine von Werdeck vom 28. (und 29.) 7. 1801. II, S. 678.
17. H. Mayer, S. 265.
18. V. 1787.
19. V. 720f.—*Heinrich von Kleist, Prinz Friedrich von Homburg,* hrsg. von Richard Samuel unter Mitwirkung von Dorothea Coverlid. (Berlin: Schmidt, 1964), S. 187. Arthur Henkel, "Traum und Gesetz in Kleists *Prinz von Homburg.*" *Die Neue Rundschau* LXXIII (1962). Wiederholt in: Heinrich von Kleist. Aufsätze und Essays. Hrsg. von Walter Müller-Seidel. (Darmstadt: Wiss. Buchgesellschaft, 1976), (Wege der Forschung 147) 593.
20. V. 1181 ff.
21. *Allerneuester Erziehungplan.*
22. Die Situation hat eine genaue Parallele in *Amphitryon.* Alkmeme hat sich selbst dazu verurteilt, nie mehr Amphitryons Bett zu nahen (V. 1331 f.). Homburgs 'unbeugsamem Willen' entspricht Alkmenes Schwur. Ihren Eid zerbricht Jupiter "kraft angeborner Macht" (V. 1333), wie der Kurfürst das Todesurteil zerreißt. Hier wie dort verhinder höhere Autorität die Vollstreckung der Selbstverurteilung.
23. [Siehen Anm. 12]—K. Mommsen, 191 f.
24. [Programmheft:] "Kleists Traum vom Prinzen Homburg." (Berlin: Schaubühne am Halleschen Ufer, 1972), 8.
25. H. Mayer, S. 262.
26. V. 1765 f.
27. V. 1799.

28. V. 1851.
29. *Penthesilea*, V. 2233; *Amphitryon*, V. 1571; *Käthchen*, I, 1 (Zeile 66).
30. V. 1591 ff.
31. V. 1386 ff.
32. An Marie von Kleist vom 10. 11. 1811.—II, S. 883.
33. II, S. 884.
34. Br. an Ulrike von Kleist vom 5. 2. 1801.—II, 628.

Adam und Frau Marthe: polare Verfahrensweisen in Kleists *Der zerbrochne Krug*

LILIAN HOVERLAND
University of Kentucky at Lexington

Im neunten Vers von Kleists *Zerbrochnem Krug* stellt der Schreiber Licht einen weitreichenden Bezug her zwischen dem Unfall des Richters Adam und dem Fall des ersten Menschen:

Ihr stammt von einem lockern Ältervater,
Der so beim Anbeginn der Dinge fiel,
Und wegen seines Falls berühmt geworden....(V. 9-11)

Die Kleist-Forschung hat die allgemeine Gültigkeit dieses Hinweises auf den Fall des ersten Menschen nicht nur für dieses Drama, sondern für Kleists Gesamtwerk dargelegt. Kleists Wort von der "gebrechlichen Einrichtung der Welt" wurde mit Adams Fall und der Vertreibung aus dem Paradies in Verbindung gebracht und eine entsprechende Verwandtschaft des *Zerbrochnen Kruges* mit dem Aufsatz zum "Marionettentheater" aufgezeigt. Der mit dem Fall gemeinte Verlust einer früheren Ganzheit, Einheit und Selbstverständlichkeit wurde von diesen Interpreten treffend erkannt. *Der zerbrochne Krug* stellt diesen gesamten Bedeutungsnexus ausdrücklich in den Mittelpunkt, und wiederholte wortwörtliche Anspielungen auf Adams Fall lassen diesen nie aus dem Gesichtskreis schwinden. So spricht Licht von dem "ersten Adamsfall, / den Ihr aus einem Bett hinaus getan" (V. 62-63), Adam erklärt zu seinem Fall: "Ich hätte Hals und Beine fast gebrochen" (V. 184), der Revisor fragt: "Herr Richter Adam. / Seid Ihr gefallen?" (V. 405-406) und schließlich erfolgt Adams eigene apodiktische Feststellung: "Ich fiel." (V. 1459)

Im Mittelpunkt des Dramas stehen nun Adams Manöver, die es sich zur Aufgabe machen, diesen Fall und vordringlich das wichtigste Indiz des Falls, das in seinen Kopf geschlagene Loch nämlich, weg zu explizieren.

Bei diesem Vorgehen bedient Adam sich der Realität auf souveräne Weise und gewinnt ihr eine Unzahl von Möglichkeiten ab. Adam agiert als sein eigener Spielleiter und Schauspieler, der in einem schon modernen Sinn— hierbei ist zum Beispiel an Pirandello zu denken—sein Stück eben hervorbringt und somit kein Endprodukt, sondern den Schöpfungsprozeß selbst vorführt. In diesem Prozeß vollzieht sich eine Neubildung der Wirklichkeit. Mit selbstzufriedenen Ausdrücken begleitet Adam seine Kreationen. So ist die Erklärung, daß er mit einem Ziegenbock am Ofen gekämpft habe, von einem "Jetzt weiß ichs" (V. 51) begleitet, und die Beteuerung, daß die Katze gerade die Perücke dazu ausersehen habe, darin fünf Junge zur Welt zu bringen, wird untermalt von einem parallelen "ich weiß nun schon" (V. 244). Adam ist offenbar erfreut über seine Erfindungskunst.

Zu dem freien Umgang mit der Realität gehört eine flexible Einstellung zur Gerechtigkeit. In Huisum gibt es laut Adam zwei Rechtskategorien: "Statuten, eigentümliche, in Huisum, / Nicht aufgeschriebene" (V. 627-628) und daneben eine zweite Erscheinungsform: denn "auch in Eurer andern Form bin ich, / Wie sie im Reich mag üblich sein, zu Hause. / ... Ich kann Recht so jetzt, jetzo so erteilen" (V. 632-633, 635). Dazu erklärt schon Delbrück, für Adam gebe es "keine absolute, sondern nur eine relative Wahrheit, für ihn als Richter kein natürliches, sondern nur ein positives Recht, das jederzeit willkürlich neu gesetzt werden kann."[1]

Adams wendiger Umgang mit der Realität in all ihren Erscheinungsformen ist nun mit einer schon von Lawrence Ryan konstatierten Subjektivität[2] in Verbindung zu bringen. Adams Erdichtungen, Witze, Verdrehungen und dunkle Anspielungen haben, wie bereits angedeutet, als ihr Ziel, die objektiv gegebenen Zeichen seines Falls—vorzüglich das Loch im Kopf also—zu übersteigen und sich in einem Bereich der rein von seinem Ich abhängigen zügellosen Sprachkunst zu bewegen. Diese freischwebende Achtlosigkeit vor dem Tatsächlichen wie auch vor jeglichem tieferen Sinn und die Verankerung allein im eigenen Ich und seinen willkürlichen Umtrieben sind als die Merkmale zu verstehen, die dem modernen gefallenen Menschen, als welcher der Adam der Komödie anzusehen ist, anhaften und sein Gefallensein recht eigentlich konstituieren. An eine solche Verantwortungslosigkeit vor dem objektiv Gegebenen ist zu denken, wenn man die allgemeiner gefaßten Bemerkungen der Kleist-Forschung erwägt, in dem Drama liege die Betonung auf "Macht und Versagen der Sprache bei der Rekonstruktion der Wirklichkeit,"[3] ja es seien eine Verselbständigung der Sprache[4] und eine Sprachskepsis[5] zu verzeichnen. Indem Adam die Sprache zu einem Werkzeug macht, das allein seinem eigenen Willen untersteht, entfernt er sich auf bewußte Weise von der Darstellung des objektiv Daseienden, von der Rekonstruktion der Wirklichkeit.

Man greift nun aber fehl, im *Zerbrochnen Krug* den generellen Ausdruck einer Sprachskepsis zu konstatieren. Der Erzfehler der übergroßen Subjektivität, der mit dem Verlust bisheriger Verständnismöglichkeiten zusammenhängt, wird zwar aufgezeigt, ja er erreicht seine volle Blüte in Adams Sprachkunststücken. Adam wird aber letzten Endes überführt und verjagt, seine Sprech— und Handlungsart sozusagen zunichte gemacht. Dagegen ist nun aber auch die Position der Krugbesitzerin Frau Marthe zu untersuchen, die eine wichtige Alternative zu dem Stil des Richters Adam darbringt und noch jenseits des Dramas gültig bleibt. Ihre Seh- und Handlungsweise, die die Forschung bisher kaum berücksichtigte, steht im Mittelpunkt des jetzigen Vortrages.

Neben den Fall des Richters Adam stellt sich ein zweiter und zwar der des Kruges. In einem "für sich" weist Adam selbst auf diese Doppelgleisigkeit: "Zwei Fälle gibts, / Mein Seel, nicht mehr, und wenns nicht biegt, so bricht." (V. 553-554) Beide Fälle verursachen ein Loch. So erklärt Walter zu Adams Wunde: "Das ist ein böses Loch, fürwahr, im Kopf, das!" (V. 1458) In dem eigentlichen Prozeß geht es aber um das in den Krug geschlagene Loch. Beide Löcher stehen natürlich in enger entstehungsbedingter wie auch thematischer Verbindung, denn derselbe Adam, der sich ein Loch am eigenen Kopf zugezogen hat, hat auch das Loch in den Krug geschlagen. Beide Löcher sind als Indizien des im thematischen Zentrum des Werkes stehenden Falls, des Bruches im bisherigen Gefüge der Dinge zu sehen. Wie sich weiter zeigen wird, besteht jedoch ein grundsätzlicher Gegensatz zwischen den Haltungen der zwei Personen, denen die Löcher jeweils zugehören.

Wenn Adam nicht nur Richter, sondern auch Beklagter ist, so geht es in der letzteren, unfreiwillig angenommenen Funktion um das Loch im Kopf: wie denn die ihm auf den Kopf und zum Loch passende Perücke das Beweisstück ist, das ihn endgültig überführt. Frau Marthe ist die Klägerin, ihr geht es aber vordringlich um das in ihren Krug geschlagene Loch. Während Adam das Loch in seinem Kopf nun verhehlen, es mit einer Perücke bedecken, es durch die unterschiedlichsten Sprachmanöver aus der Luft schaffen möchte, tritt Frau Marthe mit dem Loch in ihrem Krug auf die Bühne, das zerbrochene Gefäß zeigt sie mit betonter Haltung vor, auf es will sie die Aufmerksamkeit aller lenken. Dabei ist es unangebracht, im Sinne Grahams zu beklagen, daß für Frau Marthe nur die unmittelbar wahrnehmbare, physische Wirklichkeit von Bedeutung sei, daß ihr jegliche geistige Schau, jegliches Verständnis für sittliche oder ästhetische Kräfte unzugänglich blieben.[6] In ihrer Konzentration auf den Krug vertritt Frau Marthe vielmehr eine Position, die in dem Kreis der sie Umgebenden dringend nottut. Während Adam nämlich von dem Bruch und Fall deflektieren will und während Ruprecht, dem in sprichwörtlicher Weise von Adam Sand in die Augen gestreut wird, seinem Sehvermögen nicht traut, seine Augen aufzugeben bereit ist, als er Eve im Garten mit einem anderen Mann sprechen sieht, während diese beiden prototypisch gezeichneten Figuren also entweder von dem Geschehen ablenken oder es nicht in seiner Tatsächlichkeit wahrhaben wollen, besteht Frau Marthe auf dem objektiv Gegebenen. Statt eines Mangels ist hier eine besondere Tugend zu konstatieren.

Fernerhin beschränkt sich Frau Marthe nicht nur auf ein Beklagen des Bruches in ihrem Krug, sondern sie entwickelt ein besonderes Verfahren, das der Haltung der anderen ebenfalls entgegengestellt ist. Als Adam auf Frau Marthes Frage, ob er den Krug sehe, ungeduldig antwortet, ja, alle sähen den Krug, erwidert sie: "Nichts seht ihr, mit Verlaub, die Scherben seht ihr...." (V.646) Pointiert wendet sie sich hier gegen das zu kurz ausgerichtete Sehvermögen der anderen. So besteht sie wohl auf dem objektiven, physischen Faktum. Dieses ist für sie jedoch nicht eigentlich ausschlaggebend, denn hier ist eben—wie sie sich ausdrückt—nichts mehr zu sehen. Sie ergeht sich im weiteren vielmehr in einer detaillierten Schilderung des nicht mehr Sichtbaren, in der Erinnerung und Vorstellung aber noch Heraufzubeschwörenden und erreicht damit eine Lage der inneren Wahrnehmung, die allen anderen Personen des Dramas unbekannt ist.

Wie die Forschung bereits bestimmt hat, zeigt das von Frau Marthe beschworene Bild, die ehemalige Darstellung auf dem Krug also, eine frühere geschichtliche Welt der Harmonie und Einheit. Arntzen erklärt, es handle sich um die Darstellung der "Zeit, in der die Niederlande noch im Universalismus des mittelalterlichen Reiches aufgehoben waren, in dessen Prinzip geistlich-weltlicher Einheit, für das das Nebeneinander von Kaiser, König und Bischof auf dem Krug zeugt."[7] Die dabei im Bild gegebene Übergabe der Niederlande an Philipp II. weise jedoch schon auf den Zerfall des Reiches voraus, das Bild enthalte also nicht nur die Darstellung der geschichtlichen Einheit und Harmonie, sondern auch die Voraussetzung für deren Untergang. Dabei sei der Krug als Chiffre zu sehen, deren Bedeutung Kleist in der naiven Rede Frau Marthes versteckt habe.[8]

Frau Marthe zielt hier auf die Vergegenwärtigung eines ehemaligen Idealzustandes, der schon zur Zeit der Darstellung auf dem Krug gefährdet war und jetzt gänzlich zerstört, zerbrochen ist. Dabei kommt es ihr fortwährend darauf an, die unterschiedlichen Zustände der früheren Ganzheit und des jetzigen Zerbrochenseins miteinander zu verketten. Als Beispiel möge dieser Satz gelten: "Hier grade auf dem Loch, wo jetzo nichts, / Sind die gesamten niederländischen Provinzen / Dem span'schen Philipp übergeben worden." (V. 648-650) So geht die Schilderung weiter: von Karl V. stehen nur noch die Beine, von Philipp ist nur noch das Hinterteil zu sehen, während der Rest seines Körpers und die eben empfangene Krone zerschlagen im Topf liegen. Die Vergegenwärtigung von Bewegungen auf dem zerbrochenen Krug, die auch Philibert und Maximilian im Begriff zeigt, weiter zu fallen (V. 663), eine der Königinnen über den Bruch weinen sieht (V. 660) und einen Neugierigen das Loch anstarren läßt (V. 674), betont die Verbindungslinie zwischen dem früheren heilen und dem nunmehr zerbrochenen Zustand. Durch die Gestalten, die die Qual ob des Bruches auszudrücken scheinen, schlägt sich eine Brücke zu den jetzt durch den Fall Betroffenen. Auf dieses besondere Streben der Vergegenwärtigung gehen die Umstehenden aber nicht ein, und alle drängen Frau Marthe, von ihrem Krug doch abzulassen. So erklärt zum Beispiel Adam: "Erlaßt uns das zerscherbte Paktum, /... Uns geht das Loch—nichts die Provinzen an, / Die darauf übergeben worden sind." (V. 675, 677-678) Frau Marthe kommt es aber gerade auf diese Zweiheit an: auf das Paktum und sein Zerscherben, auf die bildliche Darstellung und das nun ihre Stelle einnehmende Loch. Mit dieser Seh- und Verständnisweise, die physisches Faktum und Ideal, Konkretes und Abstraktes, gegenwärtiges Zerbrochensein und vergangenes Ganzsein nebeneinander hinstellt und verkettet, erscheint sie als gewichtige Gegenspielerin Adams, des unverantwortlich in reiner Subjektivität befangenen Menschen, des gefallenen Erzsünders. Auf ihrer Sehweise besteht sie und setzt sich dabei in ihrer Rolle als Klägerin ausdrücklich von der für sie offenbar unzulänglichen Stellung der Richter ab:

Wieviel ihr brauchen möget, hier zu *richten,*
Das weiß ich nicht, und untersuch es nicht;
Das aber weiß ich, daß ich, um zu *klagen,*
Muß vor euch sagen dürfen, über was.
(V. 716-719; meine Hervorhebung)

Weitere Einzelheiten lassen erkennen, wie wichtig die Beziehung des jetzigen Zustandes auf den früheren ist. Der erste erwähnte Besitzer des Kruges erbeutet ihn im Gefecht mit den Spaniern, also in der durch die Geschehnisse der Krugdarstellung bedingten Periode des Kampfes zwischen Niederländern und Spaniern. Weiterhin wird die Zeitfolge kontinuierlich abgerollt, der Bezug zwischen der auf dem Krug dargestellten Übergabe der Niederlande an Philipp II. und dem jetzt geschehenen Bruch wird also auch zeitmäßig aufrechterhalten.

Die bisherige Ganzheit des Kruges wird nicht nur durch die Beschreibung seiner früheren Schönheit und durch das auf ihm selbst dargestellte Bild der geschichtlichen Einheit betont, sondern auch der Nachdruck auf der bisherigen Unzerstörbarkeit, ja 'Unverbrüchlichkeit' des Kruges weist in dieselbe Richtung. Wie Seidlin schon betont, überlebte der Krug einen Sturz aus dem Fenster, bei dem sein Besitzer den Hals brach, und eine Feuersbrunst.[9] Erst jetzt ist es Adam gelungen, den Krug tatsächlich zu zerbrechen.

Frau Marthe ist nun die Person des Dramas, die die Aufgabe der Wiederherstellung des schönen, so außerordentlich widerstandsfähigen und auf eine frühere Perfektion und Ganzheit weisenden Kruges auf sich nimmt. Adam ist hingegen für sein Zerbrechen verantwortlich. Frau Marthes Rückbesinnung auf eine frühere Ganzheit zeigt sich nun auch in einer zentralen

Sprachgewohnheit, die Adams Sprachmanövern diametral entgegengesetzt ist. Bei ihrem allerersten Auftreten wendet Frau Marthe sich gegen Veit, der ihr den Krug durch eine finanzielle Entschädigung ersetzen will. In ihrer antwortenden Schmährede zeigt sie, daß die anderen, die nicht richtig sehen können, auch nicht richtig zu sprechen wissen. So wie Frau Marthe ihrer Umgebung, die auf dem bloßen Loch besteht und nichts weiter wahrhaben will, sowohl die Vorstellung der früheren Integrität als auch die volle Bewußtheit des nunmehr zerbrochenen Zustandes aufzudringen bestrebt ist, so wie sie also eine richtige Sehweise vorführt, so demonstriert sie ein ähnlich vorgehendes richtiges Sprechen. Auch hier handelt es sich um eine ausdrückliche Zurückweisung des leichtfertigen Umganges mit dem Gegebenen und den Hinweis auf frühere Werte, Bedeutungen und Verbindungen. So wendet Frau Marthe sich gegen Veits Versicherung, es werde "sich alles hier entscheiden" (V. 416): "O ja. Entscheiden. Seht doch. Den Klugschwätzer. / Den Krug mir, den zerbrochenen, entscheiden. / Wer wird mir den geschiednen Krug entscheiden?" (V. 417-419) Hier betont Frau Marthe nicht nur den Umstand, daß der Krug auf immer geschieden und zerbrochen ist, sondern sie deutet auch an, daß mit dem Wortgebrauch der anderen Ähnliches vorgefallen ist, daß der leichtfertige Gebrauch der Sprache ihren nunmehr zersplitterten Zustand nicht in Erwägung zieht. Veit denkt bei seiner Verwendung des Stichwortes "entscheiden" nicht an dessen ursprüngliche Bedeutung, die die Rückgängigmachung einer Scheidung beinhaltet. Mit ihrem Hinweis auf diesen Wortgehalt erreicht Frau Marthe nun ein Doppeltes, das das spätere Verfahren bei der Beschreibung des Kruges vorwegnimmt. So wie Frau Marthe auf der Vorstellung der ehemaligen Ganzheit des Kruges und auf der Verbindungslinie besteht, die von dieser Ganzheit zu dem jetzigen Zerbrochensein zu ziehen ist, so führt sie einzelne Wörter, die denselben Bedeutungsnexus der Integrität und des Bruches berühren, auf ihren früheren Gehalt zurück; so stellt sie im Sprachlichen selbst Zersplittertes der ehemaligen Ganzheit entgegen und läßt die wesentliche Problematik auf potenzierte Weise zur Geltung kommen.

Dasselbe Verfahren wiederholt sich nach Veits Versicherung, er werde den Krug ersetzen. Da erwidert Frau Marthe:

Er mir den Krug ersetzen.
... Setz Er den Krug mal hin, versuch Ers mal,
Setz Er'n mal hin auf das Gesims! Ersetzen!
Den Krug, der kein Gebein zum Stehen hat,
Zum Liegen oder Sitzen hat, ersetzen!

(V. 424, 426-429)

Das ehemals zum Sitzen und Stehen sehr wohl fähige Gefäß kann nicht ersetzt werden, denn der Krug, der sogar nach dem Fall aus dem Fenster "Aufs Bein ... zu stehen" (V. 704) kam, hat jetzt "kein Gebein zum

Stehen" (V. 428) mehr. Indem Frau Marthe sich gegen Veit wendet, der leichthin von "entscheiden" und "ersetzen" spricht, geht Frau Marthe weit über den Gesichtskreis der anderen hinaus, da sie die frühere Ganzheit der Worte wie auch des Kruges im Denken und in der Vorstellung wiederbelebt und dabei die Vergangenheit sowohl als auch die Gegenwart in einem volleren Sinn zu Wort kommen läßt.

Eine Spannung zwischen diesen beiden Polen macht sich gleichwohl bemerkbar: eine Spannung, die auch Frau Marthe nicht zu lösen imstande ist. So fragt sie geringschätzig bei Veits drittem Anerbieten, sie für den Verlust zu entschädigen: "Meint Er, daß die Justiz ein Töpfer ist?" (V. 434) Etwas später erklärt sie aber in genauem Widerspruch: "Der Richter ist mein Handwerksmann," wenn es gilt, "diesen Krug hier wieder zu glasieren." (V. 493, 497) An Frau Marthes eigenen Worten läßt sich also auch das Widersinnige in dem Willen, dem Krug zu seinem früheren Zustand zurückzuverhelfen, ablesen. Und doch steht dieser Wille, zusammen mit dem ihm entgegengesetzten Vorgehen des Richters Adam, im eigentlichen Brennpunkt des Dramas.

Die Eve-Ruprecht-Handlung, obwohl für das dramatische Moment unerläßlich, bleibt in bezug auf die zentrale Thematik nebensächlich. Kleists Kürzung des Dramas und die Auslassung des Variants, der die Herstellung des Vertrauens zwischen Walter and Eve zum Gegenstand hat, mindert die Betonung von Eves Geschick und der gesamten Handlung um die Mißverständnisse zwischen Eve und Ruprecht. Graham und später auch Delbrück übergehen daher Kleists Intention, wenn sie sich gerade auf den Variant berufen und ein versöhnliches, durch ein neues Vertrauen sinnvoll gewordenes Ende davon ablesen.[10] Es war sicherlich Kleists Absicht, durch Weglassen des Variants die Nebenhandlung am Ende abzuschwächen und den Krug voll den Vordergrund gewinnen zu lassen.

In Kleists endgültiger Version wird Adam am Ende in einer schnellen Abfolge von Erklärungen als der gesuchte Krugzerbrecher entlarvt, Eve und Ruprecht versöhnen sich, aber trotz Ruprechts früherer Behauptung, es käme ihr doch nur auf die zerbrochene Hochzeit an, bleibt Frau Marthe im Laufe der abschließenden Ereignisse erstaunlich unbeteiligt. Während der letzten vier Druckseiten des Dramas, die der Aufklärung des Geschehens zwischen Eve, Adam und Ruprecht gelten, ist Frau Marthe fast gar nicht zu hören, sie zeigt keine besondere Überraschung und keine Genugtuung. Erst in der allerletzten Szene, die nach Auslassen des Variants noch größeres Gewicht erlangt, tritt Frau Marthe wieder in den Vordergrund. Nachdem der über alle Berge fliehende Adam in den Hintergrund entschwunden ist, tritt sie auf pointierte Weise nach vorn und läßt noch einmal das, was das eigentliche Zentrum des Dramas ausmacht, zu Worte kommen.

Frau Marthes Interesse gilt von Anbeginn mehr ihrem Krug, dem Titelhelden der Komödie—um mit Graham zu sprechen—als der Ermittlung des Schuldigen und dem Verhältnis zwischen Eve und Ruprecht. Das Verlangen, daß dem Krug sein Recht geschehen solle, führt schließlich sogar noch hinter das Drama. Frau Marthes Suche ist am Ende des Dramas die gleiche wie bei ihrem ersten Auftritt, ja sie wird sich jenseits des letzten Vorhangfalls fortsetzen; denn die jetzt gelöste Schuldfrage war nie die wesentliche, und ihr Krug ist noch immer zerbrochen. So ist Frau Marthe nicht bereit, ihre Klage fallenzulassen. Ganz im Gegenteil: mit ihrer unerfüllbaren Forderung wird sie zum Gericht nach Utrecht gehen und denkbarerweise dann fort und fort, von einer Instanz zur anderen *ad infinitum.* Obwohl Frau Marthe darauf besteht, daß ihr Krug nicht zu ersetzen, daß in ihrer Sache nichts zu entscheiden sei, wird sie mit ihrer Klage doch immer weiter vordringen; wohl kaum um den Rechtsfall zu erledigen, sondern um immer wieder die ehemalige Vollkommenheit ihres Kruges vor das innere Auge ihres Publikums zu stellen, um ihre Umwelt aus ihrer behaglichen und das Gebrochensein in der Welt hinnehmenden Denkweise aufzurütteln, um als Stachel ihres Bewußtseins zu fungieren.

Eine ähnliche Mission mag dem Dichter Kleist selbst vorgeschwebt haben, da er in seinem Werk immer wieder einen in sich ruhenden Zustand darstellt, der dann durch einen Fall, ein Zerbrechen, ein Entzweien gesprengt wird. Auch ihm kommt es auf die Darstellung beider Stadien an, wie es sich auf ausdrückliche Weise an dem Aufsatz zum "Marionettentheater" ablesen läßt. Hinter Frau Marthes offenbarer Einfalt und Unvernunft mag sich also eine Chiffre für die Aufgabe des Dichters verbergen, wie Kleist sie sich selbst stellte.

Frau Marthe erlangt gerade die geistige und auf das eigentlich Grundlegende dringende Schau, die die Kleist-Forschung ihr ausdrücklich abspricht. Die Interpreten der Komödie stellen immer wieder das Schuld und Fall stiftende Vorgehen des Richters Adam in den Mittelpunkt und gehen entweder auf Frau Marthe überhaupt nicht ein oder ordnen sie Adams Bezugskreis unter. Nun läßt sich aber erkennen, daß Kleist in seinem ersten Meisterwerk nicht nur das in Adam dargestellte Problem auf die Bühne bringt, sondern die Methode einer Rückgängigmachung von Adams Schuld, ein Verfahren, das eine Heilung und ein Zukitten des Bruches zum Ziel hat, ebenfalls zur Darstellung bringt. Denn Frau Marthe ist keinesfalls ein williger Repräsentant der nach dem "Fall" aus ihrer Ordnung und aus ihrem Zusammenhalt geworfenen Welt, sondern sie agiert als Gegengewicht. Immer kommt es ihr auf den Rückzug auf einen Punkt vor jeglicher Zersplitterung an: auf einen Punkt vor dem Brechen ihres Kruges, vor dem Verlust einer konkreten und zugleich idealen Sehweise, vor der Ausweitung der Wörter und ihres Gehalts in vielfache Sinnzusammenhänge. Durch eine mehrfach ansetzende Reduktion reicht sie wiederholt zurück in den früheren Zustand der Einheit, Ganzheit und Vollkommenheit, dessen Verlust das Drama beklagt.

ANMERKUNGEN

1. Hansgerd Delbrück, "Zur dramentypologischen Funktion von Sündenfall und Rechtfertigung in Kleists 'Zerbrochnem Krug'," *DVLG* 45, 1971, 706-756, S. 730.
2. Lawrence Ryan, "Kleists 'Entdeckung im Gebiete der Kunst': 'Robert Guiskard' und die Folgen" in *Gestaltungsgeschichte und Gesellschaftsgeschichte. Literatur-, kunst- und musikwissenschaftliche Studien*, Hrsg. Helmut Kreuzer in Zusammenarbeit mit Käte Hamburger, Stuttgart 1969, 242-264, hier: 261.
3. Manfred Schunicht, "Heinrich von Kleist: 'Der zerbrochne Krug'," *ZDP* 84, 1965, 550-562, S. 554.
4. Hans Joachim Schrimpf, "Kleist. Der zerbrochne Krug" in *Das deutsche Drama vom Barock bis zur Gegenwart*, 1. Band, Hrsg. Benno von Wiese, Düsseldorf 1958, 339-362, hier: 355.
5. Ewald Rösch, "Bett und Richterstuhl. Gattungsgeschichtliche Überlegungen zu Kleists Lustspiel 'Der zerbrochene Krug' " in *Kritische Bewahrung. Beiträge zur deutschen Philologie. Festschrift für Werner Schröder zum 60. Geburtstag*, Hrsg. Ernst-Joachim Schmidt, Berlin 1974, 434-475, S. 462.
6. Ilse Graham, "Der zerbrochene Krug—Titelheld von Kleists Komödie" in *Heinrich von Kleist. Aufsätze und Essays*, Hrsg. Walter Müller-Seidel, (Darmstadt, 1973²), WdF CXLVII, 272-295, S. 290.
7. Helmut Arntzen, "Kleists 'Der zerbrochene Krug' " in *Die ernste Komödie. Das deutsche Lustspiel von Lessing bis Kleist*, München 1968, 178-200, S. 188.
8. *A.a.O.*, 184.
9. Oskar Seidlin, "What the Bell Tolls in Kleist's *Der zerbrochne Krug*," *DVLG* 51, 1977, 78-97, S. 86.
10. Graham, *a.a.O.*, 289-290; Delbrück, *a.a.O.*, 753ff.

Der Zerbrochne Krug: Juggling of Authorities

WOLFGANG WITTKOWSKI
State University of New York at Albany

I have undertaken on several occasions to demonstrate that Kleist's *Amphitryon* is a satire, disguised as harmless comedy, on authority and on uncritical obedience to authority.[1] That this is also true for *Der Zerbrochne Krug* will be shown in the following discussion.

Critics have noted before that there is a curious analogy between Jupiter and Richter Adam: both become their own hanging judge (237).[2] That, however, is only half the point, the whole truth being that neither of them, although both are morally condemned, gets the punishment he justly deserves. Certainly not Jupiter, for whatever the god does is, of course, good, even if the deed would be a crime when committed by man. This is the privilege accorded to supreme authority, i.e. to God, by religious myth in Theban society.

As for Adam, he profits from the authority vested in the administrator of justice. Though he is only a village judge—"König nicht von Mazedonien" (144)—he reigns in Huisum like a petty prince. Indeed, his office is "Gottes Richtstuhl." (1100) Of course, "einzig die Ehre des Gerichts" protects him (1840 f.); but it certainly protects him well. Gerichtsrat Walter sees to it that the people continue to respect Adam even after his guilt has become obvious. (1211)

Walter's presence at the investigation contributes to the discovery of Adam's misdeed. His very name reminds us of God's *Walten*. Small wonder that so many critics have seen in him a figure of god-like superiority, an administrator of divine justice.[3] And so another analogy to Jupiter becomes clear, though only to those critics who would celebrate Alkmene's "Beschattung"[4] as piously as Amphitryon does himself, as a mark of favor and distinction.[5]

The analogy, however, can also be understood differently: disguising himself as Amphitryon, Jupiter abuses his superior powers. Nevertheless, or rather, because of this, he fails to win Alkmene's love. Jupiter then tries to reveal his true identity and fails again. Finally, he reveals himself as the Supreme Authority; and yet, he never attains the desired goal: Alkmene's love for him, not Amphitryon. Absurdly enough, he does win everyone else's praise for a deed which they, minutes earlier when he was still thought to be a mere mortal, had roundly condemned. For, strictly speaking, the father of the gods commits the same sin which Adam tries but fails to commit.

Adam, of course, is a mere mortal and anticipates and fears punishment. He forestalls identification as the culprit by hiding behind the honor of this office. Concealment is difficult, however, "ohne der Perücke Beistand" (378) and, in fact, in any other way. Adam actually reveals his true identity, out of fear, brutality, and his frivolous love of gambling. Even when there can be no more doubt that he is the culprit, his "authority," the fact that he is one of the "Honoratioren" (1838), lets him go unrecognized far too long. Finally, his detection becomes inevitable and with it the discovery that he has abused his authority, that he has denounced the government by forging a document to frighten Eve into submitting to his lust.

As for the *Gerichtsrat*, he now abuses his authority as he attempts to protect the judge from "Desertion" to keep him in public service "auf irgend einem Platze." Thus it reads in the *Variant*, Kleist's first version of the two final scenes, which is much more explicit about the part Walter really plays. It is quite apparent that the roles which he, Adam, and Jupiter play are parts in a satire of the "games authorities play," (and of the people's own share in letting them play). Without further ado, Walter concludes that "die Kassen stimmen," although Adam had repeatedly hinted at the opposite. And whom does Walter finally appoint to fill the temporarily vacant seat? "Herrn Schreiber Licht, den Würdgen" (1733 f.). Licht has helped him, and justice, and has shed light on the affair (191)—but only because "this bringer of light (-Lucifer)" he wants to be "Dorfrichter" himself (130). Secretly, in the dark, he himself has misappropriated funds for his "Zinsen und Depositionen" (149). Walter cannot know this; but he fails to investigate the whole matter as thoroughly as is his duty. In the end, Adam's prediction concerning Walter proves to be correct:

> Der Mann hat seinen Amtseid ja geschworen,
> Und praktisiert, wie wir, nach den
> Bestehenden Edikten und Gebräuchen.
>
> *(98ff.)*

Thus the triumph of the greatest impostor is complete. After all, Licht, not the *Gerichtsrat*, had been directing the show from the beginning. Witnessing his victory, the audience sees the representative of the highest authority ridiculed; a representative unaware of his true role claims in a most self-congratulatory manner to have set matters straight and to have brought about the most humane solution. When in the *Variant* the secretary Licht sanctimoniously murmurs: "Ja, wer scharfe Augen hätte" (2408), his subjunctive refers to Walter.

The general lack of "sharp eyes" among the characters has been demonstrated by Ilse Graham.[6] But why are they all unable to see the obvious? It is because they are prisoners of their own bias, which they demonstrate by their pious faith in the authority of the judge and the *Revisor*, on the one hand, and on the other—negatively—by their readiness to believe the worst of the governing powers.

After all, this whole investigation into the matter of a broken jug would not have taken place if Eve had not remained silent. But she, in fear of losing the affidavit Adam has promised her, with which to save Ruprecht from the draft and, as she believes, from duty in Asia and certain death, sees no alternative. Adam shows her a government letter, and Eve believes him although she cannot read it. She simply believes in the authority of the man who can read and who is "ihr Richter" (1390). Eve persists in believing in the letter even after Adam's boldfaced denial of the blackmail attempt which resulted in the broken jug. Finally, Adam accuses Ruprecht of the deed, the same Ruprecht for whose sake he allegedly blackmailed Eve.[7]

This is, for the time being, the end of Eve's faith in the inspector as well. As he allows Ruprecht to be condemned so that "die Ehre des Gerichts" may be saved, she screams: "Seid Ihr auch Richter?" (1889)— that is to say: are you, too, one of those appointed violators of rights who abuse their civil authority? In this case she is wrong, and yet she is more right than she knows. When finally she expresses her distrust openly, Walter allays it with a few words, while at the same time gloriously botching the Adam affair. Then he basks in the people's confidence in himself and the government. Licht is laughing up his sleeve.

The *Variant* treats this process of restoring the people's faith in their authorities thematically and elaborates it much more fully. Will the government represent the Haag merchants and send Ruprecht to Batavia? Eve insists that it will. Walter tries to convince her that she is mistaken. He offers her twenty guilders to buy Ruprecht's release if that should be necessary. But if not, she is to return the money with interest as a fine for her "böses Mißtraun". Eve is vacillating but still puts him off. This incites Walter to use his full powers of persuasion. He shows her the money:

Vollwichtig, neugeprägte Gulden sinds,
Sieh her, das Antlitz hier des Spanierkönigs:
Meinst du, daß dich der König wird betrügen?

(2369 ff.)

Notice his case of "Verfertigung der Gedanken beim Reden!"[8] Unwittingly, Walter moves from his own good intentions to those of the king, via the king's portrait.[9] And indeed, Eve's resistance collapses.[10] This eggs Walter on. He tops off his fine words with an even greater one—a word which had played a solemn role earlier, at the outset of their argument, (1951-58,2345-49): "So glaubst du jetzt, daß ich dir Wahrheit gab?" Eve fervently assents. She now seizes upon all his key words[11] and intensifies the "Verfertigung der Gedanken," i.e., the figurative interpretation of the money's meaning, to its most elevated level:

> Ob Ihr mir Wahrheit gabt? O scharfgeprägte,
> Und Gottes leuchtend Antlitz drauf. O Jesus!
> Daß ich nicht solche Münze mehr erkenne!
>
> *(2375ff.)*

Eve feels remorse. Her rapture, as always, expresses itself in religious exclamations: "O Herr Gott!" "O Jesus!" The king's face is transfigured; to her, it becomes the countenance of God. Ilse Graham emphasizes Eve's last word, "erkenne," and interprets it to mean the beginning of knowledge; but she adds, "at no point does knowledge flower into sheer faith in a spiritual reality unsupported by outward facts and signs."[12] Ironically, this is precisely what happens. Eve in her enthusiastic religious interpretation is entirely untroubled by empirical evidence or logic. The moment she mentions "erkennen," she takes leave of logic.

The inspector, his money, the king, and God become one, a sanctified authority, willed by God himself, an authority one must and may[13] and wants to trust. For Eve wants to trust. She can trust most easily in God and the life hereafter. Therefore, nothing she can say is too absurd to bring these to bear on the problem. Believing that she must conceal the truth from Ruprecht, she comforts him with the assurance that they will meet again at the resurrection; he describes her situation as "des Himmels wunderbare Fügung" (1258), rather than disbelieving what Adam has told her in the conscription matter, and this despite his obvious lasciviousness and prevarication as he tries to blackmail her.

But all this is nothing compared to the leap she takes from the portrait of the king to God, and back to the Dutch government, in the *Variant*. Just a few lines earlier she had announced with pathos that the Spaniard "versöhnt sich mit dem Niederländer nicht, und die Tyrannenrute will er wiedersich, die zerbrochene, zusammenbinden." (1962 ff.) Her people, she says, are at war with the Spanish king "weil wir was Heilges, jeglicher, wir freien Niederländer, in der Brust, des Streites wert bewahren." (1986 ff.).

Now she sets up, as the embodiment of all that is holy, the same Spaniard against whom the Dutch are defending all that is holy to them. In the name of God, the Spanish king is identified with the same Dutch government which mounts war against him. So blind is Eve in her pious devotion to the authorities that she undercuts her own pious patriotism in a comically absurd manner. And all the time, of course, we know that Walter is not the paragon of virtue he seems to be.

Kleist's theme in "Die heilige Cäcilie" and in "Der Zweikampf," both from the year 1811,[14] is religious prejudice which misleads one's consciousness, even without any bad intentions. Possibly, this and the fact that the *Variant* represents a small comedy in itself, explains why Kleist published the latter in 1811 simultaneously with, yet separately from the final version. In the *Variant*, Eve is far too explicit on matters the audience already understands. The comedy of dénouement is much too subtle to come across on stage, even in part. (How could it, if Germanists themselves read it as a serious and problematic scene?) And Eve's patriotism, her religiously elevated trust in the government, which, incidentally, is deserved for once, are not part of the work's overall thematic thrust. This deals with man's inclination to have faith in any and all authorities and to organize and reorganize reality in such a way as to keep it consistent with this faith, i.e. with our tendency to restore this faith whenever it has been undermined.

In the *Variant*, Eve's restoration of faith in the authorities takes the following form. As soon as Ruprecht goes on active duty in Utrecht, she says she will visit him and regularly bring along "von frischgekernter Butter," and "im kühlen Topf" at that. Kleist could have let these lines stand in the final text. By dropping them and the *Topf*-symbol, he made the satire unambiguous. For what remains? Walter's mishandling of the matters concerning both Adam and Licht, and his ironic, condescending recommendation that Frau Marthe should seek justice for her jug "am großen Markt zu Utrecht." "Und Dienstag ist, und Freitag, Session." That is, of course, the pottery market.[15] Walter wants Marthe to buy another jug, one with an equally attractive design and glaze: it is that simple.

Needless to say, such settlement cannot do justice to the jug. Adam should have to replace it, to say nothing of any other punishment he deserves. Moreover, the suggested purchase of a new jug while the broken one stays broken signals and symbolizes precisely the end result of the "comedy:" faith in the authorities is restored, but only superficially, only in appearance. Licht alone notices what a poor job has been done in the name of authority, but he himself is part of the authorities.

Still one might ask: does the jug signify faith in the authorities at all? Before it was broken, its owner loved the jug because of its beautiful design. And what did it show? Figures of authority engaged in a legal transaction. This design is destroyed by Judge Adam, an evil figure of authority. The authorities never bring about justice in the case. Marthe's first words prove right: the authorities are leaving the jug broken, the damage unsettled.

And Marthe is more right than she knows. She, incidentally, also understands the jug figuratively, like the wedding she now wishes to ruin like a jug (445-53), and like Eve's honor and position before the world which she wishes to restore like the jug (487-97). When Walter, in the final scene recommends that Marthe purchase a new jug, Eve's honor is no longer in need of restoration, but the power of the authorities is. Unwittingly, Marthe's very first tirade hints at this: "Ihr krugzertrümmerndes Gesindel ihr! Ihr sollt mir büßen, ihr!" Behind those exclamations rings Jehova's threat to shatter Israel like a jug if it continues to worship false judges and prophets.[16] With Spanish ferocity Marthe even demands "Peitschenhiebe" and the "Scheiterhaufen" for those who have destroyed the jug (493-5).

She herself does not, of course, think about the authorities at this point. She cannot even recognize the original violation of justice which was pictured on the unbroken jug: the Spanish king—that Philip who was the first to disregard the law so often, and his successor, the one who, as we have heard, is presently attempting to repair his "zerbrochene Tyrannenrute." For whether the ceding of Holland to Philip's Spanish crown is to be considered the ideal act of justice, signifying paradise, "Einheit der Geschichte,"[17] is highly questionable. Marthe definitely does not see it that way. She loves the picture out of pious devotion to authority and because it has had such a long history. That this history presents one big tangle of absurdities escapes everyone's notice, just as no one notices the absurdities in deed and status of the authorities.

The jug of Adam's impertinence properly "geht zu Wasser," as the proverb goes: but it does not break as it should.[18] Walter saves Adam from his just punishment. In doing so, and by appointing Licht, he actually sees to it that the jug of justice remains broken. Yet neither he himself nor anyone else in the play has any doubts about his action. Belief in the power and authority of government continues unbroken and apparently unbreakable, though cracks begin to show. Heaven shows no inclination to destroy those who pay more respect to the authorities than they should. To the extent that a crack becomes visible, it is quickly covered up. A new jug will replace the old one as though nothing had happened.

The multiple meanings contained in the metaphor of the jug fill it until all meaning is almost destroyed. Intricately and capriciously, Kleist has humor overlap with romantic irony, then dialectically reverses them into seriousness, and back again. To make matters even more complicated, Kleist's irony is both revealing and concealing.[19] Oskar Seidlin's ciphermysticism should fit in here; but I am unable to find it in the text. However, there is a case to be made for numbers. But behind them are again proverbial expressions and notions.

When the jug, which has carried water long enough, finally breaks, when the measure is full, when the time is ripe and the hour of judgment strikes, or shortly before, we may proverbially say: "It has struck twelve," or "It is five minutes to twelve." In this play, twelve is the hour of discovery and of judgment, both in actual fact and in the criminal's conscience. Whenever someone says it is eleven o'clock, or when it gets close to eleven o'clock, Adam is in danger. He much prefers to talk about an earlier time of day, such as "Glock halb sechs... am Morgen früh," for example (160), and he would much rather it was "halb... Auf eilf" than "halb ... auf zwölfe" (1398). It is eleven-thirty in the ninth scene when Eve first accuses Adam publicly (1208-14) and Walter begins to become suspicious. Quickly, Adam suggests a recess until "morgen früh, Glock neun". This time the "Kelch" passes by. But 400 lines later, that is, at about twelve o'clock, Adam is publicly found out, and it seems that finally, it has struck twelve figuratively as well.

Twelve o'clock is mentioned twice: twelve o'clock noon in the first scene: Licht and the audience have discovered that Adam is the culprit (127 f.); and twelve o'clock midnight is mentioned in the story which convicts him (1683). Unfortunately, this does not take place in the twelfth, but in the eleventh scene, so that, when it actually is twelve o'clock, it does not yet strike twelve, figuratively speaking, after all. Adam is discovered, but not punished as he deserves. Walter covers up the misdeed and wants the criminal recalled to serve in some other public function. Then follows a "Letzter Auftritt;" and now, as in the proverb, "schlägt es 13:" Walter shrugs off Marthe's question of the jug's rights with the objectively cynical recommendation that she buy another, and Marthe will do so, although she had insisted that the jug was unique.

After all that has gone before, this is scarcely surprising. The numbers, moreover, are in favor of it. Their symbolic pattern symbolizes, first, an objective world order, a powerful universal justice such as we see in Schiller's nemesis tragedy, and in *Oedipus*, the parody-prototype of this comedy. But Kleist, of course, reverses this parodically. The structure of the numerical horizon, or perhaps the people—the provenance is not clear—carries these expectations of order ad absurdum. Unnecessarily and unobtrusively, and of course without our fully realizing it, the real action moves away from what the numbers had led us to expect. Indeed, the numerical series itself finally culminates in the number thirteen, the symbol of misfortune and of extravagant deviation from justice. And as the thirteenth scene is disguised as a "Last," so the decisive deviation from justice, by Walter, occurs in a sufficiently deceptive way so that it actually appears to be a fulfillment and a restoration of justice and order.

Certain additional numerical combinations and proverbial expressions may well fit this pattern, though here I am less certain.

In scene 10, Adam seems to be conspicuously preoccupied with the number 3. His pronouncement, "Eins ist der Herr. Zwei ist das finstre Chaos. Drei ist die Welt" calls for interpretation. Does it mean: Walter transforms the chaos of justice in Huisum into an ordered universe? Hardly. Yet there is this sequence: one-two-three. And indeed, Walter is on the verge of discovery: one-two-—a third step, and Adam would be caught. Walter had heard about two blows, and has seen two wounds. The figurative three's meaning seems about to become a reality.

But at this point the judge takes over, in his usual insolent, even foolhardy manner, and drowns the fateful, concrete number two as well as its figurative meaning in that metaphysical toast. It refers to three stages of history, a concept common to the philosophical speculations on history in those days (cf. Schiller, Fichte, Kleist himself). In general, it means—as it does also in its present religious form: "coming to an end, to completion, to fulfillment." In a primitive fashion, the "one-two—you are caught" means the same, but is squelched by the pompous version of that toast. Walter puts his suspicion aside once more, and the culprit now triumphantly offers another toast, meaning "All good things come in threes;" but he elevates it to a higher level, half metaphysical, half earthy, or better, very liquid: "Drei Gläser lob ich mir. Im dritten trinkt man mit den Tropfen Sonnen, und Firmamente mit den übrigen" (1533 ff).

Indeed, Adam will not stop at three glasses, he will drink quite a bit more. And that attaches to the first toast a gloomy meaning: chaos imperceptibly tightens its grip on the world. Apparently, this happens here, at any rate, whether or not the toasts are correctly understood. And it happens because authorities such as Adam, Licht, and above all, Walter, see to it. Like so many educated, high-ranking figures which precede him in Goethe's *Wilhelm Meister* and *Wahlverwandtschaften*[20] and which follow him in 19th century German literature, Walter is blind to his own shortcomings and makes mistakes precisely because he considers himself to be practically infallible. He believes in his own authority, and others around him happily believe it as well. Such are our eternal and all too human limitations. They are serious, even dangerous. But they may be presented in a less serious vein, and we will laugh at them. That is what happens in this human comedy, this comedy of humanity. Only, our short-sightedness in real life is all too well preserved through the structure of the play: we may see its critical implications, or we may not see them; indeed, people for the most part have not seen them, since Walter's grave failure is, ironically, veiled directly and indirectly by Adam's failure on which the comedy's ploy centers. And even in Adam's case of *Fall* the grave implications are covered up.

With the imposture he attempts he nearly succeeds; he fails only in part. In our delight in the happy ending, it is easy to forget that, though unwittingly, Walter's blindness toward Adam's machinations and the judge's partial success have paved the way for chicaneries of even greater consequence. Countless "juggler's tricks" (*Gaukelspiele*) preceded this one, and innumerable others will follow. The audience is free to find such associations depressing, or instructive, or both. The grandeur of the ceremony portrayed on the jug, which Kleist took from Schiller's *Geschichte des Abfalls der Vereinigten Niederlande von der Spanischen Regierung* invites such associations. Schiller's final sentences in that passage are laconic and full of irony: "Es weinte alles, was herumstand. Es war eine unvergeßliche Stunde. Diesem rührende Gaukelspiel folgte bald ein andres."[21]

(Translated by Adrienne Ash and Charlotte Körner)

NOTES

1. "Der neue Prometheus: Kleists 'Amphitryon' zwischen Molière und Giraudoux." *Kleist und Frankreich,* (Berlin, 1968), 27-82. "The New Prometheus: Molière's and Kleist's 'Amphitryon'." *Comparative Literature Studies 8* (1971), 109-124. "Die Verschleierung der Wahrheit in und über Kleists 'Amphitryon'." *Wahrheit und Sprache. Festschrift Bert Nagel,* (Göppingen, 1972), 151-170. " 'Amphitryon': Die Kunst, Autoritätskritik durch Komödie zu verschleiern." *Molière and the Commonwealth of Letters: Patrimony and Posterity,* Jackson (1975), 175-498. *Kleists 'Amphitryon.' Materialien zur Rezeption und Interpretation,* (Berlin, 1978).
2. *Der zerbrochne Krug,* quoted from Sembdner's edition, Hanser and dtv, line numbers in parentheses. The outlines of the interpretation offered here can be found in my article "Weltdialektik und Weltüberwindung: Zur Dramaturgie Kleists." *Deutsche Dramentheorien,* R. Grimm, ed., (Frankfurt, 1972), 270-292. The expanded remarks offered here were made possible by more recent discussions on the part of Delbrück and Seidlin (footnotes 3 and 7), whose theses, nonetheless, run counter to my own.
3. Especially Walter Müller-Seidel: *Versehen und Erkennen,* (Köln, Graz, 1961), as well as Seidlin (footnote 7), and above all Hansgerd Delbrück: *Kleists Weg zur Komödie,* (Tübingen, 1974).
4. Biblical expression. Goethe makes use of it in his *Tagebuch,* July 14, 1807, where he recapitulates "die Deutung der Fabel ins Christliche," as it had been undertaken by the *Amphitryon* editor Adam Müller in a fashion which is still being followed by critics today.
5. Especially Müller-Seidel (footnote 3), but also Jochen Schmidt, *Heinrich von Kleist,* (Tübingen, 1974), who rejects Delbrück's thesis (*DVjs* 45, 1971, 706-756) in favor of the more sociological interpretations of Helmut Arntzen (*Die ernste Komödie,* München, 1968). Arntzen, however, interprets *Amphitryon* (as Schmidt does) similarly to Müller-Seidel.
6. "The Broken Pitcher: Hero of Kleist's Comedy," *MLQ* 16 (1955), 99-113; now in Ilse Graham, *Heinrich von Kleist,* (Berlin, 1977). Quotations from the latter.
7. Oskar Seidlin ("When the Bell Tolls in Kleist's *Der zerbrochne Krug,*" *DVjs* 51, 1977, pp. 78-97, here p. 91 note 15) overlooks this point which alone determines

Eve's silence before the court and thereby the entire course of the trial. His sarcastic critique of Arntzen's sociological interpretation which, it is true, is too presumptuous on many points, culminates in the quote and comment: " 'das tiefe Mißtrauen der Bauern allem gegnüber was von Oben kommt' (is that why they take their case to court and most successfully so?)."

8. Cf. Kleist's essay of the same title.
9. Delbrück treats this point in detail. He is of the opinion that to Eve, the Spanish king is "Gottes zugehöriger und wesensgleicher Gegenpart," also that her "Sünde," like everyone's sin except Walter's, is "Unglauben" toward God and authority. And further, in his view, she is referring (1.2375) to Jesus' parable of the penny, "Gebet dem Kaiser, was des Kaisers, und Gott, was Gottes ist" (96, 186).
10. "O lieber, guter, edler Herr, verzeiht mir" (158 f). Schmidt sees here a heightened awareness on Eve's part which Arntzen does not. In Schmidt's view, she recognizes that her demand for unconditional trust from Ruprecht went too far, since she herself is now in doubt. There is little support for this notion in lines 2375 ff., nor does Eve's renewed declaration of love for Ruprecht contribute anything in this direction. The fact that she begs for help on her knees, at the beginning of the scene, indicates only that she has never ceased loving Ruprecht, regardless of her apparent behavior.
11. She did this just above lines 2360 ff. as well, as did Alkmene in her decisive and much debated lines 1564 ff.
12. Ilse Graham, 38, 40.
13. Delbrück stresses this in particular (cf. footnote 7) and Seidlin agrees in principle, disregarding the comic aspect of Kleist's critical irony. In the meantime, their ranks have been joined by Peter Michelson, "Die Lügen Adams und Eves Fall." *Geist und Zeichen, Festschrift A. Henkel.* H. Auton, et al., ed. (München, 1977), 268-304.
14. Cf. Wittkowski, " 'Die heilige Cäcilie' und 'Der Zweikampf'. Kleists Legenden und die romantische Ironie." *Colloquia Germanica* (1972), 17-58.
15. Arntzen, who overemphasizes the serious aspects of the comedy, seems to have misunderstood this; yet otherwise I am in basic agreement with his interpretation (Cf. *Die ernste Komödie,* p. 196).
16. Jeremiah 19, 10-11. We owe a debt of gratitude for this important discovery to Delbrück (*Kleists Weg zur Komödie,* p. 52 f.)
17. Ilse Graham, 39; Oskar Seidlin, 88; Arntzen, 188.
18. Sembdner notes that, according to Richard F. Wilkie (*GR* 1948) Kleist borrowed several motifs and situations from Christian Felix Weise's one-act play *Der Krug geht so lange zu Wasser, bis er zerbricht, oder Der Amtmann* (1786).
19. Cf. my publications cited in footnotes 1, 2 and 14.
20. Cf. the corresponding characters from Goethe's *Novelle* and *Wahlverwandtschaften,* as well as the overview at the conclusion of my article " ' . . . daß er als Kleinod behütet werde.' 'Stifters Nachsommer.' Eine Revision." *Literaturwissenschaftliches Jahrbuch der Görresgesellschaft* (1975), 73-132.
21. It is, by the way, not clear, whether Schiller implies that the Spanish authorities are playing their juggler's tricks intentionally or not. The idea of portraying

legal symbols on a jug is found in Schiller's *Wallenstein* (*Die Piccolomini* IV, 5) along with countless other motifs that recur in Kleist's comedy: the *"Gaukelkunst"* of authorities (*Picc.* III, 1); numbers mysticism (*Picc.* II, 1); conscription; puns (the Capucine monk); the wrongful rule of a lower authority in a village; currency which bears a picture of a disputed authority figure; lament over the disintegration of public justice (all in *Wallensteins Lager*). E. Theodor Voss, "Kleists *Zerbrochener Krug* im Lichte alter und neuer Quellen" (*Wissen aus Erfahrungen*. Festschrift Herman Meyer, Hrsg. A. v. Bormann. (Niemeye: Tübingen, 1976), 338-370) refers to these works by Schiller but without drawing any conclusions, to say nothing of those I have offered above. Instead, he interprets the pictorial material as an indication that the meaning of Kleist's work is:

> "nichts Geringeres als ein die ganze Menschheit
> betreffender Prozess" "um 'Lust' und 'Pflicht',
> um 'Glück' und 'Schuld' "; "nichts Geringeres
> als die Frage . . . : war der Mensch zur Lust
> erschaffen oder zur Pflicht, war er dazu erschaffen,
> hienieden glücklich zu sein oder zu gehorchen?"
> Eve "ist jedenfalls fest davon überzeugt, daß
> Gott den Ruprecht ihr 'zur Lust erschaffen hat' "
> and she is "ja nur deshalb vor Gericht . . . , weil
> sie ihren Ruprecht vor der Pflicht, Soldat zu
> werden und vielleicht zu sterben bewahren wollte"(367-9).

This conspicuously timely definition of the problem is based on an invented alternative. It is true that Eve wants to save Ruprecht from being sent to Indonesia; but a tour of duty in his native country does not seem to her to be in any conflict with "Lust." In fact, Eve's patriotism in the *Variant* suggests that she is quite proud of her soldier-fiancé.

Novellas

Unglück und Verwirrung: Bemerkungen zu Kleists Erzählungen

BARBARA MECK
Erlangen, F.R.G.

Denkt man an Kleists Erzählungen, fallen einem automatisch Worte wie 'zwangsläufig, unaufhaltsam, unerbittlich, konfliktgeladen, konzentriert, intensiv, angespannt,' und ähnliche Charakteristika ein. Da ist kein Hauch von Besinnlichkeit oder bürgerlichgepflegtem Genre zu spüren, da fehlen termini, die sich bei andern deutschen Erzählern direkt aufdrängen, völlig. Wo wären zB. 'die stille Heiterkeit des Herzens' (Adalbert Stifter) oder 'Humor und Satire' (Wilhelm Busch), oder gar 'Langsame Entfaltung, Reifen, Ausklingen' (Goethe, Mann)?

Nein, bei Kleist geht alles rasch, verdammt gedrängt. Der Leser muß sich anstrengen, muß von vornherein die Nerven anspannen, um überhaupt bei diesem preußischen Zackzack mitzukommen. Pausen gibt es nicht. Die Handlungslinien und Charaktere überkreuzen sich, verfangen, verwirren sich und der ganze Konfliktball rollt lawinenartig ins unerbittliche Chaos ab.

Ob das nun der Tod der beiden Liebenden in "Die Verlobung in St. Domingo" oder die Ermordung von Frau, Mann und Kind in "Das Erdbeben in Chili" ist oder totale Sinnverwirrung der vier Brüder in "Die heilige Cäcilie oder die Gewalt der Musik"—immer überstürzen sich persönliche und situationsbedingte Beziehungen. Ein leichtes Abklingen, ein freundliches ritardando, eine plötzliche glückliche Wendung sind bei Kleist undenkbar. Nach dem Chaos werden dem Leser noch knapp einige sachliche Hinweise gegeben, fast wie ein amtlicher Epilog, und kommentarlos wird der betroffene Zeitgenosse ins Ungewisse entlassen. Wie man über die ganze Geschichte urteilt, ob man den Charakteren Fehler zuordnet oder nicht, ist uninteressant. Kleist dirigiert nicht vorsichtig, erzieht nicht, will den Leser nicht bilden. Er berichtet einfach sachlich seine Geschichte. So wie sie wirklich war. Und auch dort, wo es wirklich war. In Basel zB.

("Der Zweikampf"), in Oberitalien ("Das Bettelweib von Locarno") oder an den Ufern der Havel ("Michael Kohlhaas"). Nichts wird erdichtet, ersonnen, zusammenphantasiert. E.T.A. Hoffmann oder Du-bist-Orplid-mein-Land-Atmosphäre ist gänzlich unerwünscht. Nein, Kleist will immer wahr sein, streng realitätsbezogen, von unparteiischer Glaubwürdigkeit und Objektivität. Siedelt er nicht deshalb gerne seine Handlung im Historischen an? Hat ja der "Michael Kohlhaas" sogar den Untertitel 'Aus einer alten Chronik'. Da soll der Leser nach der Lektüre nicht erleichtert sagen können: "Am Schluß gibt's der Dichter endlich zu: es war alles bloß ein böser Traum."

Bei Kleist fehlt der Traum, bei Kleist ist die Realität schrecklich. Die unschuldige Littegard sitzt halb wahnsinnig im Gefängnis, das Gottesurteil war wider sie ("Der Zweikampf"); die Marquise glaubt vor Verwirrung in die Erde zu sinken, als der ihr wie ein Engel vorgekommene Graf bekennt, der Vater ihres Kindes zu sein ("Die Marquise von O..."); der Marquese haut mit dem Degen gleich einem Rasenden im leeren Spukzimmer herum und zündet sinnverwirrt sein Schloß selbst an ("Bettelweib von Locarno").

Immer grinst unausweichlich die Katastrophe im Hintergrund. Nicht auf dem Papier, im Roman, irgendwo, irgendwann, etwas das uns nicht angeht, das nur einen angenehmen Nervenkitzel, einen TV-Krimischauder bewirkt—nein! Das ganze normale Leben, die Realität, die Menschen und ihre Handlungen sind unerbittlich und ausweglos. Gefangen im Ich, gefangen im Gleis der Ereignisse. Ein Abspringen, das 'Nicht-mehr-mitmachen' des Einzelnen ist undenkbar. Jeder muß einfach, ob er will oder nicht.

Wenn O'Casey über 100 Jahre nach Kleist's Tod sagt: "Die Welt ist ein Irrenhaus," und wenn bei Kafka die Institution übermächtig, undurchschaubar nach dem Individuum greift, dann könnte Heinrich von Kleist als Herold dieser Gedanken gelten. In allen seinen Erzählungen herrscht der Ausnahmezustand, aber nicht als Ausnahme, nein, zum Normalzustand erhoben und das Lieblingsvokabular besteht aus Worten wie: betroffen, bestürzt, sinnberaubt, bewußtlos, in seiner Empfindung irre geworden, zerrissen an Leib und Seele, wahnsinnig, unglücklich.

Der Kurfürst von Sachsen kehrt nach Dresden zurück, "zerrissen an Leib und Seele" ("Michael Kohlhaas"). Mutter und Tochter rufen beide aus: "Der Graf F...!" "von einer Bestürzung in die andere geworfen." ("Die Marquise von O...")

"Seid ihr wahnsinnig?" ruft der heldenhafte Don Fernando der wütenden Menge zu, während er versucht, das Leben seiner Freunde zu retten. ("Das Erdbeben in Chili")

Die junge Mestizin Toni verliebt sich wider Willen in den Weißen Gustav von der Ried "indem sie verwirrt vor sich niedersah" und wird aus Liebe der Sache ihrer Leute untreu. Der Neger Hoango steht "bestürzt und verwirrt im Korridor mit seinem Troß von Fackeln und Bewaffneten still." Listig rettet Toni ihren Geliebten vor Hoango und ihrer ebenfalls durch die Ereignisse verwirrten Mutter—"der Alte wandte sich gegen die in Verwirrung zur Seite stehende Mutter." Doch Gustav erschießt Toni, ein Mißverständnis, und als er die Wahrheit begreift, jagt er sich eine Kugel in den Kopf, totunglücklich. ("Die Verlobung in St. Domingo")

In "Der Findling" erschrickt Nicolo, als er sich zufällig seinem Ebenbild gegenüber sieht. "Er schloß, in nicht geringer Verwirrung, die Tür wieder zu und entfernte sich." Das ist der Moment, wo Nicolo sich von der Gesellschaft, den Normen abzusondern beginnt. Hervorgerufen durch eine äußere Ausnahmesituation, nämlich sein Ebenbild zu erblicken, reagiert der junge Mann so, wie er nun zwangsläufig reagieren muß: Gefangen im eigenen Ich bringt Nicolo die "unglückliche Elvire" zu Tode, um dann von seinem Adoptivvater Piachi ermordet zu werden. Auch Piachi wird als "Unglücklicher" bezeichnet, da ihn das Gesetz wider seinen Willen vor der Hinrichtung bewahrt. Die vier Brüder in "Die Heilige Cäcilie oder die Gewalt der Musik" werden von ihrer Mutter im Irrenhaus wiedergefunden. ". . . seltsam getroffen, begab sie sich eines Tages. . . . in das Irrenhaus und bat die Vorsteher um die Gefälligkeit, ihr zu den vier unglücklichen, sinnverwirrten Männern . . . einen prüfenden Zutritt zu gestatten." Wie es zu dieser grauenvollen Umwandlung der lebenslustigen Brüder kam, bleibt letztlich ungeklärt. Es ist eine "ungeheure Begebenheit," die als solche eo ipso "unbegreiflich" sein muß. Von den Anhängern der vier Kirchenstürmerbrüder heißt es: "Durch diesen Anblick tief im Innersten verwirrt, steht der Haufen der jämmerlichen Schwärmer, seiner Anführer beraubt . . ."

Die unglückliche Littegard wird von ihrem Streiter, dem Kämmerer Friedrich von Trota angefeuert: "Bewahre deine Sinne vor Verzweiflung" und "Laß uns von zwei Gedanken, die die Sinne verwirren, den verständlicheren und begreiflicheren denken". Doch auch der vortreffliche, konservative Friedrich von Trota ist seiner bei diesen umwälzenden Ereignissen nicht mehr sicher. "Gott, Herr meines Lebens, bewahre meine Seele selbst vor Verwirrung" fleht er, und er wird nicht sinnberaubt, er wird nicht unglücklich, denn für ihn gibt es einen Halt, das Sichere, Gesetzliche, den Glauben an das Prinzip von ordo im weitesten Sinne, an Gott.

Vielleicht ist die Verwirrung der Kleistschen Figuren nur das Negativ des Goetheschen Prometheus, wenn er teils stolz, teils höhnisch, teils verzweifelt ausruft:

> Wer rettete vom Tode mich,
> Von Sklaverei?
> Hast du's nicht alles selbst vollendet,
> Heilig glühend Herz?
> Und glühtest, jung und gut,
> Betrogen, Rettungsdank
> Dem Schlafenden dadroben?

Auch Prometheus ist der Ausgestoßene, der Besondere, der durch einen Ausnahmezustand Nicht-mehr-integrierte ebenso wie der Roßhändler Kohlhaas oder die Marquise von O.... Aber während Goethe noch mit Göttern rechtet, ist Gott oder Götter, denn der absolute Gott ist verlorengegangen, für Heinrich von Kleist nur mehr ein blaßer Begriff. Seine Helden (besser: seine Figuren) müssen mit ihren schrecklich getäuschten Sinnen allein fertig werden. Hilfe von Gott oder Göttern wird nicht mehr erwartet. Hilfe von andern Menschen oder Menschengruppen endet meist tragisch. Einen Sieger gibt es nicht mehr.

Kleist's "Der Zweikampf" as Comedy

JAMES M. McGLATHERY
University of Illinois

Kleist's "Der Zweikampf" often has been called one of the weakest, or least interesting, of his stories. An obvious reason that the tale seems "un-Kleistian" is that his other works, with the exception of the comedy *Der Zerbrochne Krug*, focus upon tragic, overweening passions, while "Der Zweikampf" seems almost devoid of such eruptive and compulsive emotions. Even the villain of the piece, Count Jacob Redbeard, appears quite in control of himself and little more than an ordinary seducer and murderer. Thus, part of the explanation for some critics' deprecation of this story may be that, although it can be seen as raising momentous questions about the nature of Providence or the universe, the tale also partakes of traditions of comedy, as for example its sharing with Kleist's *Der Zerbrochne Krug* the inherently farcical theme of a seduction attempt gone awry.

One reason that blame has been leveled at "Der Zweikampf," of course, is simply that its author committed suicide not long after it presumably was written. To be sure, the last work by a writer who died in his prime often is regarded as his final statement and perhaps even his masterpiece and crowning achievement. The last year before Kleist's death, however, was clearly a time of despair for him; moreover, as his critics were aware, financial difficulties contributed to his suicide and his last writing was done under pressure of a compelling need to earn money. Thus, Kleist's earlier critics—those responsible for reviving interest in him in the second half of the nineteenth century—concentrated their efforts on finding fault with the story, since their approach to the understanding and evaluation of his works was essentially biographical.

With the arrival of what may loosely be called the existentialist period in literary criticism, opinion on "Der Zweikampf" underwent a marked change, to the point where some critics, beginning apparently with Gerhard Fricke in 1929, came to consider this tale to be "perhaps Kleist's most beautiful novella," as Fricke himself put it (p. 149). To the existentialist critic, Kleist's suicide marked the end of a tormented search for meaning in a world where positive religious faith seemed no longer possible. "Der Zweikampf," having presumably been written last, thus attracted special interest as likely to have been Kleist's ultimate statement of the problem and the final word concerning the result of his quest. To quote Denys Dyer, in his book *The Stories of Kleist*, "In *Der Zweikampf* are gathered together the basic themes of Kleist's works. It is highly appropriate that these themes should be assembled for one last time in what is arguably one of the best and most profound of his stories" (p. 175).

A position of compromise between the older view, which complained of flaws in "Der Zweikampf," and the newer, existentialist rehabilitation of it was found by John M. Ellis in an article published several years ago (*Monatshefte,* 1973). Ellis made the putative villain, Jakob Rotbart, the central figure of the story, at the expense of the tale's hero and heroine, Friedrich and Littegarde. At the same time, Ellis agreed with the existentialist view in finding the story's point to be that ". . . God's truth and goodness, even granted they exist, have become inaccessible and obscured"—for the quite different reason that "the wrong done" Jakob Rotbart (namely the Duke's arranging for his illegitimate son to succeed him instead of his half-brother Jakob) "goes unavenged" (p. 59). Although Ellis' interpretation is unlikely to convince even existentialist critics of the story, his surprising view has merit in re-opening the question of whether either Littegarde or Friedrich is worthy of interest as a central figure.

As has long been recognized, "Der Zweikampf" evidently was inspired in part by Kleist's re-telling, in his journal *Berliner Abendblätter*, of an anecdote from Froissart's *Chronique de France*. The French anecdote tells how a woman's claim to having been raped during her husband's absence was vindicated in a duel held to determine God's judgment of the matter. As we shall see, one aspect of the anecdote which may have interested Kleist is the initial suspicion that Lady Carouge had simply imagined the whole affair. At any rate, in changing the tale almost completely, Kleist made it into—above all—a gentle, touching love story.

In doing so, Kleist probably was guided by his other recognized source, the story of Renato and Eusebia in Cervantes' novel *Persiles* (Bk. II, esp. Ch. 19). There the hero fights a duel with the heroine's accuser over the latter's charge that Renato and Eusebia have been having an affair, although actually Eusebia has not even been aware that Renato is in love with her. Renato loses the duel, but with the ironic result that, precisely because he has done so, he and Eusebia eventually are married and live happily ever after. The lost duel draws the two of them together because each has felt responsible for the other's misery: he for having lost the duel and thereby having called Eusebia's honor into question, and she for having been the cause of Renato's disgrace and his resulting self-imposed exile as a chaste hermit. Kleist's basic change in the love story consists in making the heroine a young widow, and one who even at the outset is anything but unaware of the passion the hero feels for her, since she has rejected his suit out of a determination to renounce love and marriage. Equally important, Kleist borrowed from Froissart's anecdote the matter of the lady's putative sexual involvement with a second man, yet with the important difference that, as in Cervantes' story, she is not the accuser, but the accused. Finally, unlike his counterpart in Cervantes' tale, the rival in Kleist's story, far from denouncing the hero for having had an affair with the heroine, boasts instead that he has seduced her himself.

Kleist's chaste heroine, Lady Littegarde, stands accused of having engaged in a night of love-making with the local rake, her middle-aged bachelor neighbor Count Jakob Rotbart. Worse, she is suspected of denying the fact despite its bearing upon the case of the murder of Count Jakob's half-brother Duke Wilhelm von Breysach. Littegarde's devoted admirer, Friedrich von Trota, another bachelor neighbor, who holds the position of ducal president of the exchequer, takes up her cause, with the ultimate result that her virtue is vindicated. More important, perhaps, is that the accusation against Littegarde and her gallant defense by Friedrich cause her to forget her earlier resolve to become abbess of a religious foundation for women, so that in the end the young widow and her bachelor admirer marry and seem destined to live happily ever after.

Littegarde is easily recognizable as Kleist's type of highminded heroine—like Eva, Alkmene, Penthesilea, Käthchen von Heilbronn, Thusnelda, and the Marquise of O. . .—who all stand accused of having surrendered, in one way or another, to illicit desire. The heroine's emotional situation in "Der Zweikampf" may be compared best with Eva's in *Der Zerbrochne Krug*, for like her Littegarde knows that she is not guilty as charged. Indeed, Littegarde has not even, like Käthchen von Heilbronn, behaved in a manner which anyone could consider unseemly. And yet our interest nevertheless is focused—as so often in Kleist's works—on an emotional struggle within the heroine, and one which involves what may be called feelings of sexual guilt. For although in seeking von Trota's aid and accepting his offer to be her champion Littegarde was confident that her fffvirtue was beyond reproach, when God's judgment initially seems to have gone against her she evidently suffers from the tormenting thought that, despite her innocence of the specific charge, God nonetheless has found fault with her.

The explanation for Littegarde's self-doubt, as with Kleist's other heroines, may be found precisely in her excessive dedication to an ideal of chaste love. Like the Marquise of O. . ., Kleist's other young widow among his heroines, Littegarde reacted to her first husband's death by returning home to her father and putting out of mind any thought of remarrying. She resisted her father's urging that she take a husband, and only unwillingly yielded to his wish that she attend the balls held by neighboring aristocrats like Jakob Rotbart (at whose own house his initial move to seduce her was made). To be sure, when Littegarde rejected Friedrich von Trota's offer of marriage, she did so "aus Besorgnis, ihren beiden, auf die Hinterlassenschaft ihres Vermögens rechnenden Brüdern dadurch zu mißfallen" (*Werke*, II, 235, ed. Sembdner, 5th printing, 1970). Yet this consideration does not appear to have been Littegarde's original motivation in having expressed the wish, as we are told, to live "still und eingezogen auf der Burg ihres Vaters" (II, 235). On the contrary, the brothers' hopes of dividing their sister's inheritance seem to have been awakened precisely by this determination of Littegarde's not to remarry. Thus, Littegarde's decision to become abbess of a nearby religious foundation for women has its origins in her dedication to an ideal of renunciation, yet one which, in turn, appears to involve an element of sexual sublimation.

Littegarde's entry upon a career as abbess is prevented, ironically, by news of Jakob Rotbart's alibi that he was making love with her on the night of the Duke's murder. More important, Rotbart's claim moves Littegarde to turn for help and shelter to Herr von Trota, her devoted admirer, after her elderly widower father has died of shock and her brothers have turned her out of the castle. Littegarde's unconscious feelings of shame and guilt, which must lie behind her later feeling that God has found reason to judge against her, likely revolve around this urge to turn to von Trota as her angel of rescue—the role he had played once before in her life when, as they were out on a hunt, he "ihr einst . . . gegen den Anlauf eines verwundeten Ebers tüchtiger Weise das Leben gerettet" (II, 235; one thinks of the parallel scene in Kleist's play *Die Hermannsschlacht*, which occasioned Thusnelda's guilty adulterous attraction to Venditius, and also of the Marquise von O. . .'s faint in the arms of her gallant rescuer). Indeed, it was this incident which led to Friedrich's proposal and Littegarde's wavering over whether to accept or reject it. Moreover, one can hardly imagine that, once Littegarde has appealed for Friedrich's aid this second time, she could fail to reverse her decision against marrying him. Thus, Littegarde must recognize, if only unconsciously, that by seeking Friedrich's help she is in effect asking him to become her husband after all. On the conscious level, Littegarde does not seem to allow herself such thoughts, being preoccupied instead with the proud conviction that her virtue will be vindicated in the duel and that her champion therefore will be in no danger.

When God's verdict seems to go against her, considering that von Trota is mortally wounded in the duel, while Jakob Rotbart receives only a scratch, Littegarde's suppressed feelings of sexual shame and guilt begin to oppress her. This helps explain why Littegarde, although she knows she is innocent of having desired Jakob Rotbart, much less of having had relations with him, nevertheless at first behaves so strangely toward von Trota after the duel, when they are imprisoned together. For whatever reason, Littegarde obviously feels guilt for having turned to von Trota and having accepted him as her champion.

Littegarde's sublimation of desire through devotion to an ideal of chaste love was, of course, a chief factor Jakob Rotbart's mad passion to seduce her in the first place. A confirmed bachelor, Rotbart is the male counterpart of the renouncing widow, he being every bit as devoted to boasting about amorous conquests as she to pride in her chastity. It might even be said that Rotbart is virtually a projection of Littegarde's subterranean sexual guilt, in the sense that his passion for seduction mirrors her subconscious urge to surrender again to desire. At any rate, it is clear that while Littegarde's renunciation has broken many an eligible local man's heart, Rotbart's pursuits—to hear him tell it, anyway (cf. II, 230)—have cost countless women in the vicinity their virtue.

Rotbart's passion to seduce Littegarde originally was unrelated to his plan to murder his half-brother, the Duke. It may even have been coincidence that the murder took place on the same evening that Rotbart was keeping the appointment he believed he had with Littegarde (actually, of course, it was with her maid who was impersonating her without the mistress' knowledge). Whatever the case, Rotbart obviously is thrilled to be able to use the presumed visit to Littegarde as his alibi for the murder, because it gives him above all a pardonable excuse for crowing publicly about the conquest he believes he has made—which he considers all the more glorious because the woman in question was thought free of the stirrings of desire.

Littegarde's ideal of renunciation acts as a powerful erotic stimulus also upon her eventual second husband, Herr von Trota. No less than Rotbart, Friedrich burns with desire to win the charming young widow, although at the conscious level this urge takes the sublimated form of an inspiration to heroic gallantry. While Rotbart dreamed of himself as Littegarde's demonic seducer, von Trota is filled evidently with equally intense visions of himself as her angel of rescue—the stereotypical erotic sublimation fantasy in Kleist's day, and one which he used repeatedly in his works beginning with his very first play, *Die Familie Schroffenstein.*

One may wonder whether von Trota would have been nearly so devoted if Littegarde had not been thought to be so unavailable. Rotbart, for example, imagining that Littegarde had surrendered to him, did not try to communicate with her again "wahrscheinlich" as the narrator says, "aus Furcht, daß dies Abenteuer ihn zu weit führen könne..." (II, 257)—which likely means that Count Jakob began to fear that his jealously guarded bachelor status might be in jeopardy. Friedrich, of course, suffers no such attacks of bachelor cowardice, if for no other reason than that, until the very end of the story, the subject of love and marriage has not been revived between himself and Littegarde. He remains throughout the rejected suitor who devotes himself gently and subtly to winning the heart of his high-minded beloved. At the same time, like Littegarde, although to a much lesser degree, Friedrich seems unconsciously in the grips of a tension between burning desire and a need to sublimate it. This mixture of desire and its sublimation in his passion for Littegarde is perhaps best reflected in his words of self-reproach as he is recovering from his wound: ". . . ein heilloser Fehltritt in die Riemen meiner Sporen, durch den Gott mich vielleicht, ganz unabhängig von ihrer Sache, der Sünden meiner eignen Brust wegen, strafen wollte, gibt ihre blühenden Glieder der Flamme und ihr Andenken ewiger Schande preis!" (II, 249; "Fehltritt" may also be used in referring to a moral lapse).

Viewed as a love story in which shy, suppressed desire finds expression in sublime fantasies, Kleist's "Der Zweikampf" amounts to gentle, ironic comedy. The tale follows the general convention of the *Lustspiel*, in which young love—or as in this case, chaste desire—finds an obstacle in its path that must be overcome. Here, as in Lessing's comedy *Minna von Barnhelm*, the threat to Desire's triumph comes not from outside, but from within, that is, from Littegarde's high-minded decision not to remarry. Indeed, whereas Adam's attempt to seduce Eva in Kleist's *Der Zerbrochne Krug* threatened to prevent her planned marriage to Ruprecht, in "Der Zweikampf" Jakob Rotbart's need to boast about his imagined success with Littegarde, far from bidding to prevent her union with Friedrich, actually is required to bring it about.

NOTES

1. Cervantes Saavedra, Miquel de. *Die Mühen und Leiden des Persiles und der Sigismunde.* In: *Miguel de Cervantes Saavedra. Gesamtausgabe in vier Bänden,* Ed. and trans. Anton M. Rothbauer. Vol. I. Stuttgart: Henry Goverts, 1963, pp. 687-1164. (cf. Bk. 2, Chap. 19, pp. 923-28).
2. Dyer, Denys. *The Stories of Kleist. A Critical Study.* New York: Holmes & Meier, 1977.
3. Ellis, John M. "Kleist's 'Der Zweikampf,' " *Monatshefte*, 65 (1973), 48-60.
4. Fricke, Gerhard. *Gefühl und Schicksal bei Heinrich von Kleist. Studien über den inneren Vorgang im Leben und Schaffen des Dichters.* Neue Forschung 3. Berlin: Junker und Dünnhaupt, 1929.
5. Kleist, Heinrich von. "Geschichte eines merkwürdigen Zweikampfs." In: Helmut Sembdner (ed.), *Berliner Abendblätter. Herausgegeben von Heinrich von Kleist.* Stuttgart: J. G. Cotta, 1965, pp. 171-72; 175-76. (cf. also in *Heinrich von Kleist. Sämtliche Werke und Briefe.* Ed. Helmut Sembdner. 5th rev. ed. Vol. II. Munich: Hanser, 1970, pp. 288-91.

Kleist's "Der Findling"—The Pitfalls of Terseness

ROLF N. LINN
University of California
Santa Barbara

The secondary literature about Kleist's novella "Der Findling" is marked by an amazing variety of judgments and interpretations. The spectrum of opinions extends from that of Günter Blöcker at one end[1] to the virtually contrary one by Rolf Dürst on the other.[2] In between one finds those of Max Kommerell,[3] Thomas Mann,[4] Peter Dettmering,[5] Jochen Schmidt,[6] and Robert Helbling,[7] to mention just a few of those whose comments exhibit interestingly graduated viewpoints. What these representatives of a large number of Kleist aficionados and scholars have to say shall be briefly discussed here, before an attempt will be made partially to answer the questions of which aspects of the story may have encouraged the extraordinary divergences, and why they tend to slant the author's words.

For Blöcker "Der Findling" is a "perfekte Diablerie, wie es sie sonst in Kleists Werk nicht gibt."[8] It is "die Geschichte des grundlos Bösen. Die Bosheit ihres Helden ist nicht motiviert . . . sie ist einfach da, als pure, sich selbst lebende-*malizia*."[9] For this reason the story needs no psychological verisimilitude and can heap its elements of chance beyond any credibility. It is an "außer ihm liegende Macht," which plays all trumps into Nicolo's hands, Piachi and Elvire being his victims. He ruins these two, and not enough with this, he turns his stepfather into his murderer, so that Piachi, who crushes Nicolo's brain against the wall, becomes an evildoer himself. Since old Piachi refuses salvation in order to persecute his adopted son in hell one may say that cruel gods decreed for two good people a terrible fate which does not end with their death.

Max Kommerell speaks of the "Findling" only in passing and appears essentially to share Blöcker's views. But he stresses Elvire's innocence as if he suspected that someone might doubt it. "Sie war, gegen die teuflische Berechnung ihrer Seele in dem Grade wehrlos," so he says, "als sie sich musterhaft in der Erfüllung ihrer Pflicht als Gattin, der Schwermut um den Toten als dem geheimen Besitz ihrer vollkommenen Seele ergeben hatte."[10] Convincing himself Kommerell here points to a problem that did not enter Blöcker's mind.

It entered Thomas Mann's mind, however. Of course, he, too, considers Nicolo to be a scoundrel and the "Unheilbringer" of the tale, but he does not see Elvire as a model wife. Rather, he praises Kleist's moral

> "Tiefe und Finesse, welche der Dichter bewährt in der Darstellung des permanenten seelischen Ehebruchs Elvire Piachis mit dem zärtlichen Andenken an den ritterlichen Lebensretter von einst, diesem romantischen und sittlich nicht ganz einwandfreien geheimen Liebeskult, den ihr schurkischer Adoptivsohn entdeckt und den er sich durch das Blendwerk seiner Erscheinung verbrecherisch zunutze machen will."[11]

He remarks a little later that Elvire's attitude toward Nicolo is, to be sure, innocent, "unschuldig bis zur Gleichgültigkeit," but finds that through the latter's resemblance to her rescuer and the anagrammatic relation with him it is moved into a dubious light, "in ein zweifelhaftes Licht gerückt wird." Mann cautiously lets it go at insinuations, but the foster parents are no longer a unit. The foundling no longer destroys a healthy, harmonious marriage, but two people who live in an unwholesome atmosphere created by Elvire.

As Elvire loses in purity for Thomas Mann, Nicolo loses in unmotivated meanness for Dettmering. With a psychoanalytical approach this scholar avoids such problems as those of fate and morality[12] and attempts instead to lay bare the causes of the behavior of the main figures. For instance, Nicolo's precocious sexuality is explained by him as an "Ausweichen vor Elvire . . . eine Umschreibung der Tatsache, daß Nicolo an die Ödipus-Phantasie fixiert geblieben ist."[13] The young man's burning hatred for Elvire, so the analyst claims in agreement with others, stems from disgrace to which Piachi exposed him and for which he erroneously holds his stepmother responsible. But the error itself is also explained by Dettmering who sees it as the result of Elvire's lack of love for the boy Nicolo. Elvire's death cult, Nicolo's resemblance with the dead knight and the relationship of names jointly serve the feelings of lust and the need for revenge; there follows the attempted rape. When the adopted son is asked to leave the house by his father he finds himself for a second time in the situation that he was at the beginning, and he rebels.[14] The evil deeds of the foundling are made thusly plausible. They still appear unsavory, but one sees them no longer as plain actions but rather as reactions. This, to be sure, is also true for Mr. Piachi who, having lost his wife, his fortune, and his son, becomes a disappointed Michael Kohlhaas—even a super-Kohlhaas—and takes revenge on revenge. Psychoanalysis brings about a completely new distribution of guilt, if the word "guilt" may be used in this context at all.

Jochen Schmidt leads us still farther away from Blöcker, for he sees in Nicolo a parallel to Jupiter in *Amphitryon*. According to him the misdeeds of the Foundling have "symbolic" meaning for Elvire who is the central figure. Nicolo is "kein fremd von außen hereinbrechendes Schicksal, sondern eine aus dem Innern der Frau heraufbeschworene und durch sie erst lebensmächtige Erscheinung."[15] Certainly, as the double of the secretly adored Colino he represents no "Überhöhung ins Göttliche," but a "Perversion ins Teuflische, ins schlimm Zerstörerische."[16] As such he has no existence of his own, functioning only as "der vernichtende Dämon einer nichtigen Ehe."[17] With the "inversion of *Amphitryon*" and a reference to the "Marquise von O . . .," which adds little to the argument, the face of guilt is once more altered: the Piachi couple acquired their foundling and deserve him, diabolical as he may be.

Helbling understands "Der Findling" as a tale of evil which manifests itself "in crass self-interest or counterfeit emotions" of the Piachi family.[18] The three persons destined to perish misunderstand each other constantly and cannot help destroying each other. The metaphysical dimensions of Piachi's ire and revenge overshadow everything else, but they do not contravene the satanic in Nicolo so as to redeem Piachi or Elvire.

An almost diametrically opposed view to that of Blöcker's finally is to be found in the book by Rolf Dürst. Here the Piachis are in no way Nicolo's victims, rather, the latter is the victim of the heartlessness with which the Piachis treat him. The foundling has to replace the dead son, but only with regard to externals. Neither parent shows any sign of love. "So verfällt er in beiden Leidenschaften ("Bigotterie," and a "Hang für das weibliche Geschlecht") dem bloß Äußerlichen: dem Schein der Frömmigkeit und rein körperlicher Liebe."[19] The Piachis attempt to bridle these tendencies, but their success is shortlived. For a while they are deceived, but once their eyes are opened father Piachi lures the young man into a trap, exposes him to public humiliation, and kindles his hatred. Nicolo retaliates with the attempted rape of Elvire, which the old man might yet accept if Nicolo were to leave the house. But Nicolo shows his stepfather the door since, in a friendlier moment long ago, the property was given to him. Only now does Piachi have recourse to the law, and when a secret understanding between Nicolo and a bishop prevents all legal maneuvers, he uses violence. "Kleist," so Dürst summarizes his interpretation, "hat mit dem Schicksal dieser einzigen Familie die bürgerliche Gesellschaft, die Justiz, die Moral, die Kirche—sämtliche Institutionen, in deren Bahnen das moderne Leben verläuft—fragwürdig gemacht. Ihre Unzulänglichkeit ist erwiesen. Es fehlt überall das Wichtigste: das Gefühl des Herzens, die Liebe."[20]

What is the cause for the diversity of opinions regarding "Der Findling" demonstrated above? It is suggested here that among other things in this novella Kleist has given a bold portrayal of the male and female psyche, a subject, if treated with Kleistian laconicism, will set the reader's creative imagination to work, the result quite often being a spontaneous filling of interstices. Such supplementation, no matter what direction it takes, detracts from the poet's work, for his laconicism is as necessary for the sharp delineation of the characters as are their lack of communication and their unusual, but not impossible circumstances of life.

Nicolo and Elvire, it will hopefully be demonstrated, are to be understood as representatives of their sex under test conditions. Their individualities are tried by experiences and by a specific social situation to which they respond with emotional immaturity, never partaking of the feedback that the meeting of men and women usually affords. This makes them splendidly pure models—and causes their ruin.

I do not mean to deny the importance of the character of Piachi, but merely to emphasize that portion of the story that leads to the first of three deaths. Werner Hoffmeister has done ample justice to the father and husband in name only. It suffices here, therefore, to point to his function in the Elvire-Nicolo plot. There he is an initiator of action who once brings about a significant change in the relationship of stepmother and stepson. But throughout he is part of the framework which gives the novella its particular, nearly symmetrical, structure.

Piachi starts the events of "Der Findling" with an act of pity[21] and ends them with an act of brutality. Three times Nicolo throws himself at his mercy to gain his selfish ends, at the beginning, in the middle after Constanze's death, and near the end after the attempted rape. In anti-*Märchen* fashion he is twice successful and the third time unsuccessful, and his failure leads to his doom. Piachi, dismayed with his licentious son who seeks his pleasures right after Constanze's death, humiliates him during her hastened internment "before all the people" and arouses his hatred for Elvire whose indiscretion Nicolo holds wrongly responsible for the chastisement. But this brings us to the two figures on whom we wish to focus our attention.

It is necessary first to follow Elvire part-way through her life without embroidering or surmising. At the age of thirteen she is saved from a fire by a young Genovese patrician named Colino who is severely injured during the rescue. At the request of his mother she nurses her hero for three years and sees him suffer, and then die. Only near the end of the story is the reader struck by the full magnitude of the trauma experienced by the young girl. Until then he accumulates evidence without adding it up.

Two years after Colino's demise Elvire marries the much older widower Piachi who is careful never to mention the rescuer's name, since she becomes most upset when reminded of the time, "da der Jüngling für sie litt und starb." The new husband respects her feelings, having no complaints about her social performance as a wife, for she sees to his comforts, raises a niece, loves her stepson Paolo, and later receives Nicolo kindly. Nicolo's early interest in women disturbs her, but all seems well when he marries the niece Constanze, and she agrees to her husband settling a large part of their fortune upon him.

Accidentally she once encounters Nicolo disguised as a Genovese knight and faints. She never mentions the incident, which frightens him as much as her; it remains "ewiges Geheimnis." After this she just as accidentally surprises her stepson as he, right after Constanze's death, arranges for a tryst with Xaviera Tartini through the latter's maid. This, too, she keeps to herself, but she accompanies Piachi to the church where Constanze is buried and where Nicolo is publicly censured by Piachi who has found out about his son's irreverent indecency.

From this, the center and high point of the novella, Elvire's past and present are mostly revealed to us through the mediation of Nicolo. Nicolo's past contains nothing exactly paralleling Elvire's. An orphan, "God's son," he contracts a plague-like illness, recovers, takes Paolo's place who does not recover, and then grows up as a clever and unscrupulous egoist. He enters into a loveless marriage,—at the end he is willing to enter a second one for rather despicable reasons—and makes promises which he does not intend to keep, and generally appears to lead a private life of his choice while doing well in business. His cunning serves him well, until on one occasion his deception fails and his humiliation instills both hatred and desire for Elvire in him. From now on he observes her, spies on her, interprets her every move—Kunz speaks of "Innensicht" after the narrator's earlier "Außensicht" as regards the young man[22]—their lives thus become intertwined in his mind, until Elvire's last fainting spell finally removes her from his grasp.

The significant stations on the way of the ruthless active male and the seemingly apathetic female—the epithets refer to their emotional, not their social life, where they function quite normally—are three: the keyhole scene, the ivory letters scene, and the rape scene; each of these, however, entails other pertinent events which must be presented in conjunction with them.

A spiteful Nicolo once passes Elvire's room, hears words from within, and looks through the lock in the hope of discovering something that will compromise his stepmother. At first he believes not to have hoped in vain, since he sees her in ecstasy at someone's feet, whispering "Colino." However, later he stealthily visits her room and finds only the life-size picture of a young knight. Fear overcomes him and he leaves.

Curious about the identity of the knight he waits until the Piachis take a trip to the country and then shows the portrait to Xaviera and her daughter Karla. Little Karla points out the resemblance of Nicolo to the man in the picture and thereby reminds him of the incident referred to earlier where she fainted when she saw him in a Genovese costume. He believes that he has become Elvire's romantic interest and is greatly flattered. He even begins to think that perhaps it was his name rather than Colino's that he had heard her whisper.

Wishing to pursue his double game of lust and revenge further he impatiently awaits Elvire's return, but she comes back with a young relative and devotes herself to her duties as a hostess, and even after the visitor leaves she finds things to do that do not involve him. His nerves are taut. Through a combination of events, he just then comes to play with some old ivory letters which spell his name. Moving them around he is surprised to see that they also spell Colino. "... von rasenden Hoffnungen von neuem getroffen" he leaves them in this form for Elvire to notice who reacts with "beklommenem Blick," "Wehmut," tears and blushing. He suspects that she hides his own name under the transposition of letters and hopes reach new heights, while nothing happens to disabuse him.

On the next day he learns the identity of the man on the portrait, and again he feels humiliated, this time with the help of his long deceased double, but basically by Elvire. Now he promptly plans what the narrator calls the most dastardly deed ever perpetrated.

It must parenthetically be noted that the way in which he is apprised of the facts concerning Colino may well intensify his aggressiveness. It is Xaviera who informs him, and she in turn had learned the truth in the Carmelite monastery. Apparently Nicolo has long known that his stepmother goes to the Carmelites for confession and therefore asks Xaviera to make inquiries there. Kleist mentions this intriguing bit of intelligence only in passing, but that does not make it any less startling. The Carmelites are the greedy hypocrites whom Piachi detests. Their bishop's mistress is Xaviera who seduces the fifteen-year-old Nicolo "bei Gelegenheit dieser Mönchsbesuche." And yet Elvire bares her soul to these monks and receives absolution from them. What better way for her to demonstrate her emotional independence from her husband and thus her availability?

The dastardly deed follows, its description revealing one more significant point about Elvire and her Colino rites: she undresses for them. We place the last piece in the puzzle that is she and survey the young woman's entire silent ordeal. The fire and particularly the lingering death of her gallant rescuer have shocked the thirteen year old girl to such an extent that she never achieves an unequivocally normal relationship with a man. Instead she stops at the stage of the adolescent who has a "crush." She develops a cult that grants her "ecstasy," which may imply both surrogate sexuality and the satisfaction of giving a life in requital for a life lost on her account. And so she grows older, but not up.

In the final analysis she perishes because her emotional atrophy leaves her all too vulnerable to the male brute who, on his part, follows his primitive nature unbridled, does not grow up either, and never cultivates any true human intercourse. His own violent death follows; in an epilogue Piachi also dies,[23] and we lay down a fascinating study of two human beings and their powerful catalyst, which lays bare the excesses latent in us. That it does so by careful contrivance and with the utmost economy gives it its paradigmatic quality. At the same time it teases us into "fleshing it out," and the most faithful paraphrase ends up by now rendering "wie es eigentlich gewesen ist."

NOTES

1. Günter Blöcker. *Heinrich von Kleist oder das absolute Ich.* 2nd ed. (Berlin, 1962).
2. Rolf Dürst. *Heinrich von Kleist, Dichter zwischen Ursprung und Endzeit,* Diss. (Bern, 1965).
3. Max Kommerell. "Die Sprache und das Unausprechliche," *Geist und Buchstabe der Dichtung.* 3rd ed. (Frankfurt am Main, 1944). pp. 243-317.
4. Thomas Mann. "Heinrich von Kleist und seine Erzählungen," *Schriften und Reden zur Literatur, Kunst und Philosophie, III* (Frankfurt am Main, 1968), pp. 297-312.
5. Peter Dettmering. *Heinrich von Kleist—Zur Psychodynamik in seiner Dichtung* (München, 1975).
6. Jochen Schmidt. *Heinrich von Kleist—Studien zu seiner poetischen Verfahrensweise* (Tübingen, 1974).
7. Robert Helbling. *Heinrich von Kleist* (New York, 1975).
8. Blöcker. p. 133.
9. Ibid., p. 134.
10. Kommerell, p. 257.
11. Mann, p. 307.
12. The conflict between fate and free decision is often implicitly present in discussions of the "Findling." See especially Josef Kunz, "Heinrich von Kleists Novelle 'Der Findling.' Eine Interpretation," in *Festschrift für Ludwig Wolf,* ed. Werner Schröder (Neumünster, 1962), pp. 337-355.
13. Dettmering, p. 79.
14. Ibid., pp. 80 f.
15. Schmidt, p. 177.
16. Ibid., p. 178.
17. Ibid.
18. Helbling, p. 116.

19. Dürst, p. 71. Dürst claims that Piachi is critical with respect to both tendencies, but the narrator knows only of the father's attitude toward hypocrisy, and the mother's objections to an early interest in sex.
20. Ibid., p. 72.
21. Piachi's psychology at the beginning is rather complex. Cf. Werner Hoffmeister, "Heinrich von Kleists 'Findling,'" *Monatshefte,* LVIII (1966), 53.
22. Kunz, pp. 349 ff.
23. For a different interpretation of the last pages see Hoffmeister, op. cit., p. 52.

Marionettes

Heinrich von Kleist und die Marionette

WOLFGANG KUROCK
Marionettist und Lehrbeauftragter am
Figurentheaterkolleg des Deutschen Instituts
für Puppenspiel in Bochum

Als mir, nach jahrelanger praktischer Arbeit mit Tanzmarionetten, Kleists Aufsatz "Über das Marionettentheater" erneut in die Hand kam, da erschien mir das zuvor als exzentrisch beurteilte Essay plötzlich in einem völlig neuen Licht.

Während ich damals im Einklang mit der Literaturwissenschaft und gemäß der landläufigen Meinung meiner Berufskollegen die Kleistschen Forderungen zum Marionettenspiel lediglich als überspitzte Spekulation eines amateurhaften Besserwissers eingeordnet hatte,[1] so erschien es mir nun beinahe, als läse ich altvertrautes Gedankengut. Denn hier sah ich im Nachhinein alles das ausdrücklich bestätigt, was sich mir aus der Arbeitspraxis heraus an Problemlösungen angeboten hatte.

Gleich eingangs fand ich das Medium genauso beschrieben, wie ich es selber als besonders effektiv dem Publikum vorzustellen gelernt hatte: Kleine dramatische Burlesken, mit Gesang und Tanz durchwebt. Und da war keine Rede von Marionetten-Theater wie etwa vom Schauspiel von Doktor Faust oder der Historie der schönen Genoveva; Kleist spricht stets und nur von der *Tanzmarionette*. Es fiel mir besonders auf, daß Kleist genau das Prinzip des Marionettentanzes durchschaute, als er Herrn C. sagen ließ, der Maschinist brauche nicht jedes Glied der Figur im Verlaufe des Tanzes zu setzen oder zu stellen—wie es die allgemeine Ansicht zu sein scheint, daß nämlich ein "Effet" eine ganze Folge von Bewegungsabläufen auslösen kann.

Und sofort danach stieß ich auch auf den Begriff "Schwerpunkt der Bewegung,"[2] der mir, obwohl seltsam formuliert, sogleich das unaufhörliche Bemühen des Marionettenmechanikers exakt umschrieb, der bestimmte Bewegungsabläufe in seine Figur hineinlisten will: Daß nämlich die Marionette, selber ein Pendel, mit verschiedenen Gliedmaßen als Nebenpendeln und jeweils eigenen Schwerpunkten als bewegte Massen oder Formen genau die von Kleist aufgezeigten Eigenschaften ausweisen. Und wenn Kleist später noch behauptet, der Maschinist brauche nur *einen* Draht oder *einen* Faden, um den Schwerpunkt der Marionette zu regieren, während die Glieder nichts als tote Pendel bleiben und dem Gesetz der Schwerkraft (hier wäre hinzuzusetzen: . . und der Zentrifugalkraft) folgen, so läßt sich dies alles mit geeigneten Figuren ad oculos demonstrieren.

Wir finden Marionetten, die an einem Draht gespielt werden, heute noch in Belgien und Sizilien; auch in Museen sind ähnliche Techniken zu sehen, und daß diese Drahtführung durchaus legitim ist, beweist der alte französische Fachausdruck "la tringle" für diesen steifen Draht. Auf diese Weise lassen sich sinnvolle Bewegungen ausführen, das heißt: Gezielt und wiederholbar.

Wie aber ist das mit der Kontrolle der Marionette durch einen Faden? Diese Bemerkung Kleists wurde ihm stets von Fachleuten besonders angekreidet. Ich selbst habe eine solche "Ein-Faden-Führung" ebenfalls früher für unmöglich gehalten, wurde aber durch eigene Experimente eines besseren belehrt. Die Kontrolle der Figur wird dadurch sicher schwieriger, aber nicht unmöglich. Wieweit diese Technik eine Entwicklung zuläßt wie bei den vorhin gezeigten Schleuderfiguren, muß abgewartet werden.

Auch läßt sich am Objekt deutlich machen, daß Kleist mit seiner Behauptung recht hatte, durch bloße Erschütterung der Marionette sei eine tanzähnliche Bewegung zu erzielen. Es gibt sogar sogenannte Schüttelmarionetten.

Merkwürdig mutet jedoch Kleists Formulierung vom "Weg der Seele des Tänzers" an, der identisch sein soll mit der Bewegung des Schwerpunktes der Figur, und daß der Maschinist sich selbst in diesen Schwerpunkt der Tanzmarionette versetzen, d.h. selber tanzen müsse.

Die Erklärung ist naheliegend: Der Marionettist muß die Kontrolle seiner Figur solange üben, bis er sie aus dem Gefühl heraus "blind" beherrscht. Das läßt sich am praktischen Beispiel zeigen und erklären.[3]

Kleist erwähnt ferner, daß es möglich sein müsse, Marionetten durch eine Kurbel zu spielen. Solche Techniken sind der Fachwelt seit Jahrhunderten bekannt, und sie erlauben eine besonders einfache, dabei aber elegante Steuerung der Tanzfigur. Diese sogenannte Kurbelführung erläutert auf sehr eindrucksvolle Weise die Relationen zwischen den Bewegungen des Spielers und den davon abhängenden der Figur: Sie verhalten sich wie das einfache zum komplizierten, oder in Kleists gleichnishaften Worten: "Wie die Zahlen zu ihrem Logarithmus oder wie die Asymptote zur Hyperbel."

Die Qualität einer Marionette wird—neben ihrer Gestalt—vor allem nach ihrer Funktionalität beurteilt, und unter den Bewegungsfunktionen ist es die Gehbewegung, der besondere Bedeutung zugeschrieben wird, die auch seit je den Mechanikern besondere Schwierigkeiten bereitet hat. Da die Gehbewegung stets rhythmisch ist, so muß man sie auch dem Tanz zurechnen, also ist auch für sie Kleists "Schwerpunkt der Bewegung" von besonderer Bedeutung, ja geradezu der Schlüssel zum Erfolg. Hier kommt man nur durch Manipulation des Schwerpunkts in jeder Teilform zu brauchbaren Ergebnissen, und bei konsequenter Anwendung der Gesetzmäßigkeiten läßt die an sich komplizierte Gehbewegung der Marionette sich nicht nur korrekt ausführen, sondern auch fast beliebig variieren.

Den Höhepunkt dieses Aufsatzes—aus der Sicht der Marionette gesehen—stellen jedoch die Postulate Kleists zu ihrer fachgerechten Konstruktion und Gestaltung dar: "Ebenmaß, Leichtigkeit, Beweglichkeit, nur alles in einem höheren Grade, und besonders eine 'naturgemäßere Anordnung der Schwerpunkte.'" (Figur 1)

Vor allem diese Passage ist für den Marionettenpraktiker besonders bedeutsam. Zwar erscheint es selbstverständlich, daß Kleist Beweglichkeit verlangt—ein einziges verklemmtes Gelenk kann die ganze Aufführung gefährden.

Aber, warum erwähnt er Leichtigkeit? Diese Forderung hängt eng zusammen mit der darauffolgenden "naturgemäßeren Anordnung der Schwerpunkte," und die Praxis des Marionettenbaus lehrt, daß in der leichteren Form oder Figur der Schwerpunkt sich besser ins Extreme manipulieren läßt.

Dann gebraucht Kleist den Begriff: "Ebenmaß ... alles in einem höheren Grade;" Er verlangt hier wie bei der "naturgemäßeren" Anordnung der Schwerpunkte nicht ein getreues Abbild des Menschen, sondern dessen Steigerung, also geradezu hellsichtig genau das, was wir als Stilisierung, formale Interpretation oder bildnerische Verfremdung bezeichnen würden, Gesetzlichkeiten, die wir auch auf jede abstrakte Marionette anwenden können.

Es ist erstaunlich, daß anderthalb Jahrhunderte vergehen mußten, bis man Kleist beim Wort genommen und seine Gedanken in die Praxis umgesetzt hat, denn diese Grundsätze decken in ihrer fast selbstverständlichen Einfachheit und Klarheit tatsächlich jedes Problem ab, so wie dies in der Mathematik für die Axiome zutrifft. Natürlich hat Kleist damit nur das Ziel gesteckt und es den Handwerkern überlassen, den Weg dorthin zu finden—das Ziel aber war gegeben, und niemand hat es erkannt.[4]

Trotzdem wurden aber seine Ideen verwirklicht, wenn auch auf einem ganz andern Gebiet und ohne Bezug auf seinen Aufsatz: Im Kunstturnen. Hier finden wir alles das wieder, was Kleist fordert, und das in einer Präzision, einer unbewußten Anmut, einer ungezierten Grazie, die man in ihrer Vollendung als atemberaubend bezeichnen kann. Hier scheinen die Naturgesetze aufgehoben, aber nur dann, wenn der Turner sich ihnen blind

FIGURE 1. Beispiel für die "naturgemäße Anordnung der Schwerpunkte" s. die Geschichte von der Brücke über die Schlucht. Photo: Marionettenduo Bochum Wolfgang Kurock.

unterwirft, wo es notwendig ist, und nur dann selber eingreift, wo es nötig ist, durch Manipulation des Schwerpunktes und Veränderung der Pendel und Hebel optimale Effekte zu erzielen. Hier werden Kleists Postulate nicht nur dem Wort, sondern auch dem Sinne nach bestätigt.

All das wäre jedoch noch nicht so bemerkenswert, wenn Kleist sich über längere Zeit in Praxis und Theorie mit der Marionette beschäftigt, wenn er das Marionettenspiel selbst beherrscht hätte. Ich habe dazu bisher auch nicht den geringsten Anhalt gefunden und wäre für einen entspechenden Hinweis dankbar.

Es gibt aber in seinem Aufsatz Indizien dafür, daß er mit großer Wahrscheinlichkeit niemals eine Marionette in den Händen gehalten, ja sogar nicht einmal die Gelegenheit gefunden hat, dem Maschinisten hinter der Bühne bei seiner Arbeit zuzusehen.

So behauptet Kleist gleich an zwei Stellen, die Fäden der Marionette seien direkt an den Fingern des Maschinisten befestigt. Dies ist zwar eine landläufige Meinung, hält aber keiner fachlichen Prüfung stand; solche Figuren hat es in der Praxis nicht gegeben, zum mindesten nicht zu Kleists Zeit.[5]

Der andere Beweis ist fast noch stichhaltiger: Eingangs erwähnt Kleist eine Gruppe von vier Bauern, die zu einem raschen Takt die Ronde tanzten. Später führt er die Kurbel als ein Medium ein, dem in späteren Zeiten einmal Bedeutung zugemessen werden könnte, um den Tanz der Marionette zur Vollendung zu bringen. Hätte er jedoch dem Maschinisten hinter der Bühne auf die Finger gesehen, so wäre ihm sicherlich aufgefallen, daß diese ringförmig zusammengeschnürten Tanzfiguren bereits durch eine Kurbel bewegt wurden, genau so, wie man sie heute noch in Museen besichtigen kann. Was Kleist sich als eine ferne Möglichkeit darstellte, existierte schon längst in der Praxis und war den Fachleuten selbstverständlich, und der Autor hätte gewiß nicht auf dieses wichtige Glied in der Kette seiner Beweisführungen verzichtet, wenn er es nur gekannt hätte!

Wenn es schon etwas Geheimnisvolles an Kleists Aufsatz "Über das Marionettentheater" gibt, so ist es dies: Wie Millionen Zuschauer vor ihm und danach hat er vor der kleinen Bühne gesessen und dem Tanz der hölzernen Gliedermänner zugesehen—aber er allein durchschaute dieses Spiel und erkannte zwischen dem Wust von naivem Brauchtum und damals noch technischer Unvollkommenheit ganz klar das Prinzip dieser amüsanten Kleinkunst. Und wie es mir scheint, war dies nicht die Frucht intellektueller Spekulationen oder langwieriger Experimente: Es muß wie eine Erleuchtung über ihn gekommen sein. Und er sah auch ganz offenbar die Notwendigkeit ein, diese seine Erkenntnisse aufzuzeichnen und so weiterzugeben, sie dazu gleichnishaft auf den Menschen zu übertragen und diesem seine Grenzen vorzuhalten.

Sigmund Freud sagt anläßlich seiner ersten psychoanalytischen Untersuchung eines literarischen Werkes im Jahre 1907 (er besprach Wilhelm Jensens "Gradiva") dem Sinne nach, daß der Dichter unmittelbar oder intuitiv zu Einsichten gelangen könne, die der Wissenschaftler sich hart erarbeiten müsse.[6]

Dies ist sicher kein exakter Beweis, aber es sollte zu denken geben.

ANMERKUNGEN

1. Diese Fehleinschätzungen von Kleists Intentionen zur Marionette gehen in jüngster Zeit mit Sicherheit auf Max v. Boehns sogenanntes Standardwerk *Puppen und Puppenspiele* (München, 1929) zurück, in dessen 2. Band wir die unbewiesene Behauptung finden "(Kleists Aufsatz).. hat mit dem Puppen/theater nichts zu tun" (S 128). Man hat daraus ganz allgemein geschlossen, Kleist habe mit seinen Postulaten zur Marionette und zu deren Spiel am Ziel vorbeigeschossen. Liest man Kleists Aufsatz genau, so wird man finden, daß er stets von der *Tanzmarionette*, niemals jedoch von der dramatischen Theaterfigur spricht, wenn man nicht die eingangs erwähnten "kleinen dramatischen Burlesken, mit Gesang und Tanz durchwebt," dahin interpretieren will. Allerdings hat Kleist zu dieser Fehleinschäzung selbst beigetragen, indem er seinen Aufsatz überschrieb "Über das Marionetten*theater*."
2. Die exakte Formulierung könnte lauten "Schwerpunkt der bewegten Massen."
3. Man kann Maschinen oder Instrumente (und die Marionette ist streng genommen beides), die vom Ausübenden perfekt oder "blind" beherrscht werden, als eine künstliche Verlängerung *seiner Gliedmaßen* (und einer damit verbundenen Spezialisierung) bezeichnen. Durch genügend lange Übung lernt man, das technische Gerät "aus dem Gefühl heraus" zu steuern, erst dann wird die Leistung optimal sein, sie kommt aus dem Gefühlsmittel- oder -schwerpunkt, wie Kleist denn den physikalischen mit dem psychischen Schwerpunkt identifiziert. Die Richtigkeit dieser Auffassung läßt sich nur in der Praxis testen.
4. Eine ähnliche Erscheinung können wir im biologisch-technischen Bereich feststellen. Norbert Wiener hat in seiner Kybernetik abseits von jeder praktischen Nutzung die Strukturen der biologischen Steuerungen erkannt und damit den Weg für die technische Verwirklichung elektronischer Steuerungen aufgezeigt.
5. Der in den sechziger Jahren verstorbene Altmeister des volkstümlichen Marionettenspiels, Xaver Schichtl, dessen erfolgreichste Programme bezeichnenderweise aus "kleinen burlesken Szenen" und Tanznummern bestanden, pflegte gern eine Marionette mit der von ihm erfundenen "Ringfingerführung" vorzustellen. Die Fäden dieser Marionette waren an Ringen befestigt, die der Spieler auf die Finger einer Hand stecken und damit die Figur zur Bewegung brachte. Es war dies jedoch ein einmaliger Versuch.
6. Sigmund Freud, *Der Wahn und die Träume in W. Jensens "Gradiva"* (Leipzig und Wien 1907).

Marionette und Gewölbe.
Zur Differenzierung der Sinnbilder bei Kleist

SHIRO NAKAMURA
Tohoku University
Sendai, Kawauchi
JAPAN

I

Kleists bekanntesten Aufsatz "Über das Marionettentheater" hat man schon fast zu viel besprochen und benutzt. Es scheint also fast waghalsig zu sein, dem allen noch etwas hinzufügen zu wollen. Aber "merkwürdigerweise" hat nach Josef Kunz "keiner der Interpreten bisher versucht, das Gespräch 'Über das Marionettentheater' als Ganzes zu deuten."[1] Kunz hielt es für notwendig, "die bisher versäumte Aufgabe nachzuholen, nämlich die Kleistsche Abhandlung zunächst in ihrer Ganzheit zu verstehen."[2] Ebenfalls betont B.v. Wiese: "Diese kleine Schrift bedarf, trotz vieler vorausgegangener Deutungsversuche, erneut einer genauen Interpretation."[3] Solche Forderung der genauen Totalinterpretation würde bestätigen, daß man bisher dazu neigte, die Symbolik der Marionette zu eindeutig auszulegen und zu allgemein auf Kleists Gestalten anzuwenden.

Kunz selbst, trotz seines Totalinterpretationsversuchs, vernachlässigt das Paradies-Problem als Leitmotiv des Gesprächs. Wiese behauptet dagegen treffend, daß das eigentliche Thema der Kleistschen Studie das verlorene und wiederzugewinnende Paradies sei.[4] Wie man weiß, erschien dieser vortreffliche Essay in vier Fortsetzungen in den "Berliner Abendblättern." Helmut Sembdner hat zwar richtig darauf hingewiesen, daß jede Fortsetzung ein eigenes Motiv enthält und in sich abgerundet ist.[5] Aber zugleich kann man nicht übersehen, daß der Grundgedanke des Autors in jeder Fortsetzung auftaucht und fortdauernd wiederkehrt. Er erscheint nämlich schon in der ersten Nummer antizipierend-gedeutet: "Inzwischen ahndete ich bei weitem die Folgerungen noch nicht, die er (=Herr C) späterhin daraus ziehen würde." Dann in der zweiten Nummer spricht Herr C nun von dem "verriegelten Paradies." Diese nach einer kleinen rhetorischen Pause, etwas voreilig ausgesprochenen und den Gesprächspartner überraschenden Worte verraten seine eigentliche Absicht deutlich genug. Auch in der dritten Nummer, in der von der ersten Periode aller menschlichen Bildung, beschrieben im dritten Kapitel der Genesis, gesprochen wird, erscheint das Leitmotiv der Paradies-Problematik: die Geschichte von einem jungen Mann, der sein anmutig-unschuldiges Paradies plötzlich und unwiederbringlich verloren hat. Hier wird also das Paradies nicht nur ideell, sondern auch als ein konkretes Beispiel geschildert. Und in der letzten Nummer kommt man zu dem Schluß, daß im letzten Kapitel der Geschichte der Menschheit der Mensch von dem Baum der Erkenntnis wieder essen muß, um in den Stand der Unschuld zurückzukehren. Hier findet sich also die planmäßige, konsequente Entwicklung eines Gedankens, dessen Ziel zweifellos das verlorene und wiederzugewinnende Paradies ist. Dabei muß man sich allerdings hüten, das Paradies nur als theoretisch-gedankliches Problem zu behandeln. Weil hier das Gedankliche und das Ästhetische ein untrennbares Ganzes bilden, scheint es besonders nötig, dem Gedankengang immer im Zusammenhang mit dem poetischen Bild zu folgen. Sonst neigt man leicht dazu, wie es ja auch häufig geschieht, das Marionettenbild unter einer falschen Perspektive zu sehen.

Nun: was ist das ästhetische Bild, das den Gedankengang von Herrn C begleitend bestimmt und bestimmend begleitet? Es ist der Tanz. Da der eine Partner des geistvollen Gesprächs, Herr C, doch erster Tänzer der Oper ist, zieht sich der Tanz gleichsam als roter Faden durch das ganze Gespräch. Aber man sollte darunter hier nicht den Tanz als solchen oder die Summe der möglichen Arten zu tanzen verstehen. Denn es ist nur der anmutige (oder graziöse) Tanz, den Herr C bewundernd hervorhebt. Ich halte solches Begrenzen des Begriffes Tanz für nötig, um Mißbräuchen der Marionettensymbolik vorzubeugen. Tatsächlich sind fast alle Tanzbilder, die in diesem Gespräch erscheinen, mit den Attributen der Anmut, Leichtigkeit oder Ruhe wiederholt unterstrichen. Schon die erste Frage, die Herr C an seinen Partner richtet, enthält das Wort "graziös": "Er fragte mich, ob ich nicht, in der Tat, einige Bewegungen der Puppen, besonders der kleineren, im Tanz sehr graziös gefunden hatte."

Auch in den darauf folgenden Tanzbildern setzt sich dieses fort: 1. (in der ersten Nummer:) Eine Gruppe von vier Bauern tanzt die Ronde derart, daß es Teniers nicht hübscher malen kann. 2. (in der zweiten Nummer:) Die Unglücklichen, die ihre Schenkel verloren haben, können mit den mechanischen Beinen gut tanzen, und zwar mit einer Ruhe, Leichtigkeit und

Anmut, die jedes denkende Gemüt in Erstaunen setzen. 3. (in der dritten Nummer:) Ein junger Mann, über dessen Bildung eine wunderbare Anmut verbreitet ist und dem die Sicherheit der Grazie zu eigen ist — seine erste, den Dornauszieher unbewußt nachahmende Pantomime kann man wohl als eine Art anmutigen Tanzes ansehen. 4. (in der Schlußnummer:) Die Episode vom Fechtkampf mit dem Bären — darüber äußert B. v. Wiese eine interessante These: "Das vom Fechter angegriffene und dann kämpfende Tier hat Grazie, weil seine Bewegungen ohne Reflexion entspringen und daher seine Seele (vis motrix) sich in jedem Augenblick dieses Kampfes im "Schwerpunkt" der Bewegung befindet. So darf sogar dieser Kampf noch als eine Art Tanz gedeutet werden."[6] Ich habe dazu nur einiges hinzuzufügen. Dieser Kampf hat etwas Spielerisches, ist sozusagen ein spielerischer Kampf, der zum graziösen Tanz wird. Zwar greift der menschliche Fechter den Bären bald ernsthaft, bald listig an, aber der Gegner pariert nur den Stoß und verwirrt den Angreifer schließlich sogar. Seine spielerische Überlegenheit liegt wohl darin, daß er ausschließlich nur abwehrt und von seiner Seite nur angreift. Trotz oder gerade wegen des ausschließlichen Defensivspiels wird das Tier gewissermaßen "tanzend" Sieger.

Aber natürlich ist es die Marionette selbst, die als solche Anmut verkörpernde Idealtänzerin im Mittelpunkt des Gesprächs steht. Und wenn man ihre Funktion mit dem obenerwähnten ParadiesMotiv verbindet, dann erscheint sie vor uns nicht nur als anmutige Tänzerin auf einer paradiesischen Bühne, sondern auch als eine in Gottes Willen gänzlich ergebene, unschuldig-glückselige Existenz, zu der zurückzukehren man sich sehnt.

II

Es ist heute durchaus nicht selten, daß man unter dem Schwerpunkt der Marionette das sogenannte Kleistsche Gefühl versteht und das Modell der spontanen, antigraven Marionette auf Kleists Personen anwendet. Einige ältere und neuere Beispiele dafür: Bei Gerhard Fricke heißt es: "die 'antigrave' Macht des innersten, unbewußten Gefühls, das als unsichtbare Mitte die tanzende Bewältigung des Lebens ermöglicht."[7] Und bei Lawrence Ryan findet sich erneut die gleiche Ansicht: "Die gleichsam nur auf sich selber hörende, ihren Schwerpunkt in sich selbst findende Marquise läßt sich schon in mancher Beziehung mit der Kleistschen Marionette vergleichen."[8] Oder: "Lebt er (=Homburg) am Anfang nur scheinbar in der Grazie des marionettenhaften Gefühls...?"[9] Und weiter: "... die Marionettenhaftigkeit des unmittelbaren Selbstgefühls...."[10] Aber ist der Sachverhalt wirklich so? Das bekannt gewordene Kleistsche "Gefühl" scheint immer noch als effektvolle Parole zu gelten. Aber es ist ein einfaches klares Faktum, daß Kleist trotz seiner "terminologischen Sorglosigkeit"[11] seine

Lieblingsworte "Gefühl" oder "Herz" in diesem wichtigen Aufsatz niemals gebraucht. Zwar wird hier das Wort "Seele" als Schlüsselwort gebraucht. Aber man sollte ihre Begriffe nicht einfach oder vorschnell identifizieren, sondern vielmehr differenzieren, besonders weil Kleist Seele als "vis motrix" bezeichnet, sie also nicht so sehr in der personifizierenden Richtung, als vielmehr in der mechanischen Richtung erläutert.

Wie kann die Marionette, die einen Schwerpunkt hat und dem Gesetz der Gravitation folgt, "antigrav" sein? Dieses Paradoxon ist durch Formulierungen wie: "antigrave Macht des Gefühls als innerer Schwerpunkt" nicht so einfach aufzulösen. Solche Formulierung scheint mir aus einem etwas voreiligen Denken, das sich vom Text entfernt, zu stammen. Denn Herr C spricht vom anmutigen Tanz der Marionette fast immer im Zusammenhang mit dem Maschinisten. Man sollte nicht vergessen, daß der Maschinist die unerläßliche Voraussetzung für den Marionettentanz ist. Es ist zweifelsohne der verborgen regierende Maschinist, der im voraus der Marionette ihre Antigravität gibt. An einer Stelle spricht Herr C sogar vom Tanz des Maschinisten: der Maschinist versetzt sich in den Schwerpunkt der Marionette, d.h. mit anderen Worten: er tanzt. Es wäre also nicht zutreffend, wenn man dem innersten Gefühl der Marionette "die absolute Flugkraft und Unabhängigkeit vom Gesetz der Schwere"[12] zuspricht, indem man den Maschinisten ignoriert und seine Bedeutung außer acht läßt. Umgekehrt: erst durch den Maschinisten als Puppenspieler wird der Marionette die antigrave und anmutige Bewegung möglich. Ihre Antigravität bedeutet also nicht ihre Autonomie oder Spontaneität, die auf ihrem eigenen sicheren Selbstgefühl beruht. Wenn man nun jene Vorstellung vom Paradies als Leitmotiv wieder hervorruft, dann wird der göttliche Maschinist sichtbar, der die Puppen auf der himmlischen Bühne tanzen läßt. Es ist keine Willkür, unter dem verborgenen Maschinisten Gott zu verstehen. Denn am Schluß seiner Ausführungen betont Herr C gerade die wunderbarste Partnerschaft zwischen Gott und Gliedermann. Es ist aber eine andere Frage, ob dieselbe Partnerschaft auch zwischen Gott und Mensch oder zwischen Dichter und seinen Gestalten bestehen kann.[13] Ich bin etwas skeptisch darüber. Man sollte sich auch hier, mit Rücksicht auf die eigentliche Absicht des Aufsatzes, vor solcher verallgemeinernden Deutung hüten.

Man kann auch sagen, daß die Marionette mehr himmlisch-lufträumliche als irdisch-menschliche Existenz ist. Tatsächlich sagt Herr C: "Die Puppen brauchen den Boden nur, wie die Elfen, um ihn zu streifen und den Schwung der Glieder durch die augenblickliche Hemmung neu zu beleben." Sie kommen also mit der schon vorher durch die göttliche Hand gegebenen, antigraven Leichtigkeit von oben und berühren den Erdboden nur augenblicklich leicht und kehren wieder in den Luftraum zurück. Mit Recht hob man wiederholt hervor, daß Kleists Marionette mit dem Schauspiel von

Engel und Puppe in Rilkes Vierter Elegie korrespondiert. Denn auch hier "spielt der Engel (und auch die Puppe) über uns hinüber."[14] Die Marionette ist gleichsam die "Spielfigur Gottes."[15]

III

Es ist aufschlußreich, hier Paul Valérys Äußerung über den Tanz im Vergleich mit dem Gehen zu zitieren: "Das Gehen ist wie die Prosa auf ein ganz bestimmtes Objekt ausgerichtet. Es ist ein Akt, der die Erreichung eines Ziels erstrebt ... Der Tanz ist etwas ganz anderes. Es ist ein System von Akten, die aber ihren Zweck in sich selbst haben. Es führt nirgends hin...."[16] Kleists Marionette, glückselige Tänzerin im Paradies, weiß nichts vom zielbewußten "Gehen," irdischen Wollen, Suchen oder Handeln. Ihre Anmut wird eben dadurch hervorgebracht, daß sie nur spielt und tanzt. Das Gefühl, das in der Handlung eines unbeugsamen, zielbewußten Willens ausbricht und die Kleistschen Gestalten wie Penthesilea, Alkmene, Kohlhaas, oder Marquise von O ... im Innersten charakterisiert, ist daher der Marionette eigentlich fremd.

Ein weit passenderes Gleichnis für solch ein Gefühl findet man in einem anderen, gleichfalls bekannten Bild: Gewölbe oder Torbogen. Meiner Meinung nach steht die Marionette in einem gewissen Sinne dem Gewölbe-Bild diametral gegenüber. Aber seltsamerweise neigt man dazu, nur den gemeinsamen Charakterzug zwischen beiden hervorzuheben. Zum Beispiel sagt B. v. Wiese: "Die tanzende Seele der Marionette und das Gewölbe, das sich ohne Stützen hält, beides sind Kleistsche Gleichnisse für den wehrlos der Welt ausgelieferten Menschen, der den Schwerpunkt nur in sich selbst sucht, aber zugleich der widerstrebenden Schwere der Wirklichkeit ausgeliefert ist."[17] Auch an einer anderen Stelle: "Das anschauliche Gleichnis von dem Gebäude ohne Stützen, das dennoch sich hält, weil alle seine Steine auf einmal einstürzen wollen, gehört hierher wie jenes andere von der Schwerelosigkeit der Marionette...."[18] Und noch ein Beispiel bei G. Fricke: "In der Tat nähert sich das Bild (Gewölbe) in seiner Symboltiefe dem anderen berühmten Gleichnis Kleists für Wesen und Bestimmung des Menschen: der Marionette. In beiden Fällen ist es die 'antigrave' Macht des innersten, unbewußten Gefühls, das als unsichtbare Mitte dort die tanzende Bewältigung des Lebens ermöglicht, hier das in allen seinen Teilen zusammenstürzende Gefüge unbegreiflich und allmächtig trägt."[19] Wohl gibt es zwischen beiden Bildern den einen Berührungspunkt, in dem sie beide gemeinsam eine Art der Schwerelosigkeit zeigen. Aber genauer betrachtet, wird man in der scheinbaren Gemeinsamkeit einen großen Unterschied feststellen. Wie schon gesagt, ist die Marionette eine himmlisch-lufträumliche Existenz, die den Erdboden kaum braucht. Dagegen muß das Tor doch auf dem Boden stehen und hochragen. Die marionettenhafte Antigravität wird durch die göttliche Hand bewirkt. Dagegen muß das Tor sich nur mit eigener Kraft halten. Es steht nur scheinbar schwerelos. In Wahrheit: "Es steht, weil alle seine Steine auf einmal einstürzen wollen." Das bedeutet gleichsam einen inneren Spannungszustand, von dem die Marionette nichts weiß.

Auch in der Briefstelle, in der Kleist vom Würzburger Tor berichtet, liegt der Kernpunkt nicht in dem ästhetischen, schwerelosen Bild des Gewölbes, sondern in der antigraven Kraft des inneren Lebenswillens, der seine eigene zum Zerfall drängende Krise erträgt. Sich selbst in die Eigenschaft des Torbogens einfühlend, fährt Kleist in dem Bericht fort: "und ich zog aus diesem Gedanken einen unbeschreiblich erquickenden Trost, der mir bis zu dem entscheidenden Augenblick immer mit der Hoffnung zur Seite stand, daß auch ich mich halten würde, wenn alles mich sinken läßt."[20] Im gleichen Sinne von menschlicher Anstrengung wird das Gleichnis auch im neunten Auftritt von *Penthesilea* gebraucht. Mit ihm will Prothoe, indem sie das innerste Gefühl der Königin anruft, ihren Lebenswillen aufmuntern. Hier kann man sicherlich das Kleistsche "Gefühl" bzw. "Herz" mit dem Bild des Gewölbes verbinden. Man kann also das Gewölbe als Gleichnis für das irdisch-menschliche Willensgefühl ansehen, das oft die Personen Kleists bezeichnet. Aber die Marionette hat mit solcher zielbewußten, anstrengungsvollen Willensaktion nichts zu tun. Unter diesem Aspekt ist sie ein scharfer Gegensatz zum Gewölbe. Es ist also wohl nicht treffend, in Penthesilea z.B. die "Puppe mit schreckenerregender Anmut dem Abgrund entgegentanzen"[21] zu sehen.

Ich möchte behaupten, daß man die beiden Bilder, Marionette und Gewölbe, im obengenannten Sinne differenzieren und differenzierend anwenden muß. Es ist freilich nicht der Gliedermann, sondern der lebende Mensch in der irdischen Wirklichkeit, der nach seinem verlorenen Paradies sehnend verlangt. Kleist hat, wie jeder große Dichter, die volle Wahrheit der menschlichen Existenz, die, wie der Aufsatz über das Marionettentheater beschreibt, durch Bewußtsein, Reflexion oder Erkenntnis gespalten und verwirrt ist, in seinen tragischen, komischen, mitunter sogar grotesken Figuren ausgedrückt, die oft vom Begriff der Anmut der Marionette weit entfernt sind. Aber eben deshalb bleibt Kleist bis heute ständig ein aktuelles literarisches Phänomen und Problem.

ANMERKUNGEN

1. Josef Kunz, Kleists Gespräch "Über das Marionettentheater," in: *Kleists Aufsatz über das Marionettentheater. Studien und Interpretationen*, hrsg. v. Helmut Sembdner (Berlin, 1967. Im folgenden zitiert: Marionettenaufsatz, S.). 76.

2. Kunz, S. 77.
3. Benno von Wiese, "Das verlorene und wieder zu findende Paradies. Eine Studie über den Begriff der Anmut bei Goethe, Kleist und Schiller," in: *Marionettenaufsatz*, S. 203.
4. Wiese, S. 206.
5. Helmut Sembdner, Nachwort, in: *Marionettenaufsatz*, S. 222.
6. Wiese, S. 205.
7. Gerhard Fricke, "Penthesilea," in: *Das deutsche Drama I*, hsrg. v. Benno von Wiese (Düsseldorf, 1958), S. 374.
8. Lawrence Ryan, "Die Marionette und das 'unendliche Bewußtsein' bei Heinrich von Kleist," in: *Marionettenaufsatz*, S. 176.
9. Ryan, S. 191.
10. Ryan, S. 193
11. Gerhard Fricke, *Gefühl und Schicksal bei Heinrich von Kleist* (Berlin, 1929), S. 151.
12. Fricke, *Gefühl und Schicksal bei Heinrich von Kleist*, S. 152.
13. Vgl. Wiese, S. 211.
14. Verse 61-62.
15. Wiese, S. 209
16. Vgl. Karl Löwith, *Paul Valéry. Grundzüge seines philosophischen Denkens* (Göttingen, 1971), S. 52.
17. Benno von Wiese, *Die deutsche Tragödie von Lessing bis Hebbel* (Hamburg, 1948), S. 311.
18. Benno von Wiese, "Heinrich von Kleist, Tragik und Utopie," in: *Heinrich von Kleist. Vier Reden zu seinem Gedächtnis*, Hrsg. v. Walter Müller-Seidel (Berlin, 1962), S. 68.
19. Fricke, in: *Das deutsche Drama I*, S. 374.
20. Brief an Wilhelmine vom 16. November 1800.
21. Günter Blöcker, *Heinrich von Kleist oder das absolute Ich* (Berlin, 1960), S. 290.

Kleist and Mathematics: The Non-Euclidean Idea in the Conclusion of the *Marionettentheater* Essay

SYDNA STERN WEISS
Hamilton College

Heinrich von Kleist's well-known *Lebensplan* reflects a structural pattern, the triadic rhythm, which is based upon conventional, linear, rationalistic thinking, in short, Euclidean thinking. After his shattering experience with Kantian philosophy, Kleist believed his *Lebensplan* unachievable, and he pursued the goals of his more limited *Studienplan* through studies in mathematics and science. Even these studies were no peaceful acquistion of knowledge, for they took place in the charged atmosphere of the revolution in mathematics from Euclidean to non-Euclidean systems. What must have been the effect of these developments on Kleist's own thinking? It is suggested, on the basis of circumstantial evidence, that the exposure to the new mathematics led to Kleist's reinterpretation of the triadic rhythm as it appears in the conclusion of his essay, "Über das Marionettentheater" (1810).[1]

The triadic rhythm or tripartite division of history[2] as a pattern for describing the stages in the development of man is conspicuous in late 18th century philosophical and esthetic thinking. Expressed in the writings of Schelling, the Schlegels, Schiller, and Hegel, the scheme divides man's development into three phases: 1) a state of innocence or unity, 2) following the fall from grace, a state of reflection or consciousness, and 3) a final phase of entry into heaven or the millennium. Familiar with the triadic pattern in the Bible (Eden, earthly life, ascent to heaven), Kleist certainly was also acquainted with this popular interpretation of the structure of history as it was proposed by his contemporaries, among them, Adam Müller, his colleague and co-editor of the *Phöbus*.[3] The triadic concept is an optimistic view of man's development, for it posits a final unified state where all divisions and contradictions will be resolved.

The triadic rhythm is based upon Euclidean or Enlightenment thinking which is rationalistic or linear and proceeds additively to its conclusions. The goal or result of continued development in a single direction is, in terms of the pattern, paradise, or in mathematical language, infinity. Kleist's words *Studienplan, Reiseplan, Lebensplan* as well as *Ziel* and *Zweck* reflect his rationalistic, Enlightenment view of an education to be achieved through continual progress toward a definable goal:

> Ein Reisender, der das Ziel seiner Reise und den Weg zu seinem Ziele kennt, hat einen Reiseplan.... Was der Reiseplan dem Reisenden ist, das ist der Lebensplan dem Menschen. (May 1799)[4]

At this time, May of 1799, Kleist's *Lebensplan* and *Studienplan* included completion of his studies in pure mathematics and logic in Potsdam and travel to Göttingen, "um mich dort der höheren Theologie, der Mathematik, Philosophie und Physik zu widmen, zu welcher letzteren ich einen mir selbst unerklärlichen Hang habe" (March 19, 1799). In fact, he expressed confidence in his abilities in science, "weil mir keine Wissenschaft zu schwer wird; weil ich rasch darin vorrücke, weil ich manches schon aus eigener Erfindung hinzugetan habe..." (Nov. 13, 1800).

Regarding his studies in mathematics, he reported specifically that he had mastered geometric series and struggled with the irrational relationships of lines which could be viewed rationally. A. G. Kästner's indirect proofs[5] had caused him some difficulty in school, because they required that he assume as true, "was ich für falsch erkennen muß" (March 19, 1797).

For nearly two years, studies in science gave Kleist a sense of steady progress in his pursuit of *Bildung* and *Wahrheit* according to his *Studienplan* and all-encompassing *Lebensplan*. Then, in February of 1801, his emotional and intellectual well-being seemed jeopardized:

> Ich passe mich nicht unter die Menschen.... Selbst die Säule, an welcher ich mich sonst in dem Strudel des Lebens hielt, wankt—Ich meine die Liebe zu den Wissenschaften.... Das ist die Säule, welche schwankt. (Feb. 5, 1801)

Several weeks later he reported the collapse of his *Lebensplan*. He had assumed that perfectability was the final purpose of creation, ("daß die Vervollkommnung der Zweck der Schöpfung wäre."):

> Ich glaubte, daß wir einst nach dem Tod von der Stufe der Vervollkommnung, die wir auf diesem Sterne erreichten, auf einem andern weiter fortschreiten würden, und daß wir den Schatz von Wahrheiten, den wir hier sammelten,

auch dort einst brauchen könnten ... immer unaufhörlich einem höhern Grade von Bildung entgegenzuschreiten, ward bald das einzige Prinzip meiner Tätigkeit. Bildung schien mir das einzige Ziel, das des Bestrebens, Wahrheit, der einzige Reichtum, der des Besitzes würdig ist. (March 22, 1801)

Kleist's interpretation of Kantian philosophy "die neuere sogenannte Kantische Philosophie,"[6] however, led him to conclude that one could never know what truth is:

Wir können nicht entscheiden, ob das was wir Wahrheit nennen, wahrhaft Wahrheit ist, oder ob es uns nur so scheint. Ist das letzte, so ist die Wahrheit, die wir hier sammeln, nach dem Tode nicht mehr—und alles Bestreben, ein Eigentum sich zu erwerben, das uns auch in das Grab folgt, ist vergeblich—... Mein einziges, mein höchstes Ziel ist gesunken, und ich habe keines mehr. (March 22, 1801)

Kleist's *Lebensplan* with its absolute goal had collapsed; it had become meaningless. Dropping the term *Lebensplan* from his vocabulary, he spoke only of *Reise*, the purpose (*Zweck*) of which he did not know. No longer speaking of an ultimate goal, truth, and acutely aware that he had no goal (*Ziel*), "Ach, es ist der schmerzlichste Zustand, ganz ohne ein Ziel zu sein" (March 22, 1801), he settled for "Bewegung auf der Reise," motion without reference to any goal.[7]

In an attempt to salvage part of his *Studienplan*, Kleist planned to pursue mathematics and science in Paris. "In Paris werde ich schon das Studium der Naturwissenschaft fortsetzen müssen, und so werde ich wohl am Ende wieder in das alte Gleis kommen..." (June 13, 1801). En route to France, Kleist made contact with prominent scientists, "die Lehrer der Menschheit," among them Johann Blumenbach, Professor of Medicine and Natural Sciences, Göttingen; Heinrich Wrisberg, Professor of Anatomy, Göttingen; Ernst Plattner, Professor of Physiology, Leipzig; and Georg Klügel, Professor of Mathematics and Physics and a respected interpreter of Kant's treatises on mathematics, Halle.[8] Kleist also met Karl Friedrich Hindenburg, Professor of Mathematics, Leipzig, "der mir wie ein Vater so ehrwürdig war" (July 18, 1801). According to Kleist's sister Ulrike, Hindenburg and Kleist responded favorably to one another, and Hindenburg "macht[e] sich große Erwartungen von [Kleists] Reise nach Paris und seinen künftigen Leistungen."[9]

Hindenburg was the founder of the Leipzig school for *Kombinatorik* (theory of combinations) and a correspondent with Kant on mathematical subjects.[10] He and other scientists furnished Kleist with letters of introduction to their colleagues in Paris: "Ich bin an lauter Pariser Gelehrten adressiert, und die lassen einen nicht fort, ohne daß man etwas von ihnen lernt" (June 3, 1801). This strongly suggests that the young Kleist must have demonstrated understanding of those sciences which he had already studied and promise for future progress. It is likely that the recommendation of Klügel or Hindenburg actually led Kleist to Gaspard Monge, one of the founders of non-Euclidean geometry in Paris. Hindenburg must have been hoping that Kleist would bring him news of Monge's work when the former returned to Leipzig almost two years later. Kleist's dramatic description of their reunion indicates Hindenburg's expectations and his own failure to meet them. "Vorgestern faßte ich ein Herz, und ging zu Hindenburg. Da war grosse Freude. 'Nun, wie stehts in Paris um die Mathematik?'—Eine alberne Antwort von meiner Seite, und ein trauriger Blick zur Erde von der seinigen" (March 13-14, 1803).

For a sensitive intellectual, searching for a point of orientation, contact with studies in mathematics as they were being carried on by Hindenburg, Klügel, Monge, and others was like a second exposure to Kantian philosophy. Expanding on the basic work done by Sacchieri, Lambert, and Kästner,[11] these mathematicians and their contemporaries were seeking a possible proof for Euclid's Parallel Postulate.[12] The postulate states: straight lines are said to be parallel to one another, when, being in the same plane, they are incapable of meeting in a single point, however far they be produced.

Kant himself had lectured on mathematics for fifteen semesters (1755-1763).[13] J. Fang and K. P. Takayama, in their sociological history of the evolution toward non-Euclidean geometry, write, that Kant, in his dissertation of 1770, suggested "a geometry other than the Euclidean—'die höchste Geometrie'."[14] They report further that following Kant's paper, "there came a sudden increase in the production of papers and books on the subject" of the Parallel Postulate.[15] Kästner and Klügel must have known of Kant's thesis by 1780. According to Fang and Takayama, there can be no doubt of a connection between Kästner and Kant. In fact, "mathematicians and philosophers felt somehow reassured to speculate, after Kant's thesis in 1770, on the possibility of physical geometries other than the Euclidean."[16] Indeed, the very foundations of Euclidean geometry were being shaken as men like Klügel speculated "on the empirical nature of the allegedly 'self-evident-postulates and axioms, not god-send [sic], but man-made'!"[17] Mathematicians were demonstrating that Euclid's geometry was only one of many possible geometries. In "Kantian terms," Euclid's was a geometry perceived with a particular set of glasses, one which arbitrarily made parallel lines be everywhere equidistant or meet in no point. The atmosphere surrounding this revolution in mathematics was no climate for a disturbed young man seeking a set of reliable, "unsubjective" facts in science.

When Kleist arrived in Paris, he planned to spend at least a year pursuing "das Studium der Naturwissenschaften auf dieser Schule der Welt" (July 18, 1801). Signs that he would find no comfort in Paris were soon apparent. Realizing "[daß] das Wissen uns weder besser noch glücklicher [macht]" (July 29, 1801), he reflected, "Ja, wenn wir den ganzen Zusammenhang der Dinge einsehen könnten! Aber ist nicht der Anfang und das Ende jeder Wissenschaft in Dunkel gehüllt?" This observation suggests a Kantian interpretation of man's relationship to science: since the initial point remains inaccessible, man is restricted to knowing only a reflection or a segment rather than the essence of science. Man's scientific knowledge, like man's development, is, therefore, seen as confined to the middle stage of the triadic rhythm. Expanding this thought on the problematic relationship of man's finite knowledge (*Wissen*) to infinite knowledge, Kleist expressed the paradoxical ideas which are basic to the "Marionettentheater" essay. Regarding the contradictions which arise from Rousseau's assumption that sciences do not make men happier, Kleist wrote on August 15, 1801:

> Denn es mußten viele Jahrtausende vergehen, ehe soviele Kenntnisse gesammelt werden konnten, wie nötig waren, einzusehen, daß man keine haben müßte. Nun also müßte man alle Kenntnisse vergessen, den Fehler gutzumachen; und somit finge das Elend wieder vor [sic] vorn an.

As Kleist saw it, man spent centuries acquiring useless knowledge which he subsequently had to forget. But then the cycle began once more because man was driven toward knowledge. Kleist despaired so deeply at this insight that he interrupted his studies and fled Paris.

Let us recall that upon interpreting Kant's writings, Kleist gave up hope of pursuing his *Lebensplan*. Thereafter, for nearly a half year in Paris, he sought, by studying science, to regain control and order for his life. There is no proof that Kleist actually studied non-Euclidean geometry per se. However, the circumstances suggest that he came into contact with scholars who were refuting the Euclidean tradition and saying "no" to a basic tenet of geometry, namely, Euclid's Parallel Postulate. The experiences in Paris clearly reinforced Kleist's doubts and despair regarding truth as a goal of study. In October of 1801 he wrote: "Die Wissenschaften habe ich ganz aufgegeben" (Oct. 10, 1801).

Although Kleist devoted himself to literature for the remainder of his life, he never fully abandoned the sciences, but looked to them as a source for metaphors regarding his work and his relationships and as a possible escape from the complexities of his life. He chose a metaphor from mathematics in describing his dramatic figures: "[Käthchen und Penthesilea] gehören ja wie das + und das - der Algebra zusammen und sind ein und dasselbe Wesen, nur unter entgegengesetzten Beziehungen gedacht" (Dec. 8, 1808). He expressed his longing for his friend Rühle von Lilienstern in terms of a chemical reaction: "Ich wollte, ich wäre eine Säure oder ein Alkali, so hätt es doch ein Ende, wenn man aus dem Salze geschieden wäre" (Aug. 31, 1806). Another letter contains calculations regarding hydrostatics and comments on a technical design for a water pump (July 2, 1805). Stressing the equal importance of science and art, Kleist observed: "Ich kann ein Differentiale finden und einen Vers machen; sind das nicht die beiden Enden der menschlichen Fähigkeit?" (Jan. 7, 1805). In the summer of 1801 he had escaped into science; when he became ill in 1805, he considered the same escape: "Es gibt eine gute Arznei, sie heißt Versenkung, grundlose, in Beschäftigung und Wissenschaft" (Nov. 13, 1805). And shortly before his suicide, when life lay before him like a wasteland, he planned to let his art rest for a time, ". . . und mich, außer einigen Wissenschaften, in denen ich noch etwas *nachzuholen* habe, mit nichts als der Musik beschäftigen" (my italics, May, 1811). *Nachzuholen* suggests catch-up work in one's studies. There is no doubt that throughout his life, Kleist remained a "Liebhaber der Wissenschaften."[18] The *Marionettentheater* essay is the clearest evidence for this contention.

Published in 1810, "Über das Marionettentheater" begins, "Als ich den Winter 1801 in M. . . . zubrachte." Regardless of when Kleist actually wrote the essay, he chose for its internal date the winter of 1801, the final months of that crucial year in which philosophy and later science had destroyed his hopes of discovering absolute truth. It would be psychologically incomprehensible if he did not reassess the acute reversals and disappointments which he had suffered during that year. Indeed, during this winter, it is inconceivable that he did not re-examine his reaction to Kant's subjectivistic theory of time and space,[19] his experiences in Paris, and his search in science for a reliable foundation for knowledge. He may well have realized that the collapse of his rationalistic *Lebensplan* was also the breakdown of his faith in Euclidean thinking.[20] The "Marionettentheater" essay synthesizes the conventional application of the triadic rhythm to the cultural and philosophical realm with scientific concepts which Kleist must have acquired in popularized form from his contemporaries. It further records the impact of late 18th century mathematics on Kleist, a receptive intellectual with a strong affinity for science.

A structural analysis of Kleist's novella "Das Erdbeben in Chili" reveals that as early as 1807 Kleist exploited the triadic rhythm by inverting it ironically. In this tale, man's experience begins in hell (life in St. Iago and the earthquake). Precipitated by the earthquake, the middle stage, the idyllic interlude in the valley resembles life in the Garden of Eden. In the final phase, traditionally the ascent to Paradise, Kleist's figures create another hell as they massacre their fellow human beings.[21] The novella is evidence for Kleist's familiarity with the triadic pattern and for his sceptical rejection of its conventional or Euclidean sequence.

Whereas the structural principle of "Das Erdbeben in Chili" makes use of an inverted triadic rhythm, "Über das Marionettentheater" consequently reveals the outcome of a non-Euclidean interpretation of the triadic pattern according to non-Euclidean thinking. The Euclidean line extends infinitely in two directions toward a point at plus-infinity and toward one at minus-infinity ($+\infty$ and $-\infty$). Metaphorically, we may say that Eden lies at one end, earth in the middle, and heaven at the other end. The non-Euclidean line also extends infinitely in a positive and in a negative direction, but the very points at $+\infty$ and $-\infty$ coincide in what is called the "ideal point."[22] Thus, the non-Euclidean line becomes a loop, or in the language of Kleist's essay, the two points coincide, "wo die beiden Enden der ringförmigen Welt ineinander [greifen]." According to conventional thinking, one could pursue an infinite progression to its final point at infinity—or a *Lebensplan* to a goal of absolute truth. Non-Euclidean thinking incorporates the ideal point as a point on the continuous loop. The ideal point is made up of two coincident points at infinity. It is inconceivable that Klügel, Kästner, Monge, or Hindenburg did not converse with their colleagues on this new idea in mathematics. When they did so, they would inevitably have mentioned this seemingly paradoxical, yet so utterly elementary concept, and Kleist, a promising young scientist, would easily have understood it.

In the essay, the dancer, in the role of a teacher, uses the concept of a line (loop) which includes an ideal point. Indeed, the idea underlies his three analogies for explaining seeming paradoxes in which "motion" or "development" through an ideal point produces its opposite. He explains: "Doch so, wie sich der Durchschnitt zweier Linien, auf der einen Seite eines Punktes, nach dem Durchgang durch das Unendliche, plötzlich wieder auf der andern Seite einfindet. . . ." In this mathematical analogy, the dancer refers to the disappearance of the perpendicular bisector of intersecting lines on the positive side of a point and its subsequent reappearance on the negative (other) side of that point, ". . . oder das Bild des Hohlspiegels, nachdem es sich in das Unendliche entfernt hat, plötzlich wieder dicht vor uns tritt . . . ."

This analogy from physics recalls the disappearance and subsequent reappearance of an image in a concave mirror (e.g., inside of a spoon); the reflection becomes infinitely small at the ideal point and then grows large again:

> . . . so findet sich auch, wenn die Erkenntnis gleichsam durch ein Unendliches gegangen ist, die Grazie wieder ein; so daß sie, zu gleicher Zeit, in demjenigen menschlichen Körperbau am reinsten erscheint, der entweder gar keins, oder ein unendliches Bewußtsein hat, d.h. in dem Gliedermann oder in dem Gott.

This analogy from metaphysics states that the infinite development from grace through knowledge leads back to grace.[23] In non-Euclidean terms, the overall development is looplike, passing through the ideal point.

This last analogy has startling implications for the interpretation of the triadic rhythm. Regarding the middle stage when man has lost grace and is caught in a period of reflection, the dancer observes:

> Solche Mißgriffe [gestures lacking grace] ... sind unvermeidlich, seitdem wir von dem Baum der Erkenntnis gegessen haben. Doch das Paradies ist verriegelt und der Cherub hinter uns; wir müssen die Reise um die Welt machen, und sehen, ob es vielleicht von hinten irgendwo wieder offen ist.[24]

Man must continue infinitely far along the path ("die Reise um die Welt machen")—or eat again from the Tree of Knowledge—if man is to re-enter Paradise. Accordingly, the dancer replies affirmatively to the narrator's question, "müßten wir wieder von dem Baum der Erkenntnis essen, um in den Stand der Unschuld zurückzufallen?" Infinite consciousness and no consciousness ($+\infty$ and $-\infty$) are the state of existence at the ideal point ("Stand der Unschuld"), "wo die beiden Enden der ringförmigen Welt ineinander [greifen]." To a mind schooled only in the Euclidean system of thought, this interpretation of the triadic rhythm remains a paradox. To one accustomed to non-Euclidean thinking, the paradox dissolves, because the ideal point has been located on the infinite line which is a continuous loop.

It is, in retrospect, not surprising that a cultural-philosophical idea, transformed by a startling new concept in non-Euclidean thinking provided the basis for Kleist's reinterpretation of the triadic rhythm as it appears in the "Marionettentheater." If, indeed, as Kleist suggests, "ein Differentiale finden und einen Vers machen ... die beiden Enden der menschlichen Fähigkeit [sind]" (Jan. 7, 1805), is it not appropriate that a writer in whom both abilities are richly present, interpret the course of human development in metaphors which reflect the dual influence of science and philosophy on his thinking?

ACKNOWLEDGMENT

Research for this paper was carried on under a grant from the National Endowment for the Humanities.

NOTES

1. Heinrich von Kleist, *Sämtliche Werke und Briefe, Bd. II*, ed. Helmut Sembdner (Munich: Carl Hanser Verlag, 1952), pp. 335-342. References to the *Marionettentheater* essay and to Kleist's letters refer to this text. For a survey of major scholarship on the essay, see *Kleists Aufsatz über das Marionettentheater: Studien und Interpretationen*, ed. Helmut Sembdner (Berlin: Erich Schmidt Verlag, 1967).

2. Also called "die triadische Aufgliederung der Geschichte" (Josef Kunz, "Kleists Gespräch über das Marionettentheater," in Sembdner, *Kleists Aufsatz. . .*, p. 85 and "triadisches Entwicklungsschema" (Lawrence Ryan, "Die Marionette und das 'unendliche Bewußtsein' bei Heinrich von Kleist," in the same volume by Sembdner, p. 172. For an extensive discussion of the triadic concept, see Julius Peterson, *Die Sehnsucht nach dem Dritten Reich in deutscher Sage und Dichtung* (Stuttgart: J. B. Metzlersche Verlagsbuchhandlung, 1934).

3. For interpretations of the triadic rhythm by Kleist's contemporaries, see Hanna Hellmann, "Über das Marionettentheater," in Sembdner, *Kleists Aufsatz . . .*, pp. 17-31. Regarding a paradisical condition at the beginning of human history and another paradisical state at the end of mankind, Hellman quotes Müller, " 'Wir ahnen, daß sich alles Getrennte, Zerrissene, einst wieder treffen, ausgleichen und vereinigen müsse'," p. 22.

4. Kleist continues, "Ja, es ist mir so unbegreiflich, wie ein Mensch ohne Lebensplan leben könne, und ich fühle . . ., welch ein unschätzbares Glück mir mein Lebensplan gewährt . . . der Zustand, ohne Lebensplan . . . scheint mir so verächtlich, und würde mich so unglücklich machen, daß mir der Tod bei weitem wünschenswerter wäre." (May 1799)

5. Abraham G. Kästner (or Kaestner), 1719-1800, was known as the leading mathematician among poets. Gauss called him the leading poet among mathematicians.

6. Letters of March 22, 1801 and March 23, 1801 mention Kant's philosophy. For discussion, see Ernst Cassirer, "Heinrich von Kleist und die Kantische Philosophie," in *Idee und Gestalt* (Berlin: B. Cassirer, 1924).

7. In "Über die allmähliche Verfertigung der Gedanken beim Reden" (1805), in *Kleist, II*, pp. 321-327, Kleist suggests an analogous structure for thought. In the process of speaking, the conclusion of a thought becomes clear.

8. Gottfried Martin, *Arithmetik und Kombinatorik bei Kant* (Berlin: Walter de Gruyter, 1972), p. 47. Klügel had a double connection to basic work on non-Euclidean geometry. His dissertation advisor, A. G. Kästner, was a passionate bibliophile whose collection included almost all works on Euclid's Parallel Postulate which were written before 1770. In his dissertation, Klügel discussed Gerolamo Sacchieri's attempts to prove the Postulate by contradiction. For a fascinating discussion on the exchange of ideas among the mathematicians who founded non-Euclidean geometry, see J. Fang and K. P. Takayama, "Superstructural Interactions" in *Sociology of Mathematics and Mathematicians—A Prolegomenon*, Series Paideia #15 (Hauppauge, N.Y., Paideia Press, 1975), pp. 261-291.

9. Ulrike's remarks are reported in a letter (author unknown) which appears in Flodoard Freiherr von Biedermann, *Heinrich von Kleists Gespräche: Nachrichten und Überlieferungen aus seinem Umgange* (Leipzig: Hesse & Becker Verlag, n.d.), p. 55.

10. Martin, *Arithmetik*, p. 85.

11. Fang and Takayama, pp. 269-272, Martin, p. 42.

12. Except for the mathematical giants (Newton, Euler and Leibniz), every mathematician of the 17th and 18th centuries occupied himself at one time or another

with the problems of negative numbers, infinitesimal quantities, the angle formed by a tangent to a curve, and, of course, the parallel postulate (Martin, p. 67).
13. Martin, p. 14.
14. Fang and Takayama, p. 273.
15. Citing D. M. Y. Sommerville, *Bibliography of Non-Euclidean Geometry* (Chelsea, 1970), pp. 6-24, Fang and Takayama tabulate the rise in the number of such papers as follows: 1771-1780 (11); 1781-1790 (28); 1791-1800 (27); and 1801-1810 (37), p. 272.
16. Ibid., p. 280 f.
17. Ibid., p. 281.
18. Günter Blöcker, *Heinrich von Kleist oder Das absolute Ich* (Berlin: Argon Verlag, 1960), p. 58.
19. Fang and Takayama, p. 276.
20. "Having come into being in the 18th century [the great Kantian philosophical system] tied itself to Euclidism, and in fact to a doctrinaire 17th century version of it," in Salomon Bochner, *The Role of Mathematics in the Rise of Science* (Princeton: Princeton University Press, 1966), p. 203.
21. In its first appearance (*Cottas Morgenblatt,*, September, 1807), the novella was divided into twenty-nine paragraphs. Subsequently Kleist redivided the text into three paragraphs. These sections correspond to division of the text according to the phases of the triadic rhythm: 1) In St. Iago . . . schliefen sie ein, pp. 151-157; 2) Als sie erwachten . . . zur Gesellschaft zurück, pp. 158-161; and 3) Inzwischen war . . . sich freuen, pp. 161-167 in Kleist, II.
22. Dirk J. Struik, *Lectures on Analytic and Projective Geometry* (Cambridge, Mass.: Addison-Wesley Publishing Company, Inc., 1953), p. 3.
23. A comparison of the dream scenes at the beginning and end of *Prinz Friedrich von Homburg* (1811) reveals a similar looplike structure.
24. Cf. Letter of August 15, 1801, cited on p. 121 of this essay.

Schwerpunkt Kleist: Motive des Marionettentheaters im 20. Jahrhundert

RALF R. NICOLAI
The University of Georgia

Wenn auch bereits im 19. Jahrhundert verschiedentlich auf die Wichtigkeit von Kleists Aufsatz *Über das Marionettentheater* in bezug auf den idealistisch-romantischen Dreitakt hingewiesen wurde, so war es doch Hanna Hellmann vorbehalten, in ihrer Arbeit *Heinrich von Kleist. Darstellung des Problems,*[1] die Bedeutung dieses Aufsatzes voll zu würdigen. Hier wird auf Verbindungen aufmerksam gemacht, die zu Schlegel, Schleiermacher, Schelling, Novalis und Schiller bestehen, und es wird gezeigt, in welchem Maße das Erkenntnisproblem, wie es Kleist beschäftigte, als Konsequenz des Kantstudiums ausgelegt werden darf. Ferner deutet Hellmann bereits an, daß auch das Lebensgefühl Friedrich Nietzsches dem Kleists nicht unähnlich war.

Obwohl Hanna Hellmann den Marionettentheater-Aufsatz in Hinsicht auf seine Schlüsselfunktion zu einer Interpretation von Kleists sonstigem Werk überbetonte — eine Ansicht, die von Paul Böckmann im Jahre 1927 auf das richtige Maß reduziert wurde[2] — bemerkt man doch, daß viele der späteren Arbeiten zu diesem Thema gegenüber den grundlegenden Einsichten Hanna Hellmanns eher Rückschritte sind als sie Neues bringen.[3] Die sehr guten Essays von Josef Kunz, Clemens Heselhaus, Lawrence Ryan and Benno von Wiese[4] entheben von der Notwendigkeit, die divergenten Meinungen nochmals kritisch zu durchleuchten, und man darf es dabei belassen, sehr verallgemeinernd mögliche Deutungsansätze herauszustreichen.

In Kleists Aufsatz geht es letzthin um den Konflikt zwischen dem menschlichen Bewußtsein nach dem Sündenfall der Reflexion und der als Wahrheitsgrund erachteten Natur. Die Termini "Grazie," bzw. "Anmut", die nach Kleist den natürlichen Zustand ausdrücken, sind zu verstehen als Indiz der "Wesensbestimmung jenes Lebensausschnittes, der den Charakter der organischen Bindung bewahrt. Für ihn steht das Tier stellvertretend, und es teilt diese Auszeichnung mit der Pflanze."[5] Im menschlichen Dasein ist dieser Zustand — und das drückt die Episode vom Dornauszieher aus —nur möglich, wenn eine Handlung unreflektiert ist und die Bewegung aus dem natürlichen Schwerpunkt heraus erfolgt; andernfalls entsteht Ziererei. Beschränkt man die Interpretation auf die Art der Bewegung, so gehört sie lediglich in den Bereich der Ästhetik. Doch hiermit wird nur auf eine Fragestellung hingewiesen, deren Lösung in die Sphäre der Utopie verweist.

Indem der Mensch durch seine Reflexionsfähigkeit aus dem naiven Lebenszusammenhang herausgerissen wurde und sich von der Natur entfremdete, befindet er sich in einem Zustand, den die Romantik als "Verwirrung" bezeichnete. Mit der Frage danach, was der Erkenntnisvorgang bewirkt und was für eine Orientierungsmöglichkeit auf der Suche nach Wahrheit er bietet, befindet man sich auf dem Gebiet philosophischer Interpretation. Zugleich wird aber auch der psychologische Ansatz sichtbar. Mit der sich entwickelnden Fähigkeit zur Reflexion geht parallel eine Unterdrückung der Natur, bis schließlich die Naturtriebe nur noch latent vorhanden sind, d. h. auf Grund ihrer Tabuierung nicht mehr bewußt erfahren werden können. Das "letzte Kapitel von der Geschichte der Welt" bestünde dann darin, introspektiv die Natur im Selbst zu befreien, bzw. sich der verschütteten Dimensionen im Ich bewußt zu werden, und zwar nicht, um sie dadurch umso besser im Zaume zu halten, sondern um sie mit dem reflektierenden Sein zu integrieren und eine neue Harmonie zu schaffen. Der Konflikt zwischen der unterdrückten Natur und dem kontrollierenden Bewußtsein, der romantischen "Verwirrung" nicht unähnlich, schlug sich in Sigmund Freuds Begriff der "Ambivalenz" nieder.[6] Von Interesse bei einem derartigen Deutungsvorgang ist das Beispiel des fechtenden Bären. Dieser, an einem Pfahl angeschlossen, also unfrei, kann als Bild für die innere Natur des Menschen gelten. Vielleicht sagte deshalb der Erzähler: "Ich wußte nicht, ob ich träumte, da ich mich einem solchen Gegner gegenüber sah . . . .".[7] Glaubwürdig wäre eine solche Deutung auch deshalb, weil der Bär in der Mythologie, Artemis oder Diana begleitend, als lunares Tier gilt (Mutterwelt),[8] und in der Alchemie, wie Cirlot berichtet, dem *nigredo* grundliegender Materie entspricht und demzufolge als Symbol für alle Anfangsstufen, für die Instinkte und für das Un- und Unterbewußte steht.[9]

Auf die deutsche Literatur übte die im Marionettentheater angerissene Themenstellung eine beträchtliche Wirkung aus, und es überrascht nicht, daß Theodore Ziolkowski in seinem Buch *The Novels of Hermann Hesse* das ganze vierte Kapitel, mit direktem Bezug auf Kleist, einer Erklärung des triadischen Rhythmus der Menschenentwicklung widmet.[10] So tritt im Spätwerk des von der Literaturwissenschaft schon zu lange vernachlässigten Hermann Sudermann das Kleistsche Motivgut, zuweilen verflochten mit

Gedanken Nietzsches, klar zutage. 'Purzelchen' erfährt in dem gleichnamigen Roman leitmotivisch im Tanze "... das Fliegen ... das wirkliche, wahrhaftige Fliegen, das man ja nur im Traum" erlebt, und in der "Elysiumbar" tanzt sie nach einem Programm, dem teilweise ein Tableau namens *La crúche cassée* zugrunde liegt, dasselbe offensichtlich, von dem Kleist zur Niederschrift seines Lustspiels *Der zerbrochene Krug* angeregt wurde;[11] und in dem großen Roman *Der tolle Professor* steht die Suche nach dem Zentrum, um welches die intellektuelle Welt rotiert, im Brennpunkt des Geschehens — nämlich: das "traurige Handwerk" der Philosophen, "durch eine Hintertür wieder einzuschmuggeln, was sie durchs Vorderportal an die Luft gesetzt haben!" Das Resultat dieser Suche ist Professor Sieburths Werk über *Die drei Stufen der Ethik*, wobei die erste die der urwüchsigen Instinkte ist, gefolgt von der des Lebens nach der erfolgten Erziehung und den Errungenschaften "jahrtausendealter geistiger und seelischer Bildung," und schließlich die dritte Stufe als ein Höhenmenschentum, welches so weit über der Moral steht, wie die Wesen der ersten Stufe unter derselben. Sieburth stirbt vereinsamt, durch Selbstmord, ähnlich wie Kleist. Sein Lebenswerk wird dem Ofen überantwortet.[12]

Der nachhaltigste Einfluß von Kleists *Aufsatz über das Marionettentheater* wird im Werke Franz Kafkas manifest. Zunächst zum Motiv des Schwerpunktes: In bezug auf seine innere Unvollkommenheit notierte Kafka, auch er habe von Geburt aus seinen Schwerpunkt in sich — "Diesen guten Schwerpunkt habe ich noch, aber gewissermaßen nicht mehr den zugehörigen Körper. Und ein Schwerpunkt, der nichts zu arbeiten hat, wird zu Blei und steckt im Leib wie eine Flintenkugel. Jene Unvollkommenheit ist aber auch nicht verdient, ich habe ihr Entstehn ohne mein Verschulden erlitten. Darum kann ich in mir auch nirgends Reue finden ...."[13] Es besteht eine direkte Verbindung zwischen diesen Worten und denen Rotpeters, der berichtet, einer der Schüsse der Jagdexpedition, die auf dem "Anstand" lag — man beachte den Doppelsinn — habe ihn "unterhalb der Hüfte" getroffen, und jener Schuß habe verschuldet, daß er "noch heute ein wenig hinke."[14] Tatsächlich ist die Erzählung *Ein Bericht für eine Akademie* nichts anderes als Kafkas Version des *Marionettentheaters* und gleichzeitig der Schlüssel zu seinem triadisch strukturierten Werk: Der Affe verliert seine ursprüngliche, naturhafte Heimat und damit auch seine Grazie. Die menschliche Situation, die "Sekunde zwischen zwei Schritten eines Wanderers"[15] ohne Kontakt zum Ursprung oder zur absoluten Erfüllung, wurde initiiert durch das sich entwickelnde Bewußtsein und die Verlagerung des archimedischen Punktes: "Er hat den archimedischen Punkt gefunden," schrieb Kafka, "hat ihn aber gegen sich ausgenützt, offenbar hat er ihn nur unter dieser Bedingung finden dürfen,"[16] und Rotpeter konstatiert dementsprechend, seine Entscheidung, aufzuhören Affe zu sein, resultierte aus einem klaren, schönen Gedankengang, den er "irgendwie mit dem Bauch ausgeheckt haben muß, denn Affen denken mit dem Bauch,"[17] somit also mit dem Zentrum ihrer Existenz. Auch das Romanwerk Kafkas folgt diesem Schema: *Amerika* handelt von der Verstoßung aus der ursprünglichen Heimat und der Ansiedlung in einer neuen Welt; *Der Prozeß* schildert den Zustand der Verwirrung als Konflikt zwischen den sich plötzlich manifestierenden Kräften der Natur und der von der Kultur sanktionierten Lebensform; und *Das Schloß* beschreibt den verzweifelten Versuch eines Vorstoßes zum absoluten Bewußtsein, zu einer *Coincidentia oppositorum* des primitiven und des höchsten Denkens, der Einheit von Dorf und Schloß.

In der Nachkriegsliteratur rückt besonders Heinrich Böll die auf Kleist zurückgehenden Motive in eine strategische Position. In dem Roman *Ansichten eines Clowns,* der einen Wendepunkt im Schaffen Bölls darstellt, betont Hans Schnier, die im *Marionettentheater* entwickelten Theorien hätten zu fünfundneunzig Prozent für seine eigene Person Gültigkeit.[18] Die Verschiebung seines Schwerpunkts erfolgt in dem Moment, in welchem er seine Seele, personifiziert durch Marie Derkum, an die Kräfte der Religion, der Übernatur, verliert. Um seine Seele zurückzuerobern, bemüht sich Schnier um Kontakt in der ihn isolierenden Gesellschaft; er leitet dies mit einem "mehr oder weniger absichtlich" herbeigeführten Fall auf sein Knie ein, worauf er zu humpeln beginnt,[19] also seine Grazie verliert. In welchem Maße die unverfälschte Existenform des Tieres in Schnier weiterlebt, zeigt neben der Prädominanz des Lustprinzips in seinem Leben[20] seine animalische Melancholie, mit der er von Natur belastet ist,[21] sowie seine das Tierische noch übersteigende Fähigkeit, Gerüche durch das Telefon wahrzunehmen.[22] Schniers Scheitern entspricht Kleists Mutmaßung, daß die Wiederherstellung des harmonischen Urzustandes nach dem Fall wohl utopisch ist.

Die Schriftstellerin Christa Reinig geht in ihrer "exzentrischen Anatomie," dem Buch *Das große Bechterew-Tantra,* einen Schritt weiter, indem sie nämlich den Körperschwerpunkt völlig aus dem Menschen entfernt und zeitweilig nach außen verlegt: "Ich begann rückwärts zu gehen, um den Ausreißer wieder in meinen Körper zurückzubringen." Die Fixierung des Ortes, der dem Schwerpunkt adäquat ist, ist — wie sie meint — möglich vermittels der vorliegenden Literatur, und die Erzählerin verkündet, eine Lösung des Rätsels würde ihr ermöglicht, da sie eine glückliche Hand mit Büchern habe: "Es ist also nicht auf meinem Mist gewachsen, wenn ich nun verkünde: Der Körperschwerpunkt liegt am besten in der Bauchmitte ...."[23]

Eine beeindruckende Variante der Kleistschen Thematik, eingekleidet in Kafkasche Technik, bietet Ilse Aichingers Erzählung *Der Gefesselte.* Ein Mensch erwacht, nachdem er durch einen Schlag auf den Kopf (Sitz des Bewußtseins) betäubt und dann gefesselt wurde. Er entdeckt: "Alle Möglichkeiten lagen in dem Spielraum der Fesselung." Ihm wird eine "unbegreifliche Anmut der Bewegung" zuteil, er wird dem Tier ebenbürtig, wird "frei." Die Menschen aber, seine neuerlichen "Befreier," vor denen er "nicht genügend auf der Hut gewesen" war, pervertieren seine Existenz: Vor einem Kampf mit einem Wolf, ihm aufgezwungen durch einen Zirkusbesitzer, zerschneidet man ihm die Fessel und er wird wieder zum Fremden im Tierreich, zerfallen mit der Natur. Taumelnd—d. h.: ohne Grazie—greift er nun nach der Waffe und schießt dem Wolf zwischen die Augen.[24]

Anstatt der modernen Primärliteratur nachzugehen, soll kurz untersucht werden, ob und in welcher Hinsicht sich die hier behandelten Gedanken auf anderen Wissensgebieten als relevant erweisen.

Herbert Marcuse unterzog in seinem Buch *Triebstruktur und Gesellschaft* die Metapsychologie Sigmund Freuds einer Neuinterpretation und verknüpfte sie mit der sozialutopischen Auffassung einer Kultur ohne Unterdrückung. Die Psychologie wurde derart auf ihren sozio-historischen und politischen Gehalt befragt. Der Gedanke, daß eine Triebunterdrückung und Libidobeschränkung nötig sei, um Kultur zu *schaffen,* doch im Zenit der zivilisatorischen Entwicklung dem Lustprinzip wieder der Platz eingeräumt werden müsse, der ihm der Natur nach zukommt, kann mit dem Denken Kleists leicht auf einen gemeinsamen Nenner gebracht werden.[25] Marcuse macht sich, wie Freud, die Durchleuchtung des Wesens und Wirkens der *Phantasie* zur Aufgabe. Wenn die Genese der Phantasie "als Denkvorgang mit eigenen Gesetzen und eigenen Wahrheitsgehalten" in essentiellem Zusammenhang mit dem Lustprinzip steht[26] und sich der "Wahrheitswert der Phantasie... nicht nur auf die Vergangenheit, sondern ebenso auf die Zukunft" bezieht, indem sie "Formen der Freiheit und des Glücks" aufruft, die darauf Anspruch erheben, historische Wahrheit zu werden,[27] so könnte man mit Marcuse den Begriff einer Utopie, wie er sich bisher darstellte, ablehnen. Die Erfüllung der (*natur*bedingten) Phantasie mit der Negation des Leistungsprinzips, welche parallel geht "*mit* dem Fortschreiten der bewußten Ratio" und "höchste Reife der Kultur" voraussetzt,[28] läßt sich, wie Marcuse schreibt, als hypothetischer Zustand "in zwei Punkten vorstellen, die an den beiden äußersten Polen der Triebschicksale lägen: einmal am primitiven Beginn der Geschichte, das andere Mal im Stadium ihrer höchsten Reife."[29] Indem Marcuse den Ausspruch Baudelaires zitiert, die wahre Kultur läge nicht in Gas, Dampf oder Drehscheiben, sondern in der Tilgung der Ursünde — "La vraie civilisation... n'est pas dans le gaz, ni dans la vapeur, ni dans les tables tournantes. Elle est dans la diminuation des traces du péché originel" — demonstriert er, ganz im Sinne Kleists, das Schließen des Kreises, die Rückkehr zum Anfang auf höherer Stufe, als utopisch-prophetische Idee des Fortschritts.[30]

Ähnliche Denkvorgänge beschäftigen heute auch bereits die Naturwissenschaftler, wobei sich der Blickpunkt nicht nur auf die innere, sondern auch auf die den Menschen umgebende Natur richtet. Werner Heisenberg stellt seinen Überlegungen zum Naturbild der heutigen Physik und zu dem Verhältnis des Menschen zur Natur eine Stelle aus den Schriften des Chinesen Dschuang Dsi voraus, deren zentrales Thema die "reine Einfalt" ist, welche durch Arbeit mit Maschinen leicht einer "Ungewißheit in den Regungen des Geistes" weicht.[31] Diese "Ungewißheit," übersetzbar mit "Entfremdung" oder auch "Verwirrung," hat sich mittlerweile als das herrschende Grundprinzip etabliert, sozusagen als "Unbehagen in der Kultur," wobei sich das Opfer dessen kaum mehr bewußt ist. Übertroffen wird dieses Mißverhältnis nur noch von dem zwischen der Menschheit und dem ökologischen Gleichgewicht. Der allgemein gültige Gradmesser für Fortschritt und Wohlbefinden ist materieller Reichtum und die Wachstumsrate des Sozialprodukts. Ganze Tierarten werden eliminiert, Baumbestände abgeschlagen, Wasser und Luft vergiftet, Bodenschätze verschwendet. Der Biochemiker Friedrich Cramer, Direktor des Max-Planck-Instituts für experimentelle Medizin, nimmt hierzu Stellung in dem Buch *Fortschritt durch Verzicht,* indem er zu einer Rückkehr von der "offenen" zur "zyklischen" Welt aufruft, nicht zu verstehen als ein "Zurück" zur Natur, sondern als "Flucht nach vorne":

Der Aufbruch des Menschen ist endgültig, sein Heraustreten aus der Natur läßt sich nicht rückgängig machen, wir haben vom Baume der Erkenntnis gegessen und haben freiwillig das Paradies verlassen. Und wir haben viel, Unendliches dabei gewonnen. Das ROUSSEAUsche "Zurück zur Natur" kann es nicht geben, es würde Preisgabe der Kultur und Zivilisation und der größten geistigen Güter der Menschheit bedeuten. . . .

Wir erkennen nun, daß wir in unserem Verhältnis zur Natur, in den Anwendungen unseres Denkens, entscheidende Fehler gemacht haben: Während die Natur eine Gleichgewichts-Lösung für die Probleme ihres Wachstums gefunden hat, die für ihre wesentlichen Systeme einen stationären Zustand gewährleistet (Wasserkreislauf — Atmosphäre — Assimilation der Kohlensäure — Zusammenleben von Tieren und Pflanzen) bei gleichzeitiger langsamer Evolution, . . . hat der Mensch durch sein Denkvermögen und durch dessen Anwendung auf Naturvorgänge diese an vielen Stellen zerstört. . . .

Cramer betont, daß der Mensch, nachdem er die Natur verlassen hat und sich *gegen* sie stellte, sich nun *über* die Natur stellen muß:

Die Zeit ist reif dafür, daß der Mensch den Zyklus "Natur — Widernatur — Übernatur" vollendet. Unter Übernatur verstehe ich die vom Menschen bewußt gemachte Natur. Er erkennt den Anteil von Natur in sich selbst, kann ihn qualitativ und quantitativ beschreiben, er braucht ihn weder zu tabuisieren noch romantisch zu überhöhen. Er hat auch die Prinzipien der Funktion und des Entstehens der Natur und seiner selbst soweit geistig durchschaut, daß er die Zusammenhänge und Bindungen *seiner Existenz,* und damit die Bedingtheit seines Seins erkennt . . . Der Mensch kann wieder einswerden mit der

Natur, die er sich dadurch völlig aneignet, aber eben nicht aneignet im Sinne einer Eroberung, sondern einer Identifikation.[32]

Der Kleist bestätigende Satz Nietzsches, es sei "immer noch eine ganz neue und eben erst dem menschlichen Auge aufdämmernde, kaum noch deutlich erkennbare *Aufgabe, das Wissen sich einzuverleiben* und instinktiv zu machen,"[33] überschneidet sich an diesem Punkt mit der Verantwortung der Naturwissenschaften in der Ökologie und dem Aufgabenbereich der Menschheit schlechthin.

Die Bedeutung der Literatur und ganz besonders Kleists *Marionettentheater* als "Parabel für die zyklische Struktur der Welt" in diesem Kontext wurde von Cramer ausdrücklich hervorgehoben.[34] Bemerkenswert ist seine Frage, ob es wohl gelingen könne, Wissenschaft und Kunst wieder zusammenzuführen und "Denken und Fühlen in Einklang zu bringen im 'Reich des schönen Scheins'." Anknüpfend an die Gemälde Picassos, die den Höhlenzeichnungen von Lascaux frappierend ähneln, vertritt er die Auffassung, man habe es hier bereits mit einem Beispiel des Zyklischen zu tun — um die "gleichsam durch ein Unendliches" gegangene Erkenntnis. Er schreibt weiter:

> Diese Erkenntnis ist keine vernunftmäßige wissenschaftliche Erkenntnis, sondern eine ästhetische Erkenntnis, die zwischen Vernunft und Gefühl vermittelt .... Hier liegt die wahre Aufgabe der Kunst als einer Meta-Wissenschaft. Diese Meta-Wissenschaft darf, um ihre Aufgabe leisten zu können, nicht vorwissenschaftlich, also Prä-Wissenschaft sein, sondern sie muß die Welt der Realitäten voll in sich hineinnehmen... Die letzten Grenzen unserer Erkenntnis in der Kernphysik und in der Biologie scheinen mir solche Übergänge von Wissenschaft zu Meta-Wissenschaft anzuzeigen, in der nicht mehr allein die Kategorie der Rationalität gilt, sondern zusätzlich die Kategorie des Ästhetischen mitbestimmend wird.[35]

Da der Wert des Modells einer zyklischen Welt, wie es sich in Kleists *Aufsatz über das Marionettentheater* anbietet, in der Naturwissenschaft Anklang gefunden hat, darf man vielleicht noch hoffen, daß das reflektierende Wesen Mensch sein Bewußtsein in den Dienst einer Utopie stellt, anstelle durch Zerstörung und Unterdrückung seiner äußeren und inneren Natur den Urgrund zu vernichten, dem er selbst entstammt und ohne den er nicht existieren kann. Das wäre "das letzte Capitel von der Geschichte der Welt."[36]

ANMERKUNGEN

1. Der sich mit dem Aufsatz *Über das Marionettentheater* befassende Teil von Hanna Hellmanns Buch ist abgedruckt in der Jahresgabe der Heinrich-von-Kleist-Gesellschaft, *Kleists Aufsatz über das Marionettentheater. Studien und In-*

terpretationen, Hrsg. Helmut Sembdner (Berlin, 1967), S. 17-31. Kleists Aufsatz ist den kritischen Arbeiten vorausgestellt. Wo nach diesem Band zitiert wird, wird abgekürzt: *Kleist-Studien.*
2. Paul Böckmann, "Kleists Aufsatz 'Über das Marionettentheater,' " *Kleist-Studien*, S. 33.
3. So durch Friedrich Braig, *Heinrich von Kleist* (München, 1925), der versuchte, Kleist zu einem Katholiken zu reduzieren; Walter Silz, der — angeregt von Karl Schultze-Jahde — in seiner Arbeit "Die Mythe von den Marionetten" behauptet, Kleists Aufsatz sei lediglich ein geistreiches, wenn auch zum Nachdenken anreizendes Gespräch, zur "kleineren Gattung" gehörig; *Kleist-Studien*, S. 100 f., 110. James M. McGlathery will in seinem Artikel "Kleist's *Über das Marionettentheater*," *German Life and Letters* N.S. XX (July 1967, No. 4), S. 325-331, die Bewegungen der Marionetten als Totentanz und Ausdruck von Kleists Todeswunsch verstanden wissen, wogegen Karl Otto Conrady in einer gegen Wilhelm Emrich gerichteten Polemik darauf beharrte, Kleist spräche in erster Linie über Gott; vgl. Karl Otto Conrady, "Das Moralische in Kleists Erzählungen. Ein Kapitel vom Dichter ohne Gesellschaft," in: Hans Joachim Schrimpf, Hrsg., *Literatur und Gesellschaft vom neunzehnten ins zwanzigste Jahrhundert* (Bonn, 1963), S. 62, Anm., und 68, Anm.
4. Abgedruckt in *Kleist-Studien*: Josef Kunz, "Kleists Gespräch 'Über das Marionettentheater', S. 78-87; Clemens Heselhaus, "Das Kleistsche Paradox," S. 112-131; Lawrence Ryan, "Die Marionette und das 'unendliche Bewußtsein' bei Heinrich von Kleist," S. 171-195; und Benno von Wiese, "Das verlorene und wieder zu findende Paradies. Eine Studie über den Begriff der Anmut bei Goethe, Kleist und Schiller," S. 196-220. Ferner sei hingewiesen auf das Kapitel " 'Das Marionettentheater' und 'Käthchen von Heilbronn' " in dem Buch von Gerhard Fricke, *Gefühl und Schicksal bei Heinrich von Kleist* (Berlin, 1929: Neue Forschung 3), S. 150-156.
5. Kunz, *Kleist-Studien*, S. 79.
6. So in Sigmund Freud, *Totem und Tabu*, in: S. F., *Gesammelte Werke* (London: Imago Publishing Company, 1940; Neudruck: S. Fischer Verlag, Frankfurt/Main, 1968), IX, insbes. S. 26-92.
7. *Kleist-Studien*, S. 15
8. *New Larousse Encyclopedia of Mythology* (London, 1974), S. 121.
9. Juan-Eduardo Cirlot, *Diccionario de Símbolos* (Barcelona, 1969), S. 356.
10. Theodore Ziolkowski, *The Novels of Hermann Hesse. A Study in Theme and Structure* (Princeton, N.J., 1965), S. 51 ff. Es mag von Interesse sein, daß der Bär als Symbol des mütterlich-naturhaften bzw. lunaren Prinzips auch bei Hesse eine Rolle spielt. Goldmund, der als Gegenpol von Narziß der lunaren Welt zugeordnet ist, äußert kurz nach Verlassen des Klosters den Wunsch, sich in einen Bären zu verwandeln und eine Bärin zu lieben. Hermann Hesse, *Narziß und Goldmund*, in: H. H., *Gesammelte Werke* (Frankfurt/Main, 1970), VIII, S. 94.
11. Hermann Sudermann, *Purzelchen* (Stuttgart und Berlin, 1930), S. 105, 247, 256 f., 276 ff.
12. Hermann Sudermann, *Der tolle Professor* (Stuttgart und Berlin, 1930), S. 27, 61, 189-192, 536-540.
13. Franz Kafka, *Tagebücher 1910-1923* (New York, 1948), S. 688.
14. Franz Kafka, *Erzählungen* (Frankfurt/Main, 1967), S. 186.

15. Franz Kafka, *Hochzeitsvorbereitungen auf dem Lande und andere Prosa aus dem Nachlaß* (Frankfurt/Main, 1966), S. 74.
16. Ibid., S. 418.
17. Franz Kafka, *Erzählungen,* S. 188.
18. Heinrich Böll, *Ansichten eines Clowns* (München, 1973; dtv 400, 17. Aufl.), S. 153 f. Hierauf kurz: Böll.
19. Böll, S. 28.
20. Böll, S. 53 f., 101, 222.
21. Böll, S. 8, 153.
22. Böll, S. 12, 31, 34, 69, etc. Man vgl. zu diesem Thema meine Arbeit "Die Marionette als Interpretationsansatz zu Bölls *Ansichten eines Clowns,*" *The University of Dayton Review*, XI/2 (1976), S. 25-32.
23. Christa Reinig, *Das große Bechterew-Tantra* (Stierstadt/Taunus, 1970), S. 53.
24. Ilse Aichinger, *Nachricht vom Tag. Erzählungen* (Frankfurt/Main und Hamburg, 1970), S. 8 f., 15, 17 f.
25. Herbert Marcuse, *Triebstruktur und Gesellschaft* (Frankfurt/Main, 1967), S. 196; hierauf kurz; Marcuse. Dieser und der sich anschließende Teil ist auszugsweise meinem Buch *Ende oder Anfang. Zur Einheit der Gegensätze in Kafkas 'Schloss'* (München, 1977), S. 187-193 (Nachwort), entnommen.
26. Marcuse, S. 141.
27. Marcuse, S. 148.
28. Marcuse, S. 149.
29. Marcuse, S. 151.
30. Marcuse, S. 152; Charles Baudelaire, "Mon Coeur Mis a Nu" XXXII, in: C. B., *Oeuvres Posthumes,* Ed. Conard, II, S. 109.
31. Werner Heisenberg, *Das Naturbild der heutigen Physik* (Hamburg, 1970), S. 15 f.
32. Friedrich Cramer, *Fortschritt durch Verzicht* (München, 1975), S. 222 f. Hierauf kurz: Cramer.
33. Friedrich Nietzsche, *Die fröhliche Wissenschaft,* Erstes Buch, Nr. 11; in: F. N., *Werke in drei Bänden,* Hrsg. Karl Schlechta (München, 1955), II, S. 44.
34. Cramer, S. 224 ff.
35. Friedrich Cramer, "Der letzte Ausweg: Geplante Flucht nach vorn," in: *Die Zeit,* Nr. 46 (14. Nov. 1975), S. 22.
36. *Kleist-Studien,* S. 16.

Comparative Studies

Diderot and Kleist

HILDA M. BROWN
St. Hilda's College, Oxford

The profound influence exercised by Denis Diderot on German literary figures of the late 18th and early 19th century is well-documented and recognized.[1] Goethe himself in *Dichtung und Wahrheit* attests to its significance (as well as that of Rousseau) for the entire Sturm und Drang movement.[2] In their Classical period he and Schiller remained keenly interested in Diderot's works (especially *Jacques le Fataliste*), albeit Goethe had now adopted a more critical stance. It was, of course, at that time that Goethe made works like the *Essai sur la Peinture* and *Le Neveu de Rameau* available to the German public through his own translations (indeed his translation of the latter was, astonishingly, its first publication in *any* language). Nor did German enthusiasm for Diderot confine itself, around the turn of the 18th and 19th centuries, to the *Klassik*. As R. Mortier points out,[3] Fr. Schlegel was an ardent devotee of Diderot's works in general and *Jacques le Fataliste* in particular (which he described as an "arabesque"). So too was E.T.A. Hoffmann[4] and in his case the work which came in for special mention was, not surprisingly in view of its musical content, *Le Neveu de Rameau*. The rich variety and subtle complexity of Diderot's writings assured his reputation even at a period when anti-French feeling was running high in Germany and even among writers of different generations belonging to different literary movements. The works particularly favored, it is true, vary somewhat from one generation to the next: thus if a work like *Les deux amis de Bourbonne* seems to speak most powerfully to the generation of the 1770s and 1780s, (Schiller's *Die Räuber* is sometimes thought to have been inspired by the latter *conte*), then *Jacques le Fataliste*, *Le Neveu de Rameau* and the writings on art (*Salons* and *Essai sur la Peinture*) appear to command most attention for writers in the late 1790s and early 1800s and here (not for the first time) *Klassik* and *Romantik* link hands. In very general terms, one might say that the emphasis shifts away from an emotional identification with "Stoff" (e.g., the figure of the outcast from society) towards a concern with the subtleties of art-theory and artistic techniques (e.g., Diderot's use of irony which was much praised by Fr.

Schlegel, his use of particular forms like the dialogue). As F.M. Klinger, an important intermediary for Diderot in Germany, puts it in his memoirs of 1809:

> Diderot hat den Deutschen gezeigt, wie man über ästhetische Gegenstände schreiben muß. Er entwickelt uns die tiefsten Geheimnisse der Kunst so klar und deutlich, daß sie jeder versteht, sich ihrer erfreuen kann ... Der Dichter und der Philosoph gehen hier vertraulich und leicht in der schönsten Verbindung zusammen, und keiner schadet dem anderen.[5]

Coming from the man who had himself in earlier years embodied the wilder, more chaotic side of *Sturm und Drang* aspirations and whose own drama (earlier title: *Wirrwarr*) had actually given its name to the movement, this assessment demonstrates clearly the shift of emphasis which had taken place in Diderot's *Rezeption*.

Given the general awareness of the importance of Diderot's work for German letters in the period 1770-1820 to which I have briefly drawn attention, it seems no less than remarkable that its significance has not been perceived in the case of one of the greatest writers of that period, Heinrich von Kleist. In this neglect perhaps due to a longstanding preoccupation with the dramas at the expense of the prose works? One might have thought, however, that Kleist's sub-title for the *Erzählungen*—"Moralische Erzählungen"—could have provided a clue, had it not been always assumed that for this particular designation Kleist went exclusively back to the originator of the genre, Cervantes.[6] But it is surely significant that the appellation can be found for short prose works of similar length and scope in several 18th century sources and that these include Diderot himself, whose *Entretien d'un Père* and *Les deux amis de Bourbonne* appeared in collaboration with Salomon Gessner in Zürich 1773; the full title of this joint publishing venture with the best-selling Swiss writer of idylls was "Contes moraux et Nouvelles idylles de MM. D ... et Gessner." Leaving aside the very strong likelihood that Kleist knew this work at first hand on his own initiative, further connecting links could have been forged through 1) the agency of Gessner's son, Heinrich, whom Kleist got to know well while in Switzerland in 1802 and who published *Die Familie Schroffenstein* for him in 1803, and/or 2) the agency of Wieland, a close friend of Gessner's and father-in-law of Heinrich Gessner. Wieland gave an enthusiastic reception to the joint Diderot-Gessner collection in a letter to Jacobi (28 June 1772). In addition to Diderot's own use of the term "contes moraux" ("Moralische Erzählungen") it was also adopted by the German diplomat and dilettante F.W.B. Ramdohr (whom there is reason to suppose Kleist met in Paris); Ramdohr's own "Moralische Erzählungen" were the subject of a scathing review by Dorothea Schlegel in the *Athenäum* (III, i, 238 ff.) and it is more than likely that his title was derived from Diderot's example: Ramdohr met Diderot in the year of the latter's death (1784) and had written enthusiastically about his works in the *Berliner Monatschrift* of that year.

Further and more substantial manifestations of Kleist's interest in Diderot can be examined with reference to ideas and motifs contained in the *Essai sur la Peinture* which Kleist could have known in the original but with which he was undoubtedly familiar through Goethe's "translation" of 1799 in the *Propyläen* (as a translation the work is highly selective; it renders only two of Diderot's seven original sections, and that incompletely. It is furthermore equipped with a running commentary in which Goethe takes issue with particular points raised by Diderot, generally in order to refute them). In this essay Diderot spends some time arguing against the long, arid years of training spent by young painters who are obliged to practice on studio models instead of observing and recording their impressions of the "real life" going on around them. The artificiality of an art bred in such circumstances is deplored, as too is the mannerism which it inevitably produces: "Laissez-moi cette boutique de *manière*. Allez-vous-en aux Chartreux; et vous verrez la véritable attitude de la piété et de la componction ... Examinez-les bien, et vous aurez pitié de la leçon de votre insipide professeur et de l'imitation de votre insipide modèle."[7] Compare this outspoken statement about the artist's true sources of inspiration with Kleist's "Brief eines Malers an seinen Sohn" where the father takes his young painter-son to task for allowing a false piety (i.e., taking communion before setting out to paint) to come between himself and the work he is creating: "Laß dir von deinem alten Vater sagen, daß dies eine falsche, dir von der Schule, aus der du herstammst, anklebende Begeisterung ist...."[8] This chimes in particularly well with the statement on which Diderot closes the first section of his essay (entitled "Mes pensées bizarres sur le dessin"): "La manière vient du maître, de l'académie, de l'école, et même de l'antique."[9]

If Diderot and Kleist seem to be of one mind (and, incidentally, united against Goethe) on the question of the vital importance of spontaneity during the gestation of a work of art (and Kleist develops the biological analogy with a frankness that Diderot might have appreciated) and both draw up battle-lines against "academic art," another interesting parallel between the *Essai* and Kleist's contributions to the *Berliner Abendblätter* can be seen on the issue of what constitutes grace. Pursuing his train of thought concerning the natural origins and inspiration for true art, Diderot is led to consider graceful movements produced by live humans as a suitable subject for study and "imitation" instead of academic dissection of an inanimate body, the "écorché" (German "Muskelmann"). Diderot inveighs against all artificially induced academic poses adopted by models and urges instead a policy of encouraging young painters to study graceful movement via the dance—and who better can demonstate its excellence than famous dancers of the day like Vestris or Gardel?[10] It will be recalled that Kleist too was moved to invoke the great Vestris (whom he might have seen in Paris) in *Über das Marionettentheater*, when Herr C. was toying with the idea of a fully automated marionette which would surpass even the greatest human exponents of the dance-form. Diderot's development of his point about the merits of the dance by stressing the role played by gravitational forces in the production of graceful movement may well have sparked off Kleist's further elaboration of this scientific basis of graceful movement in mechanics: "Qu'une femme laisse tomber sa tête en devant, tous ses membres obéissent à ce poids; qu'elle la relève et la tienne droite, même obéissance du reste de la machine."[11] Herr C. makes the same point about the need for the limbs to act as mere pendules during a particular movement: "Da der Maschinist nun schlechthin, vermittelst des Drahtes oder Fadens, keinen anderen Punkt in seiner Gewalt hat, als diesen: so sind alle übrigen Glieder, was sie sein sollen, tot, reine Pendel, und folgen dem bloßen Gesetz der Schwere."[12] And he believes that many human dancers would do well to follow this principle. Kleist, like Diderot, deplores the artifice and mannerism ("Ziererei") which occurs in art when natural laws are neglected at the expense of reflexion or self-consciousness.

I have suggested that some interesting overlap can be found in the aesthetic theories of Diderot and Kleist which at times run so closely parallel in terms of motifs and even phraseology as to be more than coincidental. The impression that Kleist knew Diderot's writings intimately is further confirmed by an examination, necessarily brief, of Kleist's use of the dialogue form in *Über das Marionettentheater*. The form of the dialogue is one which has a considerably weaker tradition in German letters than in French: Lessing and Wieland, both significantly "Aufklärer," are notable exceptions, the former employing it for polemical and didactic purposes (cf. *Ernst und Falk*), the latter much influenced by Classical models like Plato and Lucian (cf. *Göttergespräche, Gespräche im Elysium*, etc.). German dialogue forms tend to play down artistic possibilities of the genre at the expense of discursive elements. This holds good even in the case of a Romantic exponent, Fr. Schlegel (cf. *Gespräch über die Poesie*)—significantly a Classicist by training—who is mainly concerned to expound his aesthetic theories by means of characters who are no more than mouthpieces. Kleist's employment of a highly sophisticated dialogue form—albeit in diminutive format—in his famous *Über das Marionettentheater* suggests a close study of the contributions made by the greatest exponent of the dialogue in the 18th century—Diderot. His essay follows, in compressed form, the typical French pattern of an opening "mise en scène," followed by exposition of a theory by a "Lui" (Herr C.) which is interrupted at intervals by an initially agnostic "Moi." The dramatic element, which has long been regarded as an important feature in dialogue,[13] is fully exploited, the personalities of the two disputants clearly defined and enlivened by the use of "explanatory" gesture (e.g. "Ich": "da ich den Blick schweigend zur Erde schlug"; "Er": "da er seinerseits ein wenig betreten zur Erde sah," etc.). The interpolation of anecdotes, ostensibly as supporting props for the theories advanced, but possessing an attractive independence in themselves (e.g. "Dornzieher" and bear anecdotes) is a feature very common in Diderot's dialogue (cf. *Jacques le Fataliste*) and a particularly subtle device is the contribution made by the sceptical "Ich" to support his opponent's argument, it being he who narrates the story about the youth who resembles the "Dornzieher."

Perhaps the feature which makes Kleist's dialogue most strongly resemble Diderot's sophisticated forms is the manner in which authorial perspective on the theory expounded is handled. For unlike most other examples of the genre neither Kleist's nor Diderot's dialogues are simple, clear-cut expositions of a principle in which the author is inviting his reader to share one particular point of view. Both writers employ a distinctly "polyvocal" perspective rather than the common "univocal" one found in polemical dialogue.[14] To illustrate the point in Kleist's case, one need only consider the respective standpoint adopted by "Ich" and Herr C. towards the latter's thesis that grace and human consciousness are in inverse proportion to one another. Herr C. sees this proposition in the clear-cut terms of a fanatic who has worked out his position beforehand. "Ich," as his accompanying gestures indicate (they resemble stage-direction), starts off by being highly sceptical about the grace of marionettes, but gradually he comes round to some measure of agreement with Herr C. and, as we have noticed, himself contributes the story of the self-conscious youth as a reinforcement of part of Herr C.'s argument. And when Herr C. presses his point home by producing in turn the example of the fencing bear, thus cunningly steering the argument gradually away from the human sphere, he takes "Ich" with him: "Vollkommen! rief ich, mit freudigem Beifall...." But when he introduces the next (from his point of view) logical step, i.e., the inanimate example of the marionette, Herr C. up to the very end encounters some resistance and questioning from "Ich." Certainly, he has to forgo that clear conviction from his interlocutor which had been so evident in the second story dealing with the non-human but still animate subject, the bear, "Mithin, sagte ich, ein wenig zerstreut, müßten wir wieder von dem Baum der Erkenntnis essen, um in den Stand der Unschuld zurückzufallen?" While "Ich" still hesitates, Herr C. is entirely convinced, "Allerdings, antwortete er...." And the point at issue is a sticking-point of substance. Agreement had fairly easily been reached on the question of the damaging effects of self-consciousness in man so far as grace is concerned. Again, note the concern Kleist shares with Diderot about mannerism. But it cannot easily be attained when it comes to the best means of overcoming this problem. Herr C.'s proposition that more "Erkenntnis" simply be amassed is dogmatically stated and reinforced by Biblical authority, but it scarcely seems practicable and as he himself puts it "das ist das letzte Kapitel von der Geschichte der Welt." Where does Kleist, the author, stand on all this? We cannot tell, nor does he intend us to seem him coming down clearly on one side or the other. We do not need to turn the tables round so far as to regard Herr C.'s views, as a recent commentator has done,[15] as "hochgeschraubt" and the "Ich" 's lack of conviction as a justifiable scepticism or even ridicule in what is taken to be a satire on the Berlin "Hofbühne" and Iffland in particular. But Daunicht's wrong-headed interpretation with its reversal of the roles normally allotted to the two disputants does at least invite us to examine their respective standpoints with more care than is customary and points to a large area of ambiguity in this most artistic of dialogues.[16]

Of course, it is just possible that Kleist developed the form to this point of artistry single-handed in Germany. But how much more probable it seems that he was drawn to French models and to Diderot in particular while collecting his material for the *Berliner Abendblätter*. It is interesting that he was simultaneously providing sundry translations from the French for this journal, and it is surely no accident that he was at the same time making such extensive use of associated forms like the epistle and the essay which were also forms in which French 18th century writers excelled. Of Diderot's *Le Neveu de Rameau*, which Kleist cannot have missed in Goethe's translation, a recent commentator has stressed the lack of neatly opposing views on the part of the two interlocutors,[17] and of Diderot's dialogue in general has said: "Instead of demanding a simple *either-or* decision, the dialogue shows him ideas and individuals who can be *both* this *and* that; consequently, it makes him discover the complexity of the problems at issue."[18] These statements could be applied to Kleist's masterly use of dialogue-form with equal justification and this together with the other parallels to Diderot which I have discussed above suggest that a more complete assimilation of certain aspects of Diderot's thought and art had been achieved by Kleist than by any of his predecessors in Germany.

NOTES

1. See especially the excellent work by Roland Mortier, *Diderot en Allemagne (1750-1850)*, (Paris, 1954).
2. *Aus meinem Leben, Dichtung und Wahrheit*, III, ix, ed. E. Beutler, Zürich und Stuttgart, 1962, 534.
3. Cf. Mortier, op. cit., 234 f.
4. Cf. Mortier, op. cit., 289 ff.

5. F.M. Klinger, *Betrachtungen und Gedanken* (Berlin, 1958), pp. 457-8 (based on second edition 1809, Königsberg, bei Fr. Nicolevius).
6. Cf. J.-U. Fechner, "Cervantes und Kleist—ein Kapitel europäischer Novellistik" (*Levende Talen*, 1964), 711-723. The fact, attested to by Fechner, that Kleist possessed a copy of Cervantes' tales in no way invalidates the theory that he received further stimulus to use the title by general manifestations of interest in the genre nearer his own time. Cf. too G. Dünnhaupt, "Kleists *Marquise von O . . .* and its literary debt to Cervantes," *Arcadia. Zeitschrift für vergleichende Literaturwissenschaft.* (Berlin) 10, 2. Dünnhaupt suggests that "Kleist's literary debt to Cervantes is less extensive than may have been surmised."
7. Diderot, *Oeuvres*. Ed. André Billy (Bibliothèque de la Pléiade), 1969.
8. Kleist, *Sämtliche Werke* Vol. II, Ed. H. Sembdner, 328.
9. Diderot, *Oeuvres*. ed. cit., 1119.
10. The text of the Pléiade edition has a variant reading "Marcel ou Dupré," but Goethe's translation reverts to "Vestris oder Gardel."
11. Diderot, *Oeuvres*. Ed. cit., 1119.
12. Kleist, *Sämtliche Werke* II, Ed. cit., 341-2.
13. See article on "Dialog" by Rudolf Wildbolz in *Merker-Stammler Literaturlexicon, Zweite Auflage,* (Berlin, 1958).
14. See C. Sherman, *Diderot and the Art of Dialogue*, (Geneva, 1975), 24.
15. Cf. R. Daunicht, "Heinrich von Kleists Aufsatz *Über das Marionettentheater* als Satire betrachtet," *Euphorion* 67 (1973), 306-322.
16. Cf. C. Sherman, op. cit., p. 44: "The dramatic nature of dialogue, that is, its vivacity or true-to-life quality, seems to be in inverse proportion to the clarity of its meaning or *dianoia*."
17. Cf. Sherman, op. cit., 113.
18. Cf. Sherman, op. cit., 52.

Michael Kohlhaas in New York: Kleist and E.L. Doctorow's *Ragtime*

MARION FABER
Swarthmore College

The works of Heinrich von Kleist have found a wide audience in the years since the Second World War: in the fifties, French existentialism discovered a sympathetic predecessor in the Prince of Homburg; more recently the film director Eric Rohmer has been drawn to the strange fortunes of the Marquise of O . . . And in 1974 one of Kleist's most famous tales, "Michael Kohlhaas," underwent a metamorphosis in America: the sixteenth century renegade immortalized in Kleist's 1806 novella, is alive and as well as can be expected in E.L. Doctorow's *Ragtime*, a compilation of fact and fantasy about American life in the years immediately before World War I. As yet no reviewer or critic has addressed this influence of Kleist on Doctorow's work.[1]

Ragtime is ingenious, and much of the ingeniousness lies in Doctorow's adaptation of Kleist's tale. I would like to begin by tracing the relationships in character and theme between the two works. I would then like to examine more closely some fundamental differences.

First, a brief summary of Kleist's novella: basing his tale on a true incident from the sixteenth century, Kleist relates how the horse dealer, in reality named Hans Kohlhase, seeks to regain his two black horses, abused when left hostage at the Baron Wenzel von Tronka's castle. When neither the baron nor the electors of Brandenburg or Saxony give regard to his scrupulous attempts at legal settlement, and his wife Lisbeth dies as a result of the case, Kohlhaas turns to murder and arson in order to obtain justice. The scale of violence increases, Martin Luther intercedes, political machinations result eventually in Kohlhaas being held prisoner in Dresden. Tempted to escape Kohlhaas is instead given safe conduct to Berlin by the Elector of Brandenburg. Because of an added fantastic tale involving a gypsy who gives to Kohlhaas vital information about the Saxon Elector's destiny, Kohlhaas is then unexpectedly aided by this Elector. To no avail—

after his two black stallions, in their former condition, have been duly restored to him, Kohlhaas swallows the paper with the information just before he is beheaded.

In the casual rhythm of the musical form which is its title, E.L. Doctorow's novel interweaves the lives of certain representative people in America, more exactly New York and Boston, in the years before World War I. Harry Houdini, Emma Goldman, Pierpont Morgan, a WASP family, and Jewish immigrants, all live out their intermingled destinies. The cumulative effect is the tapestry of an era. Choosing as his period the lull before the storm of World War I, Doctorow makes audible the rumblings of prewar social inequities and ideological conflicts.

The one among his figures who might most accurately be described as a hero is a fictional black ragtime pianist named Coalhouse Walker Jr. As the plot soon makes clear, this calm and proud man, advanced in years, is none other than Michael Kohlhaas reincarnated. Doctorow has, to be sure, tipped us off as to his identity as soon as the character is introduced, for his name Coalhouse is practically the same word as Kohlhaas, and transmutes the homespun German name into a parallel black American one. As "Kohl" suggests Kohlhaas' lower class origins, so "Coal" keeps Walker's blackness always before our eyes.

Doctorow, incidentally, gives two other such clues about the Teutonic ancestry of his hero: at one point, Walker tosses a message from J.P. Morgan's mansion. His missile is

> a medieval drinking stein of silver with a hunting scene in relief. The curator asked to see it and advised that it was from the seventeenth century and had belonged to Frederick, the Elector of Saxony. (231)[2]

True, Doctorow has gotten a bit ahead of himself in his centuries—it was Johann Friedrich, Elector of Saxony in the sixteenth century, to whom Kohlhaas appealed, but this hint is titillating. Shortly thereafter Doctorow also describes a portrait of Martin Luther, decorating the wall of the Pierpont Morgan mansion. (238)

I would like at this point to make a short digression regarding the significance of Coalhouse's second name, Walker. In the early nineteenth century, a black revolutionary David Walker was

> born free in Wilmington, North Carolina . . . moved to Boston and opened a secondhand clothes store . . . appeared on the Boston scene as a radical agitator . . . published *Walker's Appeal to the Colored Citizens of the World* . . . lashed out at white people whom he called "devils" and excoriated the slaveholding Christians of "this Republican land of Liberty!!!!!!"[3]

In his pamphlet Walker urged violent rebellion, which he considered the black man's religious duty. "The governors of several Southern states called their assemblies into secret session to discuss the pamphlet."[4] Thus Doctorow's protagonist unites the righteous Prussian outlaw and the black American rebel David Walker. His full name, Coalhouse Walker *Jr.*, indicates his filial relationship to these two different spiritual ancestors.

The two black horses which Michael Kohlhaas loses and regains at such tremendous cost are transformed in *Ragtime* into Walker's black Model T Ford. "His car shone. The brightwork gleamed. There was a glass windshield and a custom pantasote top." (129) The circumstances of the car's defilement are parallel: going past a volunteer fire station, Walker's Model T is stopped; he becomes the butt of the firemen's jokes. Asked to pay a toll which does not exist, he leaves his car behind. The rowdies splatter it with mud, defecate in the back seat. Like Kohlhaas, Walker is initially calm and dignified, but with each unavailing attempt to secure it, the restitution and restoration of his car grow into a burning issue. Policemen and their chiefs, lawyers (even black lawyers), district attorneys, none are willing to engage themselves in the cause of a black man. The Model T functions, as do the horses in Kleist's tale, as a recurring symbol or leitmotiv. We see the car through the eyes of another character, Younger Brother: "He noted that the hood was unlatched, and lifting and folding it back, saw that the wires had been torn from the engine." (152) The father of the family in New Rochelle also inspects the car, after the first act of murder has taken place. (174) Doctorow reasserts the relationship between Walker's provocation and its consequences. Later the car is raised from a pond for everyone to see, "like a monstrous artifact, mud dripping from its tires, water and slime pouring out of its hood." (199) Before his execution Kohlhaas finds "the two black horses, sleek with health and pawing the ground with their hooves," (170-101)[5] duly restored. Walker, too, before his voluntary gunning down, knows that a "shining black Model T Ford with a custom pantasote roof" (249) stands at the curb (though he himself never sees it). These shining black possessions, each in its day both useful and a source of prestige, loom larger and larger in their respective works. Like Kleist's horses, the Ford incorporates in its sad decline and its regained brightness the history of events. At the same time both symbols are constant reminders of an abstract, unchanging essence, ravaged externally by time and chance, but also immutable: the issue that motivates both men more than the possession itself.

There are three other important characters from "Michael Kohlhaas" who have found new life in Doctorow's work: the Baron Wenzel von Tronka has become Will Conklin, fire chief in a small New York town. Here, too, the transformation is reflected in the similarity of their names (Tr ONK a, C ONK lin). Conklin, like Tronka, is gradually abandoned by his associates because of the mammoth dimensions his practical joke has assumed. Doctorow has also followed Kleist in making the villain of the piece at the same time a comic character, more of a buffoon than a vicious devil.

Kleist:

The Junker [fell] from one fainting fit into another while two attending physicians tried to bring him around with aromatics and stimulants ... the Junker's helmet fell off several times without his missing it and was clapped back on his head by the knight walking behind him. (111-39)

Doctorow:

Conklin smelled of whiskey and the experience of being a hunted man had turned his florid face the color of veal. (183) Like all of Conklin's moves, sharing his correspondence with the authorities was a mistake ... The miserable fellow understood nothing. He drank himself into a state of torpor and became dumbly complaisant. (201)

Much like Kafka, another admirer of Kleist's, Doctorow employs a kind of tittering-on-the-brink, nervous laughter as a foil to the painful tension of events. In both cases the wheel of destiny is set in motion not by an Iago but rather by a Hanswurst.

Early in the series of attempts to settle the issue peaceably, Michael Kohlhaas' wife Lisbeth tries to petition the Elector of Brandenburg on behalf of her husband. Similarly the mother of Walker's son, Sarah, attempts to plead with the Vice President of the United States, James Sherman, on Walker's behalf. Both women meet exactly the same fate: Lisbeth "had pressed forward too boldly" and "received a blow on the chest from a lance butt" (102-29); Sarah "broke through the line" and "a militiaman ... brought the butt of his Springfield against Sarah's chest as hard as he could." (159) Describing Sarah's funeral, then, Doctorow retains the grave splendor of Kleist's narrative.

Kleist:

an oak coffin with heavy brass mountings, cushions of silk with gold and silver tassels, and a grave eight ells deep, walled with fieldstone and mortar. (103-30)

Doctorow:

The funeral ... was lavish. Sarah's coffin was bronze ... The hearse ... was railed with brass and banked with masses of flowers. Black ribbon flew from the four corners of the roof. (162)

The two women are on the side of compromise, pleading the sacrifice of principle for peace and life. But they must first submit to their men and are then crushed by the weapons of power. If there are readers for whom the heroes' offended principles do not seem to warrant such excesses, their sympathies might be enlisted by the shocking brutality of the deaths of these mild women. In each instance the death of his mate liberates the hero to become an outlaw.

The third parallel character adapted from "Michael Kohlhaas" is Martin Luther. After being rebuked by him in a public epistle, Kohlhaas visits the Reformation leader, who then intercedes for Kohlhaas. But Luther refuses to give him Holy Communion, thus ultimately denying his innocence in religious terms. His *Ragtime* counterpart is Booker T. Washington. Like the Luther who condemned the Peasant Revolt, Washington represents in this novel the conservative reformer, who seeks change within the traditional order of society or institutionalized religion. And indeed the historical Booker T. Washington

> arose as essentially the leader not of one race, but of two— a compromise between the South, the North, and the Negro. Naturally the Negros resented, at first bitterly, signs of compromise which surrendered their civil and political rights, even though this was to be exchanged for larger chances of economic development. Mr. Washington represents in Negro thought the old attitude of adjustment and submission.[6]

Despite the fact that Washington was born twenty-five years after David Walker's death, in *Ragtime* the spirit of David Walker, the revolutionary, alive in Coalhouse, can confront the spirit of Booker T. Washington, the moderate. Both Luther and Washington use virtually the same argument, the same rhetoric:

Luther:

> Kohlhaas, you who say you are sent to wield the sword of justice, what are you doing, presumptuous man, in the madness of your blind fury, you who are yourself filled with injustice from head to foot? You who lead men astray with this declaration full of untruth and cunning . . . (113-42)

Washington:

> I look about me and smell the sweat of rage, the impecunious rebellion of wild unthinking youth . . . What injustice done you, what loss you've suffered, can justify the doom you have led them into, these reckless youths? (237)

Both Kohlhaas and Walker are chastened by the words addressed to them. The radical thinkers show respect and even reverence for their Establishment leaders: Kohlhaas leaves his interview with Luther "both hands to his breast with an expression of painful emotion" (121-49) and Coalhouse Walker is moved to "tears of emotion" (238) by the disapproval of Washington. Like Luther, Washington offers to intercede. But there can be no real resolution. Neither spiritual leader, neither Luther nor Washington, can sanction an activist ideology.

In both works the figure of Kohlhaas-Coalhouse is given grandly heroic proportions. Besides calling him "one of the most upright and at the same time most terrible men of his day,' (81-9) Kleist changes the name of the historical Kohlhase— Hans—to Michael, in order to associate him with the sword-carrying Archangel Michael. Doctorow's hero, too, is set apart from other men. When Father first meets him, he reflects "that Coalhouse Walker Jr. didn't know he was a Negro." (134) Not only is his bearing proud, his performance of Scott Joplin's ragtime music has a hypnotic effect similar to Tamino's flute playing in *The Magic Flute*. Instead of bewitching animals, Coalhouse's music entrances the family:

> There seemed to be no other possibilities for life than those deliniated in the music. (132) The boy perceived it as light touching various places in space, accumulating in intricate patterns until the entire room was made to glow with its own being. (133)

These words describe an apotheosis. As he has converted all the elements of "Michael Kohlhaas" discussed thus far into the context of black culture, so too Doctorow translates those ambiguously divine overtones of Michael Kohlhaas as hero into a black equivalent. The black's ragtime music is elevated to a kind of mystical expression, and its performer, Walker, is its instrument. At the risk of going too far, we may also note that the picture of a smiling Coalhouse printed in newspapers during his notoriety shows "a circle around his head" (187)—like a halo?

There is also a stylistic affinity which deserves mention, though I do not feel it is so great as to warrant more than that. Kleist's narrative voice is low-keyed, seemingly uninvolved, allowing external signs to reveal internal states. Doctorow's style, too, is detached, cool, and intently observant. In Kleist there is an often unnerving combination of matter-of-fact tone and extreme situation. For example, the description of Lisbeth's return:

> only a few days later Sternbald entered the courtyard again, leading the wagon at a walk, inside of which the horse dealer's wife lay prostrate with a dangerous contusion of the chest. (102-29)

Thus we first learn of the tragic mishap, caught unprepared by the quotidian content of the first half of the sentence. With similar restraint, Doctorow describes one of Walker's attacks:

> One of the policemen had the presence of mind to drop to the ground. The other just stood open-mouthed as the raiders efficiently formed a line, like a firing squad, and upon signal fired their weapons in unison. The blast killed the standing policeman and shattered the windowpanes of the firehouse doors. (185)

Here the death of a policeman is juxtaposed with the shattering of glass, in a similar disproportion.

With its very short, clear sentences, Doctorow's book is highly readable, hard to put down. But if we may use his own metaphor, it is much like ragtime music, immensely engaging, but slightly mechanical and ultimately lightweight. The directness and dryness of Kleist's style are certainly reproduced in Doctorow's, but he lacks Kleist's sonority, density, complexity. Likewise, or more precisely as a consequence, Doctorow in his adaptation makes Kleist's relentlessly involuted world less disturbing. Three examples can clarify this process of simplification.

Both Kohlhaas and Walker issue several manifestos demanding justice. Although it is for both men at best a secondary objective, the beginnings of a new world order are lodged in these protests. Both outlaws establish separate societies of their own, in the Romantic tradition of Robin Hood and Karl Moor. Kohlhaas' manifestos urge all Christians to take up arms against Tronka; one is issued from the castle of Lützen, in which he has established himself:

> He summoned the people to join him to build a better order of things. With a kind of madness, the manifesto was signed: "Done at the Seat of Our Provisional World Government, the Chief Castle at Lützen." (113-41)

Instead of posting them, Walker sends his communications to the newspapers. He signs his second letter *"Coalhouse Walker, President, Provisional American Government."* (200) In *Ragtime*, an "alienist" (200) suggests that Walker's declaration shows signs of incipient madness. In Kleist the narrating voice encompasses this possibility. Doctorow is more of a partisan. Indeed, one reviewer feels that his depiction of the revolutionary could be called "left wing pastoral."[7] Not only is Kleist's hero not entirely pure in his motives, we are also shown the corruption within Kohlhaas' own band: his "lieutenant" Nagelschmidt, especially, perverts Kohlhaas' original idealistic aim, using his cause merely as an excuse to plunder. Doctorow gives us no parallel figure to Nagelschmidt. Walker is always "stern and dignified,"[8] and his men are a group of devoted and disciplined members. They think of themselves collectively as "Coalhouse," and their exuberance at their successes is never tainted by the opportunism of Kohlhaas' followers.

Secondly, the central issue itself is simplified. Both heroes seek absolute justice. Kohlhaas meets the resistance of a human world all too relative, compromising, always gray, never black or white. His goal is incommensurate with human society. Man can attain absolute justice, but does so at the cost of his life.

Walker, too, is pursuing absolute justice. To all who ask he insists that it is and can be nothing else but "the return of the Model T in exactly the same condition as when the firehorses had been driven across his path." (155) And like Kohlhaas, Walker meets a world of corruption, delays, deliberate passive aggressive behavior of officials, and technicalities of the law. (154) But when Kohlhaas surrenders, it is only the beginning of an increasingly confusing set of ramifications. We see him more and more as a victim of political intrigue: the power struggle between Saxony and Brandenburg, Nagelschmidt's proposal for escape, the Electors' future, knowledge borne by Kohlhaas, and finally the involvement of the Holy Roman Empire itself. In the process, right and wrong get hopelessly confused.

Walker remains much more a representative of the black cause, and a martyr to it. We have in *Ragtime* revolutionaries of different stamp, the Marxist Emma Goldman, the Mexican Emiliano Zapata. Walker is *Ragtime's* revolutionary against racism. He is the militant black before his time, a Black Panther in a Model T. And Walker thinks of himself in these terms, as a "servant of his color." (238) His insistence on "the truth of our manhood and the respect it demands" (238) exists within the context of a struggle against American racism. But Kohlhaas' struggle is universal. Where Walker was the president of the provisional American government, Kohlhaas claims to represent the World.

Both Kleist and Doctorow are writing quasi-historical fiction. Both writers add the element of chance or coincidence to their historical accounts. Here we have the third area of simplification in *Ragtime*.

Kleist adds to the original history of Hans Kohlhase the episode of a gypsy woman, who claims to know the future fortunes of the Electors of Saxony and Brandenburg. By coincidence, it is to Michael Kohlhaas that she gives the Saxon Elector's fate, written on a piece of paper. By coincidence, the Elector later meets Kohlhaas in a wood and learns of the first coincidence. Still later, when someone is to impersonate the gypsy in order to regain the secret paper from Kohlhaas, the woman herself is chosen. A further coincidence is her resemblance to Lisbeth and her sharing of this name. To Kohlhaas before his execution she says not farewell, but "Auf Wiedersehen," suggesting a meeting beyond the grave. There is also a host of minor unforeseen developments in the plot. All these coincidences give an otherworldly, transcending dimension to the otherwise politically explicable events. Indeed, in "Michael Kohlhaas" coincidence might be better termed fate. The roebuck comes to the electors like Birnam Wood to

Dunsinane. The universality of Kleist's novella, mentioned above, is deepened by this use of supernatural coincidence.

Doctorow also shares Kleist's predilection for coincidence; indeed, he makes of coincidence the basic structure of his book, its motivating force. But Doctorow's love of coincidence is more playful. It is a device to allow historical personalities to meet each other, and it is a fruitful one. It gives the past a new kind of accessibility. In this variation of the historical novel, the sense of truth derives not from a faithful evocation of recorded historical events, but rather from fictional manipulation of historical characters, from "ragging history"[9] to capture the spirit of an age. But Doctorow does not use coincidence to establish that precarious, confusing world of Kleist's, where supernatural forces impinge on man's will. In his player piano world, coincidence thrusts one character upon another, but it does not threaten or confuse. No otherworldly dimension confounds events.

The artistic result of these two essential simplifications, of the fact that Doctorow makes Kleist's universal tale specific, and his transcendental tale immanent, is the transformation of Kleist's tragic novella into a melodramatic episode.

By analyzing this transformation, I do not wish to suggest any failure on Doctorow's part. His is, I feel, a successful adaptation. If Doctorow owes to Kleist what is perhaps the most memorable action of the book, he has made it work there. The nineteenth-century tale is convincing in its new clothes. By restricting the action, by emphasizing its social critical aspect, Doctorow is interpreting the novella from his particular twentieth century American perspective, giving one modern instance of the universality of "Michael Kohlhaas." Bertolt Brecht once wrote that "copying is an art which the master must dominate. He must handle it skillfully, for the sole reason that otherwise he could produce nothing worth copying in its turn."[10] In bringing Michael Kohlhaas to New York, Doctorow has shown himself a master of this art.

NOTES

1. See *National Review,* August, 1975; *New York Review of Books,* August 7, 1975; *The New Yorker,* July 28, 1975; *Saturday Review,* July 26, 1975; *Time,* July 14, 1975.
2. All numbers following quotations from *Ragtime* refer to E.L. Doctorow, *Ragtime.* (New York, 1974).
3. Lerone Bennet, Jr., *Confrontation: Black and White.* (Chicago, 1965) p. 58.
4. *Ibid.*
5. Quotations from "Michael Kohlhaas" are taken from Kleist, *Die Marquise von O . . . and Other Stories,* Martin Greenberg, trans. (New York, 1962). The first

number in parentheses refers to this book. The second number refers to the German text: Kleist, *Sämtliche Werke und Briefe*, Ed. Sembdner, *(München, 1961)*.
6. *Negro Social and Political Though 1850-1920*, Ed. Howard Brotz, (New York, 1966) p. 513.
7. Jeffrey Hart, *National Review*, (August, 1975).
8. Roger Sale, *New York Review of Books*, (August 7, 1975).
9. *The New Yorker*, (July 28, 1975).
10. Bertolt Brecht, *Theaterarbeit*, quoted in Lotte Eisner, *The Haunted Screen*. (Berkeley, 1965) p. 349.

E. L. Doctorow's *Ragtime*: Kleist Revisited

ROBERT E. HELBLING
University of Utah

Upon the publication of Doctorow's novel *Ragtime*,[1] American critics and journalists were quick to praise the author's bold and clever portrayal of Americana in the Ragtime era.[2] It is startling to discover that at least one third of the book—the Coalhouse Walker episode—is an adaptation of "Michael Kohlhaas," Heinrich von Kleist's masterful novella. Doctorow himself acknowledged his indebtedness to Kleist,[3] and the journalistic critics cursorily mentioned it. But none of the reviewers has paid close attention to Coalhouse Walker's literary ancestry or the tour de force needed to convert the brooding depth and singleminded intensity of Kleist's tale into a work marked by a light ironic touch.[4] One wonders, of course, what the affinities and contrasts are between two writers of such divergent sensibilities as Kleist and Doctorow and belonging to such different literary epochs as the early nineteenth century in Germany and the late twentieth century in America. But right at the outset, the curious literary historian must admit that the panorama of problems explored by Kleist and his style of writing have proved fascinating to many succeeding generations—though not greatly to his contemporaries—and are again of particular interest to our own social and literary consciousness.

A brief search into Coalhouse Walker's literary roots will disclose some of these problems and also illustrate the parodic transformation of a masterwork almost two hundred years old which Doctorow brought off in what he calls "chronicle fiction," a blend of journalism, fiction, and mythologizing history. The Coalhouse story, moreover, gradually moves to the center stage of Doctorow's novel and unravels according to a compelling inner drive. The rest of the narrative is only loosely held together by a principle of coincidence and mere juxtaposition of events, except for a central philosophic vision expressed by the narrator that lends the disparate elements at least a semblance of intellectual unity.

A short synopsis of Kleist's "Michael Kohlhaas" will help to recall the major events in that complex tale and serve as a starting point for comparison between the two works under discussion.

Coalhouse Walker's predecessor is a sixteenth century horsedealer who, one day, is harassed by a certain Junker von Tronka with unheard-of transit formalities at the Saxon-Brandenburgian border, which he is not prepared to meet. Leaving a team of black horses and a servant behind as security, he seeks redress with various authorities, but, though vaguely listened to, he is treated as a thin-skinned trouble-maker. Meanwhile, his horses and servant are mistreated on the Junker's estate to the point of suffering the indignity of being housed in a pigsty. His wife Elisabeth naively tries to intervene on her husband's behalf before the ruler of the land but is wounded in the attempt by an overzealous guard and dies. Kohlhaas assembles a band of marauders and embarks upon a savage guerrilla-warfare in the Saxon country side. But the culprit, von Tronka, a weak and self-indulgent individual despised by his own peers, eludes him. Kohlhaas' wrath, now directed against the Saxon Elector as the embodiment of a corrupt justice, reaches megolamaniac dimensions. From his hideout he issues a manifesto, calling himself "a viceroy of the Archangel Michael, come to punish with fire and sword, for the wickedness into which the whole world was sunk, all those who should take the side of the Junker in this quarrel."[5] Martin Luther, the erstwhile firebrand, now firmly entrenched in the "establishment," calls him to Wittenberg and remonstrates with the "impious and terrible man."[6] Yet Luther relents and arranges for safepassage for Kohlhaas to Dresden so that his legal suit against von Tronka may take place, seeing that popular sentiment is on Kohlhaas' side and the smoldering revolutionary feeling might erupt into a general uprising any day. After many political maneuvers involving Saxony, Brandenburg, and the Imperial Court, Kohlhaas wins his suit against von Tronka hands down. His antagonist receives a prison term and is forced to restore the black horses to their former health. Kohlhaas himself must pay for the violence of his autonomous justice with his life. But before we reach the end of the novella, Kleist introduces an episode of an occult sort. In a lengthy flashback, we are told that after his wife's death a gypsy woman with a surprising resemblance to the dead Elisabeth, handed him in the presence of the Elector a capsule containing an apparently sinister prophecy about the future of the House of Saxony. In subsequent furtive appearances she warns Kohlhaas of his excesses, yet abets his revenge upon the Saxon Elector. Before he is led to the scaffold, Kohlhaas swallows the paper in the capsule under the very eyes of the distraught ruler, who falls prey to a languorous illness.

It is easy to detect parallels and modifications of this plot in Doctorow's novel: the "joke" played by the truculent fire chief, Willie Conklin, on the proud but unsuspecting Coalhouse; the "desecratin' " of the horse-powered

Model T;[7] Sarah's well-meant but misguided intervention and her pathetic death as a result of "police brutality;" the murderous acts of Coalhouse's band of urban guerrillas; his frustrated search for the elusive Conklin and stubborn pursuit of legal satisfaction. Equally obvious are his megalomaniac pretense in calling himself "President, Provisional American Government"[8] and his meeting with Booker T. Washington, the erstwhile reformer and elder statesman who calls him a "monstrous man" and is apprehensive about the social and racial upheaval that Coalhouse's revolt might cause, were it to go unchecked. Less obvious perhaps is the role of Pierpont Morgan as a replica of the Saxon Elector.[9] Though hardly responsible for the injustice done to the hero, Pierpont Morgan becomes, in Coalhouse's mind, the very symbol of the powers that be and their diffidence toward his plight. And when Doctorow dwells on Morgan's failing health and death, he may do so in analogy to the languorous sickness that befalls the Saxon Elector, even though Morgan's demise is not directly caused by Coalhouse's actions. Generally speaking, what Doctorow discerned in Kleist's novella is the theme of a world pervaded by bureaucratic indifference and institutionalized injustice unleashing the demons of fear, resentment, and personal violence—a perennially modern topic.

There are analogies of a more tenuous kind. The occult, for instance, plays a role in both works. In Kleist's novella it is directly connected with the hero's career through the gypsy episode; in Doctorow's, it is merely an element in the society surrounding Coalhouse. It is exemplified in Houdini's necrophiliac obsessions, but also in J. P. Morgan's belief in reincarnation and the extraordinary resemblance he detects between Henry Ford and the Pharaoh Seti I, described in two of the wittiest chapters in the book. One can go even farther and speculate that Coalhouse's persistent wooing of the taciturn and enigmatic Sarah after the fact of pregnancy has its counterpart in Kleist's "Marquise of O ...," where the hero must go through a long courtship to gain the affection of the Marquise after he has got her with child and even married her. And, finally, the survival of the illegitimate child, cared for by foster parents, bears a striking resemblance to the end of Kleist's masterful and violent novella "The Earthquake in Chile," in which human prejudice wreaks as much havoc as a natural catastrophe.

More significant and subtle, however, than these topical parallels are the character portrayal of the hero, the underlying psychology and philosophy that inform both works, certain stylistic qualities, and some affinities and contrasts in the narrative "viewpoint."

In the opening sentence of his novella, famous in German literary criticism for its directness, Kleist states that Kohlhaas was "one of the most upright and at the same time one of the most terrible men of his day."[10] He does not, however, engage in a probing psychological analysis of his hero's ambivalent state of mind, but lets his demeanor speak for itself and endows him with an aura of superiority that challenges the feudal society around him. There is a self-sufficiency and a correctness of manner in his person that contrast with the self-indulgence and insolence of the Junker and his peers, who seem not only irked by his regal bearing but also by his ownership of a team of healthy, shiny horses, status symbols in their society. Though he remains outwardly unruffled, there is a barely contained, consuming anger in Kohlhaas. After having made some legal inquiries, he returns to Tronka Castle, Kleist tells us cryptically, "with no more bitterness in his heart *than was inspired by the ordinary distress of the world.*"[11]

Coalhouse Walker in Doctorow's novel is introduced in a similar fashion. Although the setting is markedly different, the underlying psychology is the same. Coalhouse not only has a correctness of manner and dress about him, bordering on swagger, but also masters a form of superior speech that irks the white society around him and grates on the nerves of the grudgingly tolerant Father. His imitation of the more civilized mores of white society trembles on the verge of parody with its implied ridicule. His deportment seems to suggest that he is what they aspire to be. Certainly, his very bearing holds a mirror up to them, as does Kohlhaas' demeanor to the feudal lord and his retinue that harrass him. Moreover, Coalhouse Walker is the owner of a shiny Model T, a coveted status symbol in white society, that arouses the envy of Willie Conklin and his band of ruffians. Though remaining outwardly calm, Coalhouse's stubborn refusal to bow to mere force betrays his self-reliance, and, earlier, it is made clear that his self-control barely holds in check an inner energy that erupts as he subjects the piano to his will in thumping ragtime rhythms. Right from the outset we are made to feel that his self-control is the obverse of an inner drive that contains the seed of revolt.

There is an absolutist urge in both which in Kleist's hero takes on quasi-metaphysical dimensions epitomized in his claim to be the viceroy of the Archangel Michael, while Coalhouse, to be sure, remains more down to earth in proclaiming himself President of the Provisional American Government. But both launch their open revolt after their women have fallen victims to the anonymous violence of the world. There is also an ambiguity of purpose in the two that accounts for their being at once both upright and "terrible" or "monstrous." Their demand for personal legal satisfaction out of an aggrieved sense of justice and personal hurt is soon overshadowed by their claim to restore order in the world. Both become more atrocious as they become more convinced of their own righteousness. Kleist knew that it is not far from a sense of setting things aright to messianic pretense. And Doctorow obviously perceives that this all too human tendency is one of the hallmarks of our own age. Through quite audible author intervention he puts the very perceptive recognition of the "violence underlying all principle"[12] into Sarah's naive mind. On the more jocular side, he has Mother's Younger Brother break out impatiently into the disarming exclamation hurled at Coalhouse: "Is the goddamn Ford your justice?"[13]—a flippant remark that would be unthinkable in Kleist's more solemn fiction. Kleist rather states that his hero suffers from a peculiar *Verrückung*, madness. In German, the pejorative *Verrückung* is etymologically close to the mystic *Entrückung*, transfiguration. Irony ensues, for Kohlhaas has indeed been transfigured but rather in the sense of grotesque distortion. Moreover, in his edict Kohlhaas declares that he has come "to punish ... for the wickedness into which the whole world has sunk, all those who should take the side of the Junker...."[14] Both Kohlhaas and Coalhouse obviously universalize their legal dispute and wish "to claim public justice for [themselves],"[15] as Kleist remarks rather ambiguously in another place.

In both works, then, the character of the hero is only sketched in, though in bold strokes, and must be inferred from his extraordinary actions. The two writers do not dwell on their heroes' motives—on character analysis—but at strategic junctures insert reflective passages that endow their fiction with a central vision of a rather philosophic kind. Kleist has Kohlhaas muse about the "ordinary distress," the "fragile constitution," or the "monstrous disorder" of the world, epithets often encountered in his prose writings, which express a tragic awareness of the impermanence of all things, perhaps also the realization that in a world of unrelieved anguish small causes may have enormous effects—a bad joke played by a bunch of ruffians leads to destructive social upheaval. While in both works reflective statements are strewn here and there, Doctorow, in addition, reserves a special chapter for the precocious philosophic musings of the "boy," which strengthens the impression that the boy, now grown up, may be the anonymous narrator, for his voice, recorded in that chapter, sets the tone for the rest of the book. Like Kleist's hero, the boy is intensely aware of "the instability of both things and people," an experience which he translates into a series of striking analogies and images. The evanescence of life is fleetingly captured in moving pictures. Inversely, in an attempt to infuse some stability into the world of impermanence he perceives, the boy plays the same record on the Victrola over and over again, "as if to test the endurance of a duplicated event."[17] Memorable is the description of the ever changing criss-cross patterns of the tracks made by skaters in the ice, a vivid image of the coincidences that forever change the destinies of his characters "in an endless process of dissatisfaction."[18]

Doctorow goes even further in the philosophic reflections he projects into the boy's mind. He engages upon mildly existentialist considerations on the instability or indeterminacy of the human person and his consciousness of self. Starting with Ovid's *Metamorphoses* with which the grandfather stirs up the youngster's imagination, Doctorow has him gaze at himself in a mirror "until there were two selves facing one another" and "He had the dizzying feeling of separating from himself endlessly."[19] The episode, suggesting not only the predilection of some phenomenologists for mirror analogies in their attempts to describe the processes of human consciousness, also alludes to the existentialist dictum that the consciousness of self we are aware of is not identical or immediately congruent with our awareness *per se*. There is a separation or temporal lag between the "me" and the "I." More important to Doctorow's work, this existentialist notion, linked as it is in the boy's mind with the suggestion coming from Ovid's *Metamorphoses* that "everything in the world could as easily be something else,"[20] presages the duality of all the memorable characters that wander through the novel. Pierpont Morgan is as much a secretive occultist as he is a resolute exploiter of men. The domesticated Mother is gradually metamorphosed into an emancipated woman; the withdrawn Younger Brother into a blatant revolutionary. Coalhouse himself, the imitator of the life style of the "establishment," becomes its implacable enemy. The shy Sarah is suddenly capable of decisive, though misdirected, action. Houdini, the brash exhibitionist, is a scared mama's boy. They are this but they are also that, repeating in many variations the theme of duality running through Kleist's novella and announced in his terse opening sentence. Just as the little boy peering into the mirror and becoming increasingly aware of the cleavage in his consciousness, they remain partially an enigma to themselves and to us, the readers. Only Houdini and Pierpont Morgan are subjected to some tentative and rather hilarious psychoanalytic considerations. Houdini's obsession to have himself locked up in confined spaces is presented as so many attempts to get back to his mother's womb the hard way, and Pierpont Morgan's strawberry nose seems to have something to do with his feeling of isolation from the common run of men. The narrator's ironic stance toward psychoanalytic theories transpires early in the novel in his bemused portrayal of Freud's visit to the States. Rather than psychological canons, it is indeed the boy's philosophic musings that provide the clue to the narrator's vision of reality: things and men are not what they appear to be at any given moment; they can "as easily be something else;" all is flux. This Heraclitian view of reality is akin to Kleist's acute sense of the ambivalence of all things human and his general distrust of the stability of the world of appearances. And it may indeed be quite apposite in a work of chronical fiction that is supposed to record the ever-changing flux of human history.

Beyond the affinities in the two writers' philosophic outlook, it is tempting to see even in their widely differing narrative techniques certain germane intentions. By limiting themselves to reporting the manifestly "objective," both renounce to plumb the depths of the characters' consciousness, as though to suggest the impossibility of faithfully recreating subjective inner experience. The forward-pressing narrative of chronicle fiction does not lend itself to the kind of psychological introspection which, at its extreme, is embodied in the stream-of-consciousness novel. Chronicle fiction mirrors action rather than inner states of perception and requires a dynamic rather than contemplative narrative style. Doctorow uses an effective syntactic device—the omission of quotation marks around direct discourse—to accelerate the flow of his narrative. This stratagem, perhaps borrowed from certain stylish contemporary novels, allows him to merge the speakers in the story with the narrator of the story. Through the uninterrupted narrative line, what is said as much as what is done becomes part of history in the making.

Kleist obtains similar effects by using indirect discourse with obsessive frequency, a practice that elicited both the dismay and admiration of Thomas Mann. Referring to a symptomatic sentence in "The Marquise of O . . . ," he exclaimed: "Kleist succeeds in developing an indirect discourse without resorting to a single full stop: in this discourse we find no less than thirteen dependent clauses introduced by *that* and, at the end, a 'briefly, in such a manner . . .'—which, however, fails to pull the sentence up short, but instead gives rise to yet another *that* clause!"[21] The impression gained from such excessive use of indirect discourse is that the speaker has become a reporter of events in his own right and assumed some of the functions of the narrator of the story. Narrative and dialogue flow together.

The similarities end there. Syntactically, the prose of the two writers is vastly different. Kleist is known for the Germanic complexity of his syntax with its many subordinate clauses and appositions; while Doctorow uses a modern idiom of crisp independent sentences only occasionally relieved by longer, more leisurely periods. Conceivably, both writers attempt, by opposite means to be sure, to render immediate an onrush of thought, impressions and events. But, obviously, they represent two literary traditions almost two hundred years apart. It is a long way, after all, from the periodic phrases of early nineteenth century writers to the staccato style of the Hemingway generation. Nonetheless, the two styles reveal entirely different personal sensibilities.

The convolutions of Kleist's sentences, which follow a rigorous syntactic pattern, not only express effectively the involutions of political maneuvers and the meandering of the legal process; they also reflect the enmeshing of private and public concerns that leads to Kohlhaas' dramatic end in accord with that strenuous internal logic which impels the whole narrative. In Doctorow's novel events are more often juxtaposed than interlinked, at times they just happen. Chance happenings have rather the character of mere fortuitous accidents than the force of tragic incidents. This is especially true of the epic frame which surrounds the Coalhouse tale and is in part designed to lend his sedition greater social significance. In "Michael

Kohlhaas" the epic broadness of the events grows organically out of the enormity of the hero's revolt. No frame of subsidiary stories is needed.

Even if we were not acquainted with Kleist's existential problems that led to his bizarre suicide, the complex syntax of his sentences, which tries to bring order into chaos, suggests that he is desperately attached to the possibility of an ordered world and agonizes over its defects. This tension releases narrative energy which sustains his periodic style and makes him pursue a thought through a syntactical maze with singular tenacity. Conversely, Doctorow's zippily written novel, the crisp sentences that merrily jump from one observation to another, rather keep us at an ironic distance and suggest the authorial stance of a depoliticized revolutionary who is highly amused by the spectacles of madness in the world.[22] This effect is heightened by the narrator's camera technique. We follow a character until he encounters in person or reference another and the narrative flows off in a different direction. But what is more, Doctorow fastens his attention on the bizarre and delineates his characters in a caricatural, two-dimensional way. Thereby Coalhouse Walker's social revolt becomes an eccentricity among so many eccentricities.

After we have participated in Evelyn Nesbit's sensational trial, her abortive attempt at social involvement, her husband's grotesque antics in prison, Houdini's capers, Father's search for exotic experience culminating in shattering observations of Eskimo sexuality; after we have seen Freud and Jung skitter through the tunnel of love in an amusement park, become acquainted with Goldman's zany entourage, witnessed Tateh's metamorphosis from Jewish moralist to whacky film producer and been privy to J.P. Morgan's vigil in an Egyptian pyramid, well, we cannot quite take seriously Coalhouse's extraordinary revolt. The jocular treatment of most episodes and the buffooneries invest even the grimness of Coalhouse's revenge with an element of the mock serious. And the affectations of his followers—their slavish imitation of their master's sartorial consciousness and social mannerisms—suggest the rigid code and the mock ceremonials of a motorcycle gang. Finally, the taciturn Younger Brother, the explosives' maniac, who joins the band from despair after his torrid affair with Evelyn Nesbit has come to a sudden end, is another caricature of a would-be social revolutionary. It is as if the "demons" that populate Dostoevsky's novel of nineteenth century revolutionary mentality had become the "crazies" of the late sixties and early seventies of our own century.

In Doctorow's defense one must admit that the melioristic zeal of some modern terrorists has indeed some affinity in form and spirit with the insurgency of Coalhouse and his disciples. It may even be conceded that Doctorow is a moralist who knows that one way of bringing the contemporary civilization to a recognition of its follies and frustrations is through the kind of critical distance which is created by a caricatural, even grotesque, distortion of reality. More direct remonstrations might fall on deaf or annoyed ears. But the edge of his social critique is blunted precisely because be portrays his revolutionaries with caricatural archness and also surveys with curiosity the aesthetic surface of the Ragtime era. Instead of indignation about social injustice, what is created in the reader is rather a feeling of ironic bemusement about human follies and a nostalgic regret about a bygone age throbbing with scandal and excitement.

The tragic sentiment called forth by Kleist's fiction is no doubt much greater. What is indeed at stake is the perennial question of justice in all its personal, social, and even metaphysical ramifications. The ambivalence of human emotions, the juridical morass that threatens to engulf the law, the very "fragile constitution of the world" are under scrutiny, though the dénouement is at best a precarious balance between contending values. The differing portrayal of the hero's end in the two works puts into sharp focus the contrast in the authors' stance. The siege of the J. P. Morgan Library attracts a crowd of curious folk—no friends—and Coalhouse is gunned down as a common criminal would be. This is a far cry from the hero's end in Kleist's novella. As he ascends the scaffold, he is surrounded by friends and children and, mourned by the populace assembled in the town square, he goes to his death, whereupon his two sons are knighted in recognition of their father's desperate fight for justice. Kleist is obviously careful to suggest that the society around Kohlhaas clearly perceived in his uneven struggle with the "establishment" the value for which he paid with his life, namely the inviolability of his *persona* or the dignity of the individual in general, although he may have fought for the right ideal with the wrong means.

No doubt, the emotional impact of Kleist's fiction with its sudden dramatic end is greater and at the same time more thought provoking. Yet the editorial reflections which both authors infuse into their narratives are less obtrusive in Kleist's text than in Doctorow's, where at times, he quite ostensibly ventriloquizes through his characters. Kleist, for instance, shows Kohlhaas standing in front of Luther's proclamation in all his *Verderblichkeit*, i.e. perniciousness or corruptibility.[23] Doctorow puts the remark about "the self-delusion of all those who oppress humanity,"[24] into Younger Brother's mouth when the latter taunts his brother-in-law, to mention only one example.

One must concede, nonetheless, that for good reasons the narrator in Doctorow's fiction is much more prominent than in Kleist's. He is a reflective consciousness and an eloquent commentator on events. There is no doubt, parenthetically, that the little boy *is* the narrator; on the second-to-last page Doctorow slips in very cagily: "Poor Father, *I* see his final exploration,"[25] to give us more than just a hint! If, otherwise he does not let his narrator speak from the "*I*" perspective, he does so advisedly, for then the narrator's viewpoint would be too narrow for the broad panoramic frame of the whole novel. The narrator of such a many-faceted fictionalized chronicle of an age needs temporal distance from himself and the events he depicts. The mirror metaphor discussed earlier may not only be an existentialist ploy but also a device to suggest the split consciousness of the narrator: he was in the midst of things but now has a historic vision that goes beyond his earlier experience of his own self and of events. And so he can look with the same bemused irony at Coalhouse's dramatic career as he does at other happenings.

Since Kleist's novella has no frame in other major episodes, the narrator is completely absorbed by the hero's destiny and all but disappears behind the story. His viewpoint is therefore more unified and corresponds to the greater density and anxiety of Kleist's fiction. "Michael Kohlhaas" abruptly ends with the execution of the eponymous hero, Doctorow's novel trails off into faraway regions as we follow the destinies of his other characters. Younger Brother's revolutionary career and violent end repeat in a minor key Coalhouse's own fate, similar to the variations of a ragtime melody invented by a skillful improviser. No doubt, the Coalhouse tale in Doctorow's novel is itself a skillful variation on the theme of Kleist's "Michael Kohlhaas," a jazzed-up version, to be sure. But, then, jazzed-up Bach is not Bach and Kleist in "ragtime" is not Kleist. If the genius of another era cannot be duplicated, like a melody on the Victrola, with skill and proper imagination it can at least be deftly imitated. Assuredly, *Ragtime* is a stylish novel, full of ingenious and intelligent entertainment, while "Michael Kohlhaas"remains a work of dramatic power with few equals in world literature.

NOTES

1. E.L. Doctorow, *Ragtime* (New York: Random House, 1974, 1975).
2. Especially complimentary were Stanley Kauffman in *Saturday Review*, Walter Clemons in *Newsweek* and Hilton Kramer in *Commentary*; While British critics such as Russel Davies in *TLS* and Jonathan Raban in *Encounter* denounced the author's allegedly superficial sensibilities and the affectations of his style.
3. A reference to Kleist can be found in the advance publicity brochure on *Ragtime* circulated by the publisher.
4. It was only in November 1977 at the International Kleist Conference at Hofstra University that my attention was drawn to a brief but informative article by Prof. Walter L. Knorr "Doctorow and Kleist: "Kohlhaas" in *Ragtime*," in *Modern Fiction Studies*, Summer 1976, vol. 22, no. 2. My own occupation with the topic goes back to April 1976 when E.L. Doctorow, then a Visiting Professor at the University of Utah, read several passages from the ms. of *Ragtime* and I was struck by the similarities to the plot in Kleist's "Kohlhaas."

5. Heinrich von Kleist, "Michael Kohlhaas" in *The Marquise of O . . . and Other Stories*, transl. Martin Greenberg (New York: Criterion Books, 1960), p. 121, hereafter referred to as Greenberg.
6. Greenberg, p. 125.
7. Doctorow engages in an ironic wordgame with "defecatin,' " *Ragtime*, pp. 148-149, recalling perhaps the indignities Kohlhaas' horses must suffer in the pigsty at von Tronka's castle.
8. *Ragtime*, p. 237.
9. Doctorow gives us nevertheless a hint: when Coalhouse flings a tankard containing a message from the J.P. Morgan Library onto the street below, the curator recognizes it as a silver stein that once "had belonged to Frederick, the Elector of Saxony," *Ragtime*, p. 231.
10. Greenberg, p. 87.
11. Ibid., p. 92. (my italics)
12. *Ragtime*, p. 157.
13. Ibid., p. 246.
14. Greenberg, loc. cit.
15. My own translation (Greenberg translates the phrase "die öffentliche Gerechtigkeit für sich aufzufordern" somewhat lamely as "to seek justice at the law," p. 100).
16. *Ragtime*, p. 97.
17. Ibid., p. 98.
18. Ibid., p. 99.
19. Ibid., p. 98.
20. Ibid., p. 97.
21. Thomas Mann, Preface to Greenberg, pp. 14-15.
22. I am indebted for this observation to Prof. Jeffrey L. Sammons of Yale University, who made some other valuable suggestions for this article.
23. This is strangely rendered by Greenberg as "death and destruction," p. 124, in an otherwise skillful translation.
24. *Ragtime*, p. 250.
25. Ibid., p. 269.

An Echo of Kafka in Kleist

MARK HARMAN
Dartmouth College

An echo of Kafka in Kleist: If the title of this paper sounds paradoxical, it is because we usually listen to later writers for "echoes" of earlier ones. We then give substance to these "echoes" by examining possible sources, or by studying the formative influences on the later writer. Underlying this one-sided study of influence is a conception of literary history which exalts the past but ignores our own role as readers. I prefer the more dynamic model developed by the theorist Hans Robert Jauss which identifies the evolving perceptual horizon of the reading public as a dominant force in literary history.[1] We readers help shape the course of literary history. If the giants of the past become anemic classics, it is we who are responsible. As twentieth-century readers of Kleist, our vital task is to preserve the provocation of his genius.

Kafka's obsession with Kleist offers the most compelling evidence for an intellectual and artistic affinity between the two writers.[2] Kafka's encounter with Kleist's prose was intense, yet life-long. In 1911, Kafka wrote on a post-card to Max Brod: "Kleist bläst in mich wie in eine alte Schweinsblase"[3]; the following year, he asked his publisher, Ernst Rowohlt, to print his first book, *Betrachtung*, on the same tinted paper as Kleist's anecdotes;[4] in 1913, he confessed to Felice Bauer that he had already read "Michael Kohlhaas" about ten times[5] and, in the last two years before he died, he was reported to have been capable of reading the "Marquise von O . . . " aloud several times in succession.[6]

One way of approaching the intellectual and artistic affinity between the two writers is to bring our experience with Kafka to bear on Heinrich von Kleist, whom Kafka called his "blood-relative."[7] The Kafka who has radically altered our perception of literary form may help us recognize qualities of Kleist's narrative to which we would otherwise be blind.[8]

The alert eye of Albert Camus spotted the distinctive quality of Kafka's endings: "Tout l'art de Kafka est d'obliger le lecteur à relire."[9] Kafka's endings send us back to the beginning of the text. On a first reading, we often find his endings elusive, yet they somehow suggest a hint of meaning which compels us to reread. I should like to examine the ending of a short Kafka text in order to see how this rereading affects our interpretation. The scrutiny of a characteristic Kafka ending will allow us to recognize that Kleist also forces us to reread, with a similar effect.

"Ein Kommentar (Gibs auf!)"

> Es war sehr früh am Morgen, die Strassen rein und leer, ich ging zum Bahnhof. Als ich eine Turmuhr mit meiner Uhr verglich, sah ich, dass es schon viel später war, als ich geglaubt hatte, ich mußte mich sehr beeilen, der Schrecken über diese Entdeckung ließ mich im Weg unsicher werden, ich kannte mich in dieser Stadt noch nicht sehr gut aus, glücklicherweise war ein Schutzmann in der Nähe, ich lief zu ihm und fragte ihn atemlos nach dem Weg. Er lächelte und sagte: "Von mir willst Du den Weg erfahren?" "Ja", sagte ich, "da ich ihn selbst nicht finden kann". "Gibs auf, gibs auf", sagte er und wandte sich mit einem großen Schwunge ab, so wie Leute, die mit ihrem Lachen allein sein wollen.[10]

At first we are struck by the narrative coherence of the piece. The first person narrator gives a brief sketch of time and place before introducing himself and stating his destination. He is on his way to the railway station. When he glances at the clocktower and begins to hurry, we assume he is late for his train. He sees a policeman and reacts unequivocally: ". . . glücklicherweise war ein Schutzmann in der Nähe . . . ." But his enthusiastic reaction does not tell us anything about the policeman. We realize how totally dependent we are on the narrator's account of events.

Once the policeman answers the narrator's question with yet another question, we can no longer pinpoint the tone of anything that is said. The policeman's use of "du" might express contempt; but it could also be an expression of equality. The "Gibs auf, gibs auf" mystifies us because it offers no clue as to what the man should give up. We eagerly seize the narrator's description of the policeman's final gesture because we expect it to clarify the meaning of the mysterious "Gibs auf, gibs auf."

The narrator compares the policeman's sweeping movement with the parting gesture of people who want to be alone with their laughter. The comparison seems to invite us to draw on everyday psychological observation. We know from experience that people sometimes do want to be left alone with their laughter. But people feel that way for a wide variety of reasons. The final comparison gives us no inkling why the policeman wants to be alone with his laughter. In fact, we do not even know whether the policeman actually laughs. Only by way of comparison does the narrator refer to solitary laughter. The enigmatic "Gibs auf, gibs auf" remains as elusive as ever since the narrator's comparison does not allow us to infer anything about the policeman's consciousness.

We nevertheless sense that the narrator's final comparison does introduce a new element into the text. On rereading the piece, we discover the distinctive characteristic of the ending: in the final comparison, the narrator tries to describe the policeman for the first time. Hitherto he has only told us about his personal reaction to the policeman. Now, as the "Schutzmann" is turning his back, the narrator tries to extract some meaning from the sweeping movement. But we have no way of knowing whether his interpretation of the policeman's gesture is correct or not. All we can say with certainty is that the narrator's interpretation may point toward the meaning of the policeman's oracular command. The narrator himself lapses into silence, leaving us alone with the resonance of solitary laughter and the unresolved enigma of the "Gibs auf, gibs auf."

I should like to look now at a Kleistian anecdote, "Der Griffel Gottes," in the light of Kafka's paradoxical ending.

"Der Griffel Gottes"

In Polen war eine Gräfin von P. . . ., eine bejahrte Dame, die ein sehr bösartiges Leben führte, und besonders ihre Untergebenen, durch ihren Geiz und ihre Grausamkeit, bis auf das Blut quälte. Diese Dame, als sie starb, vermachte einem Kloster, das ihr die Absolution erteilt hatte, ihr Vermögen; wofür ihr das Kloster, auf dem Gottesacker, einen kostbaren, aus Erz gegossenen, Leichenstein setzen liess, auf welchem dieses Umstandes, mit vielem Gepränge, Erwähnung geschehen war. Tags darauf schlug der Blitz, das Erz schmelzend, über den Leichenstein ein, und ließ nichts, als eine Anzahl von Buchstaben stehen, die, zusammen gelesen, also lauteten: *sie ist gerichtet!*—Der Vorfall (die Schriftgelehrten mögen ihn erklären) ist gegründet; der Leichenstein existiert noch, und es leben Männer in dieser Stadt, die ihn samt der besagten Inschrift gesehen.[11]

A wicked Polish aristocrat has died, leaving money to the convent that granted her absolution. The convent erects a tombstone to commemorate her benevolence; but the grandiloquent inscription is altered by a bolt of lightning to read: *sie ist gerichtet*. The altered inscription indicates that the cruel old woman has been punished by her Creator.

But we have not reached the end of the actual text: Separated from the anecdote by a dash, a few lines authenticate the story for the news-hungry readers of the *Berliner Abendblätter*, in which the piece first appeared. Tucked away in these lines is a little phrase in parentheses which makes us question our first reading of the anecdote: "die Schriftgelehrten mögen ihn erklären". We are amazed that it should be necessary to refer the incident to "Schriftgelehrten"[12] since the altered inscription seems to state the verdict. The little phrase about the "Schriftgelehrten" sends us back to the beginning of the anecdote to discover whether we overlooked anything on a first reading.

We begin to ask ourselves why God condemns a woman who has been granted absolution. The phrase about the granting of absolution is suggestively sandwiched in between "Kloster" and "Vermögen":

> Diese Dame, als sie starb, vermachte einem Kloster, das ihr die Absolution erteilt hatte, ihr Vermögen; wofür ihr das Kloster, auf dem Gottesacker, einen kostbaren, aus Erz gegossenen, Leichenstein setzen liess, auf welchem dieses Umstandes, mit vielem Gepränge, Erwähnung geschehen war.

Yet Kleist's syntax does not state whether the old lady bequeathed her fortune to the convent in thanks for the absolution or whether a mercenary transaction was involved. The fact that the convent erects a tombstone to commemorate the old lady's benevolence does not adequately clarify its motives. Could God have condemned the woman because of the mercenary nature of the absolution which she received from the convent? Or does the altered inscription proclaim that earthly absolution cannot redeem a wicked life and that only His final judgment counts?

We can now understand why it might be necessary to have "Schriftgelehrten" unravel the theological implications of the incident. Yet we are excluded from their deliberations and have no means of answering the questions which the little phrase in parentheses at the end of Kleist's anecdote has raised. The "Schriftgelehrten" are as inaccessible to us as the consciousness of the policeman in Kafka's text.

In both Kafka's "Ein Kommentar" and Kleist's "Der Griffel Gottes" the ending points beyond the text into a realm which is fundamentally inaccessible for the reader. The techniques which the two writers use to suggest this inaccessible realm are mutually illuminating even though the narrative texture of the two pieces is very different. In each text a final phrase calls our first reading into question. Kafka's comparison points beyond the perspective of the narrator without allowing the reader to follow. Kleist's little phrase about the "Schriftgelehrten" poses questions which the text does not answer.

"Der Griffel Gottes" is a characteristic example of Kleist's prose. In the metaphysical novella, "Das Erdbeben in Chili," for instance, a pattern emerges which is similar, though far more complex. I cannot do justice here to the intricacy of one of Kleist's narrative masterpieces. Yet I shall try to suggest the contours of the reader's experience of "Das Erdbeben in Chili."

Upon a first reading of "Das Erdbeben in Chili" we want to share Jeronimo and Josephe's belief that the earthquake, which allowed them to escape certain death, was an act of divine intervention.[13] We are not grieved to hear that the archbishop, who ordered that Josephe be tried, dies an ugly death. We prefer to forget that a collapsing gable crushes the abbess who was so sympathetic to Josephe's plight. Yet once we sense that the couple's belief that they are saved is going to lead them into the hands of the mob, we can no longer ignore the evidence which contradicts their interpretation of divine will. We realize that other interpretations of God's will are equally tenable: the preacher, who arouses the crowd's thirst for blood, declares that God is punishing a city which is even more decadent than Sodom and Gomorrah.

Don Fernando does not pause to interpret the ways of God toward man; he leaps into action with the courage of a "göttlicher Held."[14] He cannot rescue Jeronimo and Josephe, whom he befriended after the earthquake, but he defends the two children, Philippe and Juan, against the frenzied mob. He manages to save Philippe, the child of the slain couple, but loses his own child, Juan. At the end of the novella, Kleist has the man of action reflect on what has happened:

> Don Fernando und Donna Elvira nahmen hierauf den kleinen Fremdling zum Pflegesohn an; und wenn Don Fernando Philippen mit Juan verglich, und wie er beide erworben hatte, so war es ihm fast, als müßt er sich freuen.[15]

We have been searching for an alternative explanation of events ever since we became disillusioned with Jeronimo and Josephe's belief that they are saved. So we might reasonably expect Don Fernando's comparison of the two children to reveal his emotional and intellectual reaction to the earthquake and its aftermath. Yet all Kleist gives us is the reference to a joy which Don Fernando nearly thinks he ought to feel. Don Fernando's response is as elusive as the narrator's final comparison in Kafka's "Ein Kommentar."

The function of Kleist's paradoxical ending becomes clear once we recognize the parallels between the anecdote, "Der Griffel Gottes," and the novella, "Das Erdbeben in Chili." On a first reading of the Kleistian anecdote, we interpret the altered inscription as an unambiguous manifestation of divine justice. We then read the little phrase about the "Schriftgelehrten" and discover that the meaning of God's intervention is by no means resolved. On reading "Das Erdbeben in Chili," we first favor the unfortunate couple's interpretation of God's will because we sympathize with their plight. We are then exposed to contradictory evidence and to an equally tenable interpretation of God's will. At the end of the novella, Kleist does not allow Don Fernando to formulate an alternative interpretation of the earthquake and its consequences. The paradoxical formulation of Don Fernando's response merely discloses an ambivalence of thought and feeling.

The ending of "Das Erdbeben in Chili" reveals Don Fernando's uncertainty and makes us uncertain about the possibility of arriving at an interpretation. The ending sends us back to the beginning of the text, fully prepared to appreciate the paradoxes which we overlooked the first time because we were so involved in Jeronimo and Josephe's fate. Kafka's "blood-relative,"[16] Heinrich von Kleist, also leaves us with paradoxes which we can savor but which we cannot get beyond.

NOTES

1. Hans Robert Jauss, *Literaturgeschichte als Provokation*, edition suhrkamp, 418 (Frankfurt/Main: Suhrkamp, 1970), pp. 144-207.
2. Oskar Walzel's perceptive review of "Der Heizer" in 1916 was the earliest attempt to sketch the Kleistian qualities of Kafka's prose, *Berliner Tageblatt*, 6 July 1916; reprinted in Jürgen Born et al., *Kafka-Symposion* (Berlin: Wagenbach, 1965), pp. 140-146. Max Brod was the first to detect a "spiritual proximity" between the lives and works of both writers, *Über Franz Kafka* (Frankfurt/Main: Fischer, 1966), pp. 37-41. Walzel's formal line of inquiry was pursued with interesting results by Helmut Lamprecht, "Mühe und Kunst des Anfangs: Versuch über Kafka und Kleist," *Neue deutsche Hefte*, 1960, 66, pp. 935-940, and Wolfgang Jahn, *Kafkas Roman "Der Verschollene,"* Germanistische Abhandlungen, Band 11 (Stuttgart: Metzler, 1965), pp. 79-83. On the other hand, Hartmut Binder, who examined the beginnings of "Das Erdbeben in Chili" and "Die Verwandlung," concluded that there was little evidence of a stylistic relationship between the two writers, *Motiv und Gestaltung bei Franz Kafka*, Abhandlungen zur Kunst-, Musik- und Literaturgeschichte, Band 37 (Bonn: Bouvier, 1966), pp. 279-286. Binder has since revised his position and in more recent work acknowledges that a stylistic affinity does indeed exist, *Kafka-Kommentar zu den Romanen, Rezensionen, Aphorismen und zum Brief an den Vater* (Munich: Winkler, 1976), pp. 384-387. The question of gesture in Kafka and Kleist, an issue touched upon by Oskar Walzel in his 1916 review, was taken up by David Edward Smith, *Gesture as a Stylistic Device in Kleist's "Michael Kohlhaas" and Kafka's "Der Prozess,"* Stanford German Studies, Vol. 11 (Bern: Lang, 1976). Interesting thematic parallels in the narratives of Kafka and Kleist are listed by Fred G. Peters, "Kafka and Kleist: a literary Relationship," *Oxford German Studies*, 1, 1966, pp. 114-162. An attempt to establish a source of Kafka's thought in the "Gedankengut" of Kleist and Romanticism was made by Ralf R. Nicolai, *Ende oder Anfang: Zur Einheit der Gegensätze in Kafkas "Schloss"* (Munich: Fink, 1977). Nicolai sees a key to Kafka's novels in the triadic scheme of existence suggested by Kleist in the *Marionettentheater* essay. I should also like to mention a paper by Beda Allemann, "Kleist und Kafka: Ein Strukturvergleich", which was delivered at the Kafka Colloquium held at the University of Paris, Sorbonne, in June 1978 and is due to be published in 1979.
3. Franz Kafka, *Briefe 1902-1924*, ed. Max Brod (Frankfurt/Main: Fischer, 1975), 27 Jan. 1911, p. 87.
4. Kafka, *Briefe*, 7 Sept. 1912, pp. 103-104.
5. Franz Kafka, *Briefe an Felice*, ed. Erich Heller and Jürgen Born (Frankfurt/Main: Fischer, 1967), 10 Feb. 1913, p. 291.

6. The reminiscences of Dora Dymant, who lived with Kafka in Berlin 1923/4, are recorded by Josef Paul Hodin, *The Dilemma of Being Modern* (London: Routledge and Paul, 1956), p. 18.
7. Kafka, *Briefe an Felice*, 2 Sept. 1913, p. 460.
8. Hans Robert Jauss expands the Formalist definition of literary evolution to embrace the historical experience mediated through the public's changing response to literature. The emphasis on literary response allows Jauss to describe theoretically how a later period can discover hitherto unrecognized qualities of earlier writers:

   > Der Abstand zwischen der aktuellen ersten Wahrnehmung eines Werks und seinen virtuellen Bedeutungen, oder anders gesagt: Der Widerstand, den das neue Werk der Erwartung seines ersten Publikums entgegensetzt, kann so groß sein, daß es eines langen Prozesses der Rezeption bedarf, um das im ersten Horizont Unerwartete und Unverfügbare einzuholen. Dabei kann es geschehen, daß eine virtuelle Bedeutung des Werks so lange unerkannt bleibt, bis die "literarische Evolution" mit der Aktualisierung einer jüngeren Form den Horizont erreicht hat, der nun erst den Zugang zum Verständnis der verkannten älteren Form finden läßt.

   Jauss, pp. 192-193.
9. Albert Camus, "L'espoir et l'absurde dans l'oeuvre de Franz Kafka", *Le mythe de Sisyphe* (Paris: Gallimard, 1942), p. 171.
10. Although Kafka's manuscript title clearly reads "Ein Kommentar," Max Brod entitled the text "Gibs auf" in his edition of *Die Erzählungen* (Frankfurt/Main, 1961), p. 377. See Heinz Politzer, *Franz Kafka: Parable and Paradox* (Ithaca: Cornell Univ. Press, 1966), p. 1ff.
11. Heinrich von Kleist, *Sämtliche Werke und Briefe*, ed. Helmut Sembdner (Munich: Hanser, 1961), 1/1, p. 263. Kleist heard a version of the anecdote through Fürst Anton Radziwill. In 1828, Radziwill told the story to Karl August Varnhagen, who recorded it. See Helmut Sembdner's notes on "Der Griffel Gottes", pp. 911-912.
12. According to Grimm's dictionary, the word "Schriftgelehrter" was brought into popular currency by Luther who used it in his translation of the Gospels to designate the learned Jewish interpreters of sacred law. "Schriftgelehrter" thus came to mean theologian. However, the earlier meaning of the word as scholar or legal expert survived alongside the narrower usage introduced by Luther. Jakob and Wilhelm Grimm, *Deutsches Wörterbuch* (Leipzig: Hirzel, 1899), IX, cols. 1743-44.
13. The chronicler's partisan comments in favor of Jeronimo and Josephe increase our sympathy for the couple: "Eine geheime Bestellung, die dem alten Don ... durch die hämische Aufmerksamkeit seines stolzen Sohnes verraten worden war ..." and also: "Durch einen glücklichen Zufall hatte Jeronimo hier die Verbindung von neuem anzuknüpfen gewusst..." Kleist, "Das Erdbeben in Chili", *Sämtliche Werke*, 1/1, p. 144.
14. Kleist, 1/1, p. 158.
15. Kleist, 1/1, p. 159.
16. Kafka, *Briefe an Felice*, 2 Sept. 1913, p. 460.

Affinities in Romanticism: Kleist's Essay "Über das Marionettentheater" and Keats's Concept of "Negative Capability"

HAL H. RENNERT
University of Florida

A comparison of Kleist's essay "Über das Marionettentheater" (1810) with Keats' "Negative Capability" letter (1817) reveals some striking similarities in how the two authors view the mind of the artist in general and the mind of the performing artist or the artist engaged in the process of creation in particular. The crux of the comparison lies in the similarity of Kleist's use of "negativer Vorteil" (the term "Vorteil" being supplied by one member of the dialogue in the essay and "negativ" being supplied by the other) and Keats' formulation of "negative capability." Both formulations are contained in rather unsystematic reflections on the state of mind of the artist; but the very spontaneity of these observations point to the workshop of both writers, where the great plays and novellas in the case of Kleist, and the great odes in the case of Keats had their origin.

With his formulation Kleist explores the advantage which a mechanical marionette or doll would have over an actual dancer if its "Maschinist" or operator were capable of delivering an exact set of instructions to a dollmaker after having fully understood the doll's center of gravity. The "Vorteil" for the human dancer would be self-knowledge and the capacity for "zieren" which, in translation, may best be rendered as self-consciousness and as affectation in its pretended form. "Negativ" in turn refers to the total and natural absence of such self-consciousness or affectation.

Keats formulates the term "negative capability" in the context of exploring the kind of mind of the artist which would most likely lead to great "achievement." Is it the kind of mind that imbues his subject with his own personality, a personality fraught with a set of certainties about life, or is it the kind of mind that does not lead to a recognition of a certain personality behind the creation? Keats weighs both sides of the question, but he clearly sides with "negative capability." But before examining more closely the meanings of "negativer Vorteil" and "negative capability" and how these paradoxical epithets emerge from their respective contexts, we must recall how in both cases it comes to such formulations in the first place.

As a point of departure for an examination of Kleist's and Keats' terms, we note that both writers reveal in the form of essay and letter a voracious drive toward the acquisition of knowledge. Such matters as the role of the artist in life, art as reflection of life, art as performance and revelation of truth and beauty are of key importance to both Kleist's and Keats' everyday concerns once a literary career was embarked upon. Especially in their letters both writers express a sense of urgency about such learning, about having to catch up, and about having to educate themselves in the shortest possible time. Both Kleist and Keats with their intimations of an early death communicate this limit of time in their letters again and again. Furthermore, both writers, once they had decided to devote their lives to literary art, which for Kleist was in 1800 and for Keats in 1817, both being in their twenty-fourth year and having come from military service as an officer in the case of Kleist and from the study of medicine as a surgeon's assistant in the case of Keats, both writers pursued their new career with the zeal of converts newly won over. As a typical example of Kleist's quest for learning he observes in a letter to Wilhelmine von Zenge in April 1801: "Aber nun will ich doch so viel Nutzen ziehn aus dieser Reise, wie ich kann, und auch in Paris etwas lernen, wenn es möglich sein wird."[1] And only a month later, from Dresden, one of Germany's cultural centers of the time, Kleist reports:

> Die Bildergalerie, die Gipsabgüsse, das Antikenkabinett, die Kupferstichsammlung, die Kirchenmusik in der katholischen Kirche, das alles waren Gegenstände bei deren Genuß man den Verstand nicht braucht, die nur auf Sinn und Herz wirken ... Wie oft, wenn ich auf meinen Spaziergängen junge Künstler sitzen fand, mit dem Brett auf dem Schoß, den Stift in der Hand, beschäftigt die schöne Natur zu kopieren, o wie oft habe ich diese glücklichen Menschen beneidet, welche kein Zweifel um das Wahre, das sich nirgends findet, bekümmert, die nur in dem Schönen leben, das sich doch zuweilen, wenn auch nur als Ideal, ihnen zeigt. Den einen fragte ich einst, ob man, wenn man sonst nicht ohne Talent sei, sich wohl im 24. Jahre noch mit Erfolg der Kunst widmen könnte? (p. 190)

Even after his so-called Kant crisis, it is characteristic of Kleist to pursue knowledge of art with great urgency. Thus, it is no accident or gratuitous attention to setting and atmosphere, but instead another instance of voracious inquisitiveness that Kleist employs the figure of the marionette in his essay.

In the essay Kleist's narrator catches fire, so to speak, when on his travels he re-encounters the leading dancer of the local opera, whom he had seen earlier at the public marionette theater, and who suggests, "daß ein Tänzer, der sich ausbilden wolle, mancherlei von ihnen [marionettes] lernen könne."[2] Thus, as he so frequently does in his letters, Kleist carefully establishes a learning situation. What exactly of the "mancherlei" was it that could enhance the dancer's and the narrator's knowledge of the dancer as a performing artist? The answer to this question is, how to achieve "Grazie" (rendered into English as meaning both gracefulness and grace). Kleist here identifies "Grazie" as the foremost quality in a dancer. But there are many other important attributes which are identified by the narrator, such as "Ebenmaß," "Beweglichkeit," and "Leichtigkeit," which, when taken together, seem to point to an ability for total concentration and intensity. Then the discussion in the essay focuses on how "Grazie" can be achieved. Here, then, the dancer suggests that if he were able to give a dollmaker an exact set of instructions as to "eine naturgemäßere Anordnung der Schwerpunkte" of such a mechanical doll, the doll would be superior in "Grazie" to a human dancer. Kleist puts it this way:

> [Narrator]: Und der Vorteil, den diese Puppe vor lebendigen Tänzern voraus haben würde?
> [Dancer]: Der Vorteil? Zuvörderst ein negativer, mein vortrefflicher Freund, nämlich dieser, dass sie sich niemals zierte. (p. 947)

The "negative Vorteil" could be achieved by a mechanical doll, because it is not hampered by self-consciousness. This self-consciousness, as Kleist puts it, would constitute a second center of gravity. If the dancer is preoccupied or distracted by a second center of gravity—expressed by Kleist as "zieren"—the dancer cannot achieve "Grazie."[3] In order to clarify the problematics of self-consciousness which in the views of both narrator and dancer is usually compounded by affectation, the narrator tells a story about a youth, who loses his natural, innocent gracefulness after he becomes aware of his similarity to the Greek statue of the youth removing a thorn. The dancer's anecdote, in turn, of a bear, who in his state of "innocence" is able to parry any thrust at him by a human fencer, also serves to illustrate the superiority of a creature which is unhampered by self-consciousness. In the wake of these clarifying examples of the youth and the bear, we become aware of Kleist's wrestling with the problem of self-knowledge, which goes far beyond the problem of self-consciousness in its complexity. In fact, prior to the clarifying discussions of the anecdotes as examples of the mechanism of interference in the process of artistic expression, the dancer points out to the narrator the following crucial background to the course of human learning and experience. With this added complexity Kleist seems to focus on one of his main themes here, which is the process of artistic creation and performance in relationship to the artist's mind:

> Es scheine, versetzte er . . . daß ich das dritte Kapitel vom ersten Buch Moses nicht mit Aufmerksamkeit gelesen; und wer diese erste Periode aller menschlichen Bildung nicht kennt, mit dem könne man nicht füglich über die folgenden, um wie viel weniger über die letzte, sprechen (p. 948)

Interpreting Kleist's concept of "negativer Vorteil" in the light of what he here establishes about the growth of the mind in relationship to artistic performance, reveals three kinds of consciousness: The first phase, in which Adam and Eve partook before eating from the tree of knowledge, is also shared by the innocent creatures such as the bear and the youth prior to his casting the fateful look into the mirror. This state of innocence, if we interpret Kleist correctly, is also shared by the marionette with its "negativer Vorteil." Clearly, "die folgenden Perioden" or the one large phase in which the narrator and his interlocutor find themselves is in the present, the pervasive here and now, or, to follow Kleist's scheme, our place between "Boden" and "Paradies," between an inanimate object and the eternal, between total unconsciousness and total consciousness. By implication, the knowledge with which a mechanical doll is created would have to be a type of redeemed knowledge from the artist in the second phase. Also by implication, Kleist saw himself in the second phase at the time of composition of the essay. The question Kleist leaves open here, which has evoked much discussion in Kleist scholarship, concerns the meaning of "das letzte Kapital von der Geschichte der Welt" as part of the final sentence of his essay: Is the third phase or "die letzte Periode" achievable for the creating or performing artist? Kleist's answer here is ambiguous and intriguing. The dancer, for one, is not without hope, when he hints at an answer: "Doch das Paradies ist verriegelt und der Cherub hinter uns; wir müssen die Reise um die Welt machen, und sehen, ob es vielleicht von hinten irgendwo wieder offen ist." (p. 948) Kleist here seems to suggest that it depends very much on what happens on this journey around the globe and whether in this travail redemption can be achieved in order to regain grace or gracefulness in spite of having once eaten from the tree of knowledge, which had resulted in the artist being struck with self-knowledge and self-consciousness. In the conclusion of the essay the image of the journey and quest around the world is expanded into an image of infinity, and the hope of attaining "Grazie" is repeated in terms of it by the dancer: "So findet sich auch, wenn die Erkenntnis gleichsam durch ein Unendliches gegangen ist, die Grazie wieder ein." (p. 951) The mind has to somehow go through the infinite in order to achieve "Grazie."

In the context of the essay it seems that one of the steps to the infinite lies in the creative act itself. In other words, one meaning of Kleist's exploration of the making of an ideally proportioned marionette is that its creator, if he has learned deeply, may be able to achieve perfection or grace in this act of re-creation. I do not think we go too far in interpreting the marionette as a symbol of art and as a symbol of the product of the soul and mind of the artist, who, having recognized the detrimental effect of self-knowledge, has endowed his creation with "negativer Vorteil."

In comparison to Kleist's formulation of "negativer Vorteil," Keats' formulation of "negative capability" also represents a culmination of numerous occasions of quests for knowledge in the poet's life. Many letters are in journal format and are imbued with his anxiety to bring a rich body of knowledge to the creative act. But it is not intellectual certainty and a neoclassical pursuit of "right reason" which Keats envisions. To his friend Reynolds he writes:

> The difference of high sensations with and without knowledge appears to me this—in the latter case we are falling continually ten thousand fathoms deep and being blown up again without wings and with all the horror of a bare-shouldered creature—in the former case, our shoulders are fledged, and we go through the same air and space without fear.[4]

In his deep conviction that his art cannot solely be an expression of "powerful feelings" as Coleridge and Wordsworth had proclaimed in the preface to the "Lyrical Ballads," Keats is more heir to the intellectuality of German Romanticism which notably Friedrich Wilhelm Schlegel and Novalis had put into practice two decades earlier. The occasion for the letter in which Keats uses the term "negative capability," was also a learning situation for Keats. He is reporting his viewing of the painting "Death on the Pale Horse" by Benjamin West and his discussions with Charles Dilke, a follower of the English philosopher and writer Godwin. In contrast to Kleist, Keats does not base his discussion on the problems of the performing artist, but more directly on the mind of the actively creative poet in relationship to his craft. Using the painting and Dilke as negative examples of what should constitute the type of art or the type of mind requisite for achievement, Keats observes:

> At once it struck me what quality went to form a Man of Achievement especially in Literature & which Shakespeare posssessed so enormously—I mean *Negative Capability*, that is when man is capable of being in uncertainties, Mysteries, doubts, without any irritable reaching after fact & reason. (p. 244)

Keats here defines what he thinks leads to great artistic achievement. Which kind of artistic predisposition or motivation produces a great work of art: is it the mind which is capable of remaining uncertain or it it what in a subsequent letter he calls the "Egotistical Sublime?" Keats pursues the foremost ingredient of achievement of the literary artist while Kleist tries to defind the foremost prerequisite of "Grazie." But the contrast is superficial: We can assume that both achievement and "Grazie" are forms of perfection and forms of quintessence of art, whether it is a dance or a poem. Thus, we are left with a remarkable similarity of the pathways Kleist and Keats takes in their formulations. Essentially, Kleist and Keats arrive at the same point, which, I believe, can be seen as a characteristic feature of Romantic thought: The artistic creation has to be free of a controlling intelligence. Neoclassic poetics would allow for the creativity of the creator's mind with which the creation is informed; Romantic poetics does not allow for such control and certainty.

In another famous letter, written a year later in Oct., 1818, Keats tries again to come to terms with the nature of the artist's mind in a similar way as in the "negative capability" letter:

> As to the poetical Character itself, (I mean that sort of which, if I am anything, I am a Member; that sort distinguished from the Wordsworthian or egotistical sublime; which is a think per se and stands alone) it is not itself—it has no self—it is everything and nothing—It has no character.... It has as much delight in conceiving an Iago as an Imogen. What shocks the virtuous philosopher, delights the chameleon Poet.... A Poet is the most unpoetical of any thing in existence; because he has no Identity—he is continually in for—and filling some other Body—the Sun, the Moon, the Sea and Men and Women who are creatures of impulse are poetical and have about them an unchangeable attribute—the poet has none. (p. 288)

Similar to Kleist's formulation, Keats sees the artist informing his creation (Kleist uses the word "versetzen," meaning to project) by being capable of being a "chameleon"; in other words by not having one certain "poetical" identity. In this connection, Keats is very critical of his friend Dilke of whom he says: "That Dilke was a Man who cannot feel he has a personal identity unless he has made up his Mind about everything." (p. 310) This, according to Keats, was the greatest stumbling block for artistic achievement: The prerequisite of the artist has to be negative capability, a relinquishing of self-knowledge and self-consciousness. This, in turn, is achieved by letting "the mind be a thoroughfare for all thoughts" and by being capable of being a chameleon poet. At the core of these reflections seems to lie Kleist's and Keats' belief that in this way concentration and intensity of lasting power in art could be achieved.

Keats' concept of the mind of the artist parallels Kleist's reflections in another remarkable way. Similar to Kleist, Keats sees a development or a three-phase evolution of life in conjunction with the growth of his mind. In one of several letters to his friend Reynolds, who as a budding writer was also concerned with the growth of his mind, Keats elaborates as follows:

> I compare human life to a large Mansion of Many Apartments, two of which I can only describe, the doors of the rest being yet shut upon me—The first we step into we call the infant or thoughtless Chamber, in which we remain as long as we do not think—We remain there a long while, and notwithstanding the doors of the second Chamber remain wide open, showing a bright appearance, we care not to hasten to it; but are at length imperceptibly impelled by the awakening of the thinking principle—within us—we no sooner get into the secnd Chamber, which I shall call the Chamber of Maiden Thought, then we become intoxicated with the light and the atmosphere, we see nothing but pleasant wonders, and think of delaying there forever in delight: However among the effects this breathing is father of is that tremendous one of sharpening one's vision into the heart and nature of Man—of convincing ones nerves that the World is full of Misery and Heartbreak, Pain, Sickness and oppression—whereby this chamber of Maiden Thought becomes gradually darkened and at the same time on all sides of it many doors are set open—but all dark—all leading to dark passages. (p. 301)

It is characteristic of Keats' rigor that he does not violate his own formulations of "irritable reaching after fact and reason" in order to explore the dark passages of the third phase of the "Mansion" of human life which he cannot know yet. He maintains "negative capability" to that extent. However, the very impetus of the letter in which Keats' description appears, seems to have been his brother Tom's fatal illness, who was shortly to die of tuberculosis, and whose condition Keats refers to twice in the letter. Additionally, Keats himself had intimations of his own early death, and his pervasive morbidity in letters as well as poems is a well documented aspect of his life and work. With these aspects in mind Keats' "dark passages" take a similar function in his exploration of the mind to Kleist's references to "Unendlichkeit." Conversely, "Unendlichkeit" partakes of the meaning of death and after-life. In the word "unendlich," which is used four times in the conclusion of Kleist's essay, death and eternity are combined into one of the most common unifying symbols of Romanticism. Although we cannot flatly equate Kleist's use of "Unendlichkeit" with Keats' morbid attraction to death, we can see in this connection one additional element of affinity between the two authors. Furthermore, it was only one year after the publication of his essay, that Kleist ended his life by his own hand.

In connection with the growth of mind, both Keats and Kleist see themselves in a continuum and being located in a second state. Not as clearly linked to innocence and loss of innocence, Keats nevertheless also seems to imply a redemptive and transcendental quality in the mysterious third stage. Keats' "Chamber of Maiden Thought" or the second stage, is directly applicable to Kleist's youth, who loses his innocence through self-knowledge and imitation.

With this discussion I hope to have reopened an exploration of Keats' and Kleist's poetics in the context of the Romantic tradition. A detailed accounting of a debt to this tradition would have been beyond the scope of this discussion. Also specifically excluded from this discussion is an exploration of the connections between Kleist's essay and the remainder of his works, which has been ably covered, notably by Heselhaus, Böckmann, and Silz.[5] In the case of Keats, the letters and poetry have most fruitfully been considered together by Bate and Wigod.[6]

Clearly the problems of self-knowledge, the formulation of the kind of artistic mind and the notion of an evolving growth of the human mind and capacity for insight, which may only find its ultimate resolution in the face of death or in the infinite, are shared by the two poets. In this sense both Kleist and Keats partake of some of the fundamental beliefs of the Romantic tradition. And as we celebrate the 200th jubilee of Kleist's birth while the twentieth century is rushing toward the ever greater possiblity of recreating human life, the meaning of Kleist's marionette assumes ever greater freshness for us.

NOTES

1. Heinrich von Kleist, *Geschichte meiner Seele: Das Lebenszeugnis* der Briefe, ed. Helmut Sembdner (Bremen: Carl Schünemann Verlag, 1959), p. 185. All reference to Kleist's letters are to this edition.
2. Heinrich von Kleist, *Sämtliche Werke*, ed. Curt Grützmacher (München: Winkler Verlag, 1967), p. 945. All references to Kleist's works are to this edition.
3. Paul Böckmann, I believe, misinterprets Kleist's use of "zieren" when he sees in it a positive quality, which Kleist's characters lack: "Schon dadurch sind sie [Käthchen, Hermann, Homburg, Kohlhaas, etc.] von den Gestalten Goethes oder Shakespeares unterschieden; sie wollen deren plastische, lebensnahe Körperlichkeit nicht besitzen, sondern folgen ihrem eigenen Gesetz, sind antigrav und können sich nicht zieren" In: *Kleists Aufsatz über das Marionettentheater*, ed. Walter Müller-Seidel (Berlin: Erich Schmidt Verlag, 1967), p. 43.
4. *The Letters of John Keats,* ed. Hyder E. Rollins (Cambridge: Harvard University Press, 1958), vol. 1, p. 277. All references to Keats' letters are to this edition.
5. *Kleists Aufsatz über das Marionettentheater: Studien und Interpretationen,* ed. Walter Müller-Seidel. This collection also contains Hanna Hellmann's pioneering study "Über das Marionettentheater" which appeared in 1911. In this study she has initiated the view of Kleist's essay as part of the philosophical, German-Romantic Tradition. I am also indebted to Geoffrey H. Hartman's essay, "Romanticism and 'Anti-Self-Consciousness' " in *Romaniticism and Consciousness,* ed. Harold Bloom (New York: W. W. Norton & Co., 1970), p. 46-56, in which he sees a connection between German and English Romanticism, but his conclusions are that Kleist achieved a "paradoxical faith" in returning to

naïvete through intellect and that in the case of Keats, "self-consciousness cannot be ovecome."
6. Walter Jackson Bate, "Negative Capability," in *John Keats*. Cambridge: The Belkap Press of Harvard University Press, 1963). The most recent work using a synthetic approach is Jacob Wigod, *The Darkening Chamber: The Growth of Tragic Consciousness in Keats*. (Salzburg: Institut für Englische Sprache und Literatur, Universität Salzburg, 1972).

Education, Linguistics and Science

Bemerkungen zum Kleistverständnis im Deutschunterricht an Gymnasien der Bundesrepublik Deutschland

KARL SCHWEIZER
Studiendirektor
Hanau, F.R.G.

Universität und Gymnasium stehen in einem Verhältnis besonderer Art zueinander: die eine Forschungsstätte in Verbindung mit der Lehre, das andere, Lehrstätte für Schüler der verschiedensten Altersstufen. An beiden Instituten unterrichten Germanisten, die die gleiche fachliche Grundausbildung durch ein Studium der Germanistik erworben haben. Der Schulgermanist unterrichtet Jungen und Mädchen im Alter von 10 bis etwa 18, 19 Jahren. Er lehrt ihnen genauso ihre Muttersprache fehlerfrei zu beherrschen, wie er sie mit dem Sprachkunstwerk vertraut zu machen versucht. Dabei stützt er sich auf Ergebnisse der Forschung, die die Universität für ihn bereit hält, setzt sie um in die Sprache der Schüler, um dadurch seine Literaturbetrachtung wissenschaftlich zu gründen, ohne selbst in erster Linie Forscher, dafür um so mehr Vermittler, Pädagoge zu sein. Seine Schüler sollen lernen, mit Texten umzugehen, sollen befähigt werden, sich kritisch mit Dichtung aus den verschiedenen Jahrhunderten auseinanderzusetzen, sollen aber auch Freude und Lust am Lesen und am Genießen der Literatur nicht verlieren. Dadurch ist sein Ansatz ein anderer als der des Forschers: er ist nicht auf der Suche nach Wahrheit, sondern vermittelt, erschließt und öffnet Vorhandenes soweit, daß junge Menschen sich mit dem Geist der betreffenden Zeit und des betreffenden Autors auseinandersetzen können.

So ist Heinrich von Kleist ein Dichter unter vielen, den der Germanist an einem Gymnasium darzustellen und dessen Werk er seinen Schülern näher zu bringen hat. Angesichts dieses Gedenkjahres lohnt es sich, die Frage zu stellen, wie wirkt Heinrich von Kleist und sein Werk heute auf junge Menschen und welchen Stellenwert hat es im Deutschunterricht an Gymnasien.

Es ist verständlich, daß die Ausführungen nicht Anspruch auf Vollständigkeit erheben können. Dies würde Umfang und Ziel des Referates überschreiten. Ich will versuchen, Tendenzen aufzuspüren, die zumindest Ansätze zu einer Antwort auf die oben gestellte Frage bringen können. Daß ich als Lehrer an einem Gymnasium auf eigene Erfahrungen und auf Gespräche mit Kollegen und Schülern zurückgreife, ist verständlich. Daß meine Ausführungen dadurch nicht ganz frei von persönlichen Eindrücken sind, bitte ich zu entschuldigen.

Im Jahre 1947 brachte Robert Ulshöfer im Klett-Verlag Stuttgart eine Zeitschrift heraus, die den Titel der "Deutschunterricht" und den Zusatz "Beiträge zu seiner Praxis und wissenschaftlichen Grundlegung" erhielt. Damit war der Ansatz gewagt, Hochschulgermanisten und Deutschlehrer an Gymnasien an einen Tisch zu bekommen. Diese Zeitschrift, Seismograph dessen, was augenblicklich an Gymnasien und Universitäten aktuell ist, könnte ebenso Spiegel sein für die Aktualität Kleists an Gymnasien der Bundesrepublik Deutschland. Schauen wir in das Gesamtregister der Jahre 1947 bis 1958. In diesem Zeitraum finden wir insgesamt 20 Aufsätze, die sich mit Kleist und seinem Werk befassen. Davon sind die Hälfte Aufsätze mit schulpraktischem Inhalt. Sie behandeln Themen, die Texte für die Oberstufe der Gymnasien betreffen, aber auch Themen, die speziell für Mittel und Unterstufe, also für Schüler zwischen 10 und 15 Jahren, geeignet sind. Besonders die Prosaschriften Kleists, Novellen und Anekdoten, werden vorwiegend von jüngeren Schülern angenommen, während ältere sich mit Dramen auseinandersetzen. Zumindest kann aus dieser Tatsache festgestellt werden, daß Kleist in dieser Zeitspanne im Gymnasium präsent gewesen ist. Man könnte in diesen Jahren von einer Kleist-Renaissance am Gymnasium und Universität sprechen. Meine eigene Berührung mit diesem Autor stammt aus den Jahren 1950-1956, während meines Studiums an der Universität Frankfurt. Was hat uns damals zu Kleist hingezogen? Er war ein Autor, der in einer Zeit des Zusammenbruchs der Werte den Einzelnen aufrief, in sich selbst ein geistiges Fundament zu schaffen, von dem aus er existieren konnte. Die Kleist-Renaissance dieser Jahre entsprang nicht einem literaturgeschichtlichen Bedürfnis, sondern einer existenziellen Notwendigkeit. Dieser Notwendigkeit entsprachen auch die Lehrpläne des Landes Hessen, die noch exakt vorschrieben, zum Beispiel den "Prinzen von Homburg," den "Michael Kohlhaas," den "Zerbrochenen Krug" und eine Reihe anderer Novellen verpflichtend zu lesen. Das heißt, durch diese Anordnung war vorausgesetzt, daß zumindest in allen hessischen Gymnasien, aber bestimmt auch in allen anderen Bundesländern Kleist zur Pflichtlektüre gehörte.

Zur 150. Wiederkehr des Todestages Heinrich von Kleists, 1961, widmete die gleiche Zeitschrift ein ganzes Heft dem "Dramatiker Heinrich von Kleist." Herausgegeben von Fritz Martini finden wir in ihm Aufsätze von Hans Schwerte über das "Käthchen von Heilbronn," von Wolfgang Wittkowski über den "Prinzen von Homburg'" von Walter Silz, New York, über die Bühnenkunst in Kleists "Prinzen von Homburg" und von Helmut Kreuzer "Hebbel und Kleist" neben einem Überblick über die Kleist-Literatur der Jahre 1955 bis 1960.

Wenn Fritz Martini in seiner Einführung in dieses Heft schreibt: "Mit den Wandlungen der gegenwärtigen Methoden und Perspektiven des Dichtungsverständnisses, die die überkommenen Auffassungen der beständigen Selbstkritik des wissenschaftlichen Denkens unterwerfen, hat die Einsicht in sein Werk andere Konturen erhalten...." dann weiß man, daß es bei diesem Heft vorwiegend um wissenschaftliche Grundlegung des Kleistverständnisses geht und weniger um schulpraktische Fragen zur Erschließung von Kleisttexten für das Gymnasium. Sollte das Fehlen schulpraktischer Aufsätze bereits hier schon Anzeichen dafür sein, daß Kleist im gymnasialen Unterricht geopfert wird zugunsten der Bewertung zeitgenössischer Autoren? Diese Schlußfolgerung ist allerdings etwas gewagt. Aber eine Tendenz wird hier schon sichtbar. Ein anderes Beispiel verstärkt diese Tendenz.

Im Oldenbourg Verlag München erscheinen seit etwa 1960 Interpretationen von Texten deutscher Dichter. Die Reihe wurde wissenschaftlich betreut von Rupert Hirschenauer und Albrecht Weber. Es waren vorwiegend Interpretationen einzelner Texte der zeitgenössischen Literatur, aber auch derjenigen vergangener Jahrhunderte. Die Reihe war gedacht für Lehrer und Schüler zugleich. Noch 1968 war man seitens des Verlages bereit, eine Interpretation von Kleists "Prinzen von Homburg" in dieser Reihe aufzunehmen. In wenigen Jahren war die gesamte Auflage der Interpretation zum "Prinzen von Homburg" vergriffen. Ein Zeichen dafür, daß bei Lehrern und Schülern ein Bedarf bestand. Zu einer Neuauflage konnte der Verlag sich bis jetzt noch nicht bereit erklären. Er glaubt, ein Bedarf für eine "Homburg"Interpretation bestehe zur Zeit nicht. Wenn dies so ist, muß man annehmen, daß eine Auseinandersetzung mit Kleist an deutschen Gymnasien nicht mehr für so wertvoll gehalten wird, wie das in den Jahren zuvor der Fall gewesen ist. Die Frage drängt sich auf: Ist Kleist ausgeklammert aus dem Literaturunterricht an deutschen Gymnasien? Ist es wirklich so, daß die Literatur mit Brecht und Böll beginnt, und was davor liegt, nur noch historischen Wert hat? Einiges zur Situation an den Gymnasien heute trägt zur Antwort auf diese Frage bei.

Zum ersten ist die Verbindlichkeit eines Stoffplanes weitgehend aufgehoben und durch Lernziele ersetzt worden. Damit obliegt es dem einzelnen Lehrer und auch dem Wunsch der Schüler, ob Kleisttexte im Unterricht besprochen werden. Bei der starken Orientierung hin zu zeitgenössischen Texten ist der Anteil an Kleistliteratur sehr gering geworden. Zum anderen ist der Begriff was denn Literatur ist, fragwürdig geworden. Er erfuhr, besonders bei jüngeren Schulgermanisten eine derartige Erweiterung, so daß Texte der Trivialliteratur genauso Gegenstand des Unterrichts sind wie die Gebrauchsprosa der Massenmedien Zeitung, Rundfunk und Fernsehen. Diese Zeiterscheinung ist sehr ernst zu nehmen, da dadurch vieles Wertvolle nicht mehr an Schüler herangetragen wird. Daß Kleist aber auch jungen Menschen heute noch etwas zu sagen hat, entdeckt man, wenn man sie mit seinem Werk konfrontiert. Wir dürfen nicht glauben, daß ihm eine Woge der Begeisterung entgegenschlägt. Für junge Menschen stellt das Eindringen in sein Werk ein hartes Stück Arbeit dar, eine Arbeit, die dann belohnt wird, wenn man feststellt, wie von Stunde zu Stunde das Interesse an ihm wächst, sein Werk sich aufschließt und aus der anfänglichen Abneigung, der reservierten Haltung, Zuneigung, ja sogar Begeisterung wird.

Zunächst, so konnte ich immer wieder feststellen, ist es Kleists Sprache, die sich wie eine unüberwindliche Wand zwischen den jungen Leser und den Autor stellt. In der Tat, sie ist in ihrer Vielschichtigkeit nicht leicht. Ein Beispiel soll dies deutlich machen. Es ist entnommen dem "Prinzen von Homburg" und steht im ersten Akt im ersten Auftritt. Ich zitiere aus der Szenenanweisung: "Ein Garten im altfranzösischen Stil. Im Hintergrund ein Schloß, von welchem eine Rampe herabführt. Es ist Nacht." Die Zeit: die Nacht vor der Schlacht bei Fehrbellin, jener Entscheidungsschlacht, bei der es um das Schicksal Brandenburgs geht. Der Prinz sitzt im Garten, traumverloren, Hohenzollern entdeckt dies und meldet es der Hofgesellschaft, unter ihr der Kurfürst selbst. Ich zitiere:

Der Graf von Hohenzollern:

Der Prinz von Homburg, unser tapferer Vetter,
Der, an der Reuter Spitze, seit drei Tagen
Den flüchtgen Schweden munter nachgesetzt,
Und sich erst heute wieder atemlos,
Im Hauptquartier zu Fehrbellin gezeigt:
Befehl ward ihm von dir, hier länger nicht
Als nur drei Fütt'rungsstunden zu verweilen,
Und gleich dem Wrangel wiederum entgegen,
Der sich am Rhyn versucht hat einzuschanzen,
Bis an die Hackelberge vorzurücken?

Der Kurfürst:

So ist's!

Hohenzollern:

Die Chefs nun sämtlicher Schwadronen,
Zum Aufbruch aus der Stadt, dem Plan gemäß,
Glock zehn zu Nacht, gemessen instruiert,
Wirft er erschöpft, gleich einem Jagdhund lechzend,
Sich auf das Stroh, um für die Schlacht, die uns
Bevor beim Strahl des Morgens steht, ein wenig
Die Glieder, die erschöpften, auszuruhn.

In der Tat, weitgespannte Sätze, deren Inhalt man beim ersten Lesen nicht schnell erfassen kann. Dazu noch eine eigenwillige Syntax, die der deutschen Grammatik widerspricht. Da beginnt die Rede des Grafen Hohenzollern mit einer Feststellung: "Der Prinz von Homburg...." und endet völlig abrupt: "Befehl ward ihm von dir...." es werden weitere Ereignisse eingeschoben, um dann zumindest nach der Interpunktion mit einer Frage zu enden, "...Bis an die Hackelberge vorzurücken?" die syntaktisch kein Fragesatz darstellt. Und weiter geht es, nach einem kurzen Einwurf des Kurfürsten "So ists" mit dem gleichen weiten Atem einer weitausladenen Rede: "Die Chefs nun sämtlicher Schwadronen...." bis "....Die Glieder die erschöpften, auszuruhen."

Diese Passage hat Spannung, zeugt von Erregung des Sprechenden, läßt teilhaben am persönlichen Engagement des Grafen und spiegelt verdeckt, jedoch kaum überhörbar etwas von dem Ergebnis des nächsten Tages wider. Diese ist die Sprache, die vom Hörer mitdenken fordert, Sprache, die sich nicht im Wohlklang erschöpft, sondern menschliches Sein widerspiegelt. Hat man dies mit jungen Menschen erarbeitet, hat man sie befähigt zu hören und zu verstehen, dann fallen die Schranken, die ihnen den Zugang zu Kleist versperrten. Das Erfreuliche ist, daß dies gelingt. Und wenn erst einmal das Interesse geweckt, dann wird zu anderen Texten, Prosa und Dramen gegriffen. Jetzt, nachdem die Sprache vertraut, dringt man ein in die Welt Kleistscher Gedanken und Ideen. Wiederum ist es der Prinz von Homburg, der fasziniert. Besonders der "sich träumende" Prinz reizt zur Identifikation. Die traumwandlerische Sicherheit, mit der er glaubt Ruhm, Ehre und Liebe zu gewinnen, ist einer Generation analog, die geneigt ist, vor gegebenen Realitäten ihre Augen zu verschließen.

Nun denn, auf deiner Kugel, Ungeheures,
Du, der der Windeshauch den Schleier heut,
Gleich einem Segel lüftet, roll heran!
Du hast mir, Glück, die Locken schon gestreift:
Ein Pfand schon warfst du.nm Vorüberschweben,
Aus deinem Füllhorn lächelne mir herab:
Heut, Kind der Götter, such ich Flüchtiges,
Ich hasche dich im Feld der Schlacht und stürze
Ganz deinen Segen mir zu Füßen um:

Wärst du auch siebenfach, mit Eisenketten,
Am schwed'schen Siegeswagen festgebunden! (I.6)

Wie erschütternd für junge Menschen zu erleben, daß diese Traumwelt jählings zusammenbricht. Wie tröstlich dann zu erfahren, daß das totale Nichts (Begegnung mit dem Grab, Szene Prinz/Kurfürstin III. 5) überwundern werden kann durch die Annahme der Wirklichkeit.

Prinz:

Das Leben nennt der Derwisch eine Reise,
Und eine kurze. Freilich! Von zwei Spannen
Diesseits der Erde nach zwei Spannen drunter.
Ich will auf halben Weg mich niederlassen!
Wer heut sein Haupt noch auf der Schulter trägt,
Hängt es schon morgen zitternd auf den Leib,
Und übermorgen liegt's bei seiner Ferse.
Zwar, eine Sonne, sagt man, scheint dort auch,
Und über buntre Felder noch, als hier:
Ich glaub's; nur schade, daß das Auge modert,
Das diese Herrlichkeit erblicken soll. (IV. 3)

Für junge Menschen ist dieser Wandel des Prinzen nur dann verständlich, wenn sie miterleben können, wie die Existenz des Prinzen durch die Begegnung mit dem Tode erschüttert worden ist. Um dieses Erlebnis wirklich glaubhaft erscheinen zu lassen, bedarf es der Auseinandersetzung mit dem "Marionettentheater." Hier liegt der Schlüssel zum Verständnis und von hier aus gelingt es auch, tiefer in die Kleistsche Gedankenwelt einzudringen. Auch die Gnade wird erkannt nicht als Willkür eines Herrschers, sondern als das, was sie im ursprünglichen Sinne ist: als bedingungslose Annahme des gegebenen Geschicks, als Einsicht in das Fehlverhalten und als freie Entscheidung ohne jeglichen Zwang einer höheren Macht.

Dies erschüttert junge Menschen. Sie alle tragen ein Stück Homburg in sich, und sie spüren, daß hier ein Autor ein sie unmittelbar angehendes Problem gestaltet hat. Dies spricht sie an. Kleist wird für sie zu einem Autor, von dem sie wissen, daß sie sich ihn erarbeiten müssen und daß er seine ganze Größe nur dem offenbart, der bereit ist, diese Arbeit auf sich zu nehmen.

Aber Kleist ist auch Kind seiner Zeit. Und welcher Autor könnte sich als politisch denkender Mensch den Zeitereignissen entziehen? Napoleon war in den ersten Jahren des beginnenden 19. Jahrhunderts die in Europa herrschende und allesbeherrschende Gestalt. Zunächst angetan von den Ideen der französischen Revolution wandelte sich die Begeisterung während der Napoleonischen Kriege in unversöhnlichen Haß gegen den Eroberer. Die "Hermannsschlacht" ist Ausdruck dieses Hasses. Sie wird heute von jungen

Menschen so wenig angenommen wie die Radikalität des Empfindens in der "Penthesilea" oder das Wüten einer alles vernichtenden Dämonie in der "Familie Schroffenstein."

Dafür gibt es aber Texte, denen sie besonders zugetan sind. Der "Zerbrochene Krug" ist ein solcher. Situations- und Wortkomik gehen hier eine glückliche Mischung ein. Aber auch hier muß man die Ebenen freilegen. Ich erinnere besonders an den zweiten Auftritt, wie hier verschiedene Handlungen gegeneinanderlaufen, vergleichbar etwa mit der Befehlsausgabe im Prinzen von Homburg (I.5). Wie Sprache, Bewegung, Gestik und Situation im Gegeneinander sich zu einem Bild der Unordnung und Erregung vereinen, ist dramaturgisch einmalig gelungen. Man freut sich über Adam, der sich immer mehr in seine Schuld verstrickt, und man bewundert den Gerichtsrat Walter, der als ruhender Pol im letzten verhindert, daß aus der Komödie eine Tragödie wird. Auch hier erkennen junge Menschen, daß Komödie nicht gleichzusetzen ist mit banalen Schwänken, daß das Lachen nicht eigentlich zur Komödie gehört, sondern sie dadurch befreiend wirkt, daß die Norm triumphiert über das Abnormale. Von den Prosaschriften sind es vor allem drei, zu denen Schüler sich hingezogen fühlen. An erster Stelle steht der "Michael Kohlhaas," an zweiter "Die Marquise von O" und an dritter "Das Bettelweib von Locarno." Diese kleine Novelle wird bereits schon in der Mittelstufe, also von Schülern der Altersstufe zwischen 12 und 14 Jahren gelesen. Auch die Kleistsche Prosa ist nicht jedem leicht zugänglich. Besonders sind es die typischen hypotaktischen Sätze, die zunächst abstoßen. Aber auch hier gelingt es, einen Zugang zu schaffen, wenn man gerade auf die Nähe der Novelle zum Drama hinweist und wenn es gelingt, das Ohr der Schüler für die spannungsgeladenen Sätze zu schärfen. Eine Erschließung der Kleistschen Novellen aufgrund der Diktion scheint mir auch hier die Methode der Wahl.

Die Syntax Kleistscher Prosa ist für junge Menschen ungewöhnlich. Sie lieben Parataxe, wehren sich gegen hypotaktischen Satzbau, weil er von ihnen Gedankenarbeit fordert, die sie nicht gerne leisten möchten. Wenn sie aber durch mehrmaliges Lesen gelernt haben, Zusammengehöriges zu erkennen und Pausen dort zu setzen, wo sie hingehören, wird ihnen die Rhythmik der Sprache vertraut. Sie spüren auch hier die Spannung, die einem Höhepunkt und einer Entladung entgegeneilt. Und der Leser wird eingestimmt, daß sich hier ein Konflikt anbahnt, der zum vordergründigen Motiv der Novelle wird. Konflikt auf der einen Seite und Spannung auf der anderen sind aber auch wesentliche Kennzeichen novellistischer Darstellung. Kleistsche Prosa ist beispielhaft für die Darstellung eines dramatischen Geschehens in epischer Form.

Ist es auch hier gelungen, den Zugang über die Sprache zu Kleists Prosaschriften zu erreichen, dann öffnet sich der Gehalt der Novellen. Der Kohlhaas, dem Unrecht geschehen aufgrund der Willkür der Junker von der

Tronkenburg und der sich dieses Recht erstreiten will, ist eine Gestalt, mit der sich junge Menschen auseinanderzusetzen bereit sind. Und wenn sie erst einmal diesen Ansatz gefunden haben, sind sie auch bereit, tiefer in die Problematik dieser Novelle einzudringen. Gerade der einzelne, dessen Weltordnung zusammengebrochen ist und der sich berufen fühlt, eine neue aus sich heraus zu schaffen, ist in seinem Ringen um absolute Werte eine Gestalt, von der man ergriffen ist und mit der man im Sinne des griechischen Philosophen Aristoteles Mitleid empfindet. Aber diese Gestalt ist kein Revolutionär, der einer Utopie nachjagt; sie beugt sich aus Einsicht einer höheren Ordnung und erkennt ihre tragische Verblendung. Und hier liegt, so glaube ich, der erzieherische Wert dieses Textes: gleich wie die Weltordnung für den einzelnen zusammenbricht, ob im "Prinzen von Homburg," im "Michael Kohlhaas" oder in der "Marquise von O": am Ende steht nicht Verzweiflung, steht nicht ein Nichts, sondern der Glaube an eine höhere Macht, die letzlich im Gefühl vieler Kleistscher Gestalten zum Durchbruch kommt und diese Gestalten zur Einsicht führt. Auch wenn diese Macht sich zeigt als "ausgleichende Gerechtigkeit" wie im "Bettelweib von Locarno."

Die Kleistsche Gedankenwelt gehört nicht der Geschichte an. Sie nur als Zeichen einer bestimmten historischen Zeit zu sehen, würde ihre hohe Aktualität gerade für die jüngere Generation verkennen. Nur müssen sie und vielleicht viele junge Germanisten an den Gymnasien unseres Landes lernen, in sie einzudringen. Diese Arbeit erhält ihren Lohn in dem Geschenk, ja in dem Vermächtnis das Kleist uns und allen folgenden Generationen hinterlassen hat. Möge der Anstoß von dieser Konferenz in alle Welt, auch in das Land hinausgehen, das Kleists Heimat war, sich mit ihm auseinanderzusetzen. Und ganz besonders sollten dies junge Menschen tun; denn Dichter wollen weniger gerühmt und mehr gelesen sein.

A Report on Two Statistical Surveys of Kleist's Syntax

TE-MAY SO
Taylor University

The uniqueness of Kleist's prose has prompted many studies of his language from various points of view. As one of those who has been moved to take a very close look at his sentence structure, I have undertaken two statistical analysis of linguistic features which have been generally accepted as being characteristics of Kleist's prose. These two features are 1) the isolation of the grammatical subject, and 2) the complexity of Kleist's syntactical structure. On both items my research is limited to the prose in the short stories, letters, anecdotes, essays, and other miscellaneous works grouped by Helmut Sembdner under the heading of "Kleine Schriften." I have used Sembner's 1965 edition of Kleist's work as the basis of the research.[1] Both statistical surveys bring into focus the grammatically independent sentences with verb-second-position.

I would first like to report about the statistical survey of the isolated grammatical subject. An example of this kind of syntactical pattern would be:

Der Junge, der bei ihm stand, *antwortete*,daß . . .
(Italics mine, Michael Kohlhaas, 14, 2 ff.)

The grammaticality of such a structure has for one time been questioned in research on Kleist.[2] German grammarians like Otto Behaghel or Paul Grebe indeed seem to suggest the notion that a sentence should normally contain the subject and the predicate following each other closely.[3] Using a generative model developed by Edward G. Fichtner[4] I have demonstrated that a sentence with an isolated grammatical subject is not ungrammatical.

A deviation from German syntax can only be said to exist in two samples found in "Michael Kohlhaas." In both cases the isolated grammatical entity is not the usual grammatical subject, but an object. This object is followed by an adverbial clause instead of the usual relative clause:

—Diesen Brief, als der Knecht gegen Abend kam,
überlieferte er ihm. . . .
(Michael Kohlhaas 76, 32f.)

The isolation of the grammatical subject emerges from the statistics as being the one with the highest frequency in comparison to other possible isolated entities such as adverb, adverbial phrase, etc. Its occurrence, however, varies in the different types of Kleist's prose:

short stories 12.78%
anecdotes 7.86%
political writings, etc................................4.85%
essays 2.46%
letters 1.17%

By relying at the percentage numbers, two things can be deduced: 1) The narrative prose with a frequency of 12.78% represents a quite different style than that of the letters with 1.17%. 2) Due to the unusually high frequency, the isolation of the grammatical subject can now be objectively pinpointed as being a prominent feature of Kleist's narrative prose. This is hardly a new statement. Many interpreters have been pointing out the use and the stylistic as well as the rhythmic value of the isolated subject, K.L. Schneider, E. Staiger, Beissner, Kahlen, etc.[5] My contribution on this particular side of the topic is in the measurability of the supplied proofs.

I find it necessary to compare the consequences of my statistics with certain views that prevail in Kleist research. One of them is the question of the generic relation between narrative and the epistolary prose. This ties in with the question about the evolution of Kleist's narrative prose. As we all know, because of the incomplete preservation of Kleist's works and writings, his letters have been considered as a stage in the development of his prose style.

Hans Joachim Kreutzer claims that Kleist's typical narrative prose matures around 1806, with the first signs being displayed in a letter written in the summer, 1801. In a footnote to this remark Kreutzer gives as an example of those "first signs" an inversion such as

Wer es [das Leben] mit Sorgfalt liebt, moralisch tot ist er schon, denn . . . .

From other examples which he indicates, Kreutzer seems to base his vision of a progressive evolution of Kleist's narrative prose on figures of speech (anaphora, chiasmus, inversion, etc.). To strengthen his statement that Kleist's narrative prose is an outgrowth of his epistolary style with a maturing date of 1806, Kreutzer further refers to another letter dated April 23, 1807. This letter displays two other features distinctive to Kleist's style: the excessive use of commas and the complexity of the sentences.[6]

Although the relation between the narrative and the epistolary prose as envisioned by Kreutzer might be true in regard to the use of the figures of speech, syntactically speaking however, I would like to offer a different view. The data compiled for the isolation of the grammatical subject suggest to me that already as early as 1799 Kleist has been using this syntactical pattern quite regularly. I would therefore be inclined to suggest that from the point of view of syntax the narrative prose cannot be considered as an outgrowth of the epistolary prose. For reasons unknown to us, Kleist uses certain syntactical patterns more often in the narrative prose than in his letters. There has never been any "beginning" of the narrative prose, it being always a part of Kleist's language. The narrative prose did not come into existence after the epistolary prose; both existed concurrently. This will be further supported by the results of the second statistic survey that I have done.

The subject of this second statistic analysis is the syntactical complexity of Kleist's sentences. As mentioned above, in corroboration of Kreutzer's (and also Kahlen's) view of a progressive development that ultimately gives birth to Kleist's narrative prose, Kreutzer has pointed out that ever since April 23, 1807, syntactical complexity had become a conspicious characteristic of Kleist's language. In measuring the syntactical complexity of Kleist's sentences I have used as a device the linguistic method developed by Edward G. Fichtner.[7] The main object of this second survey is to look for any pattern of evolution as suggested by Kahlen and Kreutzer.

In the said linguistic method, there are three variable factors governing the linguistic difficulty of a text: 1) the selection of words used in the text analysed; 2) the contents of the text analysed; 3) the syntactical structure of the sentences in the text. This last factor involves questions such as how long the sentences are, how many clauses the sentences consist of, and whether they consist of finite or nonfinite clauses. For any further details about the modus operandi of the linguistic method I refer to the paper itself.

The material on which the statistics on the syntactical complexity has been made comprises the following:

    1. Analysed in full are nineteen letters of Kleist. They range chronologically from March 13 (-18), 1793, the date of the earliest letter preserved, to November 21, 1811, the day Kleist committed suicide. Although I have tried to provide one sample for every year I made one

exception by giving no sample for the span of time between October 10, 1801 and May 13, 1805. The reason is purely arbitrary, I didn't see any compelling reason to do it. Respecting the opinions of Kahlen and Kreutzer, I have also analysed the letters which in their opinion mark the development of Kleist's narrative prose.[8]

2. As concerned short stories, every sample of each story consists of 10-15 sentences or 1-½ page(s). The "Bettelweib von Locarno" is analysed completely, however. As to "Michael Kohlhaas," three different parts of the story have been analyzed in an attempt to detect any syntactical difference among the "early " and the "late" style of Kleist's prose. The first and the second part represent the beginning and the end of the first quarter of the story. The inconclusive dispute about the date of this first quarter (whether it was written 1804 in Königsberg or 1805) does not change the fact that the first quarter of "Michael Kohlhaas" is the short story earliest written. The third sample analysed is taken from the last quarter of the story, presumably written in 1810 for the book edition. In this survey, whenever possible, the first published version of the stories have been used as the basis of the research.

The results of the second analysis are the following:

1. The letters show a much lower syntactical complexity than that evidenced in the short stories. The means of the two groups are 53.14 (letters) : 156.34 (short stories).

2. The samples of both the letters and the short stories are arranged in a chronological fashion in their respective tables. The distribution of the figures which indicate the syntactical complexity of each sample does not suggest, however, any progressive pattern of development. The letter, in particular, show quite an irregular pattern of syntactical complexity. Nothing conspicuous can be spotted, either, about the letters of 1800, 1801, 1806, and 1807.

Summary

1. Kleist achieves his distinctive style by the use of certain constructions with an exceedingly high frequency.

2. A statistical survey of the syntactical complexity of the sentences in his letters and short stories shows no distinct pattern of evolution at all.

3. Kleist's narrative prose has a predictable syntactic structure. This predictability lends the narrative prose a particular quality of uniformity and monotony. Paradoxically, a syntax with such little variation has been described as having a wide variety of literal expressiveness. Staiger, for example, interprets the isolation of the grammatical subject as an expression of the irreconcilability between men and action. Beissner as a syntactical

expression of the opposing forces against the subjective will, and finally, Schneider as a syntactical emulation of the events described by the construction itself.

ACKNOWLEDGEMENTS

This paper is based on the research done for the disseration, "Untersuchungen zur Prosa Heinrich von Kleists unter besonderer Berücksichtigung der Briefe und Novellen," submitted to the Graduate Faculty in Germanic Languages and Literatures of the City University of New York by Te-May So, 1976.

NOTES

1. *Heinrich von Kleist: Sämtliche Werke und Briefe*, 2 vols., 4th ed., Ed. Helmut Sembdner. (München: Carl Hanser, 1965). Passaged cited are from this edition.
2. See e.g. George Minde-Pouet, *Heinrich von Kleist: Seine Sprache und sein Stil— literarhistorische Forschungen* (Weimar: Emil Felber, 1807), 113: "Es wäre töricht, Kleists Wortstellung kurzweg als ein Kunstmittel seiner Sprache beziehen zu wollen. Die Unregelmässigkeit in der Stellung der Worte ist zu weit getrieben und artet nur allzu oft in Manier aus . . . ." See also Daniel Sanders, "Über die Stellung von Umstands- (oder adverbialen) Bestimmungen und Sätze zwischen dem Satzgegenstand und dem Zeitwort (Subjekt und Verbum)" *Zeitschrift für deutsche Sprache* 3, (1880) 326-32: "Es handelt sich dabei um Abweichungen von der—im Großen und Ganzen wohl begründeten—Regel, wonach im Deutschen in der gewöhnlichen Rede Umstands-Bestimmungen und -Sätze nicht zwischen das Subjekt und das Zeitwort eines Satzes zu stellen sind" (p.321).
3. Otto Behaghel, *Deutsche Syntax: Eine geschichtliche Darstellung*, Germanische Bibliothek, 1. Sammlung germanischer Elementar- und Handbücher, 1. Reihe: Grammatiken, vol. 10, 4 vols, Heidelberg: Carl-Winter's Universitäts-Buchhandlung, 1923-32, 4:46, 1462: "Das persönliche Subjekt steht im Hauptsatz *unmittelbar neben dem Verbum*, entweder ihm voraus: . . ., oder ihm nach: . . . ." (italics mine). *DUDEN Grammatik der deutschen Gegenwartssprache*, Der Grosse Duden Bd. 4,2., revised ed. Mannheim/Zürich: Bibliographisches Institut, 1966, 638, 7070.
4. Edward G. Fichtner, *English and German Syntax: A contrastive analysis on Generative-Tagmemic Principles*. (München: Wilhelm Fink, 1978).
5. Emil Staiger, "Heinrich von Kleist: Das 'Bettelweib von Lacarno': Zum Problem des dramatischen Stils," *Meisterwerke deutscher Sprache aus dem neunzehnten Jahrhundert*, 4. ed. Zürich: Atlantis, 1963, 100-17); Friedrich Beissner, "Unvorgriefliche Gedanken über den Sprachrhythmus," *Festschrift für Paul Kluckkohn und Herman Schneider: Gewidmet zu ihrem 60. Gebrutstag*, edited by

their previous students (Tübingen: J. C. B. Mohr (Paul Seibeck), 1948), 427-44; Irene Kahlen, "Der Sprachrhythmus im Prosawerk Heinrich von Kleists," (Ph.D. dissertation, Univ. of Tübingen, 1952); Karl Ludwig Schneider, *"Heinrich von Kleist: Vier Reden zu seinem Gedächtnis*, Jahresgabe der Heinrich-von-Kleist-Gesellschaft, 2. ed. (Berlin: Erich Schmidt, 1965), 27-43.

6. Hans Joachim Kreutzer, *Die dichterische Entwicklung Heinrich von Kleist: Untersuchungen zu seinen Briefen und zu Chronologie und Aufbau seiner Werke*, Philologische Studien und Quellen, Heft 41, Berlin: Erich Schmidt, 1968, 111f. About the passage from Kleist's letter, see *Heinrich von Kleist: Sämtliche Werke und Briefe*, opus cit. 2: 670,26ff; see also 2: 676,20ff. and 2: 774,5ff.

7. Edward G. Fichtner, "Syntactic Complexity: A Quantitative Measure of One Parameter of Linguistic Difficulty," A paper presented at the meeting of the Pedagogical Seminar for German Philology of the MLA Convention, San Francisco, California, 26-29 December 1975 (Mimeograph).

8. The letters are: September 19, 1800; July 21, 1801; October 10, 1801; August 31, 1806; Febr. 17, 1807; April 23, 1807; and December 22, 1807.

Heinrich von Kleist's Poetic Technique: Is It Based on the Principle of Electricity?

HERMINIO SCHMIDT
Wilfrid Laurier University

To most readers, Heinrich von Kleist is known either as a dramatic poet or as a baffling personality. Some readers would resent the effort to establish Kleist as a thinker or scientist and would not even consider interpreting his poetic writings in the light of his interest in the natural science. However, Heinrich von Kleist was in fact one of the poets who was highly stimulated by science. He was not only intensely interested but also quite well-informed in scientific matters. He himself was a thinker and scientist of some importance. Through his literary writings he tried to explain scientific speculations.

There is a reason why little attention has been focused on the interrelationship between literature and science in Germany. Wilhelm Dilthey, while laying the theoretical groundwork for the *Geisteswissenschaften* in Germany, argued quite effectively for the separation of the literary arts and the natural sciences. While this separation has been valid in his context, literary critique in Germany has not benefited from this separation.

Today it seems reasonable to suspect that 20th century literature has benefited little from Einstein's theory or from the invention of the computer. Science has become so complex, that it is beyond the horizon of the average man.[1]

In the 18th and early 19th century, science was in its infancy and still comprehensible. Literature, as a consequence, did benefit from the inventions in science, and science benefited from the speculations advanced in literature. Philosophers drew extensively from scientific observations. Poets like Goethe, Kleist, Novalis, E.T.A. Hoffmann, and many others drew heavily from the natural sciences.

Critics have either ignored Kleist's interest in science or belittled it. Consequently, large sections of Kleist's works have remained undeciphered to this day. The heavy reliance on psychological interpretation of Kleist's literary figures has caused further confusion. Hermann Weigand sums it up when he says: "Kleist Figuren lassen sich psychologisch nicht eingliedern."[2] Walter Müller-Seidel confirms that the behavior of Kleist's figures is not rationally comprehensible.[3] And Hans Joachim Kreutzer is convinced that Kleist was not interested in a realistic-psychological plot.[4]

What has been overlooked by many commentators is the fact that Kleist's dramas and stories are not about characters. They are about relations between characters. And here we have some striking similarity with the patterns observed in the sciences.[5]

The relations between these poetic figures change in the course of the poetic work, and this is distinctly pronounced. The relational pattern is basically that of attraction, repulsion, and attraction. This pattern applies, of course, to the action of most novels, but is particularly clearly defined in Kleist's novellas and dramas. The figures realign themselves continuously. By way of analogy the whole group follows a basic tendency observed in electrical experiments. Kleist has found this pattern and applied it to most of his poetic writings.

Kleist lived during a time when the German *Naturphilosophen* had developed their theory of polarities. They believed that everything in nature takes place by polar interaction. It was maintained as a fundamental principle that everything operates by the action of antagonistic forces of attraction and repulsion. It proved easy to accept this idea of a cycle at work in the macrocosm as well as the microcosm. Kleist explained: "Sieh, die Welt kommt mir vor, wie eingeschachtelt; das kleine ist dem großen ähnlich." (To Rühle, Aug. 31, 1806). For Kleist, nature was an important teacher. He writes to Wilhelmine (Nov. 16, 1800): "Einen Lehrer gibt es, der ist vortrefflich, wenn wir ihn verstehen; es ist *die Natur*."

Among the German philosophers, Schelling exerted the greatest influence on natural sciences. His *Naturphilosophie* is the unity of all natural forces. Everything takes place through contradiction, which is in the ratio of positive and negative. Matter exerts influence through attractive and repulsive forces, magnetism through opposite poles, and electricity through positive and negative channels. Kleist embraced this concept quite enthusiastically. He warned his critics: "Lächeln Sie nicht, mein Freund, es waltet ein gleiches Gesetz über die moralische wie über die physische Welt." (II, p. 308)[6]

For Kleist, polarity became the general mode of nature. Science as viewed by Newton was not universal enough. For Kleist the scientific observations in nature also applied to the relationship among mankind. With disgust he observed to Adolfine (July 29, 1801): "Ich glaube, daß Newton an dem Busen eines Mädchens nichts anderes sah, als seine krumme Linie, und daß ihm an ihrem Herzen nichts merkwürdiger war, als sein Kubikinhalt." For Kleist there was a universal law applicable to man and nature.

Kleist's basic concept is that all things in nature are built up in the same polar way. Kleist becomes quite specific about the relationship between electricity and human disease.[7] He says: "Wenn der elektrische Körper positiv ist: so flieht, aus dem unelektrischen, alles, was an natürlicher Elektrizität darin vorhanden ist, in den äußersten und entferntesten Raum desselben, und bildet, in den, jenen zunächst liegenden, Teilen eine Art von Vakuum, das sich geneigt zeigt, den Elektrizitätsüberschuß, woran jener, auf gewisse Weise, krank ist, in sich aufzunehmen." Kleist goes on to say that this extraordinary law can also be found in the moral world. It is, according to the poet, not only applicable to opinions and desires, but also to feelings, affection, and human character: "Aber das Gesetz, von dem wir sprechen, gilt nicht bloß von Meinungen und Begehrungen, sondern, auch von Gefühlen, Affeken,
Eigenschaften, und Charakteren." (II, p. 331)

A new look at Kleist's poetic faint will show how closely he adhered to the description of the electrical phenomenon. It has been observed that Kleist's dramas and novellas contain many faints.[8] Günther Blöcker[9] noted that although there are a few faints which are the result of human weakness or emotional collapses, these, however, are exceptions. According to Blöcker, Kleist's poetic faints are special phenomena. Seen in a new light,

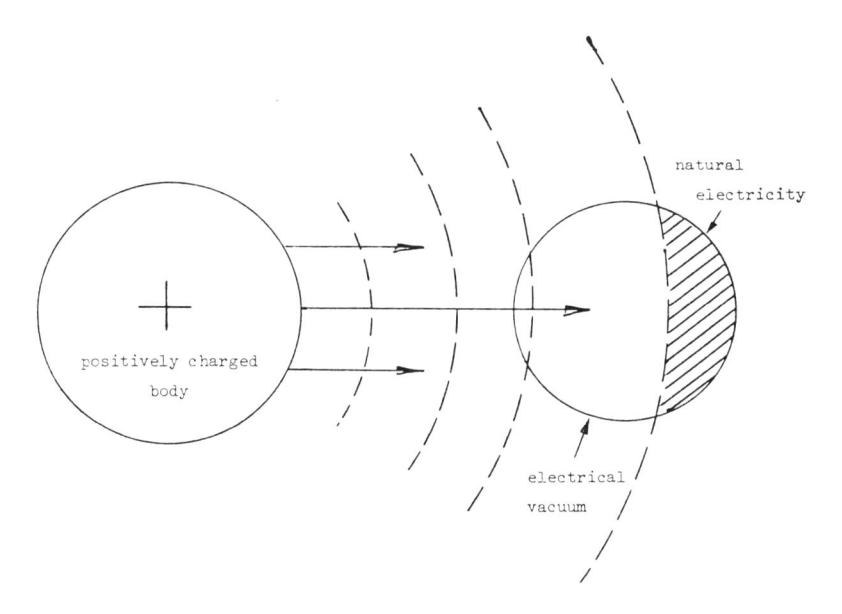

FIGURE 1.

they have striking similarities with the reactions observed in a discharging electrical jar. The Kleistsche Flasche was such an electrical jar filled with liquid or any other conducting matter. (See Figure 2.)

In the story "Der Findling," Kleist poetically incorporates this contraption. It is the principle of the Kleistsche Flasche, as originally invented by Ewald Georg von Kleist in Camin in 1745. It consisted of a jar filled with liquid and held in the hand. The hand represents one pole and the liquid in the bottle the other. Elvire in the story carries several of these bottles in her hand. She finally collapses "wie durch einen unsichtbaren Blitz getroffen." (II, p. 204)

In order to increase the electrical force of this condenser, Benjamin Franklin joined the outside of these jars together. All these bottles were brought in contact with a metal tray, a good conductor of electricity. This contraption functioned as a battery and gave off powerful sparks if approached by a grounded person (Figure 3).

A similar battery of jars is described by Heinrich von Kleist when Käthchen von Heilbronn enters her father's shop with a silver tray full of bottles and refreshments for Graf Wetter vom Strahl. The silver tray functions as an electrical conductor joining the bottles on the tray and thereby forming a Franklin-battery. Käthchen's reaction, as soon as she steps into the blacksmith shop is reminiscent of a powerful electrical shock. She collapses "als ob sie ein Blitz nieder geschmettert hätte!" (Käth. I/1, 156).

The literary application of a condenser is by no means coincidental. In the story "Michael Kohlhaas" it is a little capsule made out of lead which serves the same basic function as described earlier. This little capsule causes the same poetic faints. All figures struck in this way suffer from the same symptoms. They do not feel any pain, they can not explain what has hap-

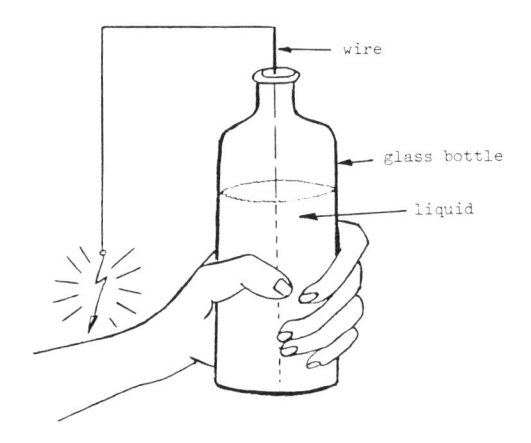

FIGURE 2. *Kleistsche Flasche (Condenser)*.

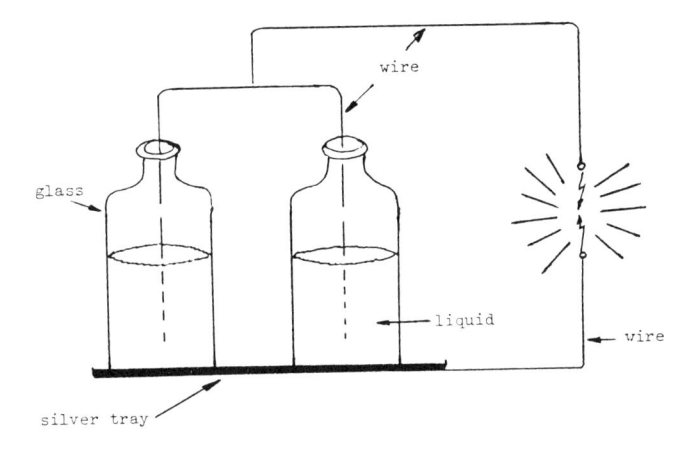

FIGURE 3. *Franklin's Battery.*

pened to them, they usually suffer from a fever and after days or weeks they regain their natural strength. In addition, they do not faint in the conventional way. They drop to the floor like a wet sack or as Kleist says, "wie ein Taschenmesser zusammenfallend."

This poetic "pocket-knife-effect" has surprising similarity to electrical shocks as observed by Benjamin Franklin and other experimenters. In his 21st *Letter on Electricity*, Franklin describes such an electrical faint caused by an electrical shock:

> A person struck in this manner collapses. The articulations suddenly lose their strength and tension so that a person drops to the floor without prior vacillation or without falling prostrate.

Similarly, Kleist's poetic figures never fall in a prostrate fashion. They drop like a garment (*Penth.* 1390), they collapse like a pocket knife (*Käth.* I/1, 165), or they simply drop into the dust. Furthermore, Franklin and others noticed that persons hit by an electrical shock never felt any pain nor could they explain what happened to them. This is exactly the case with Käthchen von Heilbronn. She does not know what has happened to her (*Käth.* III/15, 1907). Likewise Sylvester in the drama *Schroffenstein* utters, upon regaining consciousness, his surprise and disbelief (*Schroff.* II/2, 879). As soon as the Kleistsche Flasche has been discharged of the excess electricity, it needs a certain amount of time until the natural tension or the natural polarity between the inside and the outside of the jar has been regained. Regaining equilibrium is a natural process. We have a detailed technical explanation of this phenomeon in Kleist's story "Allerneuester Erziehungsplan." (II, p. 329)

In the story "Der Findling," Kleist applies this technical knowledge by having Elvire not only faint but also by having her suffer an intense fever for several days until she regains the strength "durch die natürliche Kraft ihrer Gesundheit." (II, 204) Elvire is literally and technically suffering from an excessive emptiness of her natural or electrical quality. Kleist calls this excess a "Krankheit." Käthchen von Heilbronn is suffering from a "sickness," too. After her collapse in her father's shop, she needs "sechs endlose Wochen" to regain her natural health (*Kath.* I/1, 192). Medical doctors, if they appear in a story, are usually helpless.

In contrast, the persons hit by this fever, which is preceded by fainting, regain their "natural health." This is also illustrated in the story "Michael Kohlhaas." Here it is the Kurfürst who is presumed to die, but later regains his natural health without medical attention.

From these and many more references we notice Kleist's preoccupation with the functioning of the Kleistsche Flasche. He incorporated scientific observations which he personally had made while using a friend's fully equipped laboratory (To Ulrike, Feb. 5, 1801).

Kleist's scientific incorporations are distinct from the conventional treatment of developing poetic characters as found for instance in Schiller or other writers. Kleist's figures do not develop, they react to each other. Kleist's poetic figures do not faint out of weakness or emotional stress. Instead they react to other figures as electrical bodies would react when discharged. There is little if any psychologically motivated behavior observable in the relationship between Kleist's poetic figures.

What has been demonstrated with the artificial spark from the Kleistsche Flasche holds equally true with lightning. By investigating Kleist's employment of atmospheric phenomena in his drama *Penthesilea* we find that he accurately follows the sequence of the natural phenomenon. The scientific citations and poetic incorporations prove, however, to be so extensive that it would be impossible to compress them into this short paper. I have done so in a book dealing with this subject in depth.[10] Therefore, I will be concentrating on two examples which are difficult to explain using conventional methods. They are taken from the drama *Penthesilea*.

In noticing Kleist's life-long interest in the phenomena of electricity it becomes evident that the imagery used for the Amazons is reminiscent of thunder and lightning. For instance, Penthesilea's killing of Deiphobus is described in this manner: "Und [sie] senkt, wie aus dem Firmament geholt,/Das Schwert ihm wetterstrahlend in den Hals." (*Penth.* I, 183-4) And later the Amazons are described as a storm coming up on the horizon: "An des Berges Saum—/Staub—/Staub aufqualmend, wie Gewitterwolken:/ Und, wie der Blitz vorzuckt—/Ihr ewgen Götter!/Penthesilea—" (*Penth.* III, 387-9). The reference is clearly to thunder and lightning. Lightning is an image of electricity as observed in the atmosphere. Kleist not only employs the images as many other writers have done so before him, but he adheres to the exact sequence observed in electricity. And this sequence develops into a pattern according to which all poetic figures react to each other.

It is not the image which is unique in Kleist's works, but it is the exact sequence of reactions associated with electricity to which Kleist adheres to in minute detail. It is this sequence which forms the foundation for his poetic technique.

In the drama *Penthesilea* it may be recalled that the Amazons burst into the ongoing battle between the Greeks and the Trojans with no apparent reason. In the first scene the hordes of Amazons led by Penthesilea are described as "Sturmwind" that "Weht der Trojaner Reihen vor sich her." (*Penth.* I, 35-36). In this scene we have three parties. The Greeks are fighting with the Trojans. Then the Amazons enter the ongoing battle.

Odysseus, observing this phenomenon thinks that the severity with which Penthesilea chases the Trojans must indicate that she is a potential friend of the Greeks. (*Penth.* I, 50-55) This is, however, a calculated mistake which is basic to almost all of Kleist's writings. Critics have called this "Versehen, Verkennen, Irrtum" and the like. What happens here is a personification of a natural law which is not recognized as such and therefore the poetic figures make vital mistakes.

The experimenters of the day had observed that in electrical experiments opposing poles attract one another. But they also noted that poles of the same polarity repulsed one another, the lighter one being the repulsed one.[11] If we assume that Kleist adhered to this law, then the Amazons and the Trojans should have the same polarity. The Trojans being the lesser are therefore "swept away" by the Amazons. In contrast, the Greeks and the Amazons have the opposite poles and therefore will have to attract each other as it becomes evident in the story.

In order that the attentive reader might not miss the hint, Kleist lets Diomedes tell the same story already told by Odysseus. This time the allusion to thunder and lightning as an electrical phenomenon becomes even more obvious.

> Seit jenem Tage
> Grollt über dieser Ebne unverrückt
> Die Schlacht, mit immer reger Wut, wie ein
> Gewitter, zwischen waldgekrönter Felsen Gipfeln
> Geklemmt. Als ich mit den Ätoliern gestern
> Erschien, der Unsern Reihen zu verstärken,
> Schlug sie mit Donnerkrachen eben ein,
> Als wollte sie den ganzen Griechenstamm
> Bis auf den Grund, die Wütende, zerspalten.
>
> (*Penth. I, 139-47*).

And one scene later we have to listen to a third description of the same action with unmistaken references to a violent thunderstorm:

Der Hauptmann:

Ein neuer Anfall, heiss, wie Wetterstrahl,
Schmolz, dieser wuterfüllten Mavorstöchter,
Rings der Atolier wackre Reihen hin,
Auf uns, wie Wassersturz, hernieder sie, ...

(Penth. II, 246-49).

The implication of a thunderstorm with the resulting downpour is evident in these lines.

Up till now an analogy has been traced between Penthesilea and an electrical thunderstorm. The chasing of the Trojans has been seen as a description of the law of repulsion of equal polarities. All this could be a coincidental analogy if Kleist would not be consistent in applying the law of electricity throughout his literary works. Odysseus now enters the picture and describes to his amazement the welding together of two arch enemies, namely the Trojans with the Greeks. Both were fighting with each other until the Amazons entered the fight. Now two enemies suddenly are friends. Again, Kleist uses a poetic figure to express a seemingly obvious law of nature:

Odysseus:

Soviel ich weiß, gibt es in der Natur
Kraft bloß und ihren Widerstand, nichts Drittes.

(Aber jetzt) Der Trojer wirft, gedrängt von Amazonen,
Sich hinter eines Griechen Schild, der Grieche
Befreit ihn von der Jungfrau, die ihn drängte,
Und Griech' und Trojer müssen jetzt sich fast,
Dem Raub der Helena zu Trotz, vereinen,
Um dem gemeinen Feinde zu begegnen.

(Penth. I, 125-38)

As illustrated in the two scenes from *Penthesilea*, the figures, or in this case whole armies are reacting to each other, not in accordance with an obvious rationale but in accordance with a universal law which dictates to life and matter alike. What has been illustrated in the relationship between the armies can equally be illustrated between the characters Penthesilea and Achilles. The figures react to each other not according to conventional psychological motivations but to a pattern which is mathematically exact and observable in electrical experiments. This poetic technique as used by Kleist has been recognized by another German Poet. Heinrich Heine specifically referred to Kleist when he says: "Man entdeckt in dem Menschengeiste die

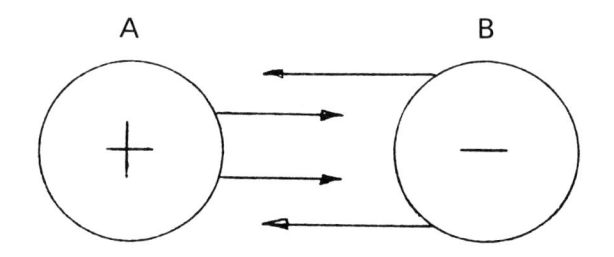

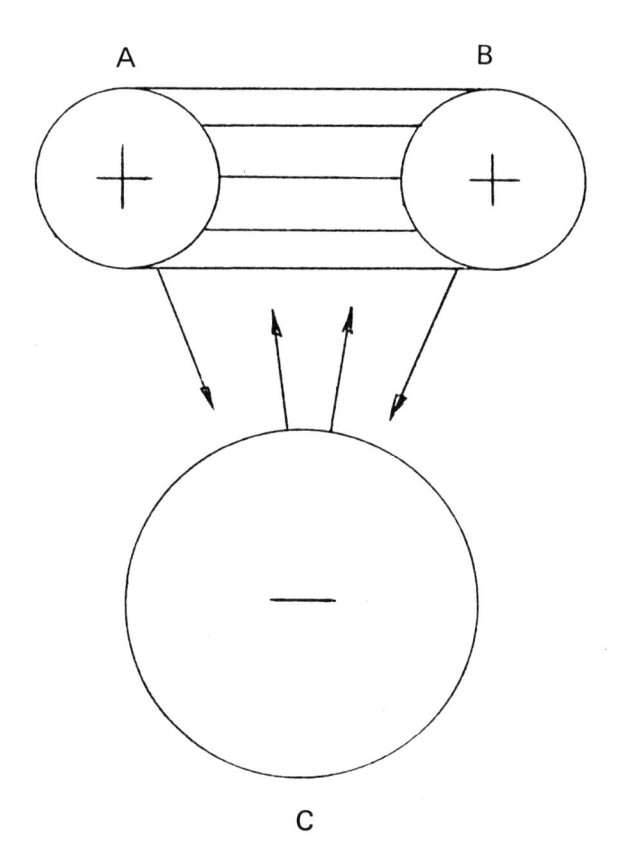

FIGURE 4.

Gesetze der Natur, Magnetismus, Elektrizität, anziehende und abstoßende Pole (Kleist)."[12]

Returning to the battle as described by Odysseus we notice a paradox. According to Odysseus' knowledge only two forces in nature exist, namely force and counter-force, but not a third one. Even to the casual reader this appears to be logical. However, according to the laws as observed in nature there is a third force in existence and Kleist brings this third force poetically to life.

In Friedrich Wilhelm Schelling's *Erster Entwurf eines Systems der Naturphilosophie* (1799) the philosopher also describes three forces: repulsion, attraction, and the gravitational force. The last one being the synthesis of the first two. Nature is a unity says Schelling. In the inorganic as well as in the organic world identical forces are at work.[13] The same observation has been made previously by Johann Carl Wilcke in 1758, in an appendix to Benjamin Franklin's translated *Letters on Electricity*. Wilcke proved with an experiment that if two bodies of opposing polarities A and B come under the influence of a stronger electrically charged body C, they will both turn into the same opposite polarity to C. However, as soon as the stronger force C is taken away, then A and B will suddenly turn against each other with now opposing polarities. In other words the third and stronger force welds together two opposing bodies.[14] (See Figure 4.)

Exactly this electrical phenomenon takes place when the enemies, the Greeks and Trojans, are suddenly united in opposition to the Amazons. Kleist knew this law from his personal experiments in a science laboratory (To Ulrike, Feb. 5, 1801). His poetic figures actually observe a seemingly strange phenomenon, but their knowledge about the underlying law is limited. They do not understand the apparent paradox of the phenomenon in front of them. This then, leads to a misunderstanding of the situation. This misunderstanding or misinterpretation by the poetic figures is central to Kleist's dramas and novellas. The figures cannot see the real meaning of the action because their mind is clouded by obvious and seemingly rational knowledge. Kleist realized this shortcoming of man very early in his life (To Wilhelmine, March 22, 1801).

The dramatic force of Kleist's poetic writing is based upon this universal law. It illustrates the struggle in nature, a cycle which is endlessly repeating itself. As a poet, Kleist has brought an abstract and philosophical problem to life. Through his allegorical figures the law of nature becomes intelligible and permits a dramatic conflict which is emotionally moving. Kleist's poetic form is difficult and recondite because the ideas are complex and difficult.

However, by recognizing Kleist's life-long interest in the laws as observed in electricity, we are able to trace the principle according to which the poet structured his works. With this principle, Heinrich von Kleist was able to create brilliantly intense novellas and dramas.

NOTES

1. Compare Aldous Huxley, *Literatur und Wissenschaft*. Transl. Herbert E. Herlitschka (München, 1963), p. 66.
2. Hermann Weigand, "Zu Kleists Käthchen von Heilbronn," *Studia Philologica et Litteraria in Honorem L. Spitzer* (Bern, 1958), p. 415.
3. Walter Müller-Seidel, *Versehen und Erkennen. Eine Studie über Heinrich von Kleist* (Köln/Graz, 1961), p. 99.
4. Hans Joachim Kreutzer, *Die dichterische Entwicklung: Heinrich von Kleist. Untersuchungen zu seinen Briefen und Aufbau seiner Werke.* (Berlin, 1968), p. 175.
5. It would be best not to use the term "character" in reference to the personae. Kleist has created these as abstractions quite on purpose.
6. All references to the text are based on Heinrich von Kleist, *Sämtliche Werke und Briefe*, Ed. H. Sembdner (Darmstadt, 1970), vols. I and II.
7. See "Allerneuester Erziehungsplan" and "Über die allmähliche Verfertigung der Gedanken beim Reden."
8. Compare also the "miraculous cure" of Berthold and Anton by Faust in Achim von Arnim's novel *Die Krohnenwächter*. Both Berthold and the child Anton are mortally "ill," one is dying of a superabundance of strength while the other is lacking the natural strength. In *Sämtliche Romane und Erzählungen*, Ed. Walter Migge (München, 1962-5), vol. I, p. 607.
9. Günter Blöcker, *Heinrich von Kleist oder Das absolute Ich* (Berlin, 1960), p. 188.
10. Herminio Schmidt, *Heinrich von Kleist: Naturwissenschaft als Dichtungsprinzip* (Paul Haupt Verlag, Bern, 1978).
11. Friedrich A.K. Gren, *Grundriss* (Halle, 1787), "Naturlehre" No. 1302.
12. Heinrich Heine, *Werke und Briefe*, Ed. Hans Kaufmann (Berlin, 1962), vol. VI, p. 383.
13. Friedrich Wilhelm Schelling, *Sämmtliche Werke* (Stuttgart, 1856-61), III, pp. 207-220.
14. Johann Carl Wilcke, *Des Herrn Benjamin Franklins Esq. Briefe von der Elektrizität. Aus dem Engländischen übersetzt, nebst Anmerkungen* (Leipzig, 1758), Anmerkung Nr. 30, p. 308.

New Perspectives

Kleist in Thun

HERMANN RESKE
Rider College

Heinrich von Kleist hatte während seines Aufenthaltes in Paris von Anfang Juni bis Mitte November 1801 das gefunden, was er auf seiner Würzburger Reise vergeblich zu finden gehofft hatte: seine Bestimmung zum Dichter. Endlich glaubt er erkannt zu haben, "was der Himmel sichtbar, unzweifelhaft von uns fordert." Um diesem Ruf folgen zu können, wünscht er sich "Freiheit, ein eigen Haus, und ein Weib," seine drei Wünsche, die er "beim Auf- und Untergange der Sonne, wie ein Mönch seine drei Gelübde," wiederholt. Mit "Freiheit" meint Kleist das tun zu dürfen, was er als gottgegebene Bestimmung erkannt zu haben glaubt, der er daher folgen muss. Der dichterische Genius regt sich. Die *Familie Schroffenstein* ist im Entstehen. Paris aber ist nicht der Ort, "ein schön Gedicht" zu schreiben. Seit der Kantkrise lehnt Kleist die Wissenschaften als Weg zur Wahrheit ab, aber er stürzt sich nicht, wie zu erwarten, kopfüber in die Kunst, wie aus den Briefen dieser Zeit hervorgeht. Er folgt seiner Bahn, aber er will sein "Ideal, das Kind seiner Liebe," nicht dem Broterwerb opfern. "Bücherschreiben für Geld—o nichts davon." Die Braut möchte er schon in das Gewölbe führen, wo er sein Kind "wie eine vestalische Priesterin das ihrige, heimlich aufbewahre bei dem Schein der Lampe." Er muß sich also zusätzlich noch nach einem Lebensunterhalt umsehen. Daher schwärmt er seiner Braut Wilhelmine von Zenge von dem "grünen Häuschen" vor, das sie empfangen soll. Ein Feld will er bebauen, einen Baum pflanzen und ein Kind zeugen. Kleist sucht Ruhe vor dem Chaos in seinem Innern, das ihn zu verzehren droht. Er glaubt, vor dem dichterischen Dämon, der ihn treibt, in ein bäuerliches Idyll flüchten zu können.

Losreißen will er sich von allen Verhältnissen, die ihn zwingen, "zu streben, zu beneiden, zu wetteifern." So fordert er die Braut geradenwegs auf, seine Bäuerin auf einem kleinen Gut zu werden, das er in der Schweiz kaufen wolle; die Arbeit müsse aber wegen der bedingten Finanzlage selbst getan werden. Man stelle sich die Generalstochter Wilhelmine von Zenge, die bereits unter Kopfschmerzen litt, wenn ihr die Sonne auf das Haupt schien, bei der Landarbeit vor! Sie sagt ab. Dennoch blieb Kleist bei seinen Plänen und kam Ende Dezember bei seinem Freund Zschokke, dem Bürger-Regierungs-Statthalter in Bern an. Dort wurde er auf das freundlichste empfangen und, was weit wichtiger ist, fand Aufnahme in Zschokkes Freundeskreis, darunter Pestalozzi und der "Buchhändler Gessner, Sohn des berühmten, der eine Wieland, Tochter des berühmten, zur Frau, und Kinder wie die lebendigen Idyllen" hatte. Weiterhin gehörte dazu das schwarze Schaf der Familie Wieland, der Sohn Ludwig, Louis genannt. Es war ein musischer Kreis, in dem Kleist sich in Bern bewegte. Erstmalig hören wir von der *Familie Schroffenstein* und dem *Zerbrochnen Krug*.

Kleist schien dieses Glück voll zu geniessen, ohne dabei seine Agrarpläne aufzugeben. Er trug sich ernstlich mit dem Gedanken, ein Gut in Gwatt anzukaufen, das ihm auch Zschokke empfohlen hatte. Der Kaufvertrag scheint so gut wie abgeschlossen gewesen zu sein, und nur ein "Mißverständnis" verzögerte seinen Umzug "aufs Land". Dieses Mißverständnis scheint Kleists eigenen Wünschen entgegengekommen zu sein, denn er verhielt sich "in allen Stücken wie der berühmte Cunctator," und schien dennoch in heiterster Stimmung. So glücklich war er, daß man es ihm an der Stirn ablesen konnte. Am ersten Februar 1802 schrieb er aus Thun an Zschokke:

> Die Leute glauben hier durchgängig, daß ich verliebt sei. Bis jetzt aber bin ich es noch in keiner Jungfrau, als etwa höchstens in die, deren Stirne mir den Abendstrahl der Sonne zurückwirft, wenn ich am Ufer des Thuner Sees stehe.

Mit der Begründung, daß die Schweiz französisch werden könne, verzichtete Kleist auf den Ankauf des Gutes in Gwatt. Was er gesucht hatte, hatte er ohnedies gefunden: Ruhe in der Natur, die "hier . . . mit Geist gearbeitet" sei. Er war überzeugt, nun seine Bestimmung gefunden zu haben und suchte sie zu erfüllen. In einem Brief an Zschokke vom zweiten März 1802 hören wir zum ersten Mal von der Aare-Insel:

> Ich habe mir eine Insel in der Aare gemietet, mit einem wohl eingerichteten Häuschen, das ich in diesem Jahr bewohnen werde . . . Ich werde in einigen Wochen einziehen.

Im gleichen Brief kündigte er an, er werde noch vor seinem Umzug auf die Insel "Geschäfte halber, auf ein paar Tage nach Bern kommen." Am 18. März berichtete er der Schwester Ulrike, daß "in Hinsicht des Geldes" in der Zukunft "zur Notdurft" für ihn gesorgt sei und daß er noch heute nach Bern abreisen werde. Diesen Hinweisen darf entnommen werden, daß Kleist die Reise nach Bern unternahm, weil er mit dem Verleger und Buchhändler Gessner geschäftlich zu tun hatte. Seine Mitteilung an Ulrike vom ersten Mai, er sei von allen Sorgen um den Hungertod befreit, obschon alles, was er erwerbe, "so grade wieder drauf geht," läßt darauf schließen, daß der Dichter bei diesem Besuch das Druckmanuskript der *Familie Schroffenstein* seinem Verleger Gessner übergab, der ihm wohl das Honorar oder wenigstens einen Teil desselben auszahlte. Diese Auffassung bestätigt auch Zschokke in seiner *Selbstschau*, in der er die Lesung des Trauerspiels vor dem Berner Freundeskreis erwähnt. Diese muß folgerichtig vor Zschokkes Abwanderung nach Schloß Biberstein im Aargau stattgefunden haben, auf der ihn Kleist und Wieland begleiteten und die am 27. März 1802 begann. Die drei Freunde trennten sich nach kurzem Aufenthalt in Aarau: Zschokke ging nach Biberstein, Wieland kehrte nach Bern zurück und Kleist bezog sein Haus auf der Insel bei Thun. Das Datum seines Einzugs kann nur vermutet werden. Stellt man in Rechnung, daß die Fußwanderung nach Aarau am 27. März begann, und daß Kleist nach Thun zurück wanderte, so kann dies kaum vor der zweiten Aprilhälfte gewesen sein.

Der erste Brief an die Schwester von der Aarinsel bei Thun vom ersten Mai 1802 sagt uns, daß er auf einer Insel bei Thun lebt, daß er froh und heiter ist und daß er verbissen arbeitet. Hier erhebt sich die Frage, an was Kleist so verbissen arbeitet, wenn, wie erwähnt, seine Tragödie bereits vor seinem Einzug in Druck gegangen war. Nach Pfuels and Tiecks Zeugnissen darf angenommen werden, daß der Dichter sich zunächst mit dem verloren gegangenen *Leopold von Oesterreich* beschäftigte. Die trostlosen politischen Verhältnisse mögen ihn dazu angeregt haben, ein ruhmreicheres Kapitel aus der Geschichte dramatisch zu gestalten. Des weiteren konzipierte er den *Zerbrochnen Krug*, für den er, gemeinsam mit den Berner Freunden, den Anstoß durch einen Kupferstich von Le Veau, "La cruche cassée," erhalten hatte und der in Zschokkes Wohnung in Bern hing. Für Wieland wurde das Thema Anlass zu einer Satire, für Zschokke zu einer idyllischen Erzählung und für Kleist zu einem Lustspiel. "Kleists *Zerbrochner Krug* hat den Preis davongetragen," sagt Zschokke in seiner *Selbstschau*. Doch all dies ist Kleist nicht genug. Er will mehr: er will die Lücke schließen, die zwischen Sophokles und Shakespeare seiner Auffassung nach klafft—und damit beginnt sein Ringen um den *Guiskard*. Wir hören darüber in einem interessanten Bericht eines jungen Mannes "aus Kleists damaligem Umgangskreis," der ohne Quellenangabe von Paul Hoffmann im Nachwort des Faksimiledruckes des *Zerbrochnen Kruges*, Weimar 1941, mitgeteilt wird. Hier lesen wir:

> Er hatte auf einer Insel der Aar ein kleines Landhaus dem unsrigen gegenüber gemietet; er brütete über einem Trauerspiel, in dem der Held auf der Bühne an der Pest stirbt. Oft sahen wir ihn stundenlang in einem brauhen Curé auf seiner Insel, mit den Armen fechtend, auf und ab rennen und deklamieren.

Dieser Bericht zeigt treffend Kleists verbissenes Ringen mit dem *Guiskard*, das hier im Mai 1802 auf der Kleist-Insel begann und im Oktober

1803 seinen tragischen Abschluss fand: "Ich habe in Paris mein Werk, so weit es fertig war, durchlesen, verworfen und verbrannt: nun ist es aus." Kleist ist es nie klar geworden, daß er mit dem *Guiskard* nicht als Dichter scheiterte, sondern daß er sich am Stoff vergriffen hatte, dass er aber mit der *Penthesilea* erfüllte, was er mit dem *Guiskard* erstrebt hatte: die griechische Tragödie mit der modernen zu verbinden.

Noch aber erfreute sich Kleist seines naturnahen Lebens auf der Insel. Die nachhaltige Wirkung dieses idyllischen Lebens läßt sich bis in Kleists späteste Werke verfolgen. Dem Gedicht "Der Schrecken im Bade" gab er bezeichnenderweise den Untertitel "Eine Idylle". "Das Erdbeben in Chili" zeigt den gejagten, besinnungslosen Menschen, der Ruhe in der offenen Natur findet. Auch da war, wie im "Schrecken im Bade," "die schöne Nacht herabgestiegen, voll wundermilden Duftes, so silberglänzend und still, wie nur ein Dichter davon träumen kann," und die Liebenden finden nach dem Zusammenbruch ihrer Welt Ruhe unter einem "Granatapfelbaum, der seine Zweige, voll duftender Früchte, weit ausbreitete." In der "Verlobung in St. Domingo" kommt das Aare-Idyll wörtlich zum Ausdruck, wenn Gustav von der Ried, gebürtiger Schweizer, Toni beschreibt, "welch ein kleines Eigentum, frei und unabhängig, er an den Ufern der Aare besitze; eine Wohnung bequem und geräumig genug, sie und auch ihre Mutter ... darin aufzunehmen." Die *Familie Schroffenstein*, obwohl vor dem Einzug auf die Insel bereits in Druck gegeben, war zweifellos in Kleists Thuner Wohnung am Tor überarbeitet worden. Sylvester scheint die Wirbel der Schadau vor Augen zu haben, wenn er sich um das Segelboot sorgt, das gefährlich schwankt und das Ufer nicht erreichen kann. Bis in den *Amphitryon* klingt die Sehnsucht nach dem verlorenen Paradies nach. Alkmene klagt über den allzu lästigen Ruhm und gerne gäbe sie das Diadem "für einen Strauss von Veilchen hin, um eine niedre Hütte eingesammelt." In dem bereits erwähnten Brief vom ersten Mai schildert Kleist sein Insel-Idyll in dichterischer Sprache, und gerade daher darf nicht übersehen werden, daß sehr häufig der Dichter mit dem Berichterstatter durchgeht:

Jetzt leb ich auf einer Insel in der Aare, am Ausfluss des Thunersees, recht eingeschlossen von Alpen, eine Viertel Meile von der Stadt. Ein kleines Häuschen an der Spitze, das wegen seiner Entlegenheit sehr wohlfeil war, habe ich für sechs Monate gemietet und bewohne es ganz allein. Auf der Insel wohnt auch weiter niemand, als nur an der andern Spitze eine kleine Fischerfamilie, mit der ich schon einmal um Mitternacht auf den See gefahren bin, wenn sie Netze einzieht und auswirft. Der Vater hat mir von zwei Töchtern eine in mein Haus gegeben, die mir die Wirtschaft führt: ein freundlich-liebliches Mädchen, das sich ausnimmt wie ihr Taufname: Mädeli. Mit der Sonne stehn wir auf, sie pflanzt mir Blumen in den Garten, bereitet mir die Küche, während ich arbeite für die Rückkehr zu Euch; dann essen wir zusammen; sonntags zieht sie ihre schöne Schwyzertracht an, ein Geschenk von mir, wir schiffen uns über, sie geht in die Kirche nach Thun, ich besteige das Schreckhorn, und nach der Andacht kehren wir beide zurück. Weiter weiß ich von der ganzen Welt nichts mehr.

Der unbefangene Leser mag dies als gegeben hinnehmen. Wer jedoch mit den geographischen Verhältnissen vertraut ist weiß, daß das Schreckhorn 69 Kilometer von Thun entfernt ist, und daß es zu Kleists Zeiten noch keinem Bergsteiger gelungen war, es zu bezwingen. Wenn also hier die Phantasie mit dem Dichter durchgeht, könnte dann nicht auch das geschilderte Liebesglück ebenfalls ein dichterischer Wunschtraum sein?

Bisher konnte das Mädeli noch nicht eindeutig eruiert werden. In der von Erich Schmidt herausgegebenen Minde-Pouetschen Gesamtausgabe von Kleists Werken befindet sich im Briefband unter No. 59 eine sich auf das Mädeli beziehende Fußnote: "Elisabeth Magdalena Stettler, 20. Juli 1777 geboren. Die Schilderung des idyllischen Zusammenlebens mit ihr und der regelmäßigen Besteigung des Schreckhorns (!), die natürlich freie Erfindung seiner dichterisch arbeitenden Phantasie ist, zeugt für die glückliche Stimmung Kleists." So weit Minde-Pouet. Hierzu hat Erich Schmidt in seinen Anmerkungen und ebenfalls unter No. 59 folgendes hinzuzufügen: "Der Name der Fischerfamilie war "Gatschet," nach Zolling ("H.v.Kleist in der Schweiz," S.63). Das klingt sehr eindeutig, und um seine Feststellung zu bekräftigen, führt er das Reisetagebuch der Friederike von Pannwitz an, einer Nichte Kleists, die mit Tante Ulrike, Kleists Schwester, 1834 eine Reise durch die Schweiz nach Nizza unternahm. Und nun hören wir seine Beweisführung:

> Wir fuhren zu Wagen den See entlang von Interlaken bis Thun, und stiegen kurz vor der Stadt aus, obgleich es regnete, um die bewußte Insel auf der Aar zu besuchen. Unser Führer führte uns nach der grösseren der beiden Inseln, die noch immer dem früheren Besitzer der beiden Inseln, Herrn Gatscher, gehört, die kleinere ist verkauft. Madame Gatscher saß im Garten, erkannte Tanten auch wieder, und sprach viel von Onkel Heinrich. Sie war so gütig, mit uns nach der kleinen Insel zu gehen, um durch ihre Verwendung uns auch das Haus öffnen zu lassen. . . .

Bezeichnend ist, daß Friederike nur von der "kleinen" und "großen" Insel spricht, nicht aber von der "Delosea-Insel". Wäre dieser Name in Thun gebräuchlich gewesen, würde er ja wohl auch von den einheimischen Führern gebraucht worden sein. Man muß zu der Annahme kommen, daß die Namensgebung ein Willkürakt Zollings war. Die von Friederike als die "kleinere" bezeichnete Insel erscheint jedoch in allen amtlichen Eintragungen als die "obere" Insel, wie bei der Durchsicht sämtlicher Kaufbriefe im Thun-Grundbuch von 1830 bis 1930 durch den Verfasser in tagelanger Arbeit festgestellt wurde. Von größerem Interesse ist die Eintragung vom 13. Oktober 1930, die erstmalig die "Besitzung am Scherzligweg" als die "sogenannte Kleist-Insel" erwähnt. Seit dieser Zeit hat sich dieser Name allgemein durchgesetzt, nicht nur im Volksmund, sondern auch bei den Behörden, auf amtlichen Stadtplänen und auf Ansichtskarten. Damit wäre die Namensbezeichnung der Insel eindeutig klargestellt.

Wie verhält es sich aber mit der von Friederike erwähnten "Madame Gatscher" in bezug auf das rätselhafte Mädeli? Der Kaufbrief vom 5. März 1830 im Thuner Grundbuch gibt an, "daß der wohlgeborene, hochgeachtete Herr, Herr Nicolaus Gatschet" die sogenannte obere Insel verkauft habe. Der von Friederike angegebene Name Gatscher ist also unrichtig. Wenn sich der unbefangene Leser aber auf die Anmerkung No. 59 von Erich Schmidt bezieht, muß er notwendigerweise den Besitzer der Insel mit dem Fischer "an der anderen Spitze" identifizieren und demgemäß glauben, daß Magdalena Gatschet Kleists Mädeli war. Jedoch ist Friederikes "Madame Gatscher," wie in den Burgerrodeln nachweisbar, eine Elisabeth Magdalena Gatschet, geborene Delosea; sie hatte den um viele Jahre älteren Nicolaus Samuel Rudolf Gatschet geheiratet, der Landvogt von Burgdorf und später Präsident des Appelationsgerichtes wurde. Somit scheidet sie also als Kleists Mädeli aus.

Wer aber war die von Zolling erwähnte Magdalena Elisabeth Stettler, welche, wie er angibt, "durch neuerliche Untersuchungen des Professors Arnold Hidber . . ." als "die" Fischertochter auf der Delosea-Insel eruiert wurde? Zolling sagt weiter, daß Hidber diese Forschungsergebnisse in den "Burgerrodeln" in Thun und Bern erzielt habe. Dem Verfasser jedoch gab die Burgerkanzlei zu Bern am 16. Januar 1969 die Auskunft, daß jegliche Nachforschungen, eine 1777 geborene Magdalena Stettler betreffend, ergebnislos geblieben seien. Sie sei weder im bürgerlichen Taufregister erwähnt, noch sei ihr Name im bürgerlichen Stammregister, Blatt "Stettler" aufzufinden. Hinzu kommt, daß in den Burgerrodeln in Bern kaum eine Fischertochter registriert sein kann. Zwar ist dort mit dem Geburtsdatum vom 20. Juli 1777 eine Elisabeth Magdalena Stettler im Staatsarchiv eingetragen, doch entstammte sie einem alten Berner Geschlecht und ist gewiss nicht die Fischertochter auf der oberen Insel.

Die Meinung des 1969 amtierenden Ortspfarrers von Thun, daß Kleists "Mädeli" möglicherweise Magdalena Furer gewesen sei, scheint keineswegs allzu abwegig. Bereits 1832 berichtete Zolling darüber:

> Da die Fischerei auf der obern Insel . . . seit Menschengedenken von der Scherzlinger Familie Furer gepachtet ist, so spricht der greise Dekan von Thun die Vermutung aus, daß Mädeli - Diminutiv von Mäde, Magdalena, und ein noch heute im Oberlande überaus verbreiteter Name - wahrscheinlich Magdalene Furer geheißen und, dieweil die Fama von ihr schweigt, keine besonders merkwürdige Zukunft verlebt habe.

Dazu sei noch bemerkt, daß in dem Kaufbrief vom 5. März 1830 der Verkäufer, Präsident Gatschet, sich die Fischereirechte vorbehielt, um seinen bisherigen Pächter im Lehenhaus abzuschirmen, und daß auch heute noch wie damals die Furers die Fischerei in Scherzligen am Thunersee und auf der Aare gepachtet haben. Das alte Familienhaus der Furers steht in Scherzligen am Ufer des Sees unmittelbar neben dem altehrwürdigen "Scherzlig-Kirchli." Im Volksmund heisst es "das alte Fischerhaus" und war bereits, wie aus einer Eintragung vom 28. März 1838 im Grundbuch Thun hervorgeht, seit 1762 im Familienbesitz, also lange vor Kleists Aufenthalt in Thun.

Stellt man nun in Rechnung, daß in Kleists Brief vom ersten Mai 1802 die Besteigung des Schreckhorns reine dichterische Fiktion ist, so darf dies ebenfalls für sein Zusammenleben mit dem Mädeli angenommen werden. Des weiteren ist zu bedenken, daß ein Zusammenleben vor den Augen des Vaters in dem puritanischen Thun allgemein als ein Skandal angesehen worden wäre. Doch die Chronik weiß darüber nichts zu berichten. Die im gleichen Brief ausgedrückte Sehnsucht nach dem Kind erscheint nicht erstmalig; Kleist hat sie mehrfach in Briefen an die Braut ausgedrückt.

Es war dem Dichter leider nicht vergönnt, längere Zeit in seinem Inselparadies zu leben. Der *Guiskard* entzog sich seinem Zugriff—und Kleist flüchtete sich nun in Krankheit. Im August schrieb er darüber seinem Schwager Wilhelm von Pannwitz; die Schwester Ulrike erfuhr davon und reiste - hilfsbereit wie immer - sofort zu ihm in die Schweiz. Bei ihrer Ankunft in Bern fand sie aber den Bruder bereits wieder gesundet und besuchte nun mit ihm "seine liebe Aar Insel," wo sie gemeinsam mehrere schöne Tage verbrachten. Mitte Oktober verliess Kleist in Begleitung seiner Schwester und des Freundes Wieland die Schweiz. Wieland blieb in Erfurt, die Geschwister reisten weiter nach Weimar, von wo Ulrike allein nach Frankfurt an der Oder zurückkehrte. Kleist aber besuchte den alten Wieland in Ossmannstedt. Dort kam es nun zu der bekannten Deklamation mehrerer Szenen des *Guiskard*, die Kleist aus dem Gedächtnis vortrug. Wieland berichtete darüber am 10. April 1804 an den Freiherrn von Wedekind:

> Ich gestehe Ihnen, daß ich erstaunt war, und ich glaube nicht zu viel zu sagen, wenn ich Sie versichere: Wenn die Geister des Aeschylus, Sophokles und Shakespeare sich vereinigten, eine Tragödie zu schaffen, so würde das sein, was Kleists "Tod des Guiskard" des Normanns, sofern das Ganze demjenigen entspräche, was er mich damals hören ließ.

Ein Jahrhundert später, am 27. Dezember 1913 schrieb Rilke an Marie von Thurn und Taxis in bezug auf den *Prinzen von Homburg* und das *Guiskard*-Fragment, wie "wunderschön" das alles sei und "blind und rein gekonnt, so aus den Tiefen einer harten Natur herausgebrochen."

Als Suchender war Kleist in die Schweiz gekommen und verbrachte seine glücklichste Schaffensperiode auf seinem "lieben Inseli." Was aber bietet sich dem heutigen Besucher, wenn er die Kleist-Insel betritt? Der inzwischen verstorbene Direktor Schütz—die Insel ist nach dem Tode seiner Witwe an den Sohn übergegangen—hat die Insel im Dezember 1939 in völlig verwahrlostem Zustand gekauft und sie wieder in das kleine Paradies verwandelt, das sie zu Kleists Zeiten war. In der Mitte errichtete er sein prächtiges Landhaus und an der westlichen Spitze ein Chalet für den Gärtner. Das Kleisthaus selbst mußte leider im Februar 1940 niedergerissen werden; doch gestaltete der Verstorbene den Platz, wo es einst gestanden hatte, zu einer würdigen Gedenkstätte. Zolling, dem es gelungen war, "die Stätte von Kleists kurzem Glück ausfindig zu machen," beschreibt das Kleisthaus als einen einstöckigen Bau aus Riegelmauern mit einem französischen Mansardendach. Der Thuner Heimatforscher Schaer-Ris berichtet von dem niedrigen Türchen, einem schmalen und nur zwei Meter hohen Gang und einer drei auf vier Meter großen Küche, sowie einem schmalen Wohnraum im Westflügel, drei auf fünf Meter groß. Die Größenmaße im ersten Stockwerk waren die gleichen und boten Raum für zwei Schlafzimmer. Hier waren die Wappen von vier Familien mit dem Datum von 1760 in die Fensterchen "gekritzt," darunter das Familienwappen der Deloseas. Sie zierten in Blei gefaßt die Wohnzimmerfenster der Schützschen Villa und sind nun als unschätzbares Geschenk der verstorbenen Frau Direktor Schütz im Besitz des Verfassers.

Warum aber konnte das Kleisthaus nicht erhalten werden? Über dan Abbruch gab es die heftigsten Kontroversen, nicht nur in mündlichen Debatten, sondern auch in der Thuner Lokalzeitung, dem Oberländer Tagblatt. Das diesbezügliche Material war dem Verfasser durch die liebenswürdige Hilfe des Heimatforschers Schwarz zugänglich. Außerdem hatte er Gelegenheit, den leidigen Streitfall mit der damaligen Besitzerin der Kleist-Insel in persönlicher Aussprache zu diskutieren. Die Kleist-Insel gehörte vor dem Ankauf durch Direktor Schütz einer Belgierin; diese hatte das Häuschen jahrelang nicht bewohnt und es leider auch nicht instand halten lassen. Durch diese jahrelange Verwahrlosung war nicht nur die Insel völlig verwildert, sondern auch das "Kleisthüsli" in einen unrettbaren Zustand geraten. Der neue Besitzer, selbst ein Kleist-Verehrer, hatte den besten Willen, wenn nur irgendmöglich, das Häuschen zu retten. Man halte sich vor Augen, daß das Gebäude unmittelbar an der Aare stand und durch das jahrelange Eindringen des Wassers der Schwamm hineingeraten war, so daß das ganze Gebälk völlig morsch war. Gutachten mehrerer Bausachverständiger erklärten einstimmg, daß eine Instandsetzung auch mit größtem Kostenaufwand nicht möglich sei. Bald darauf stürzte das Dach ein, und wie durch ein Wunder blieben die Wappenscheiben erhalten. So ist zwar das Kleisthaus verschwunden—eine Gedenkstätte aber ist uns geblieben.

Zurück zu Kleist, den wir in Ossmannstedt verließen! Wieland ermutigte ihn nach der Deklamation der Guiskard-Szenen, sein Trauerspiel zu vollenden. Kleist arbeitete wie ein Besessener und schien auch sein Ziel vor Augen zu haben, als er der Schwester schrieb, er nähere sich "allem Erdenglück." Aus vielen Gründen war aber auch sein Bleiben bei Wieland nicht von allzu langer Dauer. Über Leipzig reiste er nach Dresden, wo er die Freunde wußte: Rühle, Pfuel und die Schwestern Karoline und Henriette von Schlieben, und wo er hoffte, ungestört an seinem *Guiskard* weiter arbeiten zu können. Wieder arbeitete der Dichter mit der gleichen Verbissenheit an seinem Trauerspiel—und wieder entzog sich ihm der Stoff. Sein vergebliches Ringen brachte ihn aber der Selbstverwüstung nahe, und als seine Todessehnsucht ins Bedrohliche wuchs, war es der getreue Freund Pfuel, der ihm zur Seite stand. Was lag näher, wenn der *Guiskard* überhaupt zu vollenden war, als Kleist dort hinzuführen, wo er ihn begonnen hatte, wo er froh und glücklich gewesen war: auf sein Inseli bei Thun! So schlug Pfuel ihm eine Fußwanderung in die Schweiz vor und bot ihm an, so lange von seinem Geld zu leben, bis der *Guiskard* vollendet sei. Doch als Ulrike von den erneuten Reiseplänen erfuhr, versorgte sie den Bruder wieder einmal mit den nötigen Mitteln, obwohl sie nicht viel von dem Vorhaben hielt.

Am Tage seiner Abreise am 20. Juli 1803 in Begleitung Pfuels erreichte Kleist ein Brief Wielands, der ihn erneut anspornte, seinen *Guiskard* zu vollenden, auch wenn "der ganze Kaukasus und Atlas" auf ihn drücke. Man würde aufgrund dieser Ermutigung nun Briefe erwarten, die das gleiche Glück und die gleiche Schaffensfreude ausstrahlten, die wir von Kleists erstem Aufenthalt in der Schweiz kennen. Doch nichts davon. Nach dem Abschiedsgruß am Tag der Abreise an Ulrike hören wir nichts mehr von ihm bis zum 5. Oktober, als er ihr endlich wieder aus Genf schreibt. Da keine Briefe über diesen zweiten Schweizer Aufenthalt vorliegen, ist die Kleistforschung auf die spärlichen Angaben angewiesen, die Tieck und Bülow erst Jahre später von Pfuel erhielten. Die Freunde reisten über Bern nach Thun, wo Kleist wohl auf kurze Zeit Ruhe zur Arbeit fand. Hier hatte er den *Guiskard* begonnen und hier hoffte er ihn zu vollenden—doch wieder entzog er sich seinem Griff.

Aber es will scheinen, daß Kleist bereits hier, inspiriert durch den Freund, seine *Penthesilea* konzipierte. Wenn dem so ist, und zwei spätere Briefe sprechen für die Annahme des Verfassers (Brief vom 7. Januar 1805 an Pfuel und Brief vom Spätherbst 1807 an Marie von Kleist), so war dennoch der erneute Aufenthalt auf der Insel von grösster Wirkung. Mit der *Penthesilea* gelang Kleist, was er mit dem *Guiskard* vergeblich erstrebt hatte: "eine gewisse Entdeckung im Gebiete der Kunst"—die griechische Tragödie modern zu sehen.

Kleist und Pfuel hielten sich während dieser zweiten Schweizer Reise mehrere Male in Thun auf. Das genaue Datum des ersten Aufenthaltes ist nur ungefähr festlegbar. Ulrike berichtete nur knapp und ohne Zeitangaben über diesen Lebensabschnitt ihres Bruders, wohl aber erwähnte sie die Werdecks. Adolphine von Werdeck führte ein Reisetagebuch mit genauen Daten. Demzufolge teilte Gessner ihr am 7. August 1803 mit, daß die beiden Freunde in Bern auf die Werdecks gewartet, sich aber inzwischen nach Thun begeben hätten, um mit ihnen zusammen von dort aus weiterzureisen. Bereits am 12. August berichtete sie von einer gemeinsamen Wanderung nach den Reichenbachfällen. Danach kann also der erste Thuner Aufenthalt Kleists und Pfuels nur von kurzer Dauer gewesen sein. Das Tagebuch Adolphines enthält eine äußerst wichtige Mitteilung unterm 13. August:

> Der unschlüssige Kleist hatte zehnmal uns versichert, er würde uns nach Schwyz begleiten, und zehnmal wieder gesagt, es ginge nicht an - endlich beschloss er, nach Thun zurückzukehren, um sein Peststück (ein Trauerspiel, das dünkt mich "die Numantia" heißen sollte) zu vollenden.

Auch dieser zweite Aufenthalt war nur kurz, denn das Tagebuch berichtet, daß die Freunde sich am 21. August in einem Gasthaus in Bellinzona wieder trafen, um sich am 29. August endgültig zu trennen. Kleist und Pfuel kehrten erneut auf die Insel zurück. Dieser letzte Aufenthalt war zweifellos der längste, denn von Thun begaben sie sich über Bern nach Genf, wo wir am 5. Oktober von Kleist hören. Seit 18 Monaten hatte er mit dem *Guiskard* gerungen, und immer wieder hatte der Stoff—so glaubte er— sich seinem Zugriff versagt. Er hatte versucht, das Unerreichbare zu erreichen, bis er in Resignation und Todessehnsucht versank. Und nun schrieb er jenen einzigartigen und erschütternden Brief an die Schwester:

> Der Himmel weiß, meine teuerste Ulrike (und ich will umkommen, wenn es nicht wörtlich wahr ist), wie gern ich einen Blutstropfen aus meinem Herzen für jeden Buchstaben eines Briefes gäbe, der so anfangen könnte: "mein Gedicht ist fertig." Aber, Du weißt, wer, nach dem Sprüchwort, mehr tut als er kann. Ich habe nun ein Halbtausend hinter einander folgender Tage, die Nächte der meisten mit eingerechnet, an den Versuch gesetzt, zu so vielen Kränzen noch einen auf unsere Familie herabzuringen: jetzt ruft mir unsere heilige Schutzgöttin zu, daß es genug sei. Sie küßt mir gerührt den Schweiß von der Stirne, und tröstet mich, "wenn jeder ihrer lieben Söhne nur ebenso viel täte, so würde unserm Namen ein Platz in den Sternen nicht fehlen." Und so sei es denn genug. Das Schicksal, das den Völkern jeden Zuschuß zu ihrer Bildung zumißt, will, denke ich, die Kunst in diesem nördlichen Himmelsstrich noch nicht reifen lassen. Töricht wäre es wenigstens, wenn "ich" meine Kräfte länger an ein Werk setzen wollte, das, wie ich mich endlich überzeugen muß, für mich zu schwer ist. Ich trete vor einem zurück, der noch nicht da ist, und beuge mich, ein Jahrtausend im Voraus, vor seinem Geiste. Denn in der Reihe der menschlichen Empfindungen ist diejenige, die ich gedacht habe, unfehlbar ein Glied, und es wächst irgendwo ein Stein schon für den, der sie einst ausspricht ... Die Hölle gab mir meine halben Talente, der Himmel schenkt dem Menschen ein ganzes, oder gar keins.

Kleist verließ die Schweiz, in der er zum Dichter geworden war, nur als ein scheinbar Geschlagener. Die Niederlage war ihm zur fixen Idee geworden und führte zu einer völligen geistigen Katastrophe, aus der er sich aber, wenn auch nur langsam, erholte. Danach begann er, seinem dichterischen Ingenium zu vertrauen und schaffte nun diese einmaligen Menschen: Penthesilea, Käthchen, Eve, Alkmene, Toni, Natalie, und den Prinzen, sowie den Kurfürsten und den Kohlhaas.

Kleist hat keinen neuen Mythos gebracht, wenn nicht den Mythos der menschlichen Seele. Die Wahrheit, die er kündet, ist nicht die Wahrheit der Welt, sondern die Wahrheit eines einmaligen menschlichen Herzens. Schicksal heißt für Kleist, der Wahrheit seines Wesens folgen zu müßen. In der Wahrheit des andren zu leben, heiß für ihn: lieben. Und so schaut uns Spätgeborene der Dichter, der im Zeichen der Wahrheit starb, mit fragenden Augen an, da wir in der Verworrenheit unserer Zeit nicht müde werden, uns mißzuverstehen.

BIBLIOGRAPHIE

Bülow, Eduard von: *Heinrich von Kleists Leben und Briefe.* Berlin, 1848.
Bülow, Eduard von: "Über Heinrich von Kleists Leben." *Monatsblätter zur Allgemeinen Zeitung.* Augsburg, November 1846.
Hoffman, Paul: "Ulrike von Kleist über ihren Bruder Heinrich." In: *Euphorion* 1903.
Reske, Hermann: *Heinrich von Kleist in Thun - Die Geburt des Genius.* Paul Haupt Bern und Stuttgart, 1972.
Röhl, Hans: "Aus dem Reisetagebuch der Freifrau Adolphine von Werdeck im Sommer 1803." *Jahrbuch der Kleistgesellschaft* 1938.
Sembdner, Helmut: *Heinrich von Kleists Nachruhm.* Carl Schünemann, Bremen 1967.
Sembdner, Helmut: *Jahresbericht 1962.* Historisches Museum, Schloss Thun.
Sembdner, Helmut: Kleists Lebensspuren. Schünemann, Bremen 1957.
Zolling, Theophil: *Heinrich von Kleist in der Schweiz.* Stuttgart, 1882.
Zschokke, Heinrich: *Eine Selbstschau.* Aarau, 1842.

Literaturrezeption als Spiegel ihrer Zeit: Die Frankfurter Kleist-Feier von 1927 und die politische Rolle der Kleist-Gemeinde in der Weimarer Republik

ROLF BUSCH
Freie Universität Berlin

1. EINE DICHTERFEIER—SPIEGEL IHRER ZEIT

Eine Dichterfeier gibt exemplarisch Auskunft darüber, welche Rolle eine Gesellschaft in einer bestimmen historischen Situation einem Dichter zuzuweisen gedenkt, welche Wert- und Zielvorstellungen sie sich zu adaptieren wünscht.

"Was der Dichter unserer Zeit zu sagen hat"—darüber vermögen die Aussagen der Feiernden in der Regel herzlich wenig zu verraten, ebensowenig wie darüber, was der Gefeierte seiner eigenen Zeit mitzuteilen sich bemühte. Vielmehr treten anläßlich einer solchen Dichterfeier wie unter der Vergrößerung eines Brennglases sämtliche Tendenzen der Rezeption an die Oberfläche, die in der Gesellschaft im Moment vorhanden sind—Spiegelungen ihres Bewußteins in seiner ganzen Komplexität, Ausdruck ihres Verhältnisses zu sich selbst, zur politischen Realität, zur Kultur—und natürlich zum gefeierten Dichter.

Also leitet, in der Regel entgegen der offiziellen Fragestellung, weniger das "Was hat der Dichter uns in unserer Zeit zu sagen?" als vielmehr das "Was wünschen wir in unserer Zeit vom Dichter zu hören?" Etwas überspitzt, ist es die Frage nach dem Nutzen, die den Feiernden leitet, kann es das Benutzen des Dichters für Zwecke sein, die nicht dem Werk des Dichters, vielmehr der Gegenwart und ihrem gesellschaftlichen Bewußtsein, dem vorherrschenden, oft "falschen", d.h. ideologischen, und den nur bei Minderheiten vorhandenen Bewußtseinssträngen entlehnt sind.

Es liegt auf der Hand, nicht bei der Frage nach dem Nutzen stehenzubleiben, sondern die Zwecke zu hinterfragen, für die da einer, der—wie Heinrich von Kleist—vor 200 Jahren, vor sechs bis acht Generationen also und entsprechend vielen Kriegen, vor mindestens zwei die Welt drastisch verändernden Revolutionen, am Ende des feudal-absolutistischen und am Beginn des bürgerlichen Zeitalters geboren wurde und geschrieben hat, benutzt werden soll. Das heißt, es ist geboten, die Interessen offenzulegen, die einer hat, der eines solchen Menschen, ihn feiernd, gedenkt, also die Feiernden nach dem "cui bono?" zu fragen und dies sicher um so mehr, als der Gefeierte zu seiner Zeit wenig Gelegenheit hatte, sich feiern zu lassen, im Grunde gar keine, und gedemütigt, verlassen, ohne Lorbeerkranz, offenbar ganz und gar nutzlos in seiner Gesellschaft, jedenfalls von ihr vertoßen, nicht bloß unrühmlich, sondern nach unsern Rechtsvorstellungen eigentlich als ein des Totschlags Schuldiger und ganz zweifellos als Selbstmörder endete. Ein Gefeierter, von dem noch Generationen von potentiellen Rezipienten seiner Werke aus sehr unterschiedlichen Gründen nichts wissen wollten, bis ihn dann historische Entwicklungen nach jahrzehntelanger und durchaus auch politischer Unterdrückung ans Licht der Berühmtheit spülten. Im großen und ganzen um die Zeit seines 100. Geburtstages, konkret im Jahre 1875, bedienten sich die Beherrscher des frisch gegründeten deutschen Kaiserreiches zur 200-Jahr-Feier der Schlacht von Fehrbellin erstmals des jetzt "entdeckten" Dichters und seines "Prinzen von Homburg," und in schneller Folge kamen vier Gesamtausgaben seiner Werke auf den Buchmarkt. Die nach der Reichsgründung herrschenden Gruppen, Schichten, Klassen—wie auch immer—erkannten Kleist als brauchbar, als nützlich, als für ihre Interessen verwertbar, und seit dieser Zeit wurde er in nicht mehr gebrochener Tradition bis 1945 als ideologische "Waffe" im "Klassenkampf von oben" eingesetzt.

Wie Heinrich von Kleist dazu kam, zum Hofdichter teilweise der gleichen Schichten zu avancieren, die ihn zu seinen Lebzeiten verfemten und, soweit man das sagen kann, in den Tod getrieben hatten, was er überhaupt damit zu tun hat, als Kronzeuge des wilhelminischen Imperialismus herhalten, sich von den gleichen reaktionären gesellschaftlichen Schichten nach 1918 auf ihrem temporären Rückzug gegen die Weimarer Republik einsetzen lassen zu müssen, um nach 1933 als "Klassiker des Nationalsozialismus" zu enden—die Frage also nach der etwaigen Verantwortung des Autors und seines Werkes für seine Rezeption ist im Vergleich zu der Frage nach den Interessen der Rezipienten, nach dem historisch-gesellschaftlichen Kontext der Rezeption nebensächlich. Als Beispiel für Kleists Rolle als Hofdichter sei angeführt, daß 42 Prozent der Aufführungen des 'Prinzen von Homburg," genau 822, bis zum Ende des 1. Weltkrieges an Hoftheatern stattfanden; ein rundes Viertel, d.h. 456, fallen in die Jahre des Weltkrieges.[1] Den Ursachen für eine bestimmte Weise der Rezeption nachzugehen ist eine eminent wichtige Aufgabe, doch führt der Versuch, diese Ursachen und Zusammenhänge im Werk, beim Autor aufzuspüren, eher in die Irre, abstrahiert von der Tatsache, daß alle Rezeption Teil und Spiegel des jeweils herrschenden gesellschaftlichen Bewußtseins, Produkt des "gesellschaftlichen Seins" im Marxschen Sinne ist.

Gerade am Beispiel des Kleistschen Nationalismus läßt sich zeigen, wie eine ursprünglich fortschrittliche, den Interessen der zu Kleists Zeit herrschenden adligen Oberschichten entgegengesetzte Idee im historischen Verlauf umschlägt und 100 Jahre später zum ideologischen Werkzeug der auf imperialistische Abenteuer zielenden deutschen Oberschicht wird. "Beerbt" und politisch verwertet wurden, dies nur nebenbei, vom deutschen Faschismus unter den Dichtern nicht nur Kleist, sondern auch Goethe und Schiller,[2] unter den Komponisten nicht nur Wagner, sondern auch Schubert, Beethoven und Mozart, unter den Malern Rembrandt, Dürer und Mathias Grünewald. Walter Benjamin, der auf der Flucht vor den Nazis kurz vor Erreichen der Freiheit in den Selbstmord getrieben wurde, gibt dazu eine einfache, immer noch zutreffende Antwort:

"Auch die Toten werden vor dem Feind, wenn er siegt, nicht sicher sein.
Und dieser Feind hat zu siegen nicht aufgehört."
(Geschichtsphilosophische Thesen, VI.)

Eine Antwort, die einen freilich nicht der Pflicht entheben soll, den Ursachen jenes Siegens nachzugehen — und sei es, um ein Wiederholen zu verhindern.

Ich komme damit zum Ausgangspunkt zurück, zur Kleist-Feier als Spiegelbild der wesentlichen Tendenzen der Kleist-Rezeption zu einem bestimmten historischen Zeitpunkt. Am Beispiel der Feier der 150. Wiederkehr von Kleists Geburtstag im Oktober 1927, also vor nunmehr 50 Jahren, sollen in ihrem gesellschaftlichen Zusammenhang die wesentlichen Züge der vorherrschend antidemokratischen, klassengebundenen, teils rückwärts am Kaiserreich orientierten, teils zielstrebig auf die Machtergreifung des Faschismus hinarbeitenden Kleist-Rezeption der Weimarer Republik dargestellt werden. Die in Buchform vorliegende ideologiekritische Gesamtuntersuchung der dominierenden Kleist-Rezeption vom Kaiserreich bis zum National-sozialismus unter Heranziehung von 400 Quellen läßt die exemplarische Betrachtung der Frankfurter Kleist-Feier von 1927 gerechtfertigt erscheinen.[3] Die Kürze der hier zur Verfügung stehenden Zeit erlaubt es allerdings nicht, der notwendigen materialistischen Ableitung der in den Rezeptionsdokumenten artikulierten Ideologeme und ihres historischen Verwendungszusammenhangs den erforderlichen Raum zu widmen. Zudem müssen wohl auch—um mit Friedrich Engels zu sprechen—nicht "für all diesen urzuständlichen Blödsinn ökonomische Ursachen" gesucht werden.[4]

Wenn anläßlich der 200. Wiederkehr des Geburtstages Heinrich von Kleists Reflexionen über die Rolle angestellt werden, die Kleist und seinem Werk in der deutschen Geschichte vorwiegend zugewiesen wurde—eine schändliche Rolle, wie wir sie werten müssen—so geschieht dies nicht in der Absicht, Kleists Bild zu verdunkeln, sein Werk herabzuwürdigen—im Gegenteil: Erst die Aufklärung über die Ursachen jener den politischen Zielen des wilhelminischen Imperialismus, der antidemokratischen Kräfte in der Weimarer Republik und des Nationalsozialismus dienstbaren Kleist-Rezeption vermag uns die Geschichte sowohl als auch das Werk Kleists in seinem historischen Zusammenhang zu erhellen. Der Verdrängungsarbeit gerade der zahlreichen deutschen Germanisten gegenüber der Geschichte ihrer wissenschaftlichen Disziplin wie auch gegenüber der im Regelfall ignorierten dominierenden deutschen Kleist-Rezeption kann nicht entschieden genug entgegengetreten werden. [Nicht sonderlich hilfreich, aber immerhin ein Anfang sind in diesem Zusammenhang erste Untersuchungen englischer und amerikanischer Wissenschaftler aus der Zeit des 2. Weltkrieges, die sich u.a. mit der politischen Instrumentalisierung von Literatur durch die Nazis befassen: Eugene Newton Anderson, *Nationalism and the Cultural Crisis in Prussia 1806-1815* (New York 1939), sowie Henry Gibson Atkins: *German Literature through Nazi Eyes*, (London 1940). Die Verfasser kommen mit ihrer unhistorischen Einschätzung des Kleistschen Nationalismus und seiner Funktion in seiner Zeit nicht zurecht.]

II. DIE POLITISCHE FUNKTION DER KLEIST-GEMEINDE IN DER WEIMARER REPUBLIK

Mit dem Zusammenbruch des Kaiserreiches nach der militärischen Niederlage Deutschlands und der Ausrufung der ersten deutschen Republik ist die bis dahin vorherrschende und im Weltkrieg kulminierende Tradition der Kleist-Rezeption zunächst unterbrochen. Doch schon 1919 beschließen die national-konservativen, monarchistisch orientierten Träger der Tradition die organisierte Wiederaufnahme der Instrumentalisierung Kleists.

Am 4. März 1920 gründen sie in Berlin die Kleist-Gesellschaft mit Sitz in Frankfurt an der Oder—ein Unternehmen, für dessen Unterstützung sie trotz der schon unverkennbaren rückwärts orientierten Tendenzen der Vereinsleitung zahlreiche namhafte republikanische Künstler und Wissenschaftler gewinnen können.[5]

Mit dem Erstarken der reaktionären Kräfte in der Weimarer Republik werden im Lauf weniger Jahre die zunächst gebotenen Verschleierungsversuche überflüssig, wie u.a. die Kleist-Feier 1927 zeigt. Die politische Zielsetzung der literarischen Gesellschaft führt zu permanenten internen Konflikten und ermöglicht schließlich im Jahre 1933 die freiwillige und bewußt vollzogene Eingliederung der Rumpfgesellschaft in den Kulturbetrieb des Nationalsozialismus. Der Gründungsaufruf der Kleist-Gesellschaft nennt als wesentliches Ziel, die durch Kleist "beflügelte vaterländische Gesinnung zu fördern."[6]

Dieser noch diskrete Hinweis auf eine als solche empfundene Mangelerscheinung in der republikanischen Gegenwart gewinnt an Eindeutigkeit, wenn der gleiche Aufruf explizit an die nicht mißzuverstehende Rezeptionstradition im gerade verlorenen Krieg, d.h. an den Einsatz Kleists als ideologische Waffe anzuknüpfen versucht.

Charakteristisch für den gesamten Strang der antidemokratischen Weimarer Kleist-Rezeption ist das den Gründungsaufruf abschließende Bekenntnis:

"Zu Kleist stehen heißt deutsch sein!"

In den folgenden Jahren entfaltet diese anmaßende Parole immer offener ihren aggressiven, die Gesellschaft in "Freunde" und "Feinde" einteilenden Gehalt. In ihr kommt am kürzesten das Verschwörungsgehabe der Reaktion zum Ausdruck, die sich mehr und mehr als quasi literarische "Kampfgemeinde" versteht. Wo das Bekenntnis zu Kleist, d.h. nicht zu Kleist und seinem Werk, sondern zu einer ganz spezifischen Kleist-Rezeption der wilhelminischen Ära, als Legitimation dafür herhalten muß das Etikett "deutsch" usurpieren zu können, ist die Ausgrenzung alles dessen, was als "undeutsch," weil außerhalb der (politischen) Rezeptionstradition stehend, abqualifiziert werden kann, ein Leichtes.[7]

So spiegelt die explizite Denunzierung vermeintlicher Kleist-Gegner als "Gegner Deutschlands" nichts anderes wider als die Ablehnung der republikanischen Gesellschaft und das Warten auf den Zeitpunkt, zu dem ganz andere innen- wie außenpolitische Ziele energischer verfolgt werden können.

Die Instrumentalisierung der einzelnen Werke Kleists tritt deutlich hinter die Vereinnahmung Kleists als Autor, als Politiker in seiner Zeit zurück. Neben ebenso griffigen wie verschwommenen Formeln und überkommenen Klischees vom "Großen Unzeitgemäßen," vom "Rufer in der Wüste," "Haßwecker," "Befreier," "Retter," "Führer," "Militaristen," und "Brandstifter der ungeheuersten Feuersbrunst völkischer Rache- und Freiheits-Leidenschaft"[8] wirken gelegentliche Textbezüge nur als Dekor.

Wo man auf ein präformiertes Kleistbild bei den Gemeindemitgliedern bauen und sich des stillschweigenden politischen Einverständnisses sicher sein kann, erübrigen sich die weitere Beschäftigung mit den Werken des Dichters ebenso wie die Ausformulierung der vielen politisch doppeldeutigen Anspielungen und Appelle: Was eigentlich gemeint und beabsichtigt ist, kann unausgesprochen bleiben, da es von den Adressaten im antidemokratischen Lager ohnehin verstanden wird: die Beseitigung der verhaßten demokratischen Staatsform einerseits und die außenpolitisch-militärische Revanche andererseits.

Kennzeichnend für das politische Bewußtsein der führenden Vertreter der Kleist-Gesellschaft und der ihr verbundenen Kleist-Rezipienten ist ihre fortbestehende Identifikation mit dem wilhelminischen Deutschland. Der Verlust der alten Macht oder auch nur der alten Herrschaftsklasse und damit der Verlust der "machtgeschützten Innerlichkeit" lassen sie die militärische Niederlage als persönliche Schmach empfinden. Teilweise ökonomisch entwurzelt, von sozialer Deklassierung bedroht und politisch nach der Novemberrevolution desorientiert, suchen die bisher nach eigener Anschauung kulturtragenden Schichten ihr Heil in der rückwärts gewandten Utopie. Die Geschichte bleibt mit ihren Ursachen für die Entstehung und den Verlauf des Krieges unbegriffen, zumal die bereitgestellte "Dolchstoßlegende" als Geschichtsklitterung fraglos akzeptiert wird.

Im Innern mit einer offener erkennbaren und spürbaren Klassengesellschaft konfrontiert, deren Charakter im Kaiserreich mehr oder weniger gewaltsam unterdrückt und leichter geleugnet werden konnte, bedroht von gesellschaftlichem Abstieg und vom Machtanspruch neuer Klassen und Schichten, das Land zum Teil von ausländischen Truppen besetzt und ohne den vertrauten Schein vor allem militärischer Staatsmacht, flieht die Kleist-Gemeinde in den absurden Vergleich zwischen ihrer Gegenwart und der Zeit Kleists vor den Befreiungskriegen.

Wurde das wilhelminische Deutschland als Verwirklichung der Kleistschen Utopie reklamiert, so wird nun "Sklaverei" nach innen und außen unterstellt; man identifiziert sich mit Kleist in seinem Verhältnis zur Gesellschaft des Jahres 1811 und zur Besetzung preußisch-deutscher Gebiete durch napoleonische Truppen—mit allen Konsequenzen.

Die Wiederherstellung der alten gewaltsamen Scheinlösung der Klassenwidersprüche und die Befreiung von den Besatzungstruppen nach dem Versailler Friedensvertrag erscheinen hinter der Einvernahme eines 1811 gestorbenen Dichters als die eigentlichen Interessen der Kleist-Rezipienten. Mit dem vermeintlichen "Kulturbolschewismus" der Weimarer Republik, mit der "Proletarisierung der Bürgerlichen Kultur" jagt man ein Phantom, und mit dem Kampf gegen den sogenannten "Materialismus" der verhaßten Gegenwart versuchen die Ideologieproduzenten der Mittelschichten blind und aussichtslos ihre unhaltbare Position zwischen den antagonistischen gesellschaftlichen Klassen zu verteidigen.

Daß sich ganz andere, ganz und gar unliterarisch interessierte Kräfte des Schlachtrufs bedienen, der ursprünglich den "Prinz von Homburg" beschließt: "In Staub mit allen Feinden Brandenburgs!", jetzt aber als hohle Geste Kleistsche Feierreden zu beenden pflegt, entgeht diesen Kleist-Erben. So lächerlich uns solch markige Worte heute erscheinen mögen—der präparierte Hörer oder Leser im Jahr 1927 nimmt sie durchaus ernst und denkt sicher, was die angesprochenen "Feinde" betrifft, weniger an die im historischen Dunkel der Zeit des Großen Kurfürsten verschwundenen Zeitgenossen als vielmehr, je nach seiner subjektiven Feind-Einschätzung, an den "Franzmann" oder andere ehemalige Kriegsgegner, an die Kommunisten, die Sozialdemokraten, die Gewerkschaften, das Großkapital, die Parteien schlechthin, die Juden — oder eben "das System."

Und immerhin dauert es, auch wenn hier kein Kausalzusammenhang zwischen solch ideologischen Nebelbildungen und der Machtergreifung des Faschismus in Deutschland behauptet werden soll, nur wenige Jahre, bis die in jahrelanger Übung verbal ins Visier genommenen "Feinde Brandenburgs" tatsächlich erlegt werden, bis also die "Nebelbildungen" furchtbare materielle Gestalt annehmen.

III. DIE FRANKFURTER KLEIST-FEIER VON 1927

Im Oktober 1927, veranstalten die Kleist-Gesellschaft, die Stadt Frankfurt/Oder und die Familie von Kleist zur 150. Wiederkehr von des Dichters Geburtstag dreitägige Feiern. Den politischen Horizont der Junker-Dynastie derer von Kleist mag eine unmißverständliche Distanzierung des Familienvorstandes von einer ausnahmsweise nicht von Antidemokraten beherrschten "Kleiststiftung" aus dem Jahre 1921 illustrieren, in der ausdrücklich darauf verwiesen wird, daß es gerade die "jüdische Leitung" der Stiftung sei, die "dem Geiste Kleists" nicht entspreche.[9]

Nicht minder deutlich ist die in den Staatsfarben des Kaiserreiches (und des späteren Nazi-Deutschland) gehaltene schwarz-weiß-rote Schleife, verziert mit dem mehrfach zitierten Wunsch: "In Staub mit allen Feinden Brandenburgs!", die den Kranz schmückt, den ein Graf von Kleist-Retzow am Kleist-Denkmal im Oktober 1927 niederlegt. Und damit auch wirklich niemand mißversteht, wer mit den "Feinden" gemeint sei und was mit den französischen Besatzungstruppen im Rheinland—dem "Franzmann"—tunlichst geschehen solle, fügt dieser Graf den Germania-Vers hinzu: "Schlagt ihn tot! Das Weltgericht / fragt euch nach den Gründen nicht!" Kleist dachte, was immer davon zu halten war, damals mehr an den historischen Napoleon.

Immerhin benötigte die Offiziersdynastie von Kleist rund 100 Jahre, um sich auf ihre Art positiv des ob seiner militärischen Untauglichkeit und seines unheldischen Endes lange totgeschwiegenen Vorfahrens zu erinnern. Daß einigen Familienmitgliedern bei den Feiern eine peinliche Verwechslung des zu feiernden Objekts mit einem gleichnamigen ehemaligen Generalmajor, bzw. mit einem weniger bekannten ebenfalls dichtenden Vorfahren von Kleist (Ewald) unterläuft, sei hier nur als bezeichnende Kuriosität am Rande erwähnt.

Während der eigentlichen Festveranstaltung brechen die Widersprüche zwischen der reaktionär-traditionalistischen Kleist-Gemeinde und den demokratisch-liberalen Kleist-Rezipienten, wie sie von Anfang an schon in der Zusammensetzung der Kleist-Gesellschaft selbst angelegt waren, offen aus. Anlaß ist der Inhalt der Festrede, die vom Präsidenten der Sektion Dichtkunst der Neuen Preußischen Akademie der Wissenschaften, Wilhelm von Scholz, gehalten wird. Anknüpfend an die überlieferte Tendenz der Kleist-Rezeption bis 1918, die in vorsichtiger Form problematisiert wird, und ausgehend von der gegenwärtigen politischen Situation der Weimarer Republik in der Phase relativer innen- wie außenpolitischer Stabilisierung (Dawes-Plan 1923, Abschluß der Verträge von Rapallo 1923, Locarno 1925, Eintritt Deutschlands in den Völkerbund, 1926) weist Scholz auf die demokratischen und übernationalen Zukunftsperspektiven hin. Entsprechend hebt er bei der Entwicklung seines Kleist-Bildes mehr die Neigung des Dichters zu "Pazifismus" und "Menschheitsvaterland" hervor. Vor den in Frankfurt/Oder versammelten Spitzen der Behörden, der Militärs, der Kleist-Gesellschaft und der Familie von Kleist spricht Scholz—wie die liberal-demokratische "Frankfurter Zeitung" (Frankfurt am Main) berichtet:

> "von Europa und für Europa, und es war deutlich zu merken, daß jenes Realgymnasium und seine Versammelten solche Worte noch nicht gehört hatten. Zweifellos war diese Rede von Scholz eine gute, brauchbare und mutige Tat; sie beleuchtete ein wenig die vorsichtig unter allgemeiner Begeisterung für den Dichter Heinrich von Kleist verborgene völkisch-chauvinistische Einstellung der Feier, welche sich nicht ungern an Freiheitskriege erinnert. Auch Pfitzner wollte in diesem Sinne verstanden werden."[10]

Mit Pfitzner ist der musikalische Rahmen gemeint, der von Stücken des wenig später unter den Nationalsozialisten zu Ansehen gelangten Komponisten Pfitzner gebildet wird, darunter ein vertonter "Chor der Barden" aus der "Hermannsschlacht," aufgeführt unter Leitung des zum Ehrenmitglied der Kleist-Gesellschaft ernannten Komponisten.

Das abendliche Festbankett artet — nach dem bisherigen Verlauf der Feier begreiflich—in einen "allgemeinen wüsten Streit" zwischen Reaktionären, die Kleist als "den großen Nationalisten" preisen, und Republikanern aus, die ihn als "Weltbürger" sehen—ein Streit, der, wie die Dokumente zeigen, in der Folgezeit in der demokratischen und der republikfeindlichen Presse lautstark weitergeführt wird.

Die Diffamierungskampagne, die gegen den Festredner Wilhelm von Scholz geführt wird, macht deutlich, welche politischen Tabus der Akademiepräsident mit seiner auf Versöhnung Deutschlands mit den ehemaligen Kriegsgegnern bedachten Rede durchbrochen hat. Wie die traditionalistische Kleist-Rezeption selbst sich des Dichters zu ganz anderen politischen Zwecken bedient, soll auch die vehement geführte Kampagne nur zum Schein Scholz treffen; im Kern wird sie als grundsätzliche Abrechnung mit der Weimarer Republik, dem verhaßten "System" geführt. Die uns abstrus erscheinenden Ausfälle zeigen, welche Bedeutung der Dichter Kleist als politische Waffe und als Identifikationsobjekt gewonnen hat. Gleich dreifach werden durch die Scholz-Rede Tabus der Kleist-Gemeinde verletzt: zum einen das selbst konstruierte, tradierte Kleist-Bild, zum andern das Bild der abgelehnten demokratischen Republik und damit das immer noch geliebte Gegenbild des deutschen Kaiserreiches, und zum dritten der "Alleinvertretungsanspruch" der Kleist-Gemeinde bezüglich der Kleist-Rezeption.

In einer extrem emotionalisierten Sprache geht man zum Gegenangriff gegen die vermeintliche Fälschung der Werkauffassung vor, die als Angriff auf den toten Dichter gewertet wird: "Schwere Entgleisung," "Gaukelspiel," "ungeheurer Schimpf," "Besudeln," "Verhöhnung," "noch im Grabe," "grabschänderisch zweckhafte Verfälschung," "Vergewaltigung," "Leichenschändung" mögen als Beispiele des eingesetzten Vokabulars genügen.

Es entlarvt den pseudosakralen Charakter dieser Art Literaturrezeption, deren Anhänger eine für sie ungewohnte Kleist-Interpretation als Frevel am toten Dichter und dem Anschein nach als ihnen selbst zugefügten Schmerz empfinden. Die genaue Untersuchung des Konglomerats weist Sprache und Argumentation als die des "Unmenschen" des späteren Faschismus aus, dem Begriffe wie Internationalismus, Pazifismus, und Sozialismus gleichfalls als ideologisches Feindbild dienen. Im Zusammenhang mit dem aus dem literarisch-historischen Kontext gerissenen Kleist-Zitat: "Was aber ist Gott ein Greuel?" (Antwort: "Wenn Sklaven leben") werden Demokraten wie Scholz als "Friedensfreunde"—was pejorativ gemeint ist!—als "verköterte Menschen, die ihr sterbendes Herz dem Feind antragen, der sie mißhandelt," als 'vollkommene Kretins" in nicht mehr zu überbietender Weise diffamiert.[11]

Die sich des Dichters als Vehikel bedienende Aggression erreicht die Qualität der Morddrohung, die im historischen Zusammenhang ihrer wenig später erfolgten Umsetzung in die Wirklichkeit jeden Anflug von Lächerlichkeit ein der ihr in folgenschwerer Fehleinschätzung der politischen Lage Deutschlands in der liberal-demokratischen Presse der Zeit noch zugemessen wird. Wie man in der Zukunft mit denen zu verfahren beabsichtigt, die im beispielhaft zitierten barbarischen Jargon der "Kulturfledderei," des "Kulturbolschewismus" und des "organisierten Verbrechens am Geist" bezichtigt werden, sobald die gesellschaftlichen Verhältnisse den verblendeten Anklägern dazu die Gelegenheit bieten, kann nicht mehr mißverstanden werden.

Und all dies, wohlgemerkt, in der Reaktion auf eine alles andere als politisch-agitatorische, provokatorische Jubiläumsrede eines Schriftstellers und Kulturfunktionärs auf einen anderen Schriftsteller—eines Akademiepräsidenten, dessen Distanz zu seinen augenblicklichen Gegnern im nachhinein mit aller Vorsicht zu beurteilen ist: Es soll nicht verschwiegen werden, daß derselbe Wilhelm von Scholz genau sechs Jahre später nach der Machtübernahme des Faschismus in Deutschland selbst des Nazi-Vokabulars in erstaunlichem Maße kundig ist, als er—gemeinsam mit Rudolf G. Binding, E.G. Kolbenheyer, Otto Wirz, und Robert Fabre-Luce—sein "Bekenntnis zum neuen Deutchland" ablegt und den zur Macht gelangten Nationalsozialismus gegen die Kritik Romain Rollands verteidigt.[12]

Ein Bekenntnis zu einem Deutschland, das den in der Tat wehrlosen Dichter Heinrich von Kleist zum "Klassiker des Nationalsozialismus" erhebt und das Erbe der im wilhelminischen Imperialismus begründeten Kleist-Rezeption antritt — ein "Erbe," das wir heute zwar nicht zu übernehmen haben, das wir aber als Teil der weiterwirkenden Geschichte vorfinden und aufarbeiten müssen.

> "Die jeweils Herrschenden sind aber die Erben aller, die je gesiegt haben.(...)
> Die Beute wird, wie das immer so üblich war, im Triumphzug mitgeführt. Man bezeichnet sie als die Kulturgüter."
> *(Geschichtsphilosophische Thesen, VII.)*

So Walter Benjamin, auch zur "Klassikerpflege" der faschistischen Kunstbürokratie. Einer Klassikerbeerbung, die auch damals nicht unwidersprochen geblieben ist. Der große deutsche, im August verstorbene Philosoph und Antifaschist Ernst Bloch und der Komponist Hanns Eisler, gleichfalls zur Emigration gezwungen und bis zu seiner Bekanntschaft mit dem "Komitee für unamerikanische Umtriebe" in Amerika sicher vor der Verfolgung, gehören zu denen, die sich im antifaschistischen Kampf für eine "produktive Übernahme" des kulturellen Erbes einsetzen und seine Beschlagnahmung den Nationalsozialisten streitig zu machen versuchen.[13]

Eine kampflose Preisgabe Kleists, Schillers, und Goethes hat es nicht gegeben, weder vor noch nach 1933. Vielmehr entfalten sich in der Kleist-Rezeption einer gesellschaftlichen Minorität seit 1811 von Heinrich Heine über Gervinus und Franz Mehring, von Thomas Mann über Hans Mayer zu Ernst Fischer und Siegfried Streller, um nur einige Exponenten zu nennen, jene Tendenzen des Kleistschen Werkes, die aufgrund der konkreten historischen Entwicklung fehlen, bzw. unterdrückt werden. Auch bei der Beschäftigung mit diesen Nebensträngen der Kleist-Rezeption ist es weniger die Frage nach dem "wahren" oder "verfälschten" Kleist, die im Vordergrund stehen sollte, als vielmehr die Frage nach den Interessen der Rezipienten, nach dem "cui bono." Eine Frage, der selbstverständlich auch wir nicht ausweichen können.

ANMERKUNGEN

1. Egon-Erich Albrecht, *Heinrich von Kleists "Prinz Friedrich von Homburg" auf der deutschen Bühne* (Kiel, 1921), S.99 ff.
2. Vgl. exemplarisch die Arbeit des Reichstagsabgeordneten der NSDAP Hans Fabricius, *Schiller als Kampfgenosse Hitlers* (Bayreuth, 1932).
3. Vgl. Rolf Busch: *Imperialistische und faschistische Kleist-Rezeption. 1890-1945* (Frankfurt am Main, 1974).
4. Engels an Schmidt am 27.10.1890, nach: "Marx/Engels, Über Kunst und Literatur," Bd.1, S.100 (Berlin, 1967).
5. Aufruf der Kleist - Gesellschaft, Februar 1922:

   Die Kleist-Gesellschaft ist am 4. März 1920 in Berlin, mit dem Sitz in Frankfurt a.d. Oder, als eingetragener Verein gegründet worden. Sie ist Mittelpunkt aller Bestrebungen, die darauf abzielen, die Erinnerung an Heinrich von Kleist im deutschen Volke lebendig zu erhalten, für die Vertiefung der Volkstümlichkeit seiner Werke einzutreten, die Erkenntnis seiner dichterischen Bedeutung zu mehren und das Verständnis für seine Persönlichkeit, insbesondere die durch ihn beflügelte vaterländische Gesinnung zu fördern.

   Hatte schon die 100. Wiederkehr seines Todestages klar gezeigt, wie stark im deutschen Volke die Teilnahme für ihn war, so hat noch eindringlicher die Folgezeit und namentlich der Weltkrieg erwiesen, welche Macht der unmittelbaren Lebendigkeit Heinrich von Kleist mit seinem Geiste und seinen Werken für die Gesamtheit der Deutschen besitzt, wie er den Herzpunkt unseres eigensten Empfindens trifft. Keine Dichtungen der Vergangenheit wirken zeitgemäßer als die seinen. Keiner ruft uns mächtiger zur Selbstbesinnung und zu kühner Kraftentfaltung auf als Kleist. Von ihm können wir lernen, daß nur nationale Kunst urzeugend ist, da nur innerste Seeleneinkehr einem Volke die Kraft gibt, die zur freischaffenden Tat führt. Kleists Werke sind eine einzige Sehnsucht nach einem Leben des Menschen in Menschenwürde, Selbsterziehung und Liebe im Schutze eines von der Welt geachteten Staatswesens. Mit ihm, diesem Vertreter echten Menschentums und heißester Vaterlandsliebe, können wir die Hoffnung auf ein starkes künftiges deutsches Leben hegen und pflegen. . . .

   Trage ein jeder dazu bei, daß wir sagen können: der in seiner Zeit Unverstandene und Einsame ist mit seinem Wollen und seinen Werken für uns und die Kunst der Gegenwart ein Wegweiser geworden, ist jetzt zur höchsten Wirklichkeit erwacht, und der um sein Ziel gekämpft hat, hat nun den Sieg errungen.

Zu Kleist stehen heißt deutsch sein!

(Es folgt die Liste mit den Mitgliedern des Vorstandes):

DER VORSTAND: Dr. Arthur Graf von Posadowksy-Wehner, Staatsminister a.D., Ehrenvorsitzender; Prof. Minde-Pouet, Direktor d. Deutschen Bücherei Leipzig; Prof. Julius Petersen, Vorsitzender; Vorstandsmitglieder: Arthur Eloesser, Geschäftsführender Direktor d. Schutzverbandes deutscher Schriftsteller; Richard Groeper, Studienrat; Prof. Adolf von Harnack, Generaldir. d. Preuß. Staatsbibl.; Gerhart Hauptmann; Anton Kippenberg. Verlagsbuchhändler; Ricarda Huch; Frhr. Georg von Kleist; Max Liebermann, Präs. d. Akademie der Künste Berlin; Prof. Hans Pfitzner; Hans Reimer, Verlagsbuchhändler; Prof. Werner Richter, Min.-rat im Ministerium f. Wiss., Kunst u. Volksbildung; Paul Trautmann, Oberbürgermeister, Frankfurt/O.; Karl Zeiß, Generalintendant der Bayr. Staatstheater.

6. Ibid.
7. Hermann, Gilow, *Heinrich von Kleists Prinz Friedrich von Homburg 1821-1921. Ein geschichtlich-kritischer Rückblick*. Vortrag in der Berliner Ges. für Deutsche Philol. am 3. Nov. 1920. in: JbKG 1, 1921, S. 22-50:

(s.22) Auch wir sind oder scheinen verloren, wir sind jedenfalls entwaffnet; aber die geistigen und moralischen waffen, die uns die großen Genien des deutscher Volkes hinterlassen haben, können die Feinde uns nicht rauben. Sorgen wir nur, daß dies geistige Rüstzeug uns nicht von undeutschen Deutschen aus dem Herzen gerissen und aus der Hand geschlagen wird, daß diese Waffen nicht rosten, daß namentlich das junge Deutschland damit umzugehen lernt.

8. Wugk, Franz, *Kleist als Erzieher*. Zu seinem Geburtstag am 18. Oktober. In: *Deutsche Zeitung*, Nr. 470, 19. Okt. 1921 (Unterhaltungsbeilage):

Ehren wir Kleist, den Dichtergenius, lieben wir Kleist, den armen Dulder und Kämpfer. Aber hören wir ihn heute vor allem als den Lehrer des wahren Preußentums und Deutschtums. Mögen auch die in marxistischen und kosmopolitischen Irrlehren befangenen Volksgenossen aus Kleists Entwicklungsgang lernen, daß der Aufstieg nicht vom Patriotismus zur Weltbürgerei führt, sondern umgekehrt, aus den Niederungen des vaterlandslosen Internationalismus zu den Höhen einer eifersüchtigen, leidenschaftlichen (...) Liebe zur Heimaterde und zum eigenen *Volk*.

9. Kleist-Stiftung, in: *Neue Preußische-Kreuz-Zeitung,* Nr. 212, 9. Mai 1921:

Wir erhalten folgende Zuschrift:

Unter vorstehendem Namen besteht ein Verein unter jüdischer Leitung, die dem Geiste *Kleists* nicht entspricht. - Die Familie legt Wert darauf, bekannt zu geben, daß sie mit dieser *Kleiststiftung* nichts zu tun hat.

Der Vorstand der Familie von Kleist.

10. Der fliegende Koffer. "Zur Feier des 150. Geburtstages von Heinrich von Kleist in seiner Vaterstadt." Frankfurt: *Frankfurter Zeitung,* 18. Okt. 1927.
11. F.C. Marwede: "*Kleist.* Der Dichter der Hermannsschlacht. Zu seinem 150. Geburtstag am 18. Oktober." In: *Kösliner Zeitung,* 103. Jg., Nr. 244 vom 18. Okt. 1927.
12. *Sechs Bekenntnisse zum neuen Deutchland* (Hamburg 1933), S.27-29.
13. Ernst Bloch: "Hanns Eisler: Die Kunst zu erben." In: Die neue Weltbühne, Nr. 1, 1938.

Regie as Interpretation— Kleist's *Homburg* and *Käthchen* on the Current West German Stage

DONALD H. CROSBY
University of Connecticut

One of the numerous tragic ironies pervading the life of Heinrich von Kleist was that this born master of the theater never saw a professional performance of one of his plays. It is true that *Der zerbrochne Krug* was produced at Weimar in 1808, and that a few performances of *Das Käthchen von Heilbronn* were given in Vienna in 1810, but on neither of these occasions was the poet present—providentially, one must add, since neither production would have enhanced his self-esteem as a dramatist. *Der zerbrochne Krug*, as is well known, was sabotaged by Goethe's heavy-handed direction, whereas *Käthchen* was cut and compromised in such a way as to subvert rather than to serve its author's intentions. Not until the middle of the 19th century did Kleist's plays begin to gain acceptance, and even well into the 20th century a performance of a play other than *Der zerbrochne Krug* was a rarity. Today, in addition to the *Krug*, four other plays—*Amphitryon, Penthesilea, Das Käthchen von Heilbronn,* and *Prinz Friedrich von Homburg*— have in varying degrees acquired the status of "repertory" productions, and even Kleist's first play, *Die Familie Schroffenstein*, is given an occasional performance.

As one might have expected, the Kleist Bicentennial of 1977 brought a quickening of the pace of the production of Kleist-plays in German-speaking countries and elsewhere. Audiences in Moscow, for example, were recently treated to a rare "double bill" of Kleist "classics:" *Prinz Friedrich von Homburg* and *Der zerbrochne Krug,* performed in German on the same evening, with the same actors assuming first serious and then humorous roles! This was not a programming of convenience telescoped for a provincial audience, incidentally, but a tour production of Das Berliner deutsche Theater, which has been performing the combined program in East Berlin (to rather mixed reviews!) for the past year. In April, 1977, a production of *Penthesilea*—something of a rarity, even in Germany—was mounted, with a contemporary mise en scène, in Paris, where it was judged to be a critical if not a popular success. In our own country, new converts to Kleist can doubtless be credited both to the wide distribution of the film, "Die Marquise von O...," which even though twice removed from the formal dramatic canon is a valid representation of Kleist's dramatic genius, and to the widely acclaimed Chelsea Theater Center production of the *Prince of Homburg* in New York. Indeed, after an adaptation of this production was carried over the Public Television Network in April of 1977, an audience for Kleist's final play was created which—at least in theory—probably outnumbered the cumulative total of "live" spectators who have viewed the play in the theater during the last century!

It is to the German-speaking area we must turn, however, in order to find representative productions of Kleist's plays in the language, and, to some extent, in the tradition in which they were conceived. Of the many recent productions one might report on in this context, two can be singled out for a more detailed discussion: the 1972 production of *Prinz Friedrich von Homburg*, directed in West Berlin by Peter Stein; and the 1975 production of *Das Käthchen von Heilbronn* directed in Stuttgart by Claus Peymann. These productions merit closer attention not only because of their directorial ingenuity—that can almost be taken for granted at major West German theaters today— but because of their impact on critics and audiences alike.

To take each in turn: at first glance, a production of Kleist's *Prinz Friedrich* directed by Peter Stein might seem to be an odd, indeed a hostile pairing. Stein is, after all, one of the enfants terribles of the German theater world, arguably *primus inter pares* among a current generation of brilliant regisseurs, and best known for his iconoclastic direction of Goethe's *Tasso* in 1969. In that earlier production, Stein managed to animate Goethe's classical text with the spirit of modern political protest, a spirit distilled from the antiauthoritarian and antiwar protest of the late 1960's. The impact of Stein's production was such that no major West German theater has mounted a *Tasso* since! By comparison, Stein's direction of *Prinz Friedrich* seemed conventional, at least in the sense that it eschewed the self-conscious topicality and tendentiousness of *Tasso*. Why, then, was Stein attracted to *Prinz Friedrich* at all? One suggests that the attraction derived, first of all, from a certain consanguinity between the figures of Tasso and Homburg, the irreconcilability of their inner worlds with the societies surrounding them; and the resultant instability of temperament which leads each character to the threshold of self-destruction. It seems likely, too, that Stein felt challenged to bring directorial conviction to a text which—again, like *Tasso*—runs counter both to his modern sensibilities and his political orientation. One can hardly imagine that Peter Stein, like other intellectuals of his generation in Germany, would be much moved by lines such as Homburg's expressed intention to "glorify the splendid law of battle through a voluntary death;" nor would he be likely to be quickened by the rallying cry, "In the dust with all enemies of Brandenburg!"

Paradoxically, then, Stein was confronted with the self-imposed task of directing a play which—in part, at least—was uncongenial to him. Obviously Stein must have felt that there was a solution to this dilemma, and all evidence points to the fact that he found this solution virtually in the last lines of the play, when the bemused Prince, awakening from a faint, asks old General Kottwitz whether the spectable he is witnessing is "*ein Traum*," and the veteran officer assures him that all is a dream, "what else?" for it was precisely the dream-aspect of the play, its "other" or "higher" reality, rather than its historical milieu which dominated in the 1972 production. It was Homburg the somnambulist, the dreamer, rather than Homburg the Prussian general who fascinated Stein, and the entire production, reversing the proportions of the text, was conceived as reflecting the private, inner world of the Prince rather than the "real" world surrounding it. When the curtain rose, the spectators were confronted with a stage covered with sound-absorbing black cloth— a scenic literalization of Kleist's stage direction: "It is night." Figures appeared and disappeared noiselessly in the background as the Prince, lost in his private dream world, silently fashioned that confessional symbol of his secret ambition, the victory laurel. But before the spectator could immerse himself in this richly evocative "mood painting," an offstage voice broke the silence, announcing first the title of the play, then its author, and then proceeding to a recitation of the dedicatory poem with which Kleist prefaced his manuscript. A device of the "epic theater" perhaps? Brechtian "alienation?" or—more banally—an inspiration derived from adventure films of the 1960's (one thinks of the James Bond movies), where the action began on screen before the blaring music and endless production credits were cued in? The answer is: all of these, and more. Evidently, even expanding the "dream" dimensions of the play did not supply Stein with quite the aesthetic and intellectual distance he required: no, the play had to be 1) ascribed again, publically and unequivocally, to its author (and not to the *Regisseur!*); 2) inscribed in quotation marks, as it were; and 3) buffered by 150 years of distance. One feels, in short, that Herr Stein was trying to eat his cake and have it too, or—to change the cliché—to wash his hands of the production while still taking credit for it!

Certainly it is no coincidence that "reality" in this production, whenever it intruded into the dream-sphere, was always relativized, called into question, distorted optically or temporally. On the two occasions when Stein relieved the nocturnal (or funereal) stage setting, the ambience was strongly suggestive of the Romantic paintings of Kleist's contemporary Caspar David Friedrich. Time sequences were telescoped or even inverted to inhibit reality, such as in the "battle scene" in Act II, where a messenger reported the outcome of the battle even while it was being fought; and the Prince, occupying space in "time present," was on the stage while his actions were discussed in "time past."

Withal, Stein's conception of the play could not have been effected without an actor capable of suggesting, at all times, a somnambulant Homburg who has somehow drifted, contrary to all inclination, into the part-time role of a Prussian general. In Bruno Ganz, with whom Stein had worked closely in the past—Ganz was the Tasso of the 1969 production—Stein had precisely such an actor. Ganz—recently introduced to American audiences as the Count F... in the "Marquise von O..." film—portrayed a Homburg whose naiveté and fine-nerved sensibility made just those scenes—the opening "sleepwalking" scene, its inverted pendant at the play's close, and, above all, the notorious "fear of death" scene in Act III—just those scenes which strain the reader's (or the spectator's) credulity—into the most believable of the play. Cloaked in black, staring into the grave being opened for him, Ganz is more Hamlet than Homburg and perhaps more Kleist than either. It should come as no surprise, therefore, that his portrayal of Homburg the cavalry officer was unconvincing, quite possibly by design; one would question the wisdom of his brother officers, who, at the play's conclusion, assert their willingness to follow him into battle once more!

The final scene of the Stein *Homburg* production brought a mimetic interpolation which underscored the director's skepticism toward the conciliatory resolution which a literal-minded reading of the text implies. Stein thus aligned himself with those commentators on the play—they are not few in number—who have also questioned the believability of the final scene, where the Prince, who has already suffered through several manic oscillations between ecstasy and despair, is wrenched from the shelter of a self-willed death into a sphere of action for which he is patently ill-suited. Kleist, writing a patriotic play with topical significance, obviously had to shape his conclusion accordingly; Stein, interpreting the play from contemporary perspectives, could not accept Kleist's ending in a literal sense and hence added one of his own. Kleist's stage directions, it must be remembered, call for the Prince to gird himself for battle against the Swedes once more and to lend his voice to the martial chorus of "In Staub mit allen Feinden Brandenburgs!" In Stein's ending, by contrast, a lifelike but lifeless puppet was borne off the stage, while in a darkened corner the "real" Prince sat alone and dreaming in his private world. This mimed ending—employed with some modification in the Chelsea Theater Center production—obviously violates the letter of the text while at the same time arguably confirming its spirit. On a literal level the Prince has been restored to favor, has been crowned the victor of the Battle of Fehrbellin, and has even won his lady, but his inner conflicts have not been resolved, his psychic dissonances have not been harmonized. One suspects that the author of a famous essay on marionettes would have been inclined to applaud a conclusion which, like the final pages of his own plays and novellas, projected problems beyond the final curtain.

Just as there are parallels between *Prinz Friedrich* and the play which preceded it by only a few years, *Das Käthchen von Heilbronn*—each is a *Schauspiel* rather than a comedy or a tragedy, each springs from the final, conciliatory phase of Kleist's brief career, each finds a solution in a fairy-tale-like ending—so there are parallels, too, between the Peter Stein production of the *Prinz* and the *Käthchen* of Claus Peymann. In that recent Stuttgart production one finds the same admixture of epic theater and classical text, of "alienation" and *Werktreue* which was found, albeit in vastly different proportions, in the Berlin *Prinz von Homburg*. Yet if there are similarities between these two contemporary productions, they are akin to the resemblance of a glove to its mate after the latter has been turned inside out. In Berlin, it will be recalled, the auditorium was darkened and the stage itself draped in black; in Stuttgart the theater was garlanded with multicolored lights and the stage—crisscrossed with balancing wires familiar from the circus—covered with white cloth. In Berlin, the illusion of "distance" was created by superimposing the "credits" of the play over its muted opening; in Stuttgart the production begins with an interpolated "Vorspiel auf dem Theater," during which the titular heroine bolts onstage, pounds a brass drum, and bellows the name of the play through a megaphone! And whereas Stein's *Homburg* production skirted the core realism of the play and greatly expanded its "non-real" dimensions, Peymann's *Käthchen* slighted the Romantic, somnambulist elements of the play and substituted instead a robust realism!

Putting comparisons aside, there were striking features of Peymann's *Käthchen* which were almost certain to bewilder—and perhaps to intrigue—the spectator entering the theater armed only with textbook knowledge of Kleist's play. The first of these was the virtual obliteration of the play's chivalric framework—Kleist subtitled his play "Ein großes historisches Ritterschauspiel"—and its replacement with a modern circus montage. Medieval trappings such as castles, armor, horses, and swords are either replaced with clowns, weightlifters, and tightrope-walkers or are caricaturized. The Count von Strahl is still clad in armor, for example, but it is several times too large for him; and his sword, though doubtless constructed of *papier-mâché*, is ten feet long and made to appear to weigh several hundred pounds. And when the stage directions call for the use of horses, the knights mount bicycles adorned with horses' heads and pedal vigorously across the stage. Käthchen's father Theobald wears the raiment of the traditional circus clown, and Käthchen herself at on point performs a balancing act on the tightrope. Grouped together for purpose of resumé, these circus touches may sound like nothing more than a grab-bag of tricks designed primarily to stimulate ticket sales. In fairness to the regisseur, however, it must be remembered that *Käthchen* was written more than thirty years after Goethe's *Götz von Berlichingen* had spawned the *Ritterdrama*; hence in Kleist's time the genre had outlived itself and was ripe for spoofing. Small wonder, then, that almost all the "courtly" or "chivalric" scenes in Kleist's text—the *Fehmgericht*, the feuds, the burning castles, the grotesque *Minnedienst* in the Kunigunde episodes—were written with tongue-in-cheek. Peymann, in effect, merely substituted a modern parody of life—the distortion of a circus—for an antiquated one.

A second strking feature of this production is its repeated use of *Verfremdung*, or alienation, as a means of blurring the chronological focus of the play. In the scene before the secret tribunal—the *Fehmgericht* introduced in *Götz*—Theobald's heated attack on the character of Count von Strahl is protocolled on a clattering typewriter! A more extended example of *Verfremdung* is provided by the scene in which the demonic Kunigunde is unwittingly rescued by Count von Strahl, her feudal enemy, and decides that the most effective way of disarming the powerful knight would be to marry him. Here Peymann hit upon a pantomimic device to make her ensnarement of the Count somewhat more plausible—and much more visible—than it is in the text. As a stage musician strikes up a contemporary tango rhythm on his guitar, Kunigunde shimmies over to Strahl, engages him in a brief "boogaloo" and then, by running cords from his armor to various anchor points on the stage, literally ensnares him in a huge spider's web. Figuratively, this is precisely what happens in the play; Peymann's pantomime makes it literal—and visual. It may be asked: does this additional scene fall within the legitimate license of an interpreter, or is it merely a director's caprice? In answer, it must be recalled that no dramatist made more eloquent use of pantomine and gesture in his plays than did Kleist himself; and surely a director who adds the dimension of visual action to the printed word is acting in the spirit of the author. One cannot pass from the topic of *Verfremdung* without mention of a scene which, already in the text, has an "alienating" effect on the reader: this is the scene in the third act in which Käthchen's rescue from the burning castle is effected through the miraculous appearance, on stage, of a palm-bearing cherub! Here Peymann merely goes Kleist one better: the cherub duly appears, but it is mechanical, at least ten feet tall, and has huge flashing eyes—an altogether charming apparition!

Peymann's deft handling of the "cherub scene" illustrates his facility for turning necessity into a virtue—a sine qua non for any *Regisseur* who responds to the challenge of mounting *Das Käthchen von Heilbronn*. Kleist himself, toward the end of his life, conceded that, in order to tailor *Käthchen* to prevailing public tastes, he had compromised his original poetic conception and had thereby committed blunders (*Mißgriffe*) which he later came to lament (letter to Marie von Kleist, Summer 1811). Not the least remarkable feature of Claus Peymann's production was the director's ability to convert some of the play's palpable weaknesses into theatrical strengths. For example: the improbable switching of the two letters before the attack on Thurneck Castle; the awkward monologue of the Emperor in the final act; the unsatisfying rebuke Strahl flings into Kunigunde's teeth at the play's close—all scenes which, on the printed page, seem static or one-dimensional—are integrated under Peymann's direction into an overall conception of remarkable pace and dramatic amplitude. No review of this production would be complete without at least passing mention of Peymann's rehabilitation of the play's least believable character, Kunigunde von Thurneck, played with riveting panache by the talented actress Kirsten Dene. Part *Machtweib*, part *Märchenhexe*, this incredible amalgam of cosmetics and prosthetics somehow metamorphoses, in Frau Dene's protean performance, into an almost believable woman! Limping across a darkened stage, bent with the double burden of age and defeat, Kunigunde radiates something akin to that aura of tragedy which, in Kleist's works, lies just beneath the surface of comedy.

That the delicate balance between serious and comic elements in *Das Käthchen von Heilbronn* was otherwise not maintained in a recent Stuttgart production—and here we come to our third and final point of commentary—was, perhaps, its most serious flaw. Given the fact that *Käthchen*, as written, suggests an almost contrapuntal relationship between serious and humorous elements, one must question whether the text benefits from the humorous "enhancement" it received in this production. Sight and sound "gags" reminiscent of Karl Valentin and the Marx Brothers are, after all, more the property of the *Lustspiel* than of the *Schauspiel*. Viewed in the context of its times, Kleist's play betrays strong affinities with the Romantic genre of the *Kunstmärchen,* the re-told fairy tale. Now: fairy tales, though they may have happy endings, are rarely farcical; Peymann's production, however, at times bordered on burlesque. A *Neuinszenierung* of *Käthchen*, as we have suggested, can survive a radical change in the play's milieu; it can even tolerate a heavy dose of *Verfremdung*; it cannot, however, be transformed into what one critic of the production called "Peymann's ... Little Magic Circus"[1] and still lay claim to authenticity. Claus Peymann's production of *Das Käthchen von Heilbronn*, while at all times brilliant theater, was at some times questionable Kleist.

In conclusion, one should perhaps give a word of assurance to the traditionalists among us who would be willing to forego directorial innovation, however ingenious, and to see plays performed very much as their authors intended them to be performed. Although the German stage does appear to be dominated, at the moment, by a new vogue described by the critic Benjamin Heinrichs as "the jolly classics,"[2] there are, of course, perfectly sober and conventional performances of the "classics," including Kleist's plays, to be seen on German stages. Audiences in Berlin, for example, who found the Peter Stein production of *Homburg* at the Schaubühne too one-sided or too subjective for their tastes, had only to visit the Schillertheater in the same city to see a far more traditional interpretation of the drama as directed by Hans Litzau. And only one year before Claus Peymann unveiled his highly idiomatic *Käthchen von Heilbronn* in Stuttgart, the late Walter Felsenstein won critical encomia for an unabashedly stylized and conservative *Käthchen* at the Burgtheater in Vienna. That Kleist's plays can tolerate such an extraordinary range of interpretation is renewed testimony to the timelessness of the conflicts and the durability of the dramatic craftsmanship that is common to all his works. Two hundred years ago, the German stage was unequal to the challenge of Kleist's dramatic conceptions; today Germany's leading theaters vie with one another to test these conceptions in the crucible of changing times and tastes. The poet who wrote his plays for what Goethe disparagingly referred to as "[das] unsichtbare Theater"[3] has found his visible stage at last.

ACKNOWLEDGMENTS

Material for this paper was gathered chiefly during a research trip to West Germany and Austria in the fall and winter of 1976. The author wishes to express his appreciation for financial assistance provided by the Research Foundation of the University of Connecticut and by the Fulbright-Kommission, Bonn/Bad Godesberg. For helpful suggestions and valuable insights, the author is happy to acknowledge his indebtedness to Dr. Rolf Michaelis of *Die Zeit* and Dr. Wolfgang Kraus of the Österreichische Gesellschaft für Literatur.

NOTES

1. Jens Wendland in the *Süddeutsche Zeitung*, November 11, 1975.
2. *Die Zeit*, November 28, 1975.
3. In a letter to Adam Müller, August 28, 1807.

Thesen zur Aktualität Kleists in Westdeutschland

FRIEDRICH ROTHE
Freie Universität Berlin

Überblickt man die herausragenden Kleist-Verfilmungen und -inszenierungen seit 1969—den von der Studentenbewegung beeinflußten Kohlhaas-Film von Volker Schlöndorf "Der Rebell," Peter Steins Homburg-Inszenierung in der Schaubühne am Halleschen Ufer, Rohmers "Marquise von O..." und den neuen Film von Helma Sanders "Heinrich"—dann fällt auf, daß Kleist für die mittlere Generation in Westdeutschland wichtig geworden ist und für diese Generation der in den dreißiger Jahren Geborenen eine neue politische und gesellschaftskritische Aktualität erhalten hat.

Seit hundert Jahren etwa gehört Kleist zu den wenigen deutschen Autoren, die ohne spürbare Konjunkturen mit fast gleichbleibender Intensität zu den Literaturinteressierten unseres Landes sprechen. Für die Rezeption Kleists waren die unterschiedlichen Vorzeichen seiner Aneignung ebenso charakteristisch wie die Kontinuität der Wirkung. Trotz dieser breiten Tradition ist jedoch besonders für die Bundesrepublik die politisch-gesellschaftskritische Aktualisierung seines Lebens und Werkes durch die kritische Intelligenz etwas Neues. Denn wie bei Vielem in der Bundesrepublik wurde auch beim Umgang mit Kleist versucht die NS—"Vergangenheit" durch einen Akt der Verdrängung zu "bewältigen."

Um die Erinnerung an die NS-Propaganda, die Kleist zusammen mit Walter Flex, Schlageter und Horst Wessel als tragisch gescheiterten "Verkünder des nationalsozialistischen Deutschland" gepriesen hatte, wobei die Kleist-Gesellschaft unter ihrem Präsidenten Professor Minde-Pouet den Kleist-Kultus durch Großkundgebungen und Kleist-Feiern im ganzen Reich organisierte—um also die Erinnerung an die NS-Propaganda zu bewältigen, wurde von der westdeutschen Nachkriegsgermanistik ein neues Kleist-Bild geschaffen. Man reinigte den Dichter von den Spuren seiner politischen Verstrickung in dem Kampf gegen die napoleonische Fremdherrschaft und beschäftigte sich ausschließlich mit der Einmaligkeit seiner unglücklichen Existenzerfahrung. Die existentielle Literaturwissenschaft, die sich nach 1945 in Westdeutschland etablierte, fand in Heinrich von Kleist ihren idealen Gegenstand, der sich ihrer Methode widerstandslos zu fügen schien. Man rekurrierte auf die isolierte Stellung seiner Werke, die sich weder unter "Klassik" noch "Romantik" subsumieren lassen und machte den Selbstmord des Dichters zum Angelpunkt der Interpretation: als den Akt, worin sich sein Bewußtsein, fremd und einsam in der Zeit zu stehen, radikalisiert habe.

Den westdeutschen Literaturwissenschaftlern und einflußreichen Literaturkritikern wie Günther Blöcker, die sich mit Kleist als Vertreter eines modernen Lebensgefühls nach dem "Zusammenbruch" identifizierten, war eine politische, auf Veränderung des Bestehenden drängende Kleist-Rezeption wie die in der DDR, die in den fünfziger Jahren vom Programm der nationalen Wiedervereinigung bestimmt war, derart fremd, daß sie nicht einmal dagegen polemisierten. Typisch für die agitatorische Anwendung Kleists in der DDR war der Abdruck von Teilen des "Katechismus der Deutschen" in einem Heft der "Neuen Deutschen Literatur" (1953), das sich mit der Situation in Westdeutschland auseinandersetzte. Dieser Text, der mit den Sätzen beginnt: "Frage. Sprich, Kind, wer bist du? Antwort. Ich bin ein Deutscher. Frage. Ein Deutscher? Du scherzest. Du bist in Meißen geboren, und das Land, dem Meißen angehört, heißt Sachsen! Antwort. Ich bin in Meißen geboren, und das Land, dem Meißen angehört, heißt Sachsen; aber mein Vaterland, das Land dem Sachsen angehört, ist Deutschland, und dein Sohn, mein Vater, ist ein Deutscher,"[1] wurde als patriotischer Aufruf zum Kampf gegen die Vorherrschaft der USA in Westdeutschland und Westeuropa verstanden und eingesetzt.

Einer derart unmittelebar agitatorischen Aktualisierung Kleists steht die westdeutsche kritische Intelligenz, die sich heute mit Kleist beschäftigt, fern. Was ihre Verfilmungen und Inszenierungen vielmehr kennzeichnet, ist ihre kritische Distanz zur Politik der Linken, sosehr die Produzenten auch von den positiven Erfahrungen der Studentenbewegung von 1968/69 geprägt sein mögen. Schlöndorf, Stein und Helma Sanders interessieren sich für Kleist als einen Autor, der unter den politischen und gesellschaftlichen Verhältnissen seiner Zeit gelitten hat, sich dem Bestehenden widersetzte und trotz seiner Isolierung vom Volk, den Traum von einem deutschen Staat erdichtete, in dem die Gesellschaftsordnung in Einklang gebracht ist mit den Gefühlen des Einzelnen und das individuelle Glücksstreben dem Interesse des Staatsganzen dient. Kleists Patriotismus, sein Kampf gegen Napoleon, wird hier nicht ausgespart wie bei der früheren existentiellen Interpretation; das Hauptinteresse richtet sich jedoch—und darin sehe ich eine Distanzierung von der als rigide empfundenen politischen Praxis der Linken—auf utopische Züge in Leben und Werk Heinrich von Kleists.

Mit dieser Kleist-Rezeption verbindet sich ein Programm der Sensibilisierung, die keine romantische Flucht vor der Realität antreten sondern letztlich auf politische Veränderung hinwirken soll. Aufgrund dieses politischen Anspruchs stellen Peter Stein und Helma Sanders gerade den *Prinz von Homburg*, der seit den Gründerjahren als preußisch-deutsches Paradestück inszeniert wurde und deshalb besonders die Kritik der Linken hervorrief, ins Zentrum ihrer Kleist-Interpretation. Für sie zeigt sich die utopisch-politische Qualität des Kleistschen Werkes nicht an dem in letzter Zeit so häufig inszenierten romantischen Märchen-Drama *Käthchen von Heilbronn*, sondern an dem lehrhaften Militärstück, worin Kleist nicht ohne Trockenheit die Notwendigkeit der Subordination unter den Fürsten thematisiert. Die politische Umwertung, die Peter Stein mit seiner Inszenierung von "Kleists Traum vom Prinzen Homburg" beabsichtigt, kommt im Programmheft der Schaubühne in der Behauptung zum Ausdruck: "Kleist und seine Dichtungen verkörpern erstmalig jene Kraft und Insistenz, die die fortschrittlichen Teile der Bourgeoisie der 'deutschen Misere' entgegenzusetzen vermochten, um damit die spärlichen Anfänge von deutscher demokratischer Tradition im 19. Jahrhundert zu begründen."

Ebenfalls unter emanzipatorischem Anspruch steht Eric Rohmers Verfilmung der "Marquise von O.... ." Rohmer zeigt Kleists Erzählung als einen Emanzipationsprozeß, dessen märchenhafte Unwirklichkeit bei aller Treue zum Zeitkolorit die Richtung auf eine neue Zukunft offenhalten soll. Der Film verdeutlicht die Anstrengung der Marquise, die für sie im Rückzug auf sich selbst und der Trennung von ihrer Familie liegt, und beschreibt diesen Prozeß als Grundlage für eine neue Form der Ehe, in der die Frau dem Manne nicht unterworfen ist. Ohne Zweifel interessiert sich Rohmer vor allem für die Entwicklung der Marquise zur selbstbewußten Frau und spielt den Schluß der Erzählung nicht aus. Als ansprechender, filmischer Abglanz der gegenwärtigen Frauenbewegung wird das unbeugsame Durchsetzen weiblicher Autonomie vorgeführt, wobei die Hauptdarstellerin Edith Clever ihre Rolle in einer für die Männerwelt gewiß furchterregenden Eindringlichkeit verkörpert. Rohmer führt jedoch einen Selbsterfahrungsprozeß vor, an dessen Ende trotz aller Sensibilität nicht die Veränderung der Verhältnisse, sondern liebendes Verzeihen steht. Im Unterschied zu Peter Stein, der in seiner Inszenierung von *Kleists Traum vom Prinzen Homburg* den Prinzen seine Erhöhung als erstarrte Puppe erfahren läßt—sie wird wie eine Leiche herumgetragen—distanziert sich Rohmer nicht vom Kleistschen Schluß der Erzählung. Trotz der Faszination, die der Film auf mich ausübt, sehe ich in ihm nur eine Scheinaktualisierung. Rohmers Anspruch bei diesem Unternehmen ist fragwürdig, weil er dort, wo er, um Kleist zu aktualisieren, über ihn hinausgehen müßte, den Autor schlicht repetiert und damit das Interesse, aus dem sich die Aktualität seines Films speist, die Befreiung der Frau, letztlich verrät. Steins Homburg-Inszenierung und Helma Sanders' Kleist-Film sind für die kritische Intelligenz in Westdeutschland aktuell, weil sie die Frage nach nationaler Identität in einer Weise aufwerfen, die eine neue Diskussion dieser lange verdrängten Frage ermöglicht. Unter dem Eindruck der Herrschaft des deutschen Faschismus und aus Opposition gegen den CDU-Staat war diese Frage unter den Intellektuellen, die sich leidenschaftlich gegen die antikommunistische nationale Propaganda des Springerkonzerns wandten, tabuisiert. Um nicht mit dem imperialistischen Deutschland, das zwei Weltkriege ausgelöst hat, in einen Topf geworfen zu werden, weigerte man sich, sich mit der deutschen Geschichte auseinanderzusetzen: sie wurde als einziges Konglomerat deutscher Misere emotional abgewertet. Die wachsende politische Unterdrükung in Ost- und Westdeutschland, bei der sich die Bundesrepublik und die Regierung der DDR gegenseitig die Karten zuspielen, Ausbürgerungen und Berufsverbote im Geiste von Helsinki weitgehend tolerieren, hat jedoch dieser unpolitischen Haltung zur deutschen Geschichte entgegengewirkt. Bei vielen Intellektuellen ist ein Interesse für die Menschen erwacht, die sich in Deutschland während der ersten Hälfte des 19. Jahrhunderts gegen die Heilige Allianz der Regierungen stellten, dafür verfolgt wurden und für ein vereintes und freies Deutschland eintraten. Die Faszination, die von Kleist heute für westdeutsche Intellektuelle ausgeht, liegt nicht in der Identifikation mit seinem konservativen politischen Programm, mit den Bündnissen, die er in seinem Kampf geschlossen hat oder zu schließen versuchte; faszinierend ist sein Festhalten an dem Traum von Deutschland, in dem es keine Unterdrückung gibt und das keine anderen Völker unterdrückt, ein Traum, den er allein mit seinem Werk, in seiner Sprache zu realisieren vermochte.

Ihren Wunsch, diesen Traum zu beerben, beschreibt Helma Sanders in einem Interview, das sie zu ihrem Film "Heinrich" gegeben hat: "Deutschland ist, wie Heine sagt, ein Land 'im Luftreich des Traumes angesiedelt.' Zu Kleists Zeit bestand die deutsche Nation wie auch heute, nur in den Köpfen der Leute, nicht in der Realität. Sie war imaginär, stellt sich nur in der Sprache her. Auf diesem Gelände zwischen Polen und Frankreich, das man Deutschland nennt, ist Sprache das einzig Gemeinsame und Kleist beherrscht diese Sprache vielleicht am vollkommensten, allerdings nur in der Schrift—wenn er sie sprechen sollte, stotterte er, wohingegen er sich fließend äußern konnte, sobald er französisch sprach. Deswegen wurde er dann auch als französischer Spion verhaftet."[2]

Heinrich von Kleist, der nach den Worten Franz Mehrings "Mitleid mit dem Opfer und Haß gegen den Krebsschaden der deutschen Nation"[3] hervorruft, hält in der Tat die nationale Frage "offen" und die Auseinandersetzung mit seinem Leben und Werk stellt eindringlich die Frage nach dem, was nationale Identität in Deutschland heute bedeutet.

ANMERKUNGEN

1. Heinrich von Kleist "Katechismus der Deutschen" (Teilabdruck) in: *Neue Deutsche Literatur* Berlin/DDR: 1953, Heft 7, S. 93 f.
2. Helma Sanders "Preusse, Dichter, Selbstmoerder" in: *Berliner Hefte* Berlin: 1976, Nr. 1, S. 81 f.
3. Franz Mehring *Gesammelte Schriften* Berlin/DDR: 1961, Bd. 10, S. 324.

Unified Vision:
The Struggle for the Center

VALENTINE C. HUBBS
University of Michigan

In the critical literature on Kleist the roles of *Gefühl* and *Verstand* have undergone a long and interesting metamorphosis. Early scholarship attributed the concepts expressed by Kleist in his "Aufsatz, den sichern Weg des Glücks zu finden," to the influence of the popular philosophy of the *Aufklärung* on the young Prussian officer.[1] Later scholarship has sought to extricate the peculiarly Kleistian aspects and has emphasized the emotional tone of the essay as indicative of an underlying fear of life and the future.[2] The Kant-crisis has shared a similar fate. In the beginning it was perceived as Kleist's most important turning point, the period of his life when he repudiated the rationalism of *Aufklärung* and turned to the irrational as an infallible guide to truth.[3] *Gefühl* replaced *Verstand*. Eventually it was discovered that Kleist's over-evaluation of reason had begun to decline while he was still in his first semester of study at the university. Doubts about the actuality of the Kant crisis began to appear in the critical literature.[4] The role of *Gefühl* as an absolute guide to truth lost in acceptance, as scholars cited examples of error based upon feeling in Kleist's works. Speculation gradually found its way into most interpretations of *Verstand* and *Gefühl* until Kreutzer's philological analysis pointed the way back to more careful scholarship based upon a knowledge of the literature which Kleist had probably read and from which he had gleaned his ideas.[5]

To initiate a discussion of the roles of *Verstand* and *Gefühl* I would like to suggest that Kleist never regarded one as superior to the other, but that his particular view of these two modes of perception had been influenced by the ancient Greek *Lebensanschauung* of moderation and that this can be traced from the early "Aufsatz" to his final drama—although I do not intend to undertake such a trace in the time allotted to the reading of this paper.

It has been suggested in the critical literature that Kleist does not speak of *Verstand* and *Gefühl* in the "Aufsatz," but that this terminology is first encountered only in his early letters. Be this as it may, there are certain expressions in the "Aufsatz" which indicate that Kleist had, consciously or unconsciously, considered the differences between the two and that these differences are implicit in his arguments. He speaks of his various points as "Denkweise, oder besser Empfindungsweise," which indicates that his ideas are less the product of *Verstand* than of *Gefühl*. He regards *Vernunft* and *Herz* as the elements which, together, might enable the human being to achieve happiness. When he advises Rühle to remain on the *Mittelstraße*, he states that his *Geist* is convinced of the truth of this, but that his *Herz* constantly contradicts it. Kleist perceived the value of traveling in the fact that it resulted in a "an Herz und Geist . . . gebildeten Mann." Certainly "die ungleichartigen Gestalten" which Kleist is endeavoring to overcome are emotions, and the *Tugenden* which he enumerates as the attributes of his wise man are such which imply a balance of sentiment and reason. All these expressions imply a duality of *Gefühl* and *Verstand* as already present in Kleist's perceptions and in his thinking.

One of the latest trends in Kleist scholarship is the investigation of the mythical structure of his works and the insight which myths afford into the core of their specific nature.[6] Kleist's employing myth in his writing is just as revealing as his tendency to employ analogues of nature and of the physical and the spiritual worlds. It is, moreover, a characteristic intrinsic in his work from the beginning to the end, and the earliest mythological reference in a Kleistian work occurs in the "Aufsatz," where he paraphrases a parable from Homer's *Iliad* in order to clarify his own concept of external happiness:

> Im Vorhofe des Olymp, erzählt er, stünden zwei große Behältniße, das eine mit Genuß, das andere mit Entbehrung gefüllt. Wem die Götter, so spricht Homer, aus beiden Fäßern mit gleichem Maße meßen, der ist der Glücklichste; wem sie ungleich meßen, der ist unglücklich, doch am unglücklichsten der, dem sie nur allein aus einem Faße zumeßen (II, 308).

In retelling this myth Kleist has made a very significant change. According to Homer the most unfortunate individual is the one on whom the gods bestow only sorrow or evil; but Kleist considers him to be the most unfortunate who receives exclusively from one or the other container. Thus too much *Genuß* is just as inimical to the acquisition of happiness as too much *Entbehrung*. Happiness, or good fortune, seems then to depend upon the balancing of the scales, upon the golden mean, or upon the harmonious mixture of opposites. In another allusion to myth, the story of Polykrates, Kleist expresses the concept that life itself is subject to a certain law of balanced opposites, and that an imbalance at one period of life will be compensated for by an antithetical balance at another. This perception of harmonious mixtures of opposites is expressed in the "Aufsatz" in other ways as well. He advised Rühle to be "bescheiden und begnügsam" in his demands upon external happiness, to avoid "die schwindlichen Höhen" and to remain in the lower altitudes where the air is moderate, "nicht warm und nicht kalt, gerade so wie sie nötig ist, um frei und leicht zu atmen." The day laborer "mit mäßigen Genüssen" is happier than the rich man with his excesses:

> Also, entbehren und genießen, das wäre die Regel des äußeren Glücks, und der Weg, gleich weit entfernt von Reichtum und Armut, von Überfluß und Mangel, von Schimmer und Dunkelheit, die beglückende Mittelstraße, die wir wandern wollen. (II, 308-309).

From this early essay to his final drama Kleist apparently perceived man's happiness and good fortune in the harmony of a unified vision of the world which included both the faculties associated with the head and those associated with the heart, comingled into one balanced harmonious whole. The lack of that harmony, or the disturbance of its delicate balance, would lead to erroneous perception, improper action, and possible tragedy. Sylvester Schroffenstein, whose inner peace and harmony is manifested in the quiet atmosphere of Warwand, struggles vainly to prevent events from entering into his inner being and stirring up a turmoil which would turn his domain into violence and irrationality akin to Rupert's. In the beginning of the drama he is able to resist the corrosive influence of violent accusations and events. When he can no longer endure them, he retreats into himself, and the inner harmony of his balanced sensibilities produces a salutary effect upon him:

> Was mich freut
> Ist, daß der Geist doch mehr ist, als ich glaubte.
> Denn flieht er gleich auf einen Augenblick,
> An seinen Urquell geht er nur, zu Gott,
> Und mit Heroenkraft kehrt er zurück (896-900).

Sylvester returned to consciousness with renewed vigor and acted as he was compelled to act under the circumstances, not violently or unreasonably, like his kinsman, but calmly and circumspectly. But as the forces of inimical circumstances combined against him, he gradually lost the harmony of his inner being and became like Rupert, excessive, irrational, violent, one-sided.

Penthesilea's invective, "Verflucht das Herz, das sich nicht mäß' gen kann!" could serve as a motto to Kleist's early concept of the absolute necessity of balanced sensibilities, of a unified vision, as the *sina qua non* of infallibility and unerring action. Neither the faculties of the head nor the faculties of the heart could be permitted to assume control of the individual. *Vernunft* had to confirm *das Herz*, and also the converse was true. If they act separately, then each is flawed. When Homburg relied upon his heart as the highest authority, he erred and courted destruction. When he based his certainty that the *Kurfürst* had no intention of permitting the death sentence to be carried out upon his feeling, "Auf mein Gefühl von ihm!" his judgment was faulty. Only the harmonious combination of all his faculties, only a unified vision, can prevent error and afford inner happiness.

The harmony of a unified vision was not an ideal which Kleist postulated as an unattainable goal, a perfection for which man must strive in order to approach his moral destiny and to realize the fullest development of his innate potential. It was not the ennobling search for an ever-elusive truth of which Lessing wrote. It was an attainable something which Kleist had difficulty expressing in his early letters and essays and which resisted precise formulation in the traditional language of *Aufklärung*. He was seeking to convey an idea which still belonged to the future and for which no intellectual conceptualization in language as yet existed. Therefore he sought refuge in borrowed clichés from the popular philosophy of his age. But these clichés have obfuscated the ineffable something he was trying to express. They suggested concepts known and understood in the intellectual atmosphere of the time, yet this young man was attempting to express something quite alien to the moral concerns of *Aufklärung*. He was describing a condition of the inner being which did not belong to the metaphysical ideals of philosophy, but to the psychology of the future.

When Kleist wrote the "Aufsatz," he was convinced, or was at least trying to be convinced, that he could control this external fate by developing his mental and physical faculties. When he spoke of developing his "körperliche Kräfte," he meant his faculties of perception, seeing things in their true relationships, discovering the physical laws of nature and their connection to human life. He believed that an inner being which had achieved the stability of unified vision would be able to transcend external fate and achieve an inner happiness that was impervious to the forces of the physical world. "In mir und durch mich vergnügt, o, mein Freund! wo kann der Blitz des Schicksals mich Glücklichen treffen, wenn ich es fest im Innersten meiner Seele bewahre?" (II, 485). As an example of an individual who had achieved this desirable inner state of mind Kleist suggests Jesus Christ, who, in the face of death, comforted and forgave his enemies, smiled lovingly at his executioners, and died calmly and happily. His inner being was unaffected by outer circumstances. In this sense he was able to rise above his fate, to be untouched by it in his inner spirit. Kleist called this state of mind *Tugend*.

Although he employed the term *Tugend*, he did not have a precise notion of what it actually was, anymore than "die Philister, die von Gott reden." Clearly he was not expounding the moral philosophy of *Aufklärung,* but was attempting to express a concept which was original with him. Because he was unable to define his concept, he enumerated the various characteristics which he associated with *Tugend,* but which he had as yet never discovered combined in one person, and projected them into an ideal individual whom he called a wise man. Yet he did not conceive of wisdom as intellectual reasoning or traditional knowledge, but as implicit in the wise man's character, a result of the inner structure of his mind, which exhibited the qualities of "Edelmut, Menschenliebe, Standhaftigkeit, Bescheidenheit, Genügsamkeit, Mäßigkeit, und Gerechtigkeit." These attributes, or *Tugenden,* as Kleist called them, enabled the individual to enjoy "die Zufriedenheit unsrer selbst, . . . das Gefühl unserer durch alle Augenblicke unseres Lebens, vielleicht gegen tausend Anfechtungen und Verführungen standhaft behaupteten Würde." (II, 305). He could rejoice "in dem erfreulichen Anschauen der moralischen Schönheit unseres eigenen Wesens;" he could be happy in the inner harmony of his entire being.

During his journey to Würzburg Kleist expressed his notion of "die beglückende Mittelstraße" in an analogy which has often been interpreted to mean that he was in the process of repudiating reason and espousing feeling and emotion as the more vital elements of truth:

> Das *Enge* der Gebirge scheint überhaupt auf das Gefühl zu wirken und man findet darin viele Gefühlsphilosophen, Menschenfreunde, Freunde der Künste, besonders der Musik. Das *Weite des platten Landes* hingegen wirkt mehr auf den *Verstand* und hier findet man die Denker und Vielwisser (II, 541).

But the sentence which follows this, "Ich möchte an einem Orte geboren sein, wo die Berge nicht zu eng, die Flächen nicht zu weit sind," indicates that Kleist is still seeking the same balanced harmony of opposites that he pursued in his *Aufsatz*. It has also been suggested that Brockes himself exercised an influence upon Kleist which lured him away from university study, that Brockes, who despised rational knowledge, was directly responsible for Kleist's Kant crisis.[7] Yet Kleist admired in Brockes his balanced integration of both knowledge and feeling, which was Kleist's own goal long before he entered the university. While it is true that Brockes called scholars *Vielwisser,* and his basic principle of life was "Handeln ist besser als Wissen," that he spoke "verächtlich von der Wissenschaft," he was, nevertheless, knowledgeable about the sciences and well versed in many of them. "Von den meisten hatte er die Hauptzüge aufgefaßt, und von den andern wenigstens doch diejenigen Züge, die in sein Ganzes paßten." Here we are confronted by the very same idea of balance, expressed in somewhat different terms. Brockes appealed to Kleist because he had, so Kleist thought, achieved wholeness or inner harmony. "... denn dahin, nämlich alles in sich immer in Einheit zu bringen und zu erhalten, dahin ging sein unaufhörliches Bestreben." (II, 620) He had mastered the art of balanced sensibilities and achieved the ideal of unified vision. Even though he always spoke "wegwerfend von dem Verstande ... er ... zeigte, daß er mehr habe als andere, die damit prahlen." Brockes confirmed Kleist's original goal, to develop both heart and head in mutual harmony, and he therefore acted and reasoned correctly: "Immer seiner ersten Regung gab er sich ganz hin, das nannte er seinen Gefühlsblick, und ich selbst habe nie gefunden, daß dieser ihn getäuscht habe." (II, 620)

The prevalence of so many expressions of the *golden mean* indicates the movement of Kleist's ideas around a center. This center represents the ideal state. Happiness and virtue form one pole of that movement; the other is composed of "die wunderbar ungleichartigen Gestalten," the state of emotional turmoil which in general describes Kleist's reality. Neither pole is suitable for Kleist and he will find the center only rarely and then only in his work, not in reality. Jochen Schmidt has recently emphasized the frequent allusions in Kleist's writing to *Ruhe*;[8] Kleist longs for *Ruhe* and yet he is driven to travel. This same antithetical tendency is contained in his early craving for happiness, inner happiness, or *Ruhe*. Yet neither *Ruhe* nor *Unruhe* is the ideal state for Kleist. As Prothoe says to Penthesilea, "Freud' ist und Schmerz dir, seh' ich, gleich verderblich, / Und gleich zum Wahnsinn reißt dich beides hin." Kleist in his *Unruhe* seeks the possibility of *Ruhe,* and in his work he explores the advantages and disadvantages of both *Verstand* and *Gefühl*. His own ideal state lies between, in the center, which he could never reach, but eternally sought.

NOTES

1. About the *Aufsatz* and the letter to Martini, Joachim Maass states in his *Kleist, die Fackel Preußens* (Wien, München, Basel, 1957), p. 19, "... diese Gedanken kann man sonderlich originell kaum nennen; sie gehören zum Geistesgut der Aufklärung ... sie repräsentieren das Modedenken der Zeit, usw. ...." See also his *Kleist, die Geschichte seines Lebens* (Bern, 1977), p. 21. Cf. Friedrich Koch, *Heinrich von Kleist* (Stuttgart, 1958), p. 4 and Günter Blöcker, *Heinrich von Kleist oder das absolute Ich* (Berlin, 1960), p. 46.
2. Existential interpretations seem to have been among the first to seek other meanings behind the clichés in Kleist's *Aufsatz*. Heinz Ide, a disciple of Gerhart Fricke, says, "Die Annahme, Kleist denke 1799, dem Jahr seines Abschieds vom Militär und Beginn seines Studiums, aufklärerisch, und zwar recht flach aufklärerisch, ist psychologisch fragwürdig." *Der junge Kleist* (Würzburg, 1961), p. 15.
3. Philipp Witkop, *Heinrich von Kleist* (Leipzig, 1922), p. 47. Cf. Ernst Cassirer, "Heinrich von Kleist und die Kantische Philosophie," in *Idee und Gestalt* (Berlin, 1921), pp. 74-76.

4. Hans M. Wolff, *Heinrich von Kleist: die Geschichte seines Schaffens* (Bern, 1954), p. 115f. See also Blöcker, p. 60f.
5. Hans Joachim Kreutzer, "Die dichterische Entwicklung Heinrichs von Kleist," *Philologische Studien und Quellen* 41 (Berlin, 1968).
6. For example, V. C. Hubbs, "The Plus and Minus of Penthesilea and Käthchen," *Seminar* (Fall 1970), pp. 187-194; Robert M. Browning, "Kleist's *Käthchen* and the Monomyth," *Studies in the German Drama, a Festschrift in Honor of Walter Silz*, Eds. Donald H. Crosby and George C. Schoolfield (Chapel Hill, 1974), pp. 115-123.
7. Emil Ermatinger, *Das dichterische Kunstwerk* (Leipzig, 1921), pp. 82f.
8. Jochen Schmidt, *Heinrich von Kleist. Studien zu seiner poetischen Verfahrensweise* (Tübingen, 1974), pp. 8ff.

HEINRICH VON KLEIST
German Dramatist and Narrative Writer

A Catalogue of the
EXHIBITION
of Book, Periodical, and Film Materials

Preface

This catalogue and the exhibit in the David Filderman Gallery are the University Library's contributions to the International Conference celebrating the 200th anniversary of Heinrich von Kleist (1777-1977).

Both the catalogue and the exhibit were prepared by Ann L. Rubino, Marge Regan, and Nancy Herb of the Library's Special Collections Department, assisted by Ruth Spannhake of the Catalog Department, and Alexej Ugrinsky, Kleist Conference Coordinator. The materials have been drawn principally from the Library's collections.

CHARLES R. ANDREWS
Dean of Library Services
Hofstra University Library

Contributors to the Exhibition

AMS Press, New York, New York.

Dr. Joseph Astman, Member of the Hofstra University Kleist Conference Committee and Director of the University Center for Cultural and Intercultural Services.

Embassy of the Federal Republic of Germany, Washington, D. C.

Walter de Gruyter and Company, Publishers, Berlin, Germany.

Holmes and Meier Publishers, Inc., Africana Publishing Company, New York, New York.

Dr. Katharina Mommsen, author of *Kleists Kampf mit Goethe.*

Erich Schmidt Verlag, Berlin, Germany.

Alexej Ugrinsky, Coordinator of the Hofstra University Kleist Conference.

Introduction

(Bernd) Heinrich (Wilhelm) von Kleist was born in Frankfurt-an-der-Oder on October 18, 1777. He became one of Germany's great dramatists and a narrative writer of distinction.

When Kleist was 15 years old, he entered the Prussian Army, fought in the Rhine Campaign the following year, but gradually became dissatisfied with army life and left it in 1799, ostensibly to study science and mathematics at Frankfurt University. While at the University, he read Kant whose philosophy destroyed his faith in the value of knowledge and precipitated a crisis in his life. He fled the University in 1801 and also his fiancée, Wilhelmine von Zenge, the daughter of a general, and went to Paris and later Switzerland where he began to write plays: "Robert Guiskard", a tragedy, and "Die Familie Schroffenstein", another tragedy.

Kleist's means of support were meager, a small inheritance from his father, and continual assistance from his step-sister, Ulrike, and from friends. For the next six years he was for the most part in despair: he burned his MSS "Guiskard" (only the first act survived), resigned a civil service post in Königsberg, and was arrested and imprisoned by the French as a suspected spy.

Upon his release from the French prison, Kleist set out for Dresden. There from 1807 to 1809 he met compatible friends and was accepted in a circle of writers, painters and patrons of the arts. He became acquainted with Adam Müller, the political philosopher, and edited with him the periodical, "Phöbus" in which some of his works appeared in whole or in part. He completed "Der zerbrochene Krug", a comedy; the tragedy "Penthesilea"; the romantic drama "Das Käthchen von Heilbronn"; and the historic drama "Die Hermannsschlact"; and also reworked Molière's "Amphitryon".

In the autumn of 1809 he was in Berlin publishing a daily newspaper, the "Berliner Abendblätter" to which he contributed writings. Those political in nature created difficulties with the authorities and the paper ceased publication. When that happened, Kleist's last means of livelihood ceased too.

He was bitterly disappointed in his own life and in the lack of understanding of his contemporaries. (Goethe considered Kleist's temperament and art to suffer from unfortunate pathological excesses, a judgment which showed surprising tenacity for almost a hundred years.) He talked of suicide and sought someone to join him in self-destruction. He met such a person, Henriette Vogel, an incurably sick woman, and on November 21, 1811, he shot her first, then himself, alongside the bank of the Wannsee, near Potsdam.

Kleist felt himself to be primarily a dramatist, but his other writings, stories, poems, anecdotes, are of a high quality. As a writer, he was very much involved in the military and political events of his time and concerned about the individual in the society which was a part of them. He was influenced by Goethe and Schiller, Kant and Adam Müller. He wanted to be a great writer, but was incredibly unlucky in every venture.

Belatedly for him, his honesty, his feeling for reality, appealed to those who followed him: the realists, expressionists, nationalists, and existentialists who saw in him their prototype.

In time, in both Germany and France, Kleist has been recognized as a writer whose approach to problems in life and literature is surprisingly modern.

Anne L. Rubino

The Catalogue

BOOK MATERIALS

Kleist's Life and Times

1. BRAHM, Otto. *Das Leben Heinrich von Kleists.* 2nd. ed. Berlin: Egon Fleischel and Company, 1911. In this life of Heinrich von Kleist, the author stressed the influence of the "milieu" on Kleist, his emancipation from the "Prussian spirit", and the development in his outlook, especially from 1808 on. The book also advanced the still controversial theory of Adam Müller as Kleist's "evil genius".
2. DEICH, Aleksandr. *The Fate of Poets: Hoelderlin, Kleist, Heine.* Moscow: Art—Lit. Publishers, 1968. The first full-length study on Kleist since 1914 published in Russian. (On loan to Hofstra University Library by Alexej Ugrinsky, Kleist Conference Coordinator.)
3. HERZOG, Wilhelm. *Heinrich von Kleist: Sein Leben und sein Werk.* Mit Titelbild nach einem Portrait von Max Slevogt und einer Gravüre des Miniaturbildes aus dem Jahre 1801. München: C. H. Beck'sche Verlagsbuchhandlung, 1911. Von Kleist's life and work with a frontispiece following a portrait by Max Slevogt, not an engraving of this miniature, from the year 1801. (On loan to Hofstra University Library from Alexej Ugrinsky.)
4. HOHOFF, Curt. *Heinrich von Kleist in Selbstzeugnissen und Bilddokumenten.* Rowohlts Monographien. Herausgegeben von Kurt Kusenberg. Hamburg: Rowohlt Taschenbuch Verlag, 1958. A critical biography containing many illustrations. (On loan to Hofstra Unversity Library by Alexej Ugrinsky.)
5. KUHN-FOELIX, August. *Heinrich von Kleist.* Murnau, Germany: Ulrich Riemerschmidt Verlag, 1948. A biography.
6. VON KURENBERG, Joachim. *Heinrich von Kleist.* Ein Versuch. Hamburg: Robert Mölich Verlag, 1948. An essay on von Kleist.
7. MAASS, Joachim. *Kleist, Die Fackel Preussens.* Eine Lebensgeschichte. Wien, München, Basel: Verlag Kurt Desch, 1957. Kleist, the Prussian Torch. An informed and comprehensive biography leading to the conclusion that in Kleist the "Prussian" spirit transcended itself and found its most ethereal expression.
8. MARCH, Richard. *Heinrich von Kleist.* New Haven: Yale University Press, 1954. Short biography with chronology and list of published works.
9. MEYER-BENFEY, Heinrich. *Kleists Leben und Werke,* dem deutschen Volke dargestellt. Göttingen, Germany: Otto Hapke Verlag, 1911. Presents Kleist wrestling with a "new form of drama" and an increased concern with political problems.
10. MOMMSEN, Katharina. *Kleists Kampf mit Goethe.* (Poesie und Wissenschaft, XXVII). Heidelberg: Lothar Stiehm Verlag, 1974. Kleist's conflict with Goethe. (Presented to Hofstra University Library with the compliments of Dr. Mommsen.)

11. RAHMER, Sigismund, *Heinrich von Kleist als Mensch und Dichter, nach neuen Quellenforschungen.* Mit 2 Porträts und 1 Textabbildung. Berlin: Druck und Verlag von Georg Reimer, 1909. Heinrich von Kleist as man and writer. Rahmer opposed the notion of Kleist as a pathological talent.
12. SEMBDNER, Helmut. *Heinrich von Kleists Lebensspuren: Dokumente und Berichte der Zeitgenossen.* Zweite, veränderte und erweiterte Auflage. Sammlung Dieterich, Band 172. Bremen: Carl Schünemann Verlag, 1957. Portrait of Kleist. Letters and commentaries of Kleist's contemporaries.
13. ATKINSON, Christopher Thomas. *A History of Germany, 1715-1815.* With 35 maps and plans. New York: Barnes & Noble, Inc., 1969 reprint. Included is an account of the Prussian Military Campaign of 1793 in which Kleist took part.
14. BABBITT, Irving. *Rousseau and Romanticism.* Boston: Houghton Mifflin Co., 1919. This is a study of the great international Romantic Movement. Rousseau supplied the author with the most significant illustrations. German romanticists have been termed "twilight men." What many of them admired in woman was her unconsciousness and freedom from analysis—an admiration that was also a tribute to the "night side" of nature. It has been pointed out that as soon as the women in Kleist's plays became conscious they fell into error.
15. BÖRSCH-SUPAN, Helmut. *Caspar David Friedrich.* Translated from the German by Sarah Twohig. New York: George Braziller, 1974. Friedrich's paintings have a haunting quality, the product of an elaborate system of symbolism. Fifty-seven plates illustrate his use of tone to create symbolic yet compellingly real landscapes during the period 1797 to 1840. Von Kleist lived in Dresden from 1807 to 1809, and probably became personally acquainted with Friedrich at that time.
16. CASSIRER, Ernst. *Rousseau, Kant, Goethe.* Two Essays Translated from the German by James Gutmann, Paul Oskar Kristeller and John Herman Randall, Jr. (The History of Ideas Series.) Princeton: Princeton University Press, 1947. These essays try to illustrate, from various perspectives, the culture of the 18th century and the "climate of opinion", from which this culture arose, (which was Kleist's inheritance).
17. FRANCKE, Kuno (ed.) *The German Classics of the 19th and 20th Centuries.* Masterpieces of German Literature. Translated into English. In 20 volumes illustrated. Albany: J. B. Lyon Co., n.d. The first two volumes are given over to the works of Johann Wolfgang von Goethe poet-sage; the third to the great dramatic poet Friedrich von Schiller, and the fifth volume includes the works of Ludwig Achim von Arnim and Clemens Brentano, romanticists; all of these writers were contemporaries of von Kleist.
18. HEGEL, Georg Wilhelm Friedrich. *Lectures on the Philosophy of History.* Translated by J. Sibree. London: George Bell and Sons, 1902. Reprint of 1857 edition.
19. HEGEL, Georg Wilhelm Friedrich. *The Philosophy of History.* New York: Dover Publicatons, Inc., 1956. The heart and center of Hegel's philosophy. He put forward a philosophical framework for history, not writing history, but philosophy. These lectures were delivered in the University of Berlin between 1818-1831, but he and Kleist were contemporaries in the Romantic Movement and, although probably unaware of each other, attempted to unify opposites, the ideal and the real: Hegel in philosphy; Kleist in literature.
20. HEGEL, Georg Wilhelm Friedrich. *Vorlesungen über die Philosophie der*

Gerschichte (Georg Wilhelm Friedrich Hegel's Werke). Edited by Dr. Eduard Gans, Berlin: Verlag von Duncker und Humblot, 1848. Lectures on the philosophy of history.

21. KANT, Immanuel. *Kritik der reinen Vernunft.* Mit einer Einleitung und Anmerkungen. Herausgegeben von Dr. Erich Adickes. Berlin: Mayer & Müller, 1889. Kant's critique of pure reason. Reading of Kant destroyed Kleist's faith in the value of knowledge.

22. VON KLEIST, Franz. *Vermischte Schriften.* Berlin: bei Friedrich Maurer, 1797. Miscellaneous writings. (On loan to Hofstra University Library by Dr. Joseph Astman, Member of the Hofstra University Kleist Conference Committee and director of the UCCIS.)

23. LINDEMANN, Gottfried. *History of German Art. Painting—Sculpture—Architecture.* Translated by Tessa Sayle. New York: Praeger Publishers, 1971. Contains a chapter on 19th century art and artists in Germany. Among the artists are included some known to Kleist: Caspar David Friedrich and Phillip Otto Runge.

24. MEINECKE, Friedrich. *Das Zeitalter der deutschen Erhebung (1795-1815).* Mit einem Geleitwort von Siegfried A. Kaehler. Göttingen: Vandenhoeck & Ruprecht, 1963 reprint. Covers the generation of 1795 to 1815, a time of German rebellion and during which Kleist served in the Prussian military army.

25. MÜLLER, Adam Heinrich. *Kritische, Asthetische und Philosophische Schriften.* I und II. Kritische Ausgabe herausgegeben von Walter Schroeder und Werner Siebert. Berlin: Hermann Luchterhand Verlag, 1967. Kleist is said to have been influenced by Müller's ideas. However, it is questionable whether Kleist espoused to any appreciable degree Müller's theories, although the two men collaborated on the Phöbus.

26. MÜSEBECK, Ernst. *Gold gab ich für Eisen.* Deutschlands Schmach und Erhebung in zeitgenössischen Dokumenten, Briefen, Tagebüchern aus den Jahren 1806-1815. Berlin: Deutsches Verlagshaus Bong & Co., 1913. Germany's disgrace and rebellion as shown in contemporary documents, letters, journals, from the years 1806 to 1815.

27. PERKINS, Merle L. *Jean-Jacques Rousseau.* On the Individual and Society. Lexington: The University Press of Kentucky, 1974. Rousseau's moral and political theories.

28. POMEAU, René. *Diderot, Sa Vie, Son Oeuvre,* avec un Exposé de sa Philosophie. Collection "Philosophes". Paris: Presses Universitaires de France, 1967.

29. RICHARDS, Joyce A. *Diderot's Dilemma.* His Evaluation Regarding the Possibility of Moral Freedom in a Deterministic Universe. New York: Exposition Press, Inc., 1972. According to Diderot, a doctrine that denies man's free will destroys the concepts of virtue and vice. This was Kleist's dilemma too.

30. RUNGE, Phillip Otto. *Hinterlassene Schriften.* Herausgegeben von dessen ältestem Bruder. Zweiter Teil. Mit 1 Bild Faksimiledruck nach der Ausgabe von 1840-1841. Göttingen: Vandenhoeck & Ruprecht, 1965. Reihe Texte des 19. Jahrhunderts. These are posthumous writings.

31. TRAEGER, Jörg (ed.). *Caspar David Friedrich.* New York: Rizzoli, n.d. Friedrich was a Landscape painter whose pictures are spatial projections of time; self-portraits of a melancholy mind.

32. WALDAUER, John L. *Society and the Freedom of the Creative Man in*

Diderot's Thought. (Diderot Studies V, edited by Otis Fellows.) Genève: Librairie Droz, 1964. Diderot's impact on, and interpretaton by, contemporaries and posterity.
33. WARRACK, John Hamilton. *Carl Maria von Weber.* London: Hamish Hamilton, 1968. Weber was the most representative musician of his age (1786-1826). Kleist probably knew him, certainly about him, through Johann Ludwig Tieck, a mutual friend.

Selections from His Works

34. (VON KLEIST, Heinrich). "Kleist: Amphitryon", translated by Charles E. Passage. In *Amphitryon: Three Plays in New Verse Translation.* Chapel Hill: The University of North Carolina Press, 1974. Plautus: "Amphitruo" translated by James H. Mantinband; Molière and Kleist: "Amphitryon" translated by Charles E. Passage; together with a comprehensive account of the evolution of the Amphitryon legend and its subsequent history on the stage.
35. VON KLEIST, Heinrich. *Amphitryon.* A Comedy. Translated from the German with an introduction by Marion Sonnenfield. New York: Frederick Ungar Publishing Co., 1962.
36. (VON KLEIST, Heinrich). "Das Bettelweib von Locarno" (The Beggarwoman of Locarno). In *Heinrich von Kleists Gesammelte Schriften.* Herausgegeben von Ludwig Tieck. Dritter Theil. Berlin: Druck und Verlag von Georg Reimer, 1874. (On loan to Hofstra University Library by Dr. Joseph Astman.) There are 3 vols. to the set.
37. & 38.(VON KLEIST, Heinrich). "Briefe" (Letters). In *Heinrich von Kleists Werke.* Im Verein mit Georg Minde-Pouet, und Reinhold Steig. Leipzig: Bibliographisches Institut., n.d. The set is six volumes in all. The letters are in the first two. Georg Minde-Pouet inscribed the first volume to Dr. Astman: "To the memory of our meeting in Berlin and in the hope of a continually pleasant, scholarly and friendly relationship." (All the volumes are on loan to Hofstra University Library by Dr. Astman.)
39. VON KLEIST, Heinrich. *The Broken Jug.* Translated by Roger Jones. (Classics of Drama in English Translation). Manchester, England: Manchester University Press, 1977. Goethe produced the play at the Weimar court theatre; but the production was not a success. Goethe destroyed the flow of the one-act play by staging a three-act production. Kleist was displeased and the relationship between the two men was never easy afterwards. (Compliments of the Embassy of the Federal Republic of Germany, Washington, D. C.).
40. VON KLEIST, Heinrich. *The Broken Pitcher.* A Comedy in One Act. Translated into English Verse by Bayard Quincy Morgan. (University of North Carolina Studies in the Germanic Languages and Literatures, Number 31). Chapel Hill, North Carolina: The University of North Carolina Press, 1961.
41. (VON KLEIST, Heinrich). "Das Erdbeben in Chili". (The Earthquake in Chili). In *Heinrich von Kleist Novellen und Ästhetische Schriften.* Edited by Robert E. Helbling. New York: Oxford University Press, 1967. "Das Erdbeben" is one of the five of Kleist's stories and a few of his other writings and letters in this German edition, together with a short biography, a typology of grammatical constructions, and a bibliography.

42. (VON KLEIST, Heinrich). "Die Familie Schroffenstein". (The Schroffenstein Family). In *Heinrich von Kleists Gesammelte Schriften*. Herausgegeben von Ludwig Tieck. Erster Theil. Berlin: Druck und Verlag von Georg Reimer, 1874. This tragedy is based on an episode in the life of the 11th century Norman duke.
43. (VON KLEIST, Heinrich). "Der Findling." (The Foundling). In *Heinrich von Kleists Werke*. Im Verein mit Georg Minde-Pouet und Reinhold Steig. Sechster Band. Leipzig: Bibliographisches Institut, n.d. (On loan from Dr. Astman).
44. (VON KLEIST, Heinrich). "Germania an ihre Kinder". (Germania to her Children). Eine Ode. In *Heinrich von Kleist Sämtliche Werke und Briefe*. Herausgegeben von Helmut Sembdner. 2 vols. München: Carl Hanser Verlag, 1961.
45. (VON KLEIST, Heinrich). "Germania an ihre Kinder". In *Deutsche Gedichte in Handschriften*. Leipzig: Im Insel-Verlag, n.d. In case. Inscribed to Dr. Astman by Eva Rothe: "In memory of Germany, Jan. 1946." The handwritten facsimiles in the book are by German poets, e.g., Goethe, Schiller, Brentano, Kleist . . . . (Loaned to Hofstra University Library by Dr. Astman).
46. (VON KLEIST, Heinrich). "Gleich und Ungleich". (Like and Unlike). Eine Legende nach Hans Sachs. In *Heinrich von Kleist Gesammelte Werke*. Eingeleitet von Julius Bab. Erster Band. Berlin: Hans Heinrich Tillgner Verlag, 1923. The set consists of three volumes.
47. (VON KLEIST, Heinrich). "Die heilige Cäcilie oder die Gewalt der Musik". (St. Cecilia or The Power of Music). In *Kleists Novellen*. Im Wortlaut der ersten Fassung. Neudruck besorgt von H. Meyer-Benfey. Heidelberg: Carl Winters Universitätsbuchhandlung, 1926.
48. (VON KLEIST, Heinrich). "Die Hermannsschlacht". (The Battle of Arminius). In *Heinrich von Kleists Werke*. Im Verein mit Georg Minde-Pouet und Reinhold Steig. Herausgegeben von Erich Schmidt. Fünfter Band. Leipzig: Bibliographisches Institut, n.d. This is an historical drama which deals with the battle against the Romans in 9 A.D., but it is fiercely patriotic and anti-French. (On loan from Dr. Astman).
49. (VON KLEIST, Heinrich). "Das Käthchen von Heilbronn oder Die Feuerprobe". Ein großes historisches Ritterschauspiel. (Käthchen von Heilbronn or Ordeal by Fire). In *Heinrich von Kleist Gesammelte Werke*. Eingeleitet von Julius Bab. Zweiter Band. Berlin: Hans Heinrich Tillgner Verlag, 1923. This is a romantic drama of Käthchen's love for her idealized knight, containing elements of magic and sleep-walking.
50. VON KLEIST, Heinrich. *Le Marchand de Chevaux Michael Kohlhaas*. Illustrations de E. Dufour. Paris: Librairie Hachette, 1942. Première édition de "Michael Kohlhaas", 1810. French edition of Kleist's *The Horse Dealer, Michael Kohlhaas*. (Loaned to Hofstra University Library by Dr. Astman).
51. (VON KLEIST, Heinrich). "Die Marquise von O . . . ." (The Marquise of O . . . .). In *Heinrich von Kleists Sämtliche Werke*. Erster Band. Berlin: Globus Verlag, n.d.
52. VON KLEIST, Heinrich. *Michael Kohlhaas*. Edited by John Gearey. New York: Oxford University Press, 1967. The text of the story is in German. A critical afterword discusses some aspects of the genesis of the work. A chronology of the important dates in the life of Kleist, and a short bibliographical note, have also been provided. (On loan from Dr. Astman).
53. (VON KLEIST, Heinrich). "Penthesilea". Einleitung. In *Heinrich von Kleists*

Werke. Im Verein mit Georg Minde-Pouet und Reinhold Steig. Herausgegeben von Erich Schmidt. Vierter Band. Leipzig: Bibliographisches Institut, n.d. (On loan from Dr. Astman).
54. VON KLEIST, Heinrich. *Penthésilée*. Traduction de Julien Gracq. Paris: Librairie José Corti, 1954. French translation of Kleist's *Penthesilea*.
55. (VON KLEIST, Heinrich). "Die Bedingung des Gärtners". (The Condition of the Gardener). Eine Fabel. One of the "Politische Schriften des Jahres 1809" in *Heinrich von Kleists Werke*. Im Verein mit Georg Minde-Pouet und Reinhold Steig. Herausgegeben von Erich Schmidt. Siebenter Band. Leipzig: Bibliographisches Institut, n.d. (On loan from Dr. Astman).
56. VON KLEIST, Heinrich. *The Prince of Homburg*. A Play in Five Acts. Translated with an introduction by Charles E. Passage. (The Library of Liberal Arts). Indianapolis: The Bobbs-Merrill Company, Inc., 1956. Last and finest of Kleist's dramas.
57. (VON KLEIST, Heinrich). "Prinz Friedrich von Homburg". Ein Schauspiel. In *Heinrich von Kleists Gesammelte Schriften*. Herausgegeben von Ludwig Tieck. Zweiter Theil. Berlin: Druck und Verlag von Georg Reimer, 1874. This play is considered Kleist's outstanding dramatic achievement. (Loaned to Hofstra University by Dr. Astman).
58. (VON KLEIST, Heinrich). "Fragment aus dem Trauerspiel: Robert Guiskard, Herzog der Normänner". (Fragment from the Tragedy: Robert Guiskard, Duke of Normandy). In *Heinrich von Kleists Werke*. Im Verein mit Georg Minde-Pouet und Reinhold Steig. Herausgegeben von Erich Schmidt. Dritter Band. Leipzig: Bibliographisches Institut, n.d. Only the first act has survived. Kleist burned the rest. (On loan from Dr. Astman).
59. (VON KLEIST, Heinrich). *Plays and Novels*. Translated from the German into Russian by Boris Pasternak. Moscow: Art-Lit. Publishers, 1969. The three plays translated are: "Robert Guiskard", "Der zerbrochne Krug", and "Prinz Friedrich von Homburg". (On loan from Alexej Ugrinsky).
60. VON KLEIST, Heinrich. *Über das Marionettentheater. Aufsätze und Anekdoten*. Insel-Bücherei Nr. 481. Im Insel-Verlag zu Leipzig, 1944. Kleist's *The Marionette-theater* and other essays and anecdotes. (On loan from Alexej Ugrinsky).
61. (VON KLEIST, Heinrich). "Über das Marionettentheater". (Concerning the Marionette Theater). In *German Essays IV. Romanticism*. Kleist, Novalis, Tieck, Schlegel. Selected, edited, and annotated by Max Dufner and Valentine C. Hubbs. New York: The Macmillan Company, 1964. This is one of Kleist's aesthetical and philosophical essays. (On loan from Dr. Astman).
62. (VON KLEIST, Heinrich). "Die Verlobung in St. Domingo". (The Engagement in Santo Domingo). Herausgegeben von Helmut Sembdner. In *Heinrich von Kleist Sämtliche Werke und Briefe*. Zweiter Band. München: Carl Hanser Verlag, 1961.
63. (VON KLEIST, Heinrich). "Der Zweikampf". (The Duel). In *Heinrich von Kleist Gesammelte Werke*. Eingeleitet von Julius Bab. Dritter Band. Hans Heinrich Tillgner Verlag, 1923.

Criticism, Interpretation, Influence

64. BADEWITZ, Hans. *Kleists "Amphitryon"*. Bausteine zur Geschichte der Neueren Deutschen Literatur, XXVII. Tübingen: Max Niemeyer Verlag, 1974. A critical analysis of Kleist's *Amphitryon*.
65. BRAND, Hans Erich. *Kleist und Dostojevskij*. Extreme Formen der Wirk-

lichkeit als Ausdruckmittel religiöser Anschauungen. (Studien zur Germanistik, Anglistik und Komparistik herausgegeben von Armin Arnold, Band 4). Bonn: H. Bouvier u. Co. Verlag, 1970. Both of these writers exhibited extreme forms of reality in their works, such as expressionism, religiosity, perception.

66. BRÜGGER, Hans-Horst. *Die Briefe Heinrich von Kleists.* Abhandlung zur Erlangung der Doktorwürde der Philosophischen Fakultät der Universität Zürich. Angenommen auf Antrag von Herrn. Prof. Dr. Emil Staiger. Zürich-Höngg: Buchdruckerei A. Moos, 1946. Essays on the letters of Heinrich von Kleist.

67. CATHOLY, Eckehard, Karl Otto Conrady, Heinz Ide, and Walter Müller-Seidel. *Kleist und die Gesellschaft.* Eine Diskussion. (Jahresgabe der Heinrich-von-Kleist-Gesellschaft, 1964). Berlin: Erich Schmidt Verlag, 1965. A discussion on Kleist and society.

68. DAVID, Claude, Wolfgang Wittkowski and Laurence Ryan. *Kleist und Frankreich.* (Jahresgabe der Heinrich-von-Kleist-Gesellschaft 1968). Berlin: Erich Schmidt Verlag, 1969. Essays on Kleist's behavior in France. (Presented to Hofstra University Library with the compliments of Erich Schmidt, Publisher.)

69. DEMISCH, Heinz. *Heinrich von Kleist.* Schicksal im Zeichen der Bewußtseinsseele. Stuttgart: Verlag Freies Geistesleben, 1964. Fate as the symbol of knowledge.

70. DOCTOROW, E.L. *Ragtime.* New York: Random House, 1974. Kleist in *Michael Kohlhaas* raises the issue of a man's right to justice. Doctorow, admittedly influenced by Kleist, raises the same issue in the character of Coalhouse Walker (Kohlhaas Jr.) in *Ragtime.* (Marion Faber, Erindale College, and Robert Helbling, University of Utah, delivered two addresses on November 18, 1977, on Doctorow's *Ragtime* at the Hofstra University International Conference to commemorate the Heinrich von Kleist bicentennial.

71. DURST, Rolf. *Heinrich von Kleist. Dichter zwischen Ursprung und Endzeit.* Kleists Werk im Licht idealistischer Eschatologie. Bern: Francke Verlag, 1965. An interpretation of Kleist's works in the light of his idealistic belief about the end of the world contained in the *Marionettentheater,* with emphasis on its affinity with Hegel's philosophy of history.

72. DYER, Denys. *The Stories of Kleist: A Critical Study.* New York: Holmes and Meier Publishers, 1977. An examination of Kleist's stories against the background of his life and works. A scholarly and sensitive literary analysis. (Presented to Hofstra University Library with the compliments of Holmes and Meiers Publishers).

73. ELLIS, John Martin. *Kleist's Prinz Friedrich von Homburg.* A Critical Study. Berkeley: University of California Press, 1970. A critical interpretation of this play by Kleist.

74. EMRICH, Wilhelm, Karl Ludwig Schneider, Emil Staiger and Bennor von Wiese. *Heinrich von Kleist.* Vier Reden zu seinem Gedächtnis. (Jahresgabe der Heinrich-von-Kleist-Gesellschaft, 1962). Berlin: Erich Schmidt Verlag. Four essays in memory of von Kleist.

75. VAN DER ENG, Johannes. *Dostoevskij Romancier.* Rapports entre sa vision du monde et ses procédés littéraires. (Slavistische Drukken en Herdrukken. Uitgegeven door C.H. Van Schooneveld, Hoogleraar Te Leiden, XIII). The Hague: Mouton and Company, Publishers, 1957. An essay on Dostoevsky. Dostoevskij and Kleist have been compared as writers who shared an affinity to literature of "anguish".

76. FRICKE, Gerhard. *Gefühl und Schicksal bei Heinrich v. Kleist.* Studien über den inneren Vorgang im Leben und Schaffen des Dichters. ("Neue Forschung: Arbeiten zur Geistesgeschichte der germanischen und romanischen Völker", No. 3). Berlin: Junker Dunnhaupt Verlag, 1929. Studies on the inner life and creative work of writers. The author defines the notion of Kleist's "feeling" as an intense experience of the integrity of the self, which manifests itself increasingly in Kleist's works.
77. FRICKE, Gerhard. *Gefühl und Schicksal bei Heinrich v. Kleist.* Studien über den inneren Vorgang im Leben und Schaffen des Dichters. New York: AMS Press, 1971. Reprinted from the edition of 1929, Berlin. (Presented to Hofstra with the compliments of the AMS Press).
78. GEARY, John. *Heinrich von Kleist. A Study in Tragedy and Anxiety.* University of Pennsylvania Studies in Germanic Languages and Literature. Philadelphia: University of Pennsylvania Press, 1968. An attempt to show that the central problem in Kleist's works and literary character is a fascination with the phenomena of opposition per se rather than with a conflict between definable entities such as "feeling" and "reason" or "consciousness" and "reality".
79. VON GORDON, Wolff. *Die dramatische Handlung in Sophokles "König Oedipus" und Kleists "Der zerbrochene Krug."* Tübingen, Germany: Max Niemeyer Verlag, 1974. Dramatic performances in Sophicles' *Oedipus Rex* and Kleist's *The Broken Jug.*
80. GRAHAM, Ilse. *Heinrich von Kleist. Word into Flesh: A Poet's Quest for the Symbol.* Berlin: Walter de Gruyter, 1977. A study of Kleist scholarship from which there emerges the picture of a strikingly modern mind, a master of contemporary themes and techniques. (Presented to Hofstra University Library with the compliments of the publisher. Professor Graham of the University of London King's College delivered the opening address on the evening of November 17, 1977, at Hofstra University's International Conference to Commemorate the Heinrich von Kleist Bicentennial, 1777-1977).
81. GUNDOLF, Friedrich. *Heinrich von Kleist.* Berlin: Georg Bondi, 1932, c. 1922. Shows Kleist's affinities with modern expressionism.
82. GUNDOLF, Friedrich. *Heinrich von Kleist.* New York: AMS Press, Inc., 1970. Reprinted from the edition of 1922, Berlin. (Presented to Hofstra University Library with the compliments of the AMS Press).
83. HELBLING, Robert E. *The Major Works of Heinrich von Kleist.* New York: New Directions Publishing Corporation, 1975. A study which attempts to give a balanced and analytic view of that central theme in Kleist's Weltasschauung, its genesis in his thought, and its variations and artistic expression in his major works. (Loaned to Hofstra University Library by Alexej Ugrinsky, Kleist conference coordinator).
84. HOLZ, Hans Heinz. *Macht und Ohnmacht der Sprache.* Untersuchungen zum Sprachverständnis und Stil Heinrich von Kleists. Bücher zur Dichtkunst. Frankfurt-am-Main: Athenäum Verlag, 1962. Strength and weakness in language. An interpretation of Kleist's works on the basis of his skeptical attitude toward the communicative ability of language.
85. IDE, Heinz. *Der Junge Kleist. ". . . in dieser wandelbaren Zeit. . .".* Aus dem Göttinger Arbeitskreis. Würzburg: Holzner Verlag, 1961. The Young Kleist . . . in those changeable times. An exhaustive analysis of Kleist's letters, written prior to and immediately after the Kant crisis, on the basis of existentialist theories.
86. KANZOG, Klaus. *Prolegomena zu einer historisch-kritischen Ausgabe der*

Werke Heinrich von Kleists. Theorie und Praxis einer modernen Klassiker Edition. München: Carl Hanser Verlag, 1970. A critical discussion serving to introduce and interpret an historical-critical publication: the Works of Heinrich von Kleist.
87. KANZOG, Klaus und Hans Joachim Kreutzer (Herausgegeben). *Werke Kleists auf dem modernen Musiktheater.* (Jahresgabe der Heinrich-von-Kleist-Gesellschaft, 1973/74). Berlin: Erich Schmidt Verlag, 1977. Kleist's productions as performed in the modern musical theatre. (Presented to Hofstra University Library with the compliments of Erich Schmidt Verlag).
88. KOCH, Friedrich. *Heinrich von Kleist.* Bewußtsein und Wirklichkeit. Stuttgart: J. B. Metzlersche Verlagsbuchhandlung, 1958. An analysis of Kleist's portrayal of the clash between man's subjective "consciousness" and "reality".
89. KREUTZER, Hans Joachim. *Die dichterische Entwicklung Heinrich von Kleists.* Untersuchungen zu seinen Briefen und zur Chronologie und Aufbau seiner Werke. (Philologische Studien und Quellen herausgegeben von Wolfgang Binder, Hugo Moser, Karl Stackmann, Heft 41.) Berlin: Erich Schmidt Verlag, 1968. A thorough investigation of the sources of Kleist's works and their chronology, preceded by a survey of Kleist criticism, and followed by a discussion of his development as a writer.
90. MOERING, Michael. *Witz und Ironie in der Prosa Heinrich von Kleists.* München: Wilhelm Fink Verlag, 1972. Wit and irony in the prose of Heinrich von Kleist.
91. MÜLLER-SEIDEL, Walter. *Versehen und Erkennen.* Eine Studie über Heinrich von Kleist. Köln, Germany: Böhlau Verlag, 1961. An analysis of many formalistic an ideational aspects of Kleist's works centering on the notion that in seeking to preserve his self-identity the Kleistian character misapprehends reality and faces the danger of self-alienation, but through error arrives at greater self-possession.
92. PONGS, Hermann. *Franz Kafka. Dichter des Labyrinths.* Heidelberg: Wolfgang Rothe Verlag, 1960. Franz Kafka, writer of the complex. There is a chapter in which the author states that both Kafka and Kleist share the philosophy that feeling is of paramount importance.
93. REINERT, Claus. *Detektivliteratur bei Sophokles, Schiller und Kleist oder Das Rätsel der Wahrheit und die Abenteuer des Erkennens.* Kronberg, Germany: Scriptor Verlag, 1975. Detective literature by Sophocles, Schiller and Kleist or the mystery of reality and the adventure of knowledge.
94. RICHARDSON, Frank Charles. Kleist in France. (University of North Carolina Studies in the Germanic Languages and Literatures, No. 35.) Chapel Hill, North Carolina: University of North Carolina Press, c. 1962. An exhaustive survey and discussion of Kleist's relationship to France and the reception of his works in that country from the early 19th century to about 1960, containing a list of all translations of Kleist's works up to that time.
95. RICHARDSON, Frank Charles. *Kleist in France.* New York: AMS Press, 1969. Reprinted with the permission of the original publisher, the University of North Carolina Press, Chapel Hill edition of 1966. A reworking and bringing up to date of a doctoral dissertation under the title, "The Reception of Heinrich von Kleist in France", covering the years 1807-1959 presented in 1960 to the Horace Rackham School of Graduate Studies of the University of Michigan. (Presented to Hofstra University Library with the compliments of AMS Press.)
96. RÖBBELING, Friedrich. *Kleists Käthchen von Heilbronn.* Mit Anhang:

Abdruck der Phöbusfassung. (Bausteine zur Geschichte der neueren deutschen Literatur XII.) Tübingen: Max Niemeyer Verlag, 1973. An analysis of Kleist's *Käthchen von Heilbronn.*

97. SEMBDNER, Helmut von (Hrsg.). *Heinrich von Kleist.* Dichter über ihre Dichtungen. Verantwortliche Herausgeber Rudolf Hirsch und Werner Vortriede. München, Germany: Ernst Heimeran, 1969.

98. SEMBDNER, Helmut (Hrsg.). *Heinrich von Kleists Nachruhm.* Eine Wirkungsgeschichte in Dokumenten. Sammlung Dieterich, Band 318. Bremen: Carl Schünemann Verlag, 1967. Collection of judgments pronounced on Kleist by well-known writers, thinkers and critics in the 19th and 20th centuries.

99. SEMBDNER, Helmut (Beiträger). *Johann Daniel Falks Bearbeitung des Amphitryon-Stoffes.* Ein Beitrag zur Kleistforschung von Helmut Sembdner. (Jahresgabe der Heinrich-von-Kleist-Gesellschaft, 1969/70). Berlin: Erich Schmidt Verlag, 1971. The author's treatment of the Amphitryon theme, a contribution to the Kleist research. (Presented to Hofstra University Library with the compliments of Erich Schmidt Verlag).

100. SEMBDNER, Helmut (Hrsg.). *Kleists Aufsatz über das Marionettentheater.* Studien und Interpretationem. Mit einem Nachwort Herausgegeben von Helmut Sembdner. (Jahresgabe der Henrich-von-Kleist-Gesellschaft, 1965/66). Berlin: Erich Schmidt Verlag, 1967. Study and interpretation of Kleist's article on the Marionette theater.

101. SEMBDNER, Helmut. *Schütz-Lacrimas.* Das Leben des Romantikerfreunds, Poeten und Literaturkritikers Wilhelm von Schütz (1776-1847). Mit unbekannten Briefen und Kleist-Rezensionen. (Jahresgabe der Heinrich-von-Kleist-Gesellschaft, 1971/72). Berlin: Erich Schmidt Verlag, 1974. The life of Romanticist friend, poet and literary critic, Wilhelm von Schütz.

102. SIECK, Albrecht. *Kleists Penthesilea.* Versuch einer neuen Interpretation. (Literatur und Wirklichkeit Herausgegeben von Karl Otto Conrady, Band 14). Bonn: Bouvier Verlag Herbert Grundmann, 1976. A new interpretation of Kleist's *Penthesilea.*

103. SILZ, Walter. *Heinrich von Kleist.* Studies in his Works and Literary Character. Philadelphia: University of Pennsylvania Press, 1961. A collection of essays on various facets of Kleist's works.

104. STAHL, Ernest Leopold. *Heinrich von Kleist's Dramas.* (Modern Language Studies 4). Oxford: Basil Blackwell, 1948. A discussion of Kleist's intellectual and artistic development from the metaphysical pessimism of the early period, through the mild optimism of the *Kaethchen* to a concern with more practical, this-worldly problems in *Die Herrmannsschlacht* and *Homburg.*

105. STEIG, Reinhold. *Heinrich von Kleists Berliner Kämpfe.* Berlin und Stuttgart: Verlag von W. Spemann, 1901. Heinrich von Kleist's Prussian conflict. Valuable material attributing to Kleist the reactionary, royalist, and anti-Semitic attitudes of the conservative nobility, later conclusively disproved.

106. TURK, Horst. *Dramensprache als gesprochene Sprache.* Untersuchungen zu Kleists "Penthesilea"'. (Abhandlungen zur Kunst-Musik-und Literaturwissenschaft, Band 31). Bonn: H. Bouvier u. Co., 1965. Theater dialogue as spoken language: an interpretation of Kleist's *Penthesilia.*

107. VON REUSNER, Ernst. *Satz-Gestalt-Schicksal.* Untersuchungen über die Struktur in der Dichtung Kleists. (Quellen und Forschungen Neue Folge 6 (130)). Berlin: Walter de Gruyter and Company, c. 1961. In case. A highly theoretical and abstract discussion of the relationship between structure and

meaning in Kleist's works. (Presented to Hofstra University Library with the compliments of Walter de Gruyter and Company).

NEWSPAPER AND PERIODICAL MATERIALS

108. HENSCHEL, Arnold J. "The Primacy of Free-Will in the Mind of Kleist and in the 'Prince of Homburg' ". In *German Life and Letters*, January 1964, vol. 17, No. 2, 97-115. While other themes are important in Kleist's life, that of free-will is paramount.
109. VON KLEIST, Heinrich (Hrsg.). *Berliner Abendblätter.* 1810-11. Nachwort und Quellenregister von Helmut Sembdner, 1959. This was the first daily newspaper in Berlin and Kleist's last venture. He contributed anecdotes, some essays and anti-Napoleonic writings. He had various difficulties with the authorities on this account.
110. (VON KLEIST, Heinrich). *Berliner Hefte.* Zeitschrift für Kultur und Politik. November 1976, vol. 1. A current German periodical published in Berlin which carried in its first issue several articles on von Kleist. (Presented to Hofstra University Library with the compliments of Alexej Ugrinsky, Kleist conference coordinator).
111. (VON KLEIST, Heinrich). *Exchange/Austausch.* December 1976. A publication of Goethe House-German Cultural Institute, New York. It carried reprints of three recent newspaper articles in the *New York Post*, the *New York Times* and the *Sueddeutsche Zeitung*, respectively, "Von Kleist's 'Prince' Is Unique" by Martin Gottfried; "Rohmer's 'The Marquise of O . . .' A Witty, Joyous and Beautiful Film" by Vincent Canby; and "Herausforderung durch das Unbegreifliche", an essay by Guenter Bloecker on the occasion of the 150th anniversary of Kleist's death. (On loan from Alexej Ugrinsky).
112. VON KLEIST, Heinrich und Adam H. Müller (Hrsg.). *Phöbus.* Ein Journal für die Kunst. 1808-09. Nachwort und Kommentar von Helmut Sembdner, 1961. A distinguished literary magazine edited by von Kleist and Müller and published in Dresden. Early renditions of Kleist's works appeared in this periodical: *Penthesilea, Die Marquise von O . . ., der zerbrochene Krug, Robert Guiskard, Michael Kohlhaas, Käthchen von Heilbron*, and others.
113. POLITZER, Heinz. "Kleists Trauerspiel vom Traum: 'Prinz Friedrich von Homburg' ". In *Euphorion*, June 1970, vol. 64, No. 2, 200-20. Kleist's tragedy of a dream.
114. RESKE, Hermann. "Die Kleistische Sprache". In the *German Quarterly*, May 1963, vol. 36, No. 3, 219-35. The way Kleist used language.
115. SOKEL, Walter. "Kleist's 'Marquise of O . . .'; Kierkegaard's 'Abraham'; and Musil's 'Tonka': Three Stages of the Absurd as the Touchstone of Faith". In *Wisconsin Studies in Contemporary Literature*, Autumn, 1967, vol. 8, No. 4, 505-16. The three studies here refect a significant development in modern man's attitude toward faith.
116. STAHL, Ernest L. "Guiscard and Oedipus". In the *Tulane Drama Review*, March 1962, vol. 6, No. 3, 172-77. The problem of guilt in "Guiscard".
117. SZONDI, Peter. " 'Amphitryon', Kleist's 'Lustspiel nach Molière' ". In *Euphorion*, 1961, vol. 55, No. 3, 249-59. After the manner of Molière.
118. TATAR, Maria M. "Psychology and Poetics: J. C. Reil and Kleist's 'Prinz Friedrich von Homburg' ". In the *Germanic Review*, January 1973, vol. 48,

No. 1, 21-34. The method Dr. Reil recommended in his *Rhapsodien* for the diagnosis and treatment of persons who lapse into somnambulistic trances was used by Kleist as a source for his portrayal of Homburg's illness and cure.

119. WITTKOWSKI, Wolfgang. "Skepsis, Noblesse, Ironie". Formen des Als-Ob in Kleists 'Erdbeben' ". In *Euphorion*, 1969, vol. 63, No. 3, 247-83. Essays on the use of 'as-if' forms in Kleist's *Earthquake*.

FILM MATERIALS

120. "Marquise of O . . ." In *Exhange/Austausch*. Goethe House-German Cultural Institute, December 1976. Reprint of the October 18, 1976, *New York Times* review of the screen-play of Kleist's drama by Vincent Canby. (On loan from Alexej Ugrinsky).

121. "Die Marquise von O . . ." Kleists Novelle von Erich Rohmer inszeniert. Photographs from the film of 1976; list of performers; articles on the drama and on von Kleist by Adam Müller (1808), Wilhelm Waetzoldt, Bruno Markwardt, J. W. Goethe (1807), Max Brod, Eric Rohmer, and Peter Iden; and short chronologies of von Kleist and Rohmer. (On loan from Alexej Ugrinsky).

Alciati Emblem of the Hofstra University Library Associates—a 16th century woodcut representing a scholar at a lecturn, book illustration, German (?).

INDEX

INDEX

Aeschylus, 5, 30, 223
Aichele, Klaus 27
Aichinger, Ilse, 130, 135
Albrecht, Egon-Erich 239
Alexis, Willibald, 37
Allemann, Beda, 40, 174
Anderson, Eugene Newton, 232
Aristotle, 27, 28, 29, 31, 32, 196
Arminius the Cheruscan, 34
von Arnim, Achim, 213
von Arnim, Bettina, 37
Arnold, Heinz Ludwig, 39
Arntzen, Helmut, 62, 67, 77, 78
Ash, Adrienne, 77
Atkins, Henry Gibson, 232
Bach, Johann Sebastian, 166
Bate, Walter Jackson, 184, 185
Baudelaire, Charles Pierre, 131, 135
Bauer, Felice, 169
Beethoven, Ludwig Van, 231
Behaghel, Otto, 197, 201
Beissner, Friedrich, 198, 200, 201
Benjamin, Walter, 231, 238
Bergmann, Alfred, 40
von Biedermann, Flodoard, 125
Binder, Hartmut, 174
Binding, Rudolf G., 238
Bloch, Ernst, 238, 241
Blöcker, Günter, 93, 94, 95, 99, 115, 126, 205, 213, 252
Blumenbach, Johann, 119
Bochner, Salomon, 126
Böckmann, Paul, 127, 134, 184
von Boehn, Max, 108
Böll, Heinrich, 130, 135, 191
Born, Jürgen, 174
Braig, Friedrich, 134
Brecht, Bertold, 35, 38, 155, 191, 245
Brentano, Clemens, 10
von Brockes, Ludwig, 3, 4, 261, 262
Brod, Max, 169, 174
Brown, Hilda M., 139
Browning, Robert M., 263

von Bülow, Eduard, 227
Burckhardt, Sigurd, 38, 40
Bury, Friedrich, 49
Busch, Rolf, 39, 229, 239
Busch, Wilhelm, 83
Camus, Albert, 169, 175
Cassirer, Ernst, 125, 262
Cervantes, Miguel de, 88, 92, 140
Cirlot, Juan-Eduardo, 128, 134
Clemons, Walter, 166
Clever, Edith, 253
Coleridge, Samuel Taylor, 181
Conrady, Karl Otto, 134
Corssen, Meta 46
Coverlid, Dorothea, 57
Cramer, Friedrich 132, 133, 135
Crosby, Donald H. 243
Dahlmann, Friedrich Christoph 6
Daunicht, R. 144, 145
Davies, Russel 166
Delbrück, Hansgerd 60, 65, 67, 77, 78
DeLosea Family 222, 224
Dene, Kirsten 249
Dettmering, Peter 93, 94, 99
Diderot, Denis 139-144
Dilke, Charles 181, 182
Dilthey, Wilhelm 203
Doctorow, E.L. 147ff, 157ff.
Dostoevski, Fedor 164
Dsi, Dschuang 132
Dünnhaupt, G. 145
Dürer, Albrecht 231
Dürst, Rolf 93, 95, 99, 100
Dyer, Denys 88, 92
Dymant, Dora 175
Einstein, Albert 203
Eisler, Hanns 238
Eisner, Fritz H. 40
Ellis, John M. 40, 47, 48, 54, 56, 88, 92
Eloesser, Arthur 240
Engels, Friedrich 232, 239
Ermatinger, Emil 263
Euclid 117 ff.

Euripides 24, 29, 30, 31, 32
Faber, Marion 147
Fabre-Luce, Robert 238
Fabricius, Hans 239
Fang, J. 120. 125, 126
Fechner, J.U. 145
Felsenstein, Walter 250
Fichte, Johann Gottlieb 76
Fichtner, Edward G. 197, 199, 201, 202
Fischer, Ernst 238
Flex, Walter 251
Ford, Henry 159
Fouqué, Friedrich de la Motte 6, 35
Franklin, Benjamin 206, 207, 211
Franz Joseph 1, Emperor of Austria 36
Fricke, Gerhard 87, 88, 92, 111, 113, 115, 134
Friedrich, Elector of Saxony 167
Friedrich Wilhelm III, King of Prussia 36, 47
Friedrich Wilhelm IV, King of Prussia 36, 37
Friedrich, Caspar David 246
Freud, Sigmund 107, 108, 128, 131, 134, 162, 164
Froissart, Jean 88
Furer, Magdalena 222
Ganz, Bruno 246
Gatschet, Elisabeth Magdalena 222
Gatschet, Samuel Rudolf 222
Gervinus, Georg Gottfried 238
Gessner, Heinrich 218, 219, 226
Gessner, Salomon 5, 140
Gilow, Hermann 240
Godwin, William 181
von Goethe, Johann Wolfgang 1, 6, 7, 11, 15, 20, 21, 31, 44, 49, 50, 57, 76, 77, 83, 139, 141, 144, 184, 203, 231, 238, 243, 248, 250
Goldman, Emma 148, 154
Grabbe, Christian Dietrich 39
Graham, Ilse 3, 61, 65, 67, 71, 72, 77
Grebe, Paul 197
Greenberg, Martin 155, 167
Grimm, Jakob 175
Grimm, Wilhelm 175
Groeper, Richard 240
Grünewald, Matthias 231
Gundolf, Friedrich 11
Hamburger, Käte 67
Harman, Mark 169

von Harnack, Adolf 240
Hartman, Geoffrey 184
Hartmann, Ferdinand 57
Hauptmann, Gerhart 240
Hebbel, Friedrich 8
Hegel, Georg Wilhelm Friedrich 117
Heine, Heinrich 34, 35, 37, 40, 210, 238, 254
Heinrichs, Benjamin 250
Heisenberg, Werner 131, 135
Helbling, Robert E. 39, 93, 95, 99, 157
Heller, Erich 174
Hellmann, Hanna 125, 127, 133, 184
Hemingway, Ernest 163
Henkel, Arthur 51, 57
Henss, Rudolf 40
Heraclitus 162
Herwegh, Georg 37
Heselhaus, Clemens 127, 134, 184
Hidber, Arnold 222
Hindenburg, Karl Friedrich 119, 120, 123
Hirschenauer, Rupert 191
Hodin, Joseph Paul 175
Hoffmann, E.T.A. 84, 139, 203
Hoffman, Paul 219, 227
Hoffmeister, Werner 96
von Holtey, K. 8
Homer 258
Houdini, Harry 148, 159, 162, 164
Hoverland, Lilian 59
Hubbs, Valentine C. 257, 263
Huch, Ricarda 240
Ide, Heinz 262
Iffland, August Wilhelm 144
Jacobi, Friedrich Heinrich 140
Jauss, Hans Robert 169, 174, 175
Jensen, Wilhelm 107
Joplin, Scott 152
Jung, Carl Gustav 164
Kästner, Abraham G. 118, 120, 123, 125
Kafka, Franz 84, 129, 130, 134, 150, 169
Kahlen, Irene 198, 199, 200, 202
Kaiser, Hellmuth 56
von Kalckreuth, Friedrich Adolf 3
Kant, Immanuel 4, 5, 8, 11, 15, 20, 31, 117, 119, 120, 121, 122, 178, 257, 261
Kauffman, Stanley 166
Keats, John 177 ff.
Kippenberg, Anton 240

INDEX

Klarmann, Adolf D. 39
von Kleist, Ewald Christian 3, 236
von Kleist, Ewald Georg 206
von Kleist, Georg 240
von Kleist, Heinrich Amphitryon, 6, 27, 28, 29, 45, 57, 58, 69, 77, 95, 220, 243
    Aufsatz den sichern Weg des Glücks zu finden, 257-261
    Das Bettelweib von Locarno, 84, 195, 196, 200, 201
    Brief eines Malers an seinen Sohn, 141
    Das Erdbeben in Chili, 6, 83, 84, 122, 159, 172-175, 220
    Die Familie Schroffenstein, 5, 16, 91, 140, 195, 207, 217, 219, 220, 243
    Der Findling, 85, 93, 96, 99, 206, 208
    Geschichte meiner Seele, 6, 184
    Der Griffel Gottes, 171, 172, 173
    Die heilige Cäcilie oder die Gewalt der Musik, 73, 78, 83, 85
    Die Hermannsschlacht, 6, 33, 35-38, 90, 194
    Das Käthchen von Heilbronn, 6, 58, 134, 191, 206, 207, 208, 213, 243, 244, 247, 248, 249, 250, 253
    Leopold von Osterreich, 219
    Die Marquise von O..., 6, 27, 29, 31, 84, 95, 155, 159, 163, 167, 169, 195, 196, 244, 246, 251, 253
    Michael Kohlhaas, 6, 45, 54, 84, 147, 149, 151, 152, 154, 155, 157, 163, 166, 167, 169, 174
    Penthesilea, 6, 9, 10, 16, 27, 58, 114, 115, 195, 207-210, 220, 225, 243, 244
    Prinz Friedrich von Homburg, 6, 7, 36, 37, 41, 42, 46, 47, 56, 57, 126, 190, 192, 195, 196, 223, 230, 231, 235, 239, 240, 243, 244, 246, 247, 250, 251, 253
    Robert Guiskard, 5, 6, 27, 30, 67, 219, 220, 223, 225, 226
    Der Schrecken im Bade—Eine Idylle, 220
    Über das Marionettentheater, 9, 59, 103, 107-109, 114, 117, 122, 124, 125, 127, 129, 130, 133, 134, 142, 145, 174, 177, 184, 194
    Die Verlobung in St. Domingo, 83, 85, 220
    Der Zerbrochne Krug, 5, 27, 31, 42, 59, 60, 67, 69, 87, 89, 92, 129, 190, 195, 218, 219, 243
    Der Zweikampf, 73, 78, 84, 87, 88, 92
von Kleist, Heinrich (editor) Berliner Abendblätter, 109, 141, 144, 171
    Phöbus, 6, 57, 117
von Kleist, Marie, 6, 13, 22, 23, 56, 57, 225, 249
von Kleist, Ulrike 4, 5, 8, 9, 22, 55, 57, 208, 211, 218, 221, 223, 225
von Kleist, Wilhelmine 211
von Kleist-Retzow, Graf 235
Klinger, F.M. 140, 145
Klügel, Georg 119, 120, 123
Knorr, Walter L. 166
von Köckeritz, Karl Leopold 5
Körner, Charlotte 77
Kolbenheyer, E.G. 238
Kommerell, Max 93, 99
Kramer, Hilton 166
Kraus, Wolfgang 250
Kreutzer, Hans Joachim 67, 198, 200, 202, 204, 213, 257, 263
Kreuzer, Helmut 67, 191
Krug, Wilhelm Traugott 5
Kunz, Josef 99, 109, 114, 125, 127, 134
Kurock, Wolfgang 103
Laing, R.D. 9
Lambert, Johann Heinrich 120
Lamprecht, Helmut 174
Le Veau, Jean Jacques 219
Lefèvre, Manfred 39
Lessing, Gotthold Ephraim 3, 142, 260
Liebermann, Max 240
Linn, Rolf 35, 40, 93
Lietzau, Heinz 47
Litzau, Hans 250
Löwith, Karl 115
Lohse, Heinrich 22
Lucian 142
Luther, Martin 147, 148, 151, 158
McGlathery, James M. 87, 134
Maass, Joachim 262
Mann, Thomas 83, 93, 94, 99, 163, 238
Marcuse, Herbert 131, 135
Martin, Gottfried 125
Martini, Fritz 191
Marwede, F.C. 241
Marx, Karl 231
Marx Brothers 249

Mayer, Hans 47, 50, 54, 56, 238
Meck, Barbara 83
Mehring, Franz 238, 254
Michaelis, Rolf 250
Minde-Pouet, George 201, 221, 240, 251
Mirabeau, Comte Honoré de 40
Molière, Jean Baptiste 29, 77
Mommsen, Katharina 49, 50, 53, 56
Monge, Gaspard 120, 123
Morgan, Pierpont 148, 159, 162
Mortier, Roland 139, 144
Mozart, Wolfgang Amadeus 231
Müller, Adam 6, 77, 117, 250
Müller, Sophie 22
Müller-Seidel, Walter 57, 67, 77, 204, 213
Müller-Sternberg, Robert 39
Müller-Henning, Detlef 56
Nakamura, Shiro 109
Napoleon I, Emperor of France 5, 6, 34, 194, 235
Nesbit, Evelyn 164
Newton, Isaac 204
Nicolai, Ralf R. 127, 174
Nietzsche, Friedrich 27, 31, 127, 129, 133, 135
Novalis (Friedrich von Hardenberg) 127, 181, 203
O'Casey, Sean 84
Ovid 161, 162
von Pannwitz, Friederike 221
von Pannwitz, Karl 6
von Pannwitz, Wilhelm 223
Pestalozzi, Johann, Heinrich 218
Petersen, Julius 125, 240
Peymann, Claus 244, 247-250
Pfitzner, Hans 236, 240
von Pfuel, Ernst 3, 5, 6, 219, 225, 226
Pharaoh Seti I 159
Philip II, King of Spain 62
Picasso, Pablo 133
Pirandello, Luigi 60
Plato 142
Plattner, Ernst 119
Plautus, Titus Maccius 28
Plutarch 28
Politzer, Heinz 47, 48, 54, 56, 175
von Posadowsky-Wehner, Arthur 240
Raban, Jonathan 166
Radziwill, Anton 175

von Ramdohr, Friedrich Wilhelm Basilius 50, 57, 140, 141
Reimer, Hans 240
Reinig, Christa 130, 135
Rembrandt van Rijn 231
Rennert, Hal H. 177
Reske, Hermann 31, 217, 227
Reynolds, John Hamilton 181, 182
Richter, Werner 240
Rilke, Rainer Maria 113, 223
Röhl, Hans 227
Rösch, Ewald 67
Rohmer, Eric 31, 147, 251, 253
Rolland, Romain 238
Rothe, Friedrich 251
Rousseau, Jean Jacques 132, 139
Rowohlt, Ernst 169
Rühle von Lilienstern, Otto August 3, 6, 121, 204, 225, 258, 259
Ryan, Lawrence 41, 60, 67, 111, 115, 125, 127, 134
Saccheri, Gerolomo 120, 125
Sammons, Jeffrey L. 33, 167
Samuel, Richard 36, 40, 51, 57
Sanders, Daniel 201
Sanders, Helma 251-254
Sappho 29
Schaer-Ris, Adolf 224
Scheffner, Johann Georg 9
Schelling, Friedrich Wilhelm 117, 127, 204, 211
Schichtl, Xaver 108
von Schiller, Friedrich 1, 75-79, 117, 127, 139, 208, 231, 238
Schlageter, Albert Leo 251
von Schlegel, August Wilhelm & Friedrich 117, 127, 139, 142, 181
Schlegel, Dorothea 140
Schleiermacher, Friedrich Ernst Daniel 127
von Schlieben, Karoline & Henriette 6, 12, 22, 23, 225
Schlöndorf, Volker 251, 252
Schlütter, Hans-Jürgen 47
Schmidt, Erich 221, 222
Schmidt, Ernst-Joachim 67
Schmidt, Herminio 203, 213
Schmidt, Jochen 39, 77, 93, 95, 99, 262, 263
Schneider, Karl Ludwig 198, 201, 202

INDEX

Schrimpf, Hans Joachim 67
Sophocles 5, 30, 32, 219, 223
Staiger, Emil 198, 200, 201
Stein, Karl Freiherr vom und zum 36
Stein, Peter 47, 244-247, 250-253
Stettler, Elisabeth Magdalena 221, 222
Stifter, Adalbert 83
Stöcker, Christa 40
Strauss, Botho 54
Streller, Siegfried 238
Struik, Dirk J. 126
Sudermann, Hermann 128, 134
Takayama, K.P. 120, 125
Teniers, David 110
von Thurn und Taxis, Marie 223
Tieck, Ludwig 7, 219, 225
Trautmann, Paul 240
Ulshöfer, Robert 190
Valentin, Karl 249
Valéry, Paul 113
Varnhagen von Ense, Karl August 175
Varnhagen von Ense, Rahel 8
Varus Quintilius 34
Vellacott, Philip 32
Vogel, Henriette 6
Voss, E. Theodor 79
Wagner, Richard 231
Walker, David 148, 149, 151
Walzel, Oskar 174
Washington, Booker T. 151, 159
Weber, Albrecht 191
von Wedekind, Georg Christian 223
Weigand, Hermann 204, 213
Weise, Christian Felix 78
Vogel, Henriette 6
Voss, E. Theodor 79
Wagner, Richard 231

Walker, David 148, 149, 151
Walzel, Oskar 174
Washington, Booker T. 151, 159
Weber, Albrecht 191
von Wedekind, Georg Christian 223
Weigand, Hermann 204, 213
Weise, Christian Felix 78
Weiss, Sydna Stern 117
Wendland, Jens 250
von Werdeck, Adolphine 12, 22, 23, 57, 204, 226
Wessel, Horst 251
West, Benjamin 181
Wieland, Christoph Martin 5, 30, 140, 142, 219, 223, 224
Wieland, Louise 5
Wieland, Ludwig 218
Wiener, Norbert 108
von Wiese, Benno 67, 109, 111, 113, 115, 127, 134
Wigod, Jacob 184
Wilcke, Johann Carl 211, 213
Wildbolz, Rudolf 145
Wilkie, Richard F. 78
Wirz, Otto 238
Wittkowski, Wolfgang 69, 191
Wolff, Hans M. 263
Wordsworth, William 21, 181, 182
Wrisberg, Heinrich 119
Wugk, Franz 240
Zapata, Emiliano 154
Zeiss, Karl 240
von Zenge, Wilhelmine 3, 4, 5, 22, 23, 178, 204, 217
Ziolkowski, Theodore 128, 134
Zolling, Theophil 221, 227
Zschokke, Heinrich 5, 218, 219, 227